PRISMATIC ECOLOGY

Prismatic Ecology

ECOTHEORY BEYOND GREEN

Jeffrey Jerome Cohen

Editor

Foreword by
Lawrence Buell

UNIVERSITY OF MINNESOTA PRESS

MINNEAPOLIS • LONDON

An earlier version of "White" was previously published as Bernd Herzogenrath, "The Weather of Music: Sounding Nature in the Twentieth and Twenty-first Century," from *Deleuze/Guattari and Ecology,* edited by Bernd Herzogenrath (2009). Reprinted with permission of Palgrave Macmillan.

A different version of "Grey" was published as Jeffrey J. Cohen, "Undead," *Journal of the Fantastic in the Arts* 23, no. 3 (2012). Reprinted with permission of *Journal of the Fantastic in the Arts.*

Published by the University of Minnesota Press
111 Third Avenue South, Suite 290
Minneapolis, MN 55401-2520
http://www.upress.umn.edu

Library of Congress Cataloging-in-Publication Data
Prismatic ecology : ecotheory beyond green / Jeffrey Jerome Cohen, editor ; foreword by Lawrence Buell.
Includes bibliographical references and index.
ISBN 978-0-8166-7997-3 (hc : alk. paper)
ISBN 978-0-8166-7998-0 (pb : alk. paper)
1. Philosophy of nature. 2. Ecology—Philosophy.
3. Colors—Miscellanea. I. Cohen,
Jeffrey Jerome, editor.
BD581.P745 2013
304.2—dc23
2013032556

Printed in the United States of America on acid-free paper

The University of Minnesota is an equal-opportunity educator and employer.

20 19 18 17 16 15 14 13   10 9 8 7 6 5 4 3 2 1

This volume is dedicated to my family:

WENDY, KATHERINE, ALEX.

You explored the terrains that gave rise to this project with me,
and the prospect of our future journeys carries me along.

CONTENTS

FOREWORD
LAWRENCE BUELL

Just as you were perhaps starting to wonder if significant further break-throughs might still be possible after two decades of rapid ecocritical advance from Anglo-American cottage industry to worldwide movement, along comes this new book whose collective accomplishment any author would envy: to develop an insight of the most elementary yet far-reaching importance that had previously been hidden in plain sight, the specious-ness of reducing "ecology" or "ecocriticism" to "green."

No doubt I was especially susceptible to conversion from having just returned from the white world of prewinter Svalbard in the Norwegian far far north to encounter the Arctic imaginary of *Prismatic Ecology*'s opening chapter. But I wager that every other reader who delves into this collection will share my epiphanic "aha!" reaction, even when they find themselves taking issue with this or that particular argument down the line. "Of course! Why didn't I think of that before?"

As the authors go on to show, ecological variegations beyond green hardly stop with white. Why not red (blood)? Why not brown (the Mis-sissippi Delta)? Why not violet-black (the deep sea)? For that matter— another insight for which polar experience prepares you—why not UV? For just because it is invisible to the human eye does not mean it is not constitutive, penetrating you even when you are not aware. Conversely, other chapters show, the problem with "green" is not only that it has been oversold as a lumping term, thereby foreshortening one's sense of other spectrum/spectral possibilities. Ecology as green also perpetuates the implication of binary nature–culture separation (simplistic for both sides of the human–nonhuman divide) and understates the potential for self-intoxicated fetishization of greenery as such, especially when channeled into out-of-control feats of bioengineering.

Some readers may complain that ecotheoretical revisionism through a prismatic lens amounts to a kind of phenomenological skewing of its own by an overprivileging of the visual bias seemingly wired into human perception, "the nobility of sight" as Hans Jonas called it—accentuated further in extrospective works of literature, painting, even sculpture.[1] But I think that the aesthetic that these authors loosely share refutes such possible carping in advance by avoiding magisterial claims about sightedness (Arctic sound figures centrally in "White," for instance); by stretching to include the invisible portions of the spectrum; and by the loosely shared aesthetic-epistemological frame nowhere better summed up than near the start of "Orange": "Color itself might best be modeled as a multispecies sensory process or network that generates biosemiotic-material effects that then take on a metaphorical life of their own as they are translated to different registers."

Beyond its dispute with green exclusivism, another, slightly less novel but maybe even more consequential way through which this book might signal a significant new turn for ecocriticism is by lightening up on the save-the-world moral earnestness so salient in ecocriticism's defining episodes so far: first-wave back-to-nature deep ecologism, second-wave environmental justice revisionism, and the newer-wave worlding of ecocriticism under the signs of ecoglobalism and postcolonialism. The more venturesomely ludic side of the work of Tim Morton and Stacy Alaimo—both of them also contributors to *Prismatic Ecology,* and the two major ecocritics most cited by the other contributors—is extensively on display here. The ensuing tendencies at various points toward skittery counterintuitive associationism will not be to everyone's taste. But anyone who comes to this book with an open mind desiring to see it expanded is certain to find much to energize him or her in the way of range and acuity of its textual engagements, both canonical and otherwise (Old English lyric and Icelandic saga to Spenserian sonnet to Karen Tei Yamashita, Samuel Delany, and zombie film), and in its interdisciplinary erudition (the history of orange as exotic commodity and icon, the mineralogy of gold and the somber history of its extraction, the possible correlation between autism and ecosublimity, the deep-sea phenomenon of bioluminescence, the relation between Schelling's *Naturphilosophie* and the discovery of ultraviolet—and much more).

But I do not want to leave the impression of an intellectual centrifuge without center. On the contrary. To be sure, a group of discrete essays by a score of individual authors cannot be expected to yield anything like programmatic coherence. Still, despite the marked differences of method and argument as well as of course subject and archive, they seem, as a group, to orient themselves within a common gravitational field as regards the concept of the ecological vis-à-vis culture—a commonality, furthermore, that might wind up amounting to this book's single most important impact on future ecocritical practice. At first, ecocriticism sought to take humankind—and the study of literature and the arts—back to nature. Then it renounced the holistic and/or binary thinking that seemed to energize those efforts and, during its ecojustice and postcolonial phases, tended to reconceive "nature" as product through a social constructivist lens. These chapters by and large take a different position perhaps best summed up in "Black": that "the winning move" lies "not in abandoning the concept of nature but in abandoning the idea that *culture* is something outside *nature*." Again: "To think societies is not to think something distinct from ecology but to think particular ecological formations."

This seems to amount both to an advance and to a return of sorts. It is an advance in the sense of getting past all that long-since-tired recitation of how the industrial age erased the nature–culture borderline, if indeed that had not already happened centuries if not millennia before. Yet it also seems a sort of return in the sense of entertaining a new kind of ecological holism, a post-humanist one, one that grants culture to nonhumans even as it insists that humanness including human "culture" is embedded in ecological process.

Can this revisionist ontology deliver a better ethics—not to mention politics—for the Anthropocene? That is a huge and unanswerable question. It is huge because humankind surely does need a Copernican revolution in the ethical arena to cope with the effects of the earlier Copernican revolution in science if humanity and the biosphere are to make it without horrendous cost into the twenty-second century. But it is unanswerable because although such a revolution may in fact be starting to happen, not even the youngest reader of these words will probably ever know, any more than Copernicus or Newton a century later could have predicted the Internet or the smart phone. Rachel Carson's *Silent Spring* is, after all, only fifty years old at this moment of writing. But if I am right in my description of this collection's loosely shared persuasion, and if the best insights here gain the traction that they deserve, then at least we can say that ecocriticism—whatever its eventual payoff direct or indirect as an intervention in the public sphere more generally—is moving toward a more auspicious conception of ontology and aesthetics than it has achieved thus far.

Note

1. Hans Jonas, *The Phenomenon of Life: Toward a Philosophical Biology* (Chicago: University of Chicago Press, 1966), 135–56.

ACKNOWLEDGMENTS

That color might do more than describe an inert property held by various things—that it might designate an environmental actant, with material effects—is an insight that has long been imaginable within ecotheory, but that possibility has often been circumscribed by an intense focus on the shade of green. Roam a wide terrain like the lithic reds near Sedona, the luminous beige on blue of the southeastern coast of Australia, the volcanic black and glacial white of Iceland, or the messy polychromes of Murray Hill, and hue's vibrancy becomes something more than an extraneous supplement that arrives belatedly to a substance, body, object. Color marks a restlessness, an inherent vivacity, within matter. It invites contemplation of the complicated agency of the stones, animals, plants, forces, architectures, palpable and invisible elements that compose ecologies: of their beauty, their fragility and resilience, their ability to sustain relations far deeper than anything analysis can plumb. Color is yet another rebuke to our inveterate anthropocentricity.

I brought the idea for this rainbow collection of essays to Richard Morrison at the University of Minnesota Press in the spring of 2011 and—as has always been the case—he was immediately supportive. Eighteen months later, the book enters production, my fourth in partnership with the press. Richard has my lasting gratitude for enabling *Prismatic Ecology* to thrive. His feedback at both early and advanced stages has been invaluable, and his enthusiasm sustaining. The contributors to this volume are a superb group of scholars and writers. Despite our swift schedule, they

have always been on time, willing to take creative risks, and full of astonishing verve. I cannot imagine working with a more inspirational group.
Special thanks to Larry Buell for composing so generous a foreword,
and to Serenella Iovino and Serpil Oppermann for their shimmering
onword. As a reader of the manuscript as well as spur to thinking creatively
about the book's mission, Karl Steel has been a full partner in the project;
I also thank the second, anonymous reader for valuable feedback. Haylie
Swenson composed the excellent index.

Funding to work on this project derived from the generous support of
both the American Council of Learned Societies and the John Simon
Guggenheim Foundation. In these days of diminishing resources for
humanities research, these two foundations are stalwarts. I also thank
my research assistant Emily Russell for her care in ensuring each chapter
was properly formatted and all small errors corrected. A conversation
on an airplane with Liza Blake helped me to imagine the contours of
this book. Lowell Duckert has been a constant and valued companion on
ecotheoretical endeavors. The colloquy that unfolded in my spring 2011
seminar "Objects, Ethics, and Agency" assisted in framing *Prismatic Ecology*. I thank the always amazing graduate students at George Washington
University for their enthusiasm for object-oriented ecologies.

Ecology's Rainbow

JEFFREY JEROME COHEN

"Composition" . . . underlines that things have to be put together
(Latin *componere*) while retaining their heterogeneity. Also, it is
connected with composure; it has clear roots in art, painting,
music, theater, dance, and thus is associated with choreography
and scenography; it is not too far from "compromise" and
"compromising," retaining a certain diplomatic and prudential
flavor. Speaking of flavor, it carries with it the pungent but
ecologically correct smell of "compost," itself due to the active
"de-composition" of many invisible agents.

—BRUNO LATOUR, "An Attempt at a
'Compositionist Manifesto'"

Prismatic Composition 1, ca. 1360–1375

An artist has painted an artist preparing to paint.[1] He sits at his desk, blankness of a white page attending. A world awaits composition—but not ex
nihilo. The artist is surrounded by floating bowls of color, each evocative
of materialities to come: two shades of yellow (one for hair, one for furni-
ture); a brown and verdant mélange for backgrounds and shadows; forest
green and orange mixed with crimson for vegetal flourishes; blue-tinged
violet, a shade for stockings and intricate manuscript borders; a lush red
for robes and the outline of a historiated capital. The rainbow of oversized
paint vessels holds the tints that the illuminator has actually employed to
compose this scene. *In a brown study,* as the saying goes: the perspective
here is not one of detached mastery (since its enmeshed framing emphasizes that "things have to be put together," it is difficult to find a stable outside to this meditation on composition).[2] The illustration instead offers an

implicative prospect, an extemporal dreaming: possibility through relation, collaborative engagement, emergence within material constraint.[3]

The mise-en-scène stresses that color is formative, the substrate as
well as conveyor of an intricate world. The white vellum is a collaborative
space as well as a substantial thing (skin from a grazing sheep; a blankness
that is not infinitely malleable; an object with ample properties and built-
in constraints). This mundane materiality is also evident in the fact that
the artist has mixed his colors from environmental compounds become
cultural actants. His artistic alliances are crafted with precise combinations of pulverized minerals, juice pressed from harvested berries, oak
gall boiled in water and mixed with powdered eggshells, common ash, rare
pollen, acidic urine. His pigments loom in enormous bowls, probably the
shells of mussels, harvested from the shore. They are larger than the artist,
importunate in their heft. Color is not some intangible quality that arrives
belatedly to the composition but a material impress, an agency and partner, a thing made of other things through which worlds arrive.

This medieval illustration of chromatic efficacy is placed within a large
letter C. Part of a fourteenth-century encyclopedia entry, the illuminated
capital introduces the Latin word *COLOR*. James le Palmer never finished his impossibly ambitious compilation of knowledge, the *Omne
Bonum*. Composition is exhausting. No matter how variegated the scheme,
more of the world remains to be gathered. No matter how capacious, taxonomy necessarily remains incomplete: you cannot fold the world into
an alphabet, or a palette. A white page rests in the middle of COLOR's en-
closing C.[4]

And bright white, as we know, needs only a transparent prism to begin
the work of diffraction, renewal, and multihued composition.

Prismatic Composition 2, ca. 2012

Like our medieval illuminator, the Dublin artist John Ryan paints color's
compositional agency. His pieces are sculptural, emphasizing the sub-
stantiality of hue, a phenomenon too often associated with mere light.
Ryan's installations stress that the artist cannot fully direct raw paint's flow,
thereby granting an elemental purposefulness to art's material base. Ryan
works mainly in luminous monochrome. His sturdy swathes of brushed
pigment capture a transmutation from liquid to solid, the congealing of

Figure 1. James le Palmer, "Color." British Library Royal 6 E VI f. 329. Copyright The British Library Board. All rights reserved.

color's vibrant materiality.[5] His large-scale installation "Polyptych," for example, concatenates lustrous accretions of oil paint, acetate sheets, and screws that fasten the various components into multihued assemblages. The masses of color artfully curved across these transparent sheets are heavy yet radiant, as vivacious as lichens, fungi, and epiphytes. Nothing is represented in these assemblages, but much comes into being. Color is allowed its dignity, its elemental ability to produce affect and sensation. The room in which these thick hues hang becomes a polychromatic, ecstatic ecology (from οἶκος: a fundamental unit, a household, a collectivizing space, a gathering of people and things). Through lively profusion Ryan's compositions open new ways of apprehending, feeling, imagining, narrating. A biome of hue.

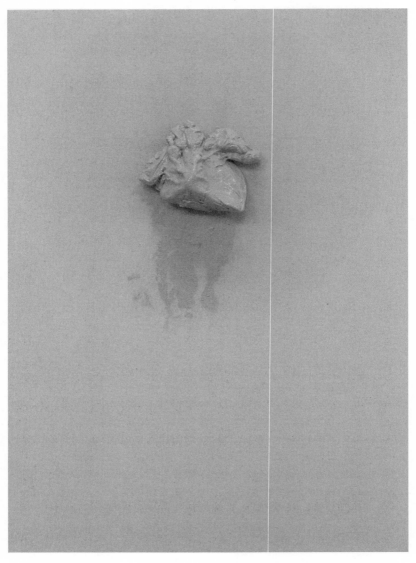

Figure 2. "God Is a Place," by John Ryan. Printed by kind permission of the artist.

Prismatic Composition 3, ca. 1700 BCE–5700 CE

An intimate of the restless glaciations of the Laurentide ice sheet, the Mississippi is an earth artist, but its projects take so long to execute that humans have a difficult time discerning their genius. The river composes with ice, stone, potent flows of water, heterogeneous biosystems, and tumbling sediment. Its current installation curves sinuously across 2,320 miles, extensively terraforms, slowly alters the Gulf of Mexico through delta formation, and constantly extends land into what had been sea. Every millennium or so the Mississippi undergoes avulsion, suddenly emptying itself somewhere else along the coast, leaving fertile bayous in its wake. Humans have attempted frequent domestication of the river. Dams, dikes, and levees modify its flow; industrial pollutants darken its currents; its waters are employed as an aqueous highway for the transport of goods. Yet the Mississippi is inassimilable. An incessant flow of objects, animals, elements, and forces not reducible to human use-value, the powerful river exerts a relentless agency easily readable in its engendered worlds. Its artist's colors derive from a fluvial spectrum that tends mostly to deep green, dim blue, and murky brown, but with glistening patches of yellow, some infrequent deep reds, and from time to time even violet.

Green Criticism

As they compose their worlds, the anonymous medieval illuminator, John Ryan, and the Mississippi River feature green prominently in their creative palates, but as one hue among many. Green dominates our thinking about ecology like no other, as if the color were the only organic hue, a blazon for nature itself. This verdant link makes a certain amount of sense. Chlorophyll deployed to harvest solar energy renders leaves and grasses green (even if they are also yellow, red, orange, purple, winter brown). The forest is predominantly a Green World. The color is lush, fecund, vigorous. Yet a preponderance of green prevents the eye from noticing that the aerial is as much a part of an ecology as the arboreal—and that when the heavens viridesce the tint presages tornado, not green peace. No woodland is monochrome (gray of tree bark, yellow penetration of solar spangles, crimson for low-hanging berries, beige for humus, black for birds, mushrooms, and snakes). Shadow itself is ecological: the umbra of plants, planets, stones creates ephemeral biosystems where questions of light matter more than specificities of hue.[6] Green has become our synonym for sustainability, but such a colorful ascription begs the question of exactly what mode of being we are attempting to sustain, and at what environmental cost.[7]

Green has long been the favored color of ecocriticism.[8] A green reading offers an environment-minded analysis of literature and culture, and is typically concerned with how nature is represented within a text and how modes of human inhabitance unfold within an imagined natural world. Like queer, feminist, and critical race analyses, green readings are inherently presentist and possess an admirably activist bent. Yet green readings have a tendency to reproduce what Bruno Latour calls the Great Bifurcation, a split between nature and culture that founds a structurating antinomy even in the face of constitutive and intractable hybridities.[9] Assuming such a split can lead to analyses stressing anthropocentric and detached concepts like stewardship, preservation, and prescriptive modes of environmental management.[10] Green analysis often focuses on the destabilizing encroachment of industrialized society into wild spaces, the restorative and even ecstatic powers of unblemished landscapes, and the companionless dignity of nonhuman creatures. Woodlands, serene waterscapes, sublime vistas, and charismatic megafauna feature prominently. Blending the romantic, the pastoral, and the georgic, green ecologies tend to dwell on the innate plenitude that nature offers, mourning its commodification and disruption. Such readings demonstrate a quiet faith in the totality envisioned by Deep Ecology, in a world that if left to its primordial solitude would abide in lasting stability.[11]

But green is also complicated. It is the hue of simple creatures like algae, and of flora indifferent to the lumbering of mammals, organisms without which large-scale aerobic life would be impossible. The green revolution was not without cost: the Great Oxygenation Event, the environmental introduction of oxygen into the atmosphere by photosynthetic creatures 2.4 billion years ago, triggered a mass extinction of anaerobic earth dwellers. This excess of oxygen also enabled thousands of new forms of minerals to flourish. The color is emblematic for the various Green Parties of the United States and Europe, some of which offer a traditional humanist politics of conservation, while others embrace ecoanarchism and radically open-ended structures for the emergence of new modes of life. Blending blue and yellow in varying proportions, green is a composite color that arrives in a multitude of shades. Many of these variations do not easily fit within my swift description of green criticism. Green modes of interpretation are powerfully attractive partly because they are not easily reduced to a facile program of analysis. The best green criticism is ceaseless in its natality. It does not necessarily know its conclusions in advance, but collaborates with text and world to craft something unpredetermined. Yet the color green too frequently signifies a return, however belatedly, to the verdancy of an unspoiled world, to whatever remnants of a lost paradise might be reclaimed. Classical and medieval myths of a golden age have been replaced by dreams of a primordial verdure, the Green Eden in which humans took no more from the land than they needed, and a sustainable mode of earthly inhabitance flourished. A corollary to such thinking renders indigenous peoples possessors of an ecological wisdom otherwise lost, so that native peoples are assumed to be closer to the land. Such reductivism represents contemporaries as living fossils, as if they existed out of time. Indigeneity (an almost impossible category: only Africa has indigenous humans) comes to represent a prehistory in which humans dwelled in a state of enchantment, were childlike in their simplicity, and because of their innocence from technology had not yet become ecologically alienated.[12] Yet some American Indians run casinos. Australia's largest native animals were hunted to extinction soon after Aboriginal peoples arrived, a swift disappearance that does not well accord with the assumption that natural equilibrium is the primeval state of hunter-gatherers or early agriculturalists.

Bright Green

As Timothy Morton points out, a preponderance of ecocritical writing is conducted in the shade of "bright green," a hue that tends to be "affirmative, extraverted and masculine" as well as "sunny, straightforward, ableist, holistic, hearty, and 'healthy.'"[13] Bright green is also too solitary, a romantic color through which individuals commune with nature and arrive at personal revelations and solipsistic calm—as if nature were an angel or messenger. To obtain such revelatory power the wilderness must be imagined as a purified place to which one travels rather than dwells always within: separate from the human, empty, foundationally pure. Yet as Stephen J. Pyne details, landscapes that arriving Europeans perceived as untouched had been profoundly reconfigured by fire regimes, such as those pre-Contact peoples in Australia developed to manage the diverse environments in which they dwelled.[14] Lawrence Buell has written compellingly of how ecofeminism and environmental justice—among many other movements within ecological theory—can move us beyond the lonely limits of some green ardors toward more communal and collaborative formations.[15] Yet even a feminist, postcolonial, or queer ecocriticism is not necessarily an analysis that moves beyond green.[16] Verdant, parklike, and unpopulated, Spaceship Earth (that green, blue, and white marble suspended in a cosmic sea of black) offers too bounded, too totalized, and too self-contained a vision.[17] To compose (write, paint, envision, act) ecologically is to build-in openness, and therefore vulnerability.

It is not easy being viridescent. Bright green criticism emphasizes balance, the innate, the primal, landscapes with few people, macrosystems, the unrefined. What of the catastrophic, the disruptive, urban ecologies, the eruptive, heterogeneous microclimates, inhumanly vast or tiny scales of being and time, the mixed spaces where the separation of nature and culture are impossible to maintain? Underneath every field stretches an unplumbable cosmos of primordial stone, worms, recent debris, reservoirs of natural and manufactured chemicals, poisonous and fertile muck. In a green Arcadia what do we make of the airplane, graves, gamma rays, bacteria, invasive bamboo accidentally planted as an ornament, inorganic agency, the crater become a lake, the invisibly advancing or receding glacier, relentless lunar pull, electronic realms, prehistoric flora lingering as plastic refuse, lost supercontinents, parasites, inorganic compounds that act like living creatures, species undergoing sudden change? Other colors may be necessary to trace the impress and interspaces created by ecologies that cannot be easily accommodated within the bucolic expanses of green readings, or at least within those that possess a utopian emphasis on homeostasis, order, and the implicit benevolence of an unexamined force labeled Nature. What of the ocean's violet turbulence, the beige fecundity of excrement, the blue solitude of the wandering iceberg, the mineral excrescence of a gray city, the polychromatic lives of objects that may or may not demonstrate an interest in connecting to human spaces? Nature is not a creature of seclusion and solace, but a concept for repeated interrogation, a term without transparent explanatory force. The chapters of this volume argue that breaking monochromatic light into a multitude of colors offers a suggestive entryway into nonanthropocentric ecologies, where the *oikos* is not so much a bounded home as an ever-unfinished world.

Ursula K. Heise has demonstrated that, contrary to a belief long cherished in environmental studies, an attachment to the local does not necessarily foster the globalized ethic of care demanded in a transnational age.[18] Her notion of ecocosmopolitanism is useful for broadening critical perspectives, substituting a view from a planet at risk for the boundedness of small citizenships. But a sense of planet will not in the end be capacious enough. Space is as multiple as it is disorderly. Moving beyond the near-to-hand and pastoral (i.e., bright green) locales that are the focus of much environmental criticism requires emphasizing the *cosmos* in ecocosmopolitanism—yet not in the classic sense of a tidy and beautiful whole (Greek *kosmos* means "order, ornament"). Latour coined the "dirty" term *kakosmos* to describe the tangled, fecund, and irregular pluriverse humans inhabit along with lively and agency-filled objects, materials, and forces.[19] A middle space, unbounded, perturbed, contingent. "Contingency," observes Michel Serres, "means common tangency," haptic entanglement of body and world, knotted and multidimensional admixture, so that "knowing things requires one first of all to place oneself between them."[20]

Multihued Agency

Following colors in their materiality as entry into this messy intricacy, the contributors to this volume follow the human and nonhuman actors with which the ecokakosmopolitan is always in alliance: mysterious forces, object and organisms that do not fully disclose themselves, radiation, black holes, distant arms of the galaxy and event horizons, shit and muck, the ephemeral and the volatile, disability, distillation, capitalism as an ordering system, domestication, alien substances, supernovas, urban sprawls, the undead, lost worlds, networks of travel or sonority, human difference, negativity, depression, the aurora borealis, deep-sea dwellers, luminescence for no audience, feedback loops, alien metals, soundscapes, slaughterhouses, environmental justice, chimeras, the vegetal, the indistinct, the solitary, failure, queerness, violence, swamps, an errancy of earth and seas and skies.[21] The spectrum is an unfinishable totality, an open expanse that gathers for a while a range of possible relations, always in excess of what a human perceives (ultraviolet and beyond, infrared and beyond). No Green Eden here, but a restless expanse of multihued contaminations, impurities, hybridity, monstrosity, contagion, interruption, hesitation, enmeshment, refraction, unexpected relations, and wonder. A swirl of colors, a torrent, a muddy river.

Perhaps it was surprising to see the Mississippi appear alongside a medieval illuminator and a Dublin painter as the third artist in the chromatic vignettes with which this introductory chapter opens. To claim a river can create is perhaps to subscribe to a naive animism; to believe that rivers compose might be to project human qualities on indifferent things; to call ancient fluvial terraforming a mode of earth art could ascribe desire to matter devoid of will. Yet what is at stake in limiting agency to an origin in human volition—as if we intend much of what we accomplish? The profundity of climate change in the Anthropocene argues against such easy alignment. Causes tend to be known retroactively when they are known at all, traced back through multiple threads of effect, through volatile knots of human and inhuman actors operating in alliance as well as at odds with each other. When Jane Bennett maps the intricacies of the American power grid during a substantial blackout, no single intention—or single actor, or single failing—can be found to trigger the spiral of effects that collapsed a network.[22] "Human" is one among a wide many. No observer can even conceptualize this shifting mesh of power lines, generators, engineers, distribution nodes, consumers, conveyors, geographic expanses, appliances, managers, weather, and electrical flow in its entirety: there is no divine or objective perspective on a web within of such deep relation. Agency is distributed among multifarious relations and not necessarily knowable in advance: actions that unfold along the grid surprise and then confound. This *agentism* is a form of activism: only in admitting that the inhuman is not ours to control, possesses desires and even will, can we apprehend the environment disanthropocentrically, in a teetering mode that renders human centrality a problem rather than a starting point.[23] As Andrew Pickering observes, "Instead of seeing dualist detachment and domination as a move, a tactic, a ploy, and a very specific way of living in the flow of becoming, we tend to mistake it for the world itself."[24] The power grid is, like a desert or a pond or a household, itself an open system composed of biological, inorganic, natural, and technological actors, an untidy and dispersive entanglement similar to what Pickering calls a mangle, Latour a network, Morton a mesh, Stacy Alaimo transcorporeality, Tim Ingold a meshwork, Gilles Deleuze and Félix Guattari an assemblage, Graham Harman (working in a register with far greater emphasis on the integrity of objects, but one in deep sympathy with network theory) the quadruple object, mapped via ontography.[25] Such a web might also be called an environment (from a Middle English noun that means *circuit*, itself from an Old French verb that means *to veer*) or an ecosystem (a fragile co-dwelling of organisms, things, and elements in relation). These motion-filled metaphors might seem too much like forceful rivers, animated by relentless flow. Yet nonhuman things do not thereby vanish into a swirl of primordial possibility, as if nothing possessed integrity. Instead the human and the nonhuman are granted the ability to forge multiple connections, to sustain (or break) transformative relations, to bring about the new thing, to create, to vanish, to surprise. Even rivers on the move possess their submerged stones, overhanging cliffs, vorticose shallows, lush bayous, obscure thrivings.

Rainbow and Arrow

A natural phenomenon as simple as a rainbow, sudden child of a pluvial prism, illustrates well how ensnarled relations among human actors and inhuman actants may be. This ethereal spectrum shimmers when a tumble of raindrops refracts and reflects daylight back to an observer at an angle of 42 degrees. For the sun's white brilliance to separate into its constituent colors, its rays must arrive from directly behind the perceiver. The source of a rainbow's luminosity therefore cannot be glimpsed at the same time as the rainbow itself. A rainbow must also be constantly renewed to remain visible. Once the mist or showers stop, the bow is gone. The rainbow that we glimpse one moment is the gift of different water than that of the previous moment. But these ethereal bands of color are even more complicated. Like the horizon, rainbows are perspectival and therefore exist in no particular location. Since the angle of ocular perception cannot precisely coincide for any two onlookers, to stand in a slightly different place yields a different arc. As Giovanni Battista Vico proved long ago, each eye of the same observer beholds a divergent rainbow, a fact that can be proved by closing one at a time, causing the bow to "jump." As Philip Fisher observes, because the rainbow is an optical effect that depends on a specific kind of visual apparatus to come into being, "without observers, there are no rainbows."[26] The celestial band of hues shimmers through a particular biology without which it cannot exist. A rainbow forms when the organic and the inorganic, eye and sunlight, matter and energy are brought into a sudden relation that changes the quality of light itself. The rainbow exists as an object, but an interstitial one, at a meeting place of relations and materiality. A rainbow is an alliance: solar gleam, errant cloud, waterdrops in motion, captivated human, changed world. We could diagram the conditions necessary to observe a rainbow, placing the human in the middle, the sun directly behind, and a plummet of refracting raindrops above. Yet this totality is impossible as a lived perspective. When we see the rainbow we are enmeshed within refracted light from an obscured source. The arc of radiant colors is a medial thing, a cocreation. Its polychromatic curve arrives through optical and biological intimacy with color, through a prismatic impress that engenders ecological composition. We behold the rainbow by living with its cloudbursts and sunlight, by attuning ourselves to our dwelling within a particular environmental space. The result of finding ourselves in the company of this rare object is wonder, an aesthetic experience essential to thought (cognition begins when we are struck by a thing that has called attention to itself).[27] Its contingency or mutuality (which also might be called a *composition* in Latour's sense, a placing together that retains difference) renders the pluvial prism no less real.

Messenger

"Iris" is therefore the Greek and Latin word for rainbow; a noun designating the colored ring in the human eye; and the name of a messenger who connects heaven and earth, human and nonhuman realms. Intimates of the elements as well as objects in abiding human relation, rainbows hint at the complexities that dwell both within and beyond green ecologies. Following the path of the arc's rain as it cascades to the earth and feeds a small stream, we may find ourselves propelled along creeks to bourns, tributaries, headwaters, all the way to the torrential roll of the Mississippi. A traditional ecocritical reading of this mightiest of American rivers would likely focus on what might be called the "River as It Was," a Green Mississippi that comprises a small Gaia, a bounded and balanced system existing in placid indifference to the human world. Indigenous peoples may have fished along its banks or coursed its restless waters in small boats, but this is the river before industry arrives—before anyone thought to dam its flow, harness its force, or redirect its course. An Edenic space, a waterway of innate plenitude, the Green Mississippi runs outside cataclysm or imbalance, runs outside history. Such a river never existed. Its waters perpetually erode the earth, reshaping the kaleidoscope of biomes that cluster along its long path. The massive amounts of silt it moves downstream have altered the Gulf of Mexico profoundly. Catastrophe flows at vitality's side.

The Mississippi can be a languid sweep, abounding in aesthetic power and serene plenty. But the river is also place of danger: drought, flood, scouring force, hazardous currents, cataclysmic changes of course. This perilous waterway is similar to what Steve Mentz calls a blue ecology.[28] Mentz employs the term to designate an environmental cultural studies focused on the ocean. "The sea is not our home," he writes, and when we venture on its waves we face extinction, a "bitter ecology of salt."[29] Yet his marinal insights are also true of some fresh and brackish waters. Though they differ in scale and dynamism and do not therefore necessarily convey the same hazards—shallow and local spaces against the ocean's universalism, vastness, and profundity—no water offers a safe or permanent habitation to terrestrial creatures. The Blue Mississippi (or Old Blue, as the river is sometimes called) is an aqueous surge that cannot be our home. We are earthbound creatures. Submergence is our demise, the ruin of those who think ecology's *oikos* is anthropocentric, that its inhuman force may be domesticated into lasting or comfortable shelter. Water is a deep and alien world, filled with animals we might harvest but only at our peril. A river, like the ocean, swallows. It is no Eden.

Pollution, silt, and swift force ensure that the roiled depths of the Mississippi are murky. This fast-moving flow is too powerful to gain a secure epistemological foothold within: it keeps knocking foundations loose, keeps disturbing what we know. The Muddy Mississippi is the brown river, a place of interstices, mixing, hybridity, autonomy, cogency. The closer to the sea it flows the more impure it becomes, culminating in an estuary that combines saltwater with fresh and everything with mud. *Estuary* comes from the Latin word *aestus,* a boiling, a tide. It is etymologically related to the words for summer (*aestas*) and building (*aedes,* and thereby "edify"):

time and tide in composition. Estuaries are places of precarious existence (not every organism can adapt to brackish flow). They are also stone-producing factories. Much of our terrestrial lithic inheritance derives from alluvial deposits that have been enfolded into landmasses as the continents drift the seas. The Brown Mississippi transports us into geologic time frames, into a temporal scale so vast that the agency of the river becomes palpable as it terraforms two thousand miles of land, scattering sediment into the Gulf of Mexico and giving birth to future bedrock. Within this fluvial timescale, the river's desires also become more evident: "The Mississippi wants to move."[30] Engineers and city planners have long battled the river, erecting artificial levees atop the natural embankments of riparian New Orleans. The strategy has never worked. The river keeps rising, so that the levee walls loom so high that cargo ships now pass overhead relative to the city streets. The desire of the Muddy Mississippi is to pour into the Atchafalaya River and surge into the Gulf a few hundred miles west of its current delta. A long history of the river demonstrates that such shifts in its course are inevitable. Yet because a change in the Mississippi's flow would mean that New Orleans would lose its freshwater supply (and thereby the shipping and industrial production that sustains the city), a prolonged battle has been waged against the current's agency. Instead of living with the muddy river, those dwelling in New Orleans have attempted its domestication. The river continues to rise and to eat away at its constraining levees, sometimes with disastrous results.[31] As Hurricane Katrina well illustrated, those who pay the highest price (loss of home, loss of livelihood, loss of life) when such domination fails are those who are civilly disempowered, minorities and the poor. The Muddy Mississippi demands attention to inhuman timescales, but its flow is not oblivious to environmental justice.

The River that Is: the Brown Mississippi, with its murk, lithic factory of an estuary, strong currents, peril, and geological temporality. What of the River to Be? An ecosystem is an oikosystem, a *dwelling* system. Is there a wider way to conceptualize ecology, one that embraces the harmonies of green, the dangers of blue, and the difficult admixtures of brown, but recognizes that there is not sufficient dwelling space in any of these hues? Green loves nature left to itself; blue traces spaces inimical to home building, brown leaves some cities dry, others inundated, nothing much affirmed.

A more prospective palette emerges when these colors are allowed contiguity and contingency, joining them to others. The colors of the prism are manifold, nebulous, less easy to divide than we think. Indigo dwells between blue and violet because Isaac Newton liked the color of an imported dye. The human eye perceives a limited spectrum; some animals behold more than we can. Every hue, real or imagined, bodes a world.

Prospect

A rainbow promises. The skyborne arc is a biblical sign of covenant, of God's pledge not to scour the world's entirety again. Despite this assurance, though, its curve threatens. The *bow* or *arcus* in the sky is named after a martial weapon, what grows tight to let fly the deadly arrow. Sometimes the rainbow is a symbol of harmony, yet it is also provisional, perspectival, fleeting, messy. It is also a little embarrassing. We associate rainbows with the juvenile. Color is often denigrated this way, to attenuate its power. Bright tone, like the wonder it inspires, is relegated to children. Rainbows have therefore become trippy, a symbol of queer alliance, of nonnormative occupation of space. By refracting light into manifold colors and gathering those hues and their observers into a temporary community, rainbows have diverse material effects.

And they also remain themselves. Though they appear in the heavens, rainbows are indifferent to allegory. No arc in the sky can portend safety, can promise futurity. The deluge will arrive. Clouds do what clouds do, light's relentless agency and energy persist whether observed or not, forces and objects among other forces and objects, entering into all kinds of relations with each other, unconcerned with us. I write these lines by hand in the wake of a derecho, the arc-shaped spawn of anthropogenic climate change that cut a destructive swath from Chicago through West Virginia to Washington, D.C., in the summer of 2012. Our house lost power for a week. Many less fortunate people lost their dwellings, even their lives. A meteorological sympathy we have built into our technology rendered the radar representation of the derecho's spearhead an enormous rainbow that moved swiftly across the continent, smashing trees as it relentlessly coursed.

Yet the rainbow is also a partner. It requires our eyes. With it we compose. An object in perpetual motion, the rainbow is ephemeral, but perceived because it touches, excites, compels. The rainbow is what we behold when we realize we live in the thickness of things, in a world where the sun and the rain and our eyes and our skin and our desires are part of a system without a totality, without an outside. A rainbow's arc is a dispersal of color, but its curve is made possible only through a gathering of the elements. Love, desire, agency, human, and nonhuman alliances: as Empedocles wrote long ago, reflecting on how the world came to be composed, the binding of the elements, of the primal materiality of the cosmos, is *philia*.[32]

There is no over the rainbow. The arc recedes as we draw close. Or, better, the rainbow is at once intimate and distinct, a partner in composition as well as an energetic object that retains its integrity, inexhaustibility, mystery. Because I cannot speak this ecological vision any better, I close with Derek Jarman's meditation from *Chroma,* the book of poetry and color that he composed while dying, as gift and as future. *Chroma* is itself a prism, gathering the world beneath its radiant colors, from White and Shadow through Rose, Blue, and Isaac Newton to Iridescence and Translucence. The rainbow Jarman envisions as the volume draws to its end, as his life draws to its end, is elemental. It bridges like and unlike, culture and nature, promise and indifference, human and inhuman, oil and water: "Who has not gazed in wonder at the snaky shimmer of petrol patterns on a puddle, thrown a stone into them and watched the colours emerge out of the ripples, or marvelled at the bright rainbow arcing momentarily in the burst of sunlight against the dark storm clouds?"[33]

And the binding of the elements is love.

Notes

1. The image I am discussing is from the *Omne Bonum* of James le Palmer, now held in the British Library and cataloged as Royal 6 E VI f. 329. The electronic record for the manuscript may be found here: http://www.bl.uk/catalogues/illu minatedmanuscripts/record.asp?MSID=7788&CollID=16&NStart=60506.

2. See Bruno Latour, "An Attempt at a Compositionist Manifesto," *New Literary History* 41 (2010): 473.

3. In thinking about a perspective of mastery versus a surrender to transformative relation, I have in mind Andrew Pickering's paradigmatic reading of Willem de Kooning and Piet Mondrian in "New Ontologies," in *The Mangle in Practice: Science, Society, and Becoming,* ed. Andrew Pickering and Keith Guzik (Durham, N.C.: Duke University Press, 2008), 1–14, as well as the two strangely convergent, anxious terms for domination and management in Simon C. Estok, *Ecocriticism*

and Shakespeare: Reading Ecophobia (New York: Palgrave Macmillan, 2011) and David Batchelor, *Chromophobia* (London: Reaktion Books, 2000).

4. Le Palmer's multitude of entries for "A" run the gamut from *absolutio* (absolution), *acutus sapor* (intense flavor), and *advocatus* (lawyer) to *adulterium* (adultery), *agere* (to act), *alea* (dice), and *aqua* (water). B is nearly as copious in its gathering of natural and social terms, C and D even more expansive. Yet by the time the encyclopedist arrives at letter N, his energy has flagged. A single entry per letter henceforth appears. Le Palmer's encyclopedia is thoroughly examined by Lucy Freeman Dandler in *Omne Bonum: A Fourteenth-Century Encyclopedia of Universal Knowledge* (London: Harbey Miller, 1996–99), 2 vols.

5. "Vibrant" or "vital" materiality is Jane Bennett's useful entryway into the agency of matter in her book *Vibrant Matter: A Political Ecology of Things* (Durham, N.C.: Duke University Press, 2010). See also the copious work being conducted under the descriptor of the "new materialism," such as *New Materialisms: Ontology, Agency, and Politics,* ed. Diana Coole and Samantha Frost (Durham, N.C.: Duke University Press, 2010) and *Material Feminisms,* ed. Stacy Alaimo and Susan Hekman (Bloomington: Indiana University Press, 2008). I would like to thank Michael O'Rourke for introducing me to John Ryan, and the artist himself for sharing his work with me and discussing its aims.

6. For an ecological phenomenology of shadow, see David Abram, *Becoming Animal: An Earthly Cosmology* (New York: Vintage Books, 2010), 13–24.

7. Most scholarship on sustainability either takes it for granted as a self-evident goal or critiques it as a mode for living with minimal change of habit. For a sophisticated rereading of its key concepts (including energy, expenditure, and excess), see Allan Stoekl, *Bataille's Peak: Energy, Religion, and Postsustainability* (Minneapolis: University of Minnesota Press, 2007), as well as the essays published in the *PMLA* "Sustainability" cluster (vol. 127 [2012]: 558–606).

8. A selective overview of the field and survey of some early key texts may be found in *The Green Studies Reader: From Romanticism to Ecocriticism,* ed. Laurence Coupe (London: Routledge, 2000). It would be difficult today to begin such a volume with the eighteenth century, since ecocritical modes have been profoundly influential in the early modern and (increasingly) medieval periods. Some scholars distinguish between ecocriticism as literature-focused and green cultural studies as more capacious in its analytic scope (e.g., Graham Huggan and Helen Tiffin, *Postcolonial Ecocriticism: Literature, Animals, and the Environment* [London: Routledge, 2010], 24), but that distinction seldom holds in scholarly practice, which tends inherently to the interdisciplinary.

9. Latour argues against the factual neutrality of science as much as he does the self-evidence of nature. In addition to his "Compositionist Manifesto," see

also "Why Has Critique Run out of Steam? From Matters of Fact to Matters of Concern," *Critical Inquiry* 30 (2004): 225–48; *We Have Never Been Modern,* trans. Catherine Porter (Cambridge, Mass.: Harvard University Press, 1993); and especially *Politics of Nature: How to Bring the Sciences into Democracy,* trans. Catherine Porter (Cambridge, Mass.: Harvard University Press, 2004), where Latour describes the death of Pan and argues that "ecology dissolves nature's contours and redistributes its agents" (21). See also Émilie Hache and Bruno Latour, "Morality or Moralism? An Exercise in Sensitization," trans. Patrick Camiller, *Common Knowledge* 16, no. 2 (2010): 311–30. For a seminal example of a green criticism that at once complicates the color by critically revaluating Romanticism's "ever green" language yet remains wholly invested in a self-evident and keenly demarcated nature, see Jonathan Bate, *Romantic Ecology: Wordsworth and the Environmental Tradition* (London: Routledge, 1991).

    10. Greg Garrard calls it "anthropocentric managerialism" and points out that its too easy indictment tends to privilege intuition and "modern reconstructions of . . . 'primal' religions" over science (*Ecocriticism* [London: Routledge, 2010], 23). Cf. Lynn White Jr., who aligns a tendency toward the domination of nature with Christianity and finds an alternative in Francis of Assisi ("The Historical Roots of Our Ecological Crisis," *Science* 155 [1967]: 1203–7, reprinted in *The Ecocriticism Reader,* ed. Cheryll Glotfelty and Harold Fromm [Athens: University of Georgia Press, 1996]: 3–14). A balanced emphasis on science and indigenous practices as postcolonial, mediated, and local ways of knowing may be found in Julie Cruikshank, *Do Glaciers Listen? Local Knowledge, Colonial Encounters, and Social Imagination* (Seattle: University of Washington Press, 2005); yet like all the work so far cited, Cruikshank's is almost unremitting in its anthropocentricity. For a bracing examination of what the world would look like from a disanthropocentric point of view, see Ian Bogost, *Alien Phenomenology, or What It's Like to Be a Thing* (Minneapolis: University of Minnesota Press, 2012). Bogost's work is allied with the movement known as object-oriented ontology. Heavily indebted to the philosophy of Levi Bryant, Graham Harman, and Timothy Morton, its influence is evident throughout this introduction as well as the volume as a whole.

    11. Most famously, this totality becomes James Lovelock's Gaia, the earth considered as a single organism. "Deep ecology" itself is associated with the work of Gary Snyder and Arne Naess. Within such totalized models, disequilibrium-prone humans can easily become not a part of the system but a virus or cancer (leading to a call for their eradication so that Mother Earth can recover). The gendering of the planet as feminine, moreover, can also play into its exploitation, as Val Plumwood and Carolyn Merchant have argued. For a good overview of the strengths and weaknesses of green approaches in the encounter with historically

diverse literature that stresses unease rather than balance, see Gillian Rudd, *Greenery: Ecocritical Readings of Late Medieval English Literature* (Manchester: Manchester University Press, 2007), especially 1–19.

12. Drawing on the work of Shepard Krech III (*The Ecological Indian: Myth and History* [New York: Norton, 1999]), Lawrence Buell aptly labels this figure "the paradigmatic 'ecological Indian,' the model minority sage of green wisdom," and the "eco-sensitive indigene" (*The Future of Environmental Criticism: Environmental Crisis and the Literary Imagination* [Oxford: Blackwell, 2004], 23–24).

13. Timothy Morton, *The Ecological Thought* (Cambridge, Mass.: Harvard University Press, 2010), 16. Morton's idea of a "dark ecology," with its uncertainties, implicatedness, and refusal to offer a metaposition, has much resonance throughout this volume.

14. Pyne makes this point repeatedly throughout the series of volumes he has dubbed the "Cycle of Fire," but see especially *Burning Bush: A Fire History of Australia* (New York: Henry Holt, 1991). Stephanie Trigg and I have followed this fiery line more closely in our essay "Fire," *postmedieval* 4 (2013): 80–92.

15. See Buell's magisterial *The Future of Environmental Criticism*, 97–127. For an inspirational enacting of this envisioned future, as well as a meditation on some alternatives, see Serpil Oppermann, Ufuk Özdağ, Nevin Özkan, and Scott Slovic, eds., *The Future of Ecocriticism: New Horizons* (Newcastle upon Tyne: Cambridge Scholars, 2011).

16. Compare, for example, the otherwise excellent collection of essays *Queer Ecologies: Sex, Nature, Politics and Desire,* ed. Catriona Mortimer-Sandilands and Bruce Erickson (Bloomington: University of Indiana Press, 2010), with its recurring oppositions between sex and nature, nature and environment, the natural world and the human constitution of that world (e.g., "Introduction," 5), to the thoroughgoing posthumanism of *Queering the Non/Human,* ed. Noreen Giffney and Myra J. Hird (Farnham, UK: Ashgate, 2008).

17. For a short history of the contradictory meanings of the image of the earth as viewed from space, see Garrard, *Ecocriticism*, 160–62.

18. Ursula K. Heise, *Sense of Place and Sense of Planet: The Environmental Imagination of the Global* (Oxford: Oxford University Press, 2008). For an explication of ecocosmopolitanism, see especially 57–67. Heise stresses the human–nonhuman alliances on which this sense is built at 157–59.

19. See Latour, *Politics of Nature,* 99; Latour, "Compositionist Manifesto," 481.

20. Michel Serres, *The Five Senses: A Philosophy of Mingled Bodies,* trans. Margaret Sankey and Peter Cowley (London: Continuum, 2008), 80.

21. This list in part details the contents of this collection of essays, but also fore-grounds some of the critical approaches that many of the essays have in common—especially those critical modes that have been labeled the new materialisms and object-oriented ontology.

22. See Bennett's discussion of assemblages, distributed agency, thing-power, and a massive blackout in *Vibrant Matter,* 23–38; compare what she writes about something so obviously animated (electricity) to the life she finds even in the crystals that compose metal (52–61). Although his approach is very different, for a detailed consideration of life as non-self-evident and not reducible to biology, see Eugene Thacker, *After Life* (Chicago: University of Chicago Press, 2010).

23. The ethics of this objectal agency are explored in the collection *Animal, Vegetable, Mineral: Ethics and Objects,* ed. Jeffrey J. Cohen (New York: Oliphaunt/punctum books, 2012).

24. Pickering, "New Ontologies," 4.

25. See Andrew Pickering, *The Mangle of Practice: Time, Agency, and Science* (Chicago: University of Chicago Press, 1995); Bruno Latour, *Reassembling the Social* (Oxford: Oxford University Press, 2005); Morton, *Ecological Thought;* Stacy Alaimo, *Bodily Natures: Science, Environment, and the Material Self* (Bloomington: Indiana University Press, 2010); Tim Ingold, *Being Alive: Essays on Movement, Knowledge, and Description* (London: Routledge, 2011); Gilles Deleuze and Félix Guattari, *A Thousand Plateaus: Capitalism and Schizophrenia,* trans. Brian Massumi (Minneapolis: University of Minnesota Press, 1987), as well as the inspirational essays assembled in *Deleuze/Guattari and Ecology,* ed. Bernd Herzogenrath (New York: Palgrave Macmillan, 2009); and Graham Harman, *The Quadruple Object* (Alresford, UK: Zero Books, 2011). Examples of this kind of dispersive intimacy could be multiplied across material, bodily, and network theory, but these are some articulations that have aided me in this project.

26. Rainbows are in this way a phenomenon that marks a relation between eye and landscape, a meeting place rather than an autonomous thing. Fisher therefore writes that "on an uninhabited planet there would continue to be sun and rain, stars and snow, but there would be no rainbow and no horizon." See Philip Fisher, *Wonder, the Rainbow, and the Aesthetics of Rare Experiences* (Cambridge, Mass.: Harvard University Press, 1998), 37, 122–23.

27. Fisher writes, "Rare objects . . . elicit from us an activity . . . the activity is, of course intellectual. . . . Wonder begins with something imposed on us for thought" (*Wonder, the Rainbow, and the Aesthetics of Rare Experiences,* 40).

28. Steve Mentz, *At the Bottom of Shakespeare's Ocean* (London: Continuum, 2009). Against a landlocked green perspective, a blue ecology conveys what Mentz calls the "real taste of ocean . . . a sharp tang of nonhuman immensity" (1) that wrenches us violently from our "landed perspectives" (3).

29. Mentz, *At the Bottom,* 18. Cf. "the ocean is no place to live. . . . Long ago we crawled out of the water. We can't go back" (96). The book's closing section ("Toward a Blue Cultural Studies") is as beautiful as it is compelling. See also Dan Brayton, *Shakespeare's Ocean: An Ecocritical Exploration* (Charlottesville: University of Virginia Press, 2012), who writes of green's terrestrial bias and writes of "chlorophilia—an inability to look beyond the imagery of the land and its leafy green oak. Green is indeed a vital color, but it is not nature's only shade" (37).

30. Pickering, "New Ontologies," 6.

31. This account of the Mississippi's flow and the war of the engineers to constrain it is based on Pickering, "New Ontologies," 5–13; and John McPhee, "Atchafalya: The Control of Nature," *New Yorker,* February 23, 1987, http://www .newyorker.com/archive/1987/02/23/1987_02_23_039_TNY_CARDS_000 347146?currentPage=all.

32. An excellent and easily accessible introduction to the work of Empedocles (including the surviving Greek fragments and an English translation) may be found at http://classicpersuasion.org/pw/empedocles/.

33. From "Iridescence" in Derek Jarman, *Chroma: A Book of Color* (Minneapolis: University of Minnesota Press, 2010).

White

BERND HERZOGENRATH

What is a white ecology? What does it look like, what does it contain? What is covered, what is left out? In a way, is not a white ecology—at least in the political, racial sense—what has been there, always, what is silently (or not so silently) practiced as the default mode of ecology? Is not green the new white, in such a way that ecology as we know it is firmly set and rooted in the Western Christian—white—tradition of Metaphysics?

On the other hand, a white ecology could also mean an ecology that encompasses many different ecologies. Like white encompasses the colors of the spectrum, a white ecology might provide a context in which different eco*logics* (different ecological fields, such as human, viral, chemical, etc., that all follow their own logics and trajectories) resonate with each other. An ecology motivated by the philosophy of Gilles Deleuze and Félix Guattari, I argue, can provide such a space—it is basically a call to think complexity, and to complex thinking, a way to think the environment as a negotiation of dynamic arrangements of cultural *and* natural forces, of both nonhuman and human stressors and tensors, both of which are informed and "intelligent." It refers to a pragmatic unfolding of these infinitely complex arrangements, and as such can rest solely on neither a theory of cultural constructivism nor natural or biological determinism. Deleuze and Guattari provide a useful toolbox for such a project—Guattari has even called for, in his book *Chaosmosis,* "a science of ecosystems" and a "generalized ecology—or ecosophy."[1]

Guattari points out the relevance of a *generalized* ecology: not just "one world—one ecology." It may thus be important to turn an eco*logics*—a "generalized" environmental studies (by definition both local *and* global)— into a "general project" that traverses philosophy, sociology, linguistics, politics, art, history, the hard and soft sciences, drawing not on linear dynamics but on chaos- and complexity theory, propagating logics of open systems (with a minimum of structural stability) and morphogeneses that link various fields of research within a chaotic, ecosophic, and ecological reference. The perspective point of such an ecologics has nothing of a technophobic Luddism, and it comes without the regressive *eco*logical rhetorics found in some of the more "conservative" strands of environmental studies. Neither does it follow the one-way logic of social|linguistic constructivism encountered in much of a more "traditional" ecocriticism:

> The ecocritic wants to track environmental ideas and representations wherever they appear, to see more clearly a debate which seems to be taking place, often part-concealed, in a great many cultural spaces. Most of all, ecocriticism seeks to evaluate texts and ideas in terms of their coherence and usefulness as responses to environmental crisis.[2]

Unlike the majority of "traditional" ecological or ecocritical approaches, a Deleuzian and Guattarian version of ecology does not see "nature" as a single and unified totality; it does not at all rhyme with Al Gore's fantasy of The World Formerly Known as the Harmonious Universe, thrown out of its proper balance by mankind, the dominator and exploiter, and to be *re*stored by man, its steward. Nature, seen as a dynamic, open, and turbulent whole, is posed not in balance but more in what Ludwig von Bertalanffy has termed "Fließgleichgewicht" (flowing, turbulent balance).[3]

Guattari, then, at the end of *Chaosmosis*, comes to criticize the ecological movement in France precisely for its narrow pragmatics. He also scolds the movement's tendency to make "ecology" refer to nature only, when what is needed as well is a cultural ecology, whose development has been increasingly at the center of cultural studies. "Nature," "landscape," "environment"—in postmodern times, all these terms and their connotations can no longer be restricted to what one once called "the natural." Seemingly clear-cut categories such as nature and man, human and nonhuman, are no

longer tenable and cannot anymore be grounded in an essentialist separation, as Deleuze states, "now that any distinction between nature and artifice
is becoming blurred."[4] The Deleuzian and Guattarian model of ecology
affords a single mode of articulating cultural, environmental, and evolutionary relations within ecological systems and makes room for conceptualiz-
ing a general, nonanthropomorphic affectivity within dynamic systems.

Genesis in White

I want to start with a little story of white—two stories, in fact . . . two
"founding myths."

In the Beginning was the Word, and the Word was with God, and the
Word was God. But where did the word fall, where did it leave its trace?
Where did it echo, resonate? So, before the word, there must have been
some background, some canvas, some blank page? As Deleuze and Guattari have it, "Significance is never without a *white wall* upon which it
inscribes its signs and redundancies."[5] So, in the beginning was the White.
Uniform, indistinctive whiteness. And God wrote. The omniscient author
had no writer's block. Facing the absolute whiteness, always following
the Golden Ratio, he separated light from darkness, the waters from the
land, night from day, and so on. So from uniform whiteness, different colors, objects, things—life emerged, because God spoke or wrote the word.
God was the word.

So much for the Hebrew Bible and the book of John. But even later
in the New Testament, everything starts with—or against the background
of—whiteness. When the world was white with winter came the infant
Lord to earth. But, according to Friedrich Nietzsche's Zarathustra, the
Christian winter also encourages an all-too-stable, rigid, and unflexible
mode of thought:

> But when the winter comes . . . , then verily, not only the block-
> heads say, "Does not everything stand still?"
> "At bottom everything stands still"—that is truly a winter
> doctrine.[6]

White is the standard, the non plus ultra, the default. In the beginning was
the White. In the beginning was the WASP. Or, as Deleuze and Guattari
state in their chapter "Faciality," "the face is Christ . . . Jesus Christ Superstar:

he invented the facialization of the entire body and transmitted it everywhere"[7]—thus the dominant face is white, the white of the European Christian. In this WASP story of Genesis, white plays an important role, as the *Urgrund* of Creation. Important, but silent and mute. A whiteness that is in itself *un*formed, but has to be *in*formed by a great artist, in order to come to life.

White as the absolute—the absolute purity, from which life began, with which all started, animated by the word, the spirit. There is a tradition here that resonates through the history of Western (White) Metaphysics. Note John Locke, who conceives of the human mind as "white paper, void of all characters." Or G. W. F. Hegel, who talks about "the void of the Absolute, in which pure identity, formless whiteness, is produced" . . . this whiteness is "absolutely monochromatic."[8] In such an encompassing whiteness, the white itself does not move—it is indeed moved, informed, by a First Mover|Informer: God. In this white Genesis, God's working material, the white canvas or blank page, is *"either* an undifferentiated ground, a formless nonbeing, or an abyss without differences and without properties, *or* a supremely individuated Being and an intensely personalized Form. Without this Being or this Form, you will have only chaos."[9] This alternative is based on the *"hylomorphic* model,"[10] a doctrine going back to Aristotle, which claims that every "body" is the result of an imposition of a transcendent *form* (or *soul*) on chaotic or passive *matter*.

However, one might also tell a different story of creation, and of a different whiteness. Not one where force and agency come from the outside, but one where life emerges autopoetically. Nietzsche's Zarathustra, in the quotation mentioned above, goes on and counters the (Christian) "winter doctrine": "O my brothers is everything not in flux now? Have not all railings and bridges fallen into the water?"[11] Note, for example, Lucretius and Epicurus. Here the beginning of creation is envisaged as a steady and regular fall of atoms. Boring. Monochromatic monotony. We can imagine this as absolute, undifferentiated whiteness. The kind of whiteness David Batchelor refers to in his book *Chromophobia*, the clinical monochromatic whiteness of a toilet high on disinfectants, or a designer kitchen, where "no eating, no drinking, no pissing" takes place.[12] But then, suddenly, out of its own spontaneous mood, one of these white atoms swerves a bit—the *clinamen*. Bumps against the others, crashes into more, and the whole regularity suddenly becomes turbulent. Creative chaos. Self-organizing patterns—newness emerges. The once-monochromatic whiteness differentiates itself.

This creative swerve is a notion that becomes a driving force in modern art. Against Hegel's "chalk-like dead appearance" of the white color,[13] Wassily Kandinsky poses the following epiphany:

> Suddenly, all nature seemed to me white; white (great silence—full of possibilities) displayed itself everywhere and expanded visibly. . . . This discovery was of enormous importance for me. I felt, with an exactitude I had never yet experienced, that the principal tone, the innate inner character of color, can be redefined ad infinitum by its different uses.[14]

And John Cage, for his composition "Music for Piano," focused on the notes "suggested" by the imperfections of the paper, the self-differentiating molecular whiteness of molar white. Just like there is no silence, there is no such thing as undifferentiated whiteness. In fact, Cage's "4:33" was triggered by this very observation he made when seeing Robert Rauschenberg's white paintings: these were not just "simply white" but "airports for the lights, shadows and particles."[15]

The story of the *clinamen* is a story that does without an outside, organizing force. In line with this Lucretian notion, for Deleuze, matter is "molecular material" equipped with the capacity for self-organization[16]—matter is *alive, informed* rather than *informe* ("formless"): "matter . . . is not dead, brute, homogeneous matter, but a matter-movement bearing singularities or haecceities, qualities and even operations."[17] True to the dictum of chaos physics and complexity theory, two disciplines that underlie much of Deleuze's thought, its autopoietic (i.e., self-organizing, without any external agent) capacities reveal themselves at states "far from equilibrium," when matter crosses thresholds (e.g., phase states). These capacities are hidden at a state of equilibrium, yet it is exactly this state of equilibrium that in the "traditional sciences" is regularly taken as *the* characteristic and essential feature of matter. Thus strategies of slowing down, stabilizing, and homogenizing matter result in an account of matter as passive, chaotic, and "stupid"—a mere mass or object to be "informed" by an outside spirit, force, subject, or God.

A Deleuzian ("white") ecology is preoccupied with "intelligent matter" and supports a belief in the force and richness of matter itself: one that is not dominated by form, one that does not need form to be imposed on it to become alive but is in and of itself animate and informed. Matter engenders its own formations and differentiations because it carries them in itself, as potentialities, so that form|soul|mind is not something *external* to matter but *coextensive* with it. Such a turn toward matter and materiality suggests a decided move against the constructivist, impoverished concept of matter as passive and chaotic, where an "organizing" and transcendent agent is needed for making matter work, making it alive—if matter is passive, it cannot by itself account for the emergence of newness; if matter is chaotic, it cannot by itself account for order. The form–matter division is never absolute, since it "leaves many things, active and affective, by the wayside." Not only does it "assume . . . a fixed form and a matter deemed homogeneous"[18]—for Deleuze, matter is not *inert* in the first place but *informed,* for it consistently contains and produces emergent structures and potentials. The hylomorphic model emphasizes the *constituted* individual item, and thus ignores the very *process* by which this item comes to be.

Such a "white" mode of ecology, focusing on the autopoietic potential of matter as outlined in the research conducted by chaos and complexity theory—see, for example, the work of Michel Serres, Ilya Prigogine, and Isabelle Stengers and Humberto Maturana and Francisco Varela[19]—*can* account for the world's order and creativity without taking recourse to essentialism or determinism, nor to any transcendentalisms, since "life" for Deleuze is the very property of matter itself. Thus "instead of imposing a form upon a matter: what one addresses is less a matter submitted to laws than a materiality possessing a *nomos.*"[20]

Ice and Snow

Back to a beginning. The story of Genesis, now from a geologic viewpoint. Again, according to some theories, recognizable life starts with the big white. Seven hundred million years ago, the world's surface was covered with ice, which turned the globe into a giant snowball, as the geologist Paul Hoffmann has it. A Giant (Abominable?) Snowball called Earth.

Still, more than 10 percent of the world's land mass is permanently covered with ice—glaciated. Starting from the poles, the ice crept through the oceans, shock-freezing them, and eventually also covered the land.

Underwater volcanoes, after millions of years under the ice, eventually made their gases break through the frost cover, and after some centuries turned the atmosphere into a hothouse, or a fiery furnace. Out of fire and ice—according to Hoffmann—out of catastrophic events, complex life as we know it today emerged.

Ice—a crystalline inorganic solid, less dense than water, prone to powerful expansion. Ice is a shape shifter; it can take the shape of snowflakes, icicles, hail, pack ice, and glaciers. And there is nothing undifferentiated and monochrome about it—it changes color, depending on its "ingredients," and also because it reflects the light of its surroundings: "airports for the lights, shadows and particles." And it is also not static. Like glass, and rocks, ice moves . . . what seems to be a static idler only appears so to the human eye, simply because our perception is too fast to notice the slow but constant movement of the ice, either as it expands or as it moves along in glaciers because of the different aggregate states of the ice: the bigger, harder blocks on top slide on the more watery basement like a belly ride on a gigantic slushy.

Alaska

Like in Alaska, the most northern, and also most western part of the United States, with its subpolar climate. By now concentrating on "white-ecological" intersections of "natural" and "cultural" ecologies in the work of the Alaskan composer John Luther Adams, I would like to enfold a complex ecosystem here in which nature percolates into culture, and vice versa, resonating in each other. Ice as a habitat, ice as a "vital force," but sonorous ice also triggering linguistic theories of climate-dependent languages, and the Alaskan landscape—natural and cultural—stimulating the site-specific "sonic geography" of Adams. Snow muffles every sound, and the sound of glaciers, of ice cracking, of the land's inhabitants form a complex sonic landscape into which the work of Adams taps, but which he also then reinserts into and as a "real part" of the Alaskan landscape. Deleuze and Guattari, when describing an ice desert, might be talking about "Adams country" as well:

> There is an extraordinarily fine topology that relies not on points or objects but rather on haecceities, on sets of relations (winds, undulations of snow or sand, the song of the sand or the creaking

of ice, the tactile qualities of both). It is a tactile space, or rather "haptic," a sonorous much more than a visual space.[21]

The Inuit—so a much-cherished myth (and a myth is what it is!) goes— have quite a lot of words for snow (and ice, one might presume). Theories go from twenty-one words up to more than hundred. (Kate Bush counts 50 *Words for Snow*, a good average calculation.) There are even more linguistic theories connected to the cold, snowy, and icy habitat: in the nineteenth century, there were linguistic models that connected the quality of vowels to certain climatic conditions: since with "dark" vowels such as *a, o,* or *u,* you have to open the mouth more than with "light" vowels such as *e* and *i,* the dark vowels were thought to appear more often in languages located in places with hot climates (so as to let more air in), whereas the light vowels were the cultural property of cold places (maybe in order not to hurt your teeth by having to open the mouth more than necessary).

So, in tune with the "sonic geography" that Adams has conceptualized with regard to his music, the white landscape has already given rise to a—albeit mythical—"climatic linguistics." Another, more "imperial linguistics"—and "white" in the racial sense—is also in place when talking about Alaska. Alaska is also a "white continent" in the sense that the landscape's whiteness has invited "imperial inscriptions" insofar as the polar regions have been taken as a blank space of exploration for white people, who do not necessarily acknowledge that the regions have long been inhabited. As a kind of "multichromatic white" counterweight, Adams uses native Alaskan voices and ritual traditions in his work, together with "field recordings" of native animals, and the sound of glaciers and weather events.

Adams, according to Alex Ross "one of the most original musical thinkers of the new century,"[22] is a singular voice in contemporary music. Like Henry David Thoreau, Charles Ives, and John Cage before him, Adams inhabits both the periphery and the center of his times. Adams lives and works in Alaska, and his music echoes the open spaces of the far North. However, he is anything but a regionalist. He aspires to integrate his art into the larger fabric of life, believing that "music can provide a sounding model for the renewal of human consciousness and culture."[23] Adams does not *represent* nature through music. He creates tonal territories that resonate *with* nature—immersive listening experiences that evoke limit-less distance, suspended time, deep longing, and even transcendence. As the composer writes about the northern landscape: "The feeling of end-less space is exhilarating. *This* is what I want to find in music!"[24]

Adams's explorations began some thirty-five years ago, with a cycle called *songbirdsongs,* setting his "translations" of bird songs within open-ended musical landscapes. During the last few years, Adams has added a scientific perspective to his fascination with nature, which also reflects his stance toward the relationship between the "two cultures":

> Science examines the way things are. Art imagines how things *might* be. Both begin with perception and aspire to achieve understanding. Both science and art search for truth. Whether we regard truth as objective and demonstrable or subjective and provisional, both science and art can lead us toward a broader and deeper understanding of reality. Even as they augment our understanding, science and art heighten our sense of wonder at the strange beauty, astonishing complexity and miraculous unity of creation.[25]

Thus *Strange and Sacred Noise,* for example, an extended ritual for percus-sion, is inspired by elemental noise in nature and by chaos theory, blend-ing the composer's ideal of "sonic geography" with "sonic geometry"—mathematical forms (fractal geometry, the Cantor set, the Koch snow-flake) made palpable in sound, true to Cage's dictum that "the function of the artist is to imitate nature in her manner of operation"[26]—nature is not static, regular, monochromatic but dynamic, in flux, turbulent.

Adams—much like Deleuze—is interested in "the relations between the arts, science, and philosophy. There is no order of priority among those disciplines for both Deleuze and Adams."[27] The relationship is not a simple one-sided affair—as Adams has recently stated in a video clip, "Art and science have lots to say to one another. What is music but audible physics?"[28] Whereas science involves the creation of functions, of a pro-positional mapping of the world, and art involves the creation of blocs of sensation (or affects and percepts), philosophy involves the invention of concepts. According to Deleuze|Guattari, philosophy, art, and science

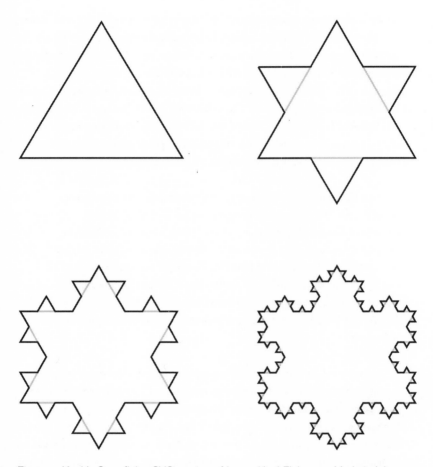

Figure 1. Koch's Snowflake. SVG version of Image:KochFlake.png. Made in Inkscape with the L-System effect. Wikimedia Commons.

are defined by their relation to chaos. Whereas science "relinquishes the infinite in order to gain reference," by creating definitions, functions, and propositions, art, on the other hand, "wants to create the finite that restores the infinite"[29]—and it was exactly this creation of *finite* objects that bothered Cage (e.g., in "4:33"), a problem that Adams ingeniously "fixed" in his installation *The Place Where You Go to Listen*. In contrast, "philosophy wants to save the infinite by giving it consistency."[30] Yet, since "sciences, arts, and philosophies are equally creative," it might be fruitful, as Deleuze proposes, "to pose the question of echoes and resonances between them"[31]— to pose the question of their ecology, which is what much of Adams's work does.

Nietzsche, in his unpublished early notebooks, dating from the period of his *Unfashionable Observations* (1872–73), relates the true philosopher to the scientist and the artist as listener (it is as if Cage is present in these lines): "The concept of the philosopher . . . : he tries to let all the sounds of the world reverberate in him and to place this comprehensive sound outside himself into concepts"[32] . . . whereas the artist lets the tones of the world resonate within him and projects them through percepts and affects. So, the sound-art practice of Adams becomes research and philosophy, and vice versa—John Luther Adams, artist–philosopher–scientist.

Rainer Maria Rilke, in his 1919 essay "Primal Sound" (*Urgeräusch* in the German original) described an experience he had as a young boy, when introduced to a phonograph for the first time, seeing how the needle produced sounds out of grooves in a wax cylinder, grooves that the recording of actual sounds had put there in the first place. Years later, while attending anatomical lectures in Paris, Rilke connected the lines of coronal suture of the human skull to his childhood observations—"I knew at once what it reminded me of: one of those unforgotten grooves, which had been scratched in a little wax cylinder by the point of a bristle!"[33] From this incident, Rilke derives the following "experimental set-up":

> The coronal suture of the skull (this would first have to be investigated) has—let us assume—a certain similarity to the closely wavy line which the needle of a phonograph engraves on the receiving, rotating cylinder of the apparatus. What if one changed the needle and directed it on its return journey along a tracing which was not derived from the graphic translation of a sound, but existed of itself naturally—well: to put it plainly, along the coronal suture, for example. What would happen?[34]

Rilke's obvious answer, is, of course: noise, music—sound! Probing farther, Rilke asks himself, "What variety of lines then, occurring anywhere, could one not put under the needle and try out? Is there any contour that one could not, in a sense, complete in this way and then experience it, as it makes itself felt, thus transformed, in another field of sense?"[35] Although this sounds rather anthropocentric, it should be noted that Rilke is not so much interested in the skull as a container for an only-human intelligence but simply in its "sonorous materiality," thus opening up nonhuman vectors pointing at a more-than-human sonic ecology. In a letter, Rilke specifies this idea. Writing to Dieter Bassermann, Rilke speculates on

> set[ting] to sound the countless signatures of Creation which in the skeleton, in minerals . . . in a thousand places persist in their remarkable versions and variations. The grain in wood, the gait of an insect: our eye is practiced in following and ascertaining them. What a gift to our hearing were we to succeed in transmuting this zigzag . . . into auditory events![36]

And with Nietzsche, we could add: "Images in human eyes! This dominates all human nature: from the *eye*! The *ear* hears sounds! A completely different, wonderful conception of the same world."[37] It is such an unheard-of world that Adams's music makes come to life—and in 2010 he was awarded the Nemmers Prize in Music Composition "for melding the physical and musical worlds into a unique artistic vision that transcends stylistic boundaries."[38]

Adams lives and works in Fairbanks, Alaska, approximately 125 miles south of the Arctic. Adams's work is highly influenced by his environment, this "hyperborean zone, far from the temperate regions,"[39] far from equilibrium. Adams, it has to be noted, is also an environmental activist and founder of Alaska's Green Party. Mitchell Morris thus dubs Adams a "Green composer,"[40] referring, however, to the notion of ecology as in *Deep* Ecology, whereas I would place Adams firmly within a Deleuzian ecology based on a nondualist ontology.[41] From his early works on he has always pointed out that he wants his music to be understood as an interaction with nature—as a site-specific "contact" with the environment that he calls "sonic geography."[42]

Adams's sonic geography comprises a cycle called *songbirdsongs* (1974–80), consisting of various imitations of Alaskan birds reminiscent of Olivier Messiaen's *Catalogues d'oiseaux*. Although Adams in the compositional process and the transcription brings birdsong on a "human scale" in terms of tempo, modulation, pitch, and so on, he conceptualizes the different melodies—or "refrains"—as a "tool kit," so that during the performance, an ever-new aggregation of phrases and motifs comes into existence, an open system, undetermined in combination, length, intonation, tempi, and so on. *Earth and the Great Weather* (1990–93), an evening-long piece, was "conceived as a journey through the physical, cultural and spiritual land-scapes of the Arctic," a traversing of smooth "Eskimo space."[43] Far from exoticizing Alaskan culture, Adams here merges original compositions in-spired by Alaska Native drumming, spoken recitations in English and Native languages, as well as natural sounds of wind, melting glaciers, thunder that are electronically altered and recomposed, to create a musical landscape that includes native, modern, human, and nonhuman sounds in a larger sonic ecology. In a further step, Adams combined his sonic geography with the concept of what he calls "sonic geometry."[44] Adams is more and more interested in the "noisier" sounds of nature and refers to findings of chaos theory and fractal geometry to find sonic equivalents for nature's modus operandi—*Strange and Sacred Noise* (1991–97) is an example of this ap-proach.[45] To date, the culmination of Adams's sonic geography|geometry has been his recent project *The Place Where You Go to Listen*, the title of which refers to an Inuit legend according to which the shamans hear the wisdom of the world in (and get their knowledge from) the whisper of the wind and the murmur of the waves, being sensitive to what Deleuze, with reference to G. W. Leibniz, calls "little perceptions."[46]

Adams aims at realizing a "musical ecosystem, . . . A work of art . . . that is directly connected to the real world in which we live and resonates sym-pathetically with that world and with the forces of nature."[47] Adams does not only *imitate* nature in its manner of operation, like Cage still does, he taps into nature's dynamic processes *themselves* to generate sound and light. Adams developed this project in close collaboration with geologists and physicists—as Adams stated in an interview, "At a certain level, it was like . . . they were the boys in the band."[48]

As Deleuze specified in one of his seminars, "Between a philosophical concept, a painted line and a musical sonorous bloc, resonances emerge, very, very strange correspondences that one shouldn't even theorize, I think, and which I would prefer to call 'affective' . . . these are privileged

moments."[49] These moments privilege an affect where thought and sensation merge into a very specific way of "doing thinking" *beyond* representation and categorization, a moment that might be called "contemplation,"
which also fittingly describes the audience's approach to Adams's *Place
Where You Go to Listen,* which transforms the rhythms of night and day, the
phases of the moon, the weather, earthquake data, and disturbances in the
earth's magnetic field into an ever-changing ecosystem of sound and light.
As Deleuze and Guattari argue in *What Is Philosophy?,* "Philosophy needs
a nonphilosophy that comprehends it; it needs a nonphilosophical com-
prehension just as art needs nonart and science needs nonscience."[50]

In Adams's installation, real-time data from meteorological stations all
over Alaska and from the five stations of the Alaska Earthquake Information Center are collected, coordinated, and made audible through pink-
noise filters (pink noise is white noise without the higher frequencies,
so that it sounds rather like natural sounds of wind and surf. Pink noise
also occurs in many physical, biological, and economic systems). As Curt
Szuberla, one of the physicists involved in the project, explains, "The
strings and bells and drumheads are plucked, bashed and banged based
on the geophysical data streams. And the geophysical data streams . . . are
the fingers and mallets and bells that hit things and make things sound."[51]
The Place Where You Go to Listen is a permanent installation at the University of Alaska Museum of the North in Fairbanks, where sound and light
are generated in real time through data processing of the day and night
rhythms, the rhythm of the seasons, of the moon phases, the weather
conditions, and the seismic flows of the magnetic field of the earth—
nature itself, as well as the music it produces, operates according to its own
times and speeds (and slownesses). Hours, even days (and more) might
pass between perceivable seismic changes or changes in the magnetic field
of the earth. *The Place* is an open system, a machinic aggregation operating according to what Deleuze calls "differences of level, temperature,
pressure, tension, potential, *difference of intensity*"[52]—just like the weather.
Adams's noise-filter-machine is plugged into the sun-machine, and also
into the wind-machine, rain-machine, and so on; these in turn couple to
form the weather-machine. Digital machines cut into the flows of nature, but
within a machine|nature ecology|ontology that is not based on the strict
separation of these two spheres, where nature is either a fixed, unchanging

essence or the mere retro-effect of culture and representation, but an ecology|ontology of dynamics and production. Adams's installation thus presents "modes of individuation beyond those of things, persons or subjects: the individuation, say, of a time of day, of a region, a climate."[53]

The Place Where You Go to Listen focuses on nature as process and *event*—in an almost Stoic emphasis on *becoming* versus *being,* Adams privileges time-sensitive *dynamics,* not clear-cut *states.* In his study *La théorie des incorporels dans l'ancien stoicisme,* to which Deleuze refers in *Logic of Sense,* Emile Bréhier states that, according to Stoic "thought, one should not say, 'the tree is green,' but 'the tree greens' . . . what is expressed in this proposition is not a property, such as 'a body is hot,' but an event, such as 'a body becomes hot.'"[54] This *becoming,* writes Deleuze, passes the line "between the sensible and the intelligible, or between the soul and the body"—or nature and culture—and places itself "between things and events."[55] By getting rid of the *is* of representational thought, where an object's quality is at least potentially related to a subject that expresses this quality as an attribute, by replacing fixity with process as both the subject's and the world's "manner of operation," these "infinitive-becomings have no subject: they refer only to an 'it' of the event."[56] Adams's installation goes farther in the direction of the event than, for example, Ives and even Cage—although these two composers had also already pondered the conflict between the processuality of nature and the means of art. Ives asked himself:

> A painter paints a sunset—can he paint the setting sun? . . . [Is] [t]here . . . an analogy . . . between both the state and power of artistic perceptions and the law of perpetual change, that ever-flowing stream, partly biological, partly cosmic, ever going on in ourselves, in nature, in all life?[57]

Ives tried to master this problematics by way of the ever-increasing complexification of his compositorial means. Cage also emphasized that he did not think it correct to say "the world as it *is*"—

> it *is* not, it becomes! It moves, it changes! It doesn't wait for us to change . . . it is more mobile than you can imagine. You're getting

closer to this reality when you say as it "presents itself"; that means that it is not there, existing as an object. The world, the real is not an object. It is a process.[58]

But—Ives was still the subject in control of chaos, and Cage, despite all indeterminacy, regretted that he was still creating "clear-cut" objects. Adam solves this problem by leaving the executing|processing energy to the nonhuman processual forces themselves. Music and environment thus become an ecosystem of a dynamics of acoustic and optic resonances interacting in|with an environment in constant flux. Music in this sense thus for Adams becomes something entirely different than a "means" of human communication about an external world:

> If music grounded in tone is a means of sending messages to the world, then music grounded in noise is a means of receiving messages *from* the world. . . . As we listen carefully to noise, the whole world becomes music. Rather than a vehicle for self-expression, music becomes a mode of awareness.[59]

Thus *The Place Where You Go to Listen* leaves the conceptualization of a music *about* nature, of music as a way to *represent* nature and landscape, on which, for example, Ives still relied, and creates music as a part of nature, as coextensive with the environment—"Through attentive and sustained listening to the resonances of this place, I hope to make music which belongs here, somewhat like the plants and the birds."[60] Even more direct than Cage, Adams emphasizes nature's "manner of operation" in not only taking it as a model but by directly "accessing" and relating to the becoming of a site-specific environment and creating works that *are* this relation—a music of place, of a place where you go to listen.

A "white ecology" according to Adams's "sonic ecology" thus draws on the resonances between human and nonhuman eco*logics,* makes those resonances perceivable. As Adams himself states, "The challenge for artists today is to move beyond self-expression and beyond anthropocentric views of history, to re-imagine and re-create our relationships with this planet and all those (human and other-than-human) with whom we share it."[61]

Even if Adams does not explicitly refer to Thoreau, his work is indebted to Thoreau's sound aesthetics—even more so, I argue, than Ives's or even Cage's work. And Adams's work is also indebted to Thoreau's sense of ecology—an ecology similar to the kind of "white ecology" I have tried to outline here, based on a decidedly *nondualistic* and *processual* ontology. As for Adams, music already for Thoreau is part of the environment—nature has no need to be translated or represented, nature and the environment already *sound,* already *express themselves.* In *Walden,* Thoreau writes that "making the yellow soil express its summer thought in bean leaves and blossoms rather than in wormwood and piper and millet grass, making the earth say beans instead of grass—this was my daily work."[62] If Thoreau calls this natural expression by the name of "saying," he is evoking a correspondence between "expression" and "production" of—a correspondence that goes far beyond the level of representation. The expression of nature on the side of production arrives in the subject as impression, so that from the perspective of culture, what we call representation is already rooted in nature—"every word is rooted in the soil, is indeed flowery and verdurous."[63]

Imagine Thoreau, playing not only the "telegraph harp" but also the "ice-gong"—banging on the frozen surface of Walden Pond with diverse materials, at different points on the pond, being joined by Cage and Adams . . . the American beginnings of a "white ecology."

Notes

1. Félix Guattari, *Chaosmosis: An Ethico-Aesthetic Paradigm,* trans. Paul Bains and Julian Pefanis (Bloomington: Indiana University Press, 1995), 91.

2. Richard Kerridge and Neil Sammels, eds., *Writing the Environment: Ecocriticism and Literature* (London: Zed Books, 1998), 5.

3. . . . and what in the English translation curiously goes as "steady state" (Ludwig von Bertalanffy, *General Systems Theory: Foundations, Development, Applications* [New York: George Braziller, 1969], 41).

4. Gilles Deleuze, *Negotiations, 1972–1990,* trans. Marting Joughin (New York: Columbia University Press, 1997), 155.

5. Gilles Deleuze and Félix Guattari, *A Thousand Plateaus: Capitalism and Schizophrenia,* trans. Brian Massumi (Minneapolis: University of Minnesota Press, 1987), 167.

6. Friedrich Nietzsche, *Thus Spoke Zarathustra,* trans. Walter Kaufmann (New York: Penguin, 1978), 200.

7. Deleuze and Guattari, *Thousand Plateaus*, 176.

8. John Locke, *An Essay concerning Human Understanding*, ed. Roger Wool-house (Harmondsworth: Penguin, 1997), 109; G. W. F. Hegel, *Phenomenology of Spirit*, trans. A. V. Millner (Oxford: Oxford University Press, 1977), 31.

9. Gilles Deleuze, *Logic of Sense*, ed. Constantin V. Boundas, trans. Mark Lester, with Charles Stivale (New York: Columbia University Press, 1990), 108.

10. Deleuze and Guattari, *Thousand Plateaus*, 408.

11. Nietzsche, *Thus Spoke Zarathustra*, 200.

12. David Batchelor, *Chromophobia* (London: Reaktion Books, 2000), 19.

13. G. W. F. Hegel, *Aesthetics: Lectures on Fine Art*, vol. 2, trans. T. M. Knox (Oxford: Oxford University Press, 1975), 776.

14. Wassily Kandinsky, "Cologne Lecture," in *Complete Writings on Art*, ed. Kenneth C. Lindsay and Peter Vergo (Boston: Da Capo, 1982), 398.

15. John Cage, *Silence* (Hanover, N.H.: Wesleyan University Press, 1973), 102.

16. Deleuze and Guattari, *Thousand Plateaus*, 342.

17. Ibid., 512.

18. Ibid., 408.

19. Ilya Prigogine and Isabelle Stengers, *Order out of Chaos: Man's New Dialogue with Nature* (London: Flamingo, 1984); Humberto R. Maturana and Francisco J. Varela's coauthored books *The Tree of Knowledge: Biological Roots of Human Understanding* (Boston: Shambhala, 1987), and *Autopoiesis and Cognition: The Realization of the Living* (Dordrecht: Kluwer Academic, 1980); Michel Serres, *Genesis* (Ann Arbor: University of Michigan Press, 1995); and Serra, *The Birth of Physics* (Manchester, UK: Clinamen, 2000).

20. Deleuze and Guattari, *Thousand Plateaus*, 408. Deleuze and Guattari refer to Gilbert Simondon's study *L'individu et sa genése physico-biologique* (Paris: PUF, 1964), in which Simondon attempts to explain individuation—the genesis of an individual—as a self-organizing process of *pre-individual* singularities and differences. According to Deleuze, what Simondon elaborates in his book is "a whole ontology, according to which Being is never One." Note the remarkable affinity with Deleuze's own ontology (Gilles Deleuze, "On Gilbert Simondon," in *Desert Islands and Other Texts, 1953–1974*, ed. David Lapoujade, trans. Michael Taormina [Cambridge, Mass.: MIT Press/Semiotext(e), 2004], 89). Simondon himself addresses the political implications of the hylomorphic model when he states that "form corresponds to what the man in command has thought to himself, and must express in a positive manner when he gives orders" (quoted in Deleuze and Guattari, *Thousand Plateaus*, 555n33).

21. Deleuze and Guattari, *Thousand Plateaus*, 421.

22. Alex Ross, "Song of the Earth," in *The Farthest Place: The Music of John Luther Adams,* ed. Bernd Herzogenrath (Boston: Northeastern University Press, 2012), 14.

23. John Luther Adams, *The Place Where You Go to Listen: In Search of an Ecology of Music* (Middletown, Conn.: Wesleyan University Press, 2009), 1.

24. John Luther Adams, *Winter Music: Composing the North* (Middletown, Conn.: Wesleyan University Press, 2004), 69.

25. Adams, *Place Where You Go,* 10.

26. Cage, *Silence,* 194.

27. Deleuze, *Negotiations,* 123.

28. John Luther Adams, "Sonic Geography of Alaska" (dir. Steve Elkins), http:// vimeo.com/3019076 (accessed May 10, 2012).

29. Deleuze, *Negotiations,* 197.

30. Gilles Deleuze and Félix Guattari, *What Is Philosophy?,* trans. H. Tomlinson and G. Burchell (New York: Columbia University Press, 1994), 197.

31. Deleuze, *Negotiations,* 5, 123.

32. Friedrich Nietzsche, *Writings from the Early Notebooks,* ed. Raymond Geuss and Alexander Nehamas (Cambridge: Cambridge University Press, 2009), 115.

33. Rainer Maria Rilke, "Primal Sound," in *The Book of Music and Nature: An Anthology of Sounds, Words, Thoughts,* ed. David Rothenberg and Martha Ulvaeus (Middletown, Conn.: Wesleyan University Press, 2001), 22.

34. Ibid., 23.

35. Ibid.

36. Rainer Maria Rilke, *Letters of Rainer Maria Rilke,* vol. 2, *1910–26,* trans. Jane Bannard Greene and M. D. Herter Norton (New York: Norton, 1969), 391–92.

37. Nietzsche, *Writings,* 113.

38. Nemmers Prize Committee Announcement, http://www.music.northwestern.edu/about/prizes/nemmers-prize/2010-press-release.html (accessed May 10, 2012).

39. Gilles Deleuze, *Essays Critical and Clinical,* trans. Daniel W. Smith and Michael Greco (Minneapolis: University of Minnesota Press, 1997), 82.

40. Mitchell Morris, "Ectopian Sound or The Music of John Luther Adams and Strong Environmentalism," in *Crosscurrents and Counterpoints,* ed. Per F. Broman et al. (Göteborg: University of Göteborg Press, 1998), 131.

41. Such a nondualist ontology—what I here call a "white ecology"—is also what Hanjo Berressem calls a "flat ecology" (see Berressem's "Structural Couplings: Radical Constructivism and a Deleuzian Eco*logics,*" in *Deleuze/Guattari and Ecology,* ed. Bernd Herzogenrath [Houndmills: Palgrave, 2009], 57–101).

42. John Luther Adams, "Resonance of Place," *North American Review* 279, no. 1 (1994): 8.

43. John Luther Adams, "Sonic Geography of the Arctic: An Interview with Gayle Young," 1988, http://www.johnlutheradams.com/interview/gayleyoung .html (accessed July 9, 2013); Deleuze and Guattari, *Thousand Plateaus,* 494. In fact, the first movement of *Earth and the Great Weather* is already named "The Place Where You Go to Listen."

44. John Luther Adams, "Strange and Sacred Noise," in *Northern Soundscapes,* vol. 1 of *Yearbook of Soundscape Studies,* ed. R. Murray Schafer and Helmi Järviluoma (Tampere: University of Tampere, 1998), 143–46.

45. *Strange and Sacred Noise* is a concert-length cycle of six movements for percussion quartet. Its first and last movements (". . . dust into dust . . ." and ". . . dust rising . . .") are based on the Cantor set and Cantor dust (the two-dimensional version of the Cantor set). These fractals model the behavior of electrical noise, which Adams takes as a diagram for the percussion set to explore the dynamic form of the Cantor dust. See Sabine Feisst, "Music as Place, Place as Music: The Sonic Geography of John Luther Adams," in *The Farthest Place: The Music of John Luther Adams,* ed. Bernd Herzogenrath (Boston: Northeastern University Press, 2012), 23–47.

46. Gilles Deleuze, *Difference and Repetition,* trans. Paul Patton (New York: Columbia University Press, 1994), 213. A direct Leibnizian reference can be found in his *New Essays on Human Understanding,* 2nd ed., ed. and trans. Peter Remnant and Jonathan Bennett (New York: Cambridge University Press, 1996). "To hear this noise as we do, we must hear the parts which make up this whole, that is the noise of each wave, although each of these little noises makes itself known only when combined confusedly with all the others, and would not be noticed if the wave which made it were by itself . . . we must have some perception of each of these noises, however faint they may be; otherwise there would be no perception of a hundred thousand waves, since a hundred thousand nothings cannot make something" (55). Such a "sonorous ocean," it can be argued, the becoming-perceptible of micro-sounds underneath the (human) radar, also provides a more materialist version of the Pythagorean idea of "sphere music": contrary to a harmonious universe rotating according to "well-tempered" intervals, it would refer to the multiplicity of sounds of the world—nature changes constantly, everything moves, and everything that moves oscillates according to a certain frequency, the total result of which would be "white noise" (the murmur of the universe).

47. John Luther Adams, quoted in Amy Mayer, "Northern Exposure: A Museum Exhibit Converts Activity in the Alaskan Environment into an Ever Changing Sound Show," *Boston Globe,* April 16, 2006.

48. Radio interview with Amy Mayer, *Living on Earth,* www.loe.org/shows/ segments.htm?programID=06-P13-00016&segmentID=5 (accessed May 10, 2012).

49. My translation of: "Alors je dirais que le concept philosophique n'est pas seulement source d'opinion quelconque, il est source de transmission très particulière, ou entre un concept philosophique, une ligne picturale, un bloc sonore musical, s'établissent des correspondances, des correspondances très très curieuses, que à mon avis il ne faut même pas théoriser, que je préférerais appeler l'affectif en général. . . . Là c'est des moments privilégiés" (Gilles Deleuze, "Image Mouvement Image Temps," Cours Vincennes—St Denis: le plan—02/11/1983, www.web deleuze.com/php/texte.php?cle=69&groupe= Image%20Mouvement%20Image %20Temps&langue=1 [accessed May 10, 2012]).

50. Deleuze and Guattari, *What Is Philosophy?*, 218.

51. Quoted in Mayer, *Living on Earth*.

52. Deleuze, *Difference and Repetition*, 222.

53. Deleuze, *Negotiations*, 26.

54. Emile Bréhier, *La théorie des incorporels dans l'ancien stoicisme* (Paris: Librairie Philosophique J. Vrin, 1970), 20–21. My translation of: "On ne doit pas dire, pensaient-ils: 'L'arbre est vert,' mais: 'L'arbre verdoie'. . . . Ce qui s'exprime dans le jugement, ce n'est pas une propriété comme: un corps est chaud, mais une évènement comme: un corps s'échauffe."

55. Gilles Deleuze, *Dialogues* (New York: Columbia University Press, 1987), 63.

56. Ibid., 64.

57. Charles Ives, *Essays before a Sonata, the Majority, and Other Writings,* ed. Howard Boatwright (New York: Norton, 1999), 71.

58. John Cage, *For the Birds: John Cage in Conversation with Daniel Charles* (Boston: Marion Boyars, 1981), 80.

59. John Luther Adams, "In Search of an Ecology of Music," 2006, http:// www.johnlutheradams.com/writings/ecology.html (accessed May 10, 2012).

60. Adams, "Resonance of Place," 8.

61. Adams, *Winter Music,* 128.

62. Henry David Thoreau, *The Illustrated Walden,* ed. J. Lyndon Shanley (Princeton, N.J.: Princeton University Press, 1973), 157.

63. Henry David Thoreau, *The Journal of Henry David Thoreau,* ed. Bradford Torrey and Francis H. Allen (New York: Dover, 1962), 1:386.

Red

TOBIAS MENELY AND MARGARET RONDA

> If I said fire, if I said blood welling from a cut—
> . . . Red, I said. Sudden, red.
>
> —ROBERT HASS, "The Problem of Describing Color"

Cavel West

During its years of operation, the Cavel West slaughterhouse in Redmond, Oregon, killed up to five hundred horses a week and shipped the meat to European and Japanese markets. Cavel West was owned by a Belgian company, Velda Group, which ran several horse-slaughtering facilities in the United States and Canada. Its manager, Pascal Derde, described the speed and transnational scope of the plant's slaughtering operation this way: "Killed on Friday, processed Monday, Thursday we load the truck, and then it's flown to Europe. Monday it's sold in Belgium, Tuesday eaten, Wednesday it's back in the soil."[1] Derde's description of an efficient, waste-free globalized circuit of capitalist production, circulation, and consumption elides a more disturbing reality: Cavel West was notorious in the Redmond area not only for the stench it produced but also for the blood, tissue, and contaminated sludge that entered local waterways, sometimes overwhelming the wastewater facility. Such problems are endemic to areas around horse-slaughter plants, where blood and tissue are a common sight in local streams, even spilling from taps and bubbling up in bathtubs. For years, Redmond residents had protested the plant's environmental abuses, but to no avail. The plant gained further notoriety when it was revealed that many of the slaughtered horses had been rounded up by the Bureau of Land Management under the aegis of a program originally intended to protect them.

On July 21, 1997, the Cavel West slaughterhouse burned to the ground. Later in July, a communiqué was sent from the Animal Liberation Front and Earth Liberation Front (ELF) to the media, claiming responsibility for the fire. According to the communiqué, the fire was set with three electrically timed incendiary devices and "35 gallons of vegan jello" (identified by authorities as a blend of soap, gasoline, and diesel); in addition, they left "two gallons of muriatic acid" to taint any remaining horse flesh. The arson, the activists claimed, "would bring to a screeching halt what countless protests and letter-writing campaigns could never stop."[2] Part of a string of ELF arsons in the Pacific Northwest in the late 1990s, the Cavel West fire is considered by radical environmentalists to be one of the most successful acts of "ecotage." Will Potter, in his study of radical ecoactivism, *Green Is the New Red,* describes its status among activists as "folkloric."[3] Not only did it cause $1.4 million in damages, but it led to the plant's permanent closure and drew national attention to the environmental issues involved in the industrial rendering of horse meat. The incident also highlighted the rise in the United States of a radical, underground movement carrying out direct action aimed at environmentally destructive corporations and a juridical order dedicated to protecting private property. What its participants describe as "ecodefense," the state has characterized as "ecoterrorism." By March 2001 the ELF was named the greatest domestic terrorist threat by the FBI.

The Sign of Red

In this chapter, we read the story of Cavel West—the slaughterhouse and the global market, the blaze of resistance in the name of the nonhuman, and the state's hyperactive response—in terms of a dialectic of appearance and nonappearance, which we associate with the sign of red. The philosopher Charles Sanders Peirce returned often to the semiotic primacy of red. "First, imagine a person in a dreamy state," he writes in "What Is a Sign?" "Let us suppose he is thinking of nothing but a red color. Not thinking about it, either, that is, not asking nor answering any questions about it, not even saying to himself that it pleases him, but just contemplating it, as his fancy brings it up."[4] Redness is an example of "firstness," which Peirce elsewhere defines as "a degree of disturbance of your consciousness. The quality of red is not thought of as belonging to you, or as attached to liveries.

It is simply a peculiar positive possibility regardless of anything else."[5] In laying the groundwork for a theory of signs, Peirce repeatedly refers to the color red as an instance of primordial vividness, an apprehensible quality distinguishable from the given forms it takes. This phenomenological "possibility"—the availability of red to "fancy," its elemental potential as sign, separable from its "object"—is the first condition of semiotic activity, as it comes to manifest, say, in the red hourglass of the female black widow spider, the red flag of the revolutionary, and, symbolically, in the words themselves: red, rojo, rouge. Attesting to this semiotic primacy, "red" is the only color word for which there is an evident Proto-Indo-European root (*reudh*); in the Middle Ages, red and not black was considered the opposite of white; and the Berlin-Kay hypothesis identified red, after black and white, as the most basic color term across languages.[6]

Two conditions underlie the semiotic conspicuousness of red. First, red appears at the longest wavelengths of the visible spectrum of light and is considered the most acutely noticeable color to those mammals and birds capable of perceiving it. This vividness is physiological but also environmental. On our verdant, terraqueous earth, green and blue are the hues of contexts, enveloping atmospheres, whereas red, in most natural environments, signals disturbance and rupture. Red is the most prevalent color of "aposematism"—from the Greek *apo-* (away) and *sema* (sign)—as in the bright body of the granular poison frog, the hairs of the velvet ant, and the bands of the coral snake. In these cases, red stands, conspicuously, for an otherwise invisible threat, much as a stop sign warns of danger. The second set of conditions for the semiotics of red is associative. Red is the hue of burning wood and of blood exposed to oxygen, and is thus widely linked with fiery destruction and the violent breaching of boundary, "nature red in tooth and claw." The association of red with political radicalism— whether republican, anarchist, or socialist—is long-standing and pervasive. The *Oxford English Dictionary* traces the correlation between red and revolution in Europe to the thirteenth century and the use of the red flag as a signal of defiance to the sixteenth century. In the 1790s the sans-culottes wore the bonnet rouge, and red came to be associated with socialism during the brief establishment of the "Red Republic" in France in 1848.

Red marks kairotic condensation, rift and inversion, beginnings and endings, the red earth from which Adam and the animals are created and the red skies that presage the imminence of Judgment Day. Because of its vividness, red is often the sign of what remains otherwise unseen: the absent cause, the hidden poison, the underground resistance. It signifies in extremis, borders and their rupture, consolidating but also interrupting the symbolic order. In what follows, we examine blood and fire, the symbolic status of creaturely consanguinity and radical political action, but also the disappearance of red, the nonsignification of limit, violence, and risk in the Anthropocene. Red ecology, as we characterize it, draws on the semiotic and symbolic conspicuousness of red to turn attention to the otherwise invisible sites, the slaughterhouse and the market, where organisms and ecological matter are transformed into commodities. It is attuned, dialectically, to the reemergence of red, from horse blood in the waterways to the sparks of revolutionary action, but also to the possibility that these red alerts will fail to illuminate the crises of the present.

Blood: Sacrifice and the Slaughterhouse

According to the second chapter of Genesis, the first man was a clod of red earth—*adamah* in Hebrew, part of a semantic constellation that includes *edom* (red) and *dam* (blood)—animated by divine breath: "The LORD God formed the man [*adam*] from the dust of the ground [*adamah*] and breathed into his nostrils the breath of life, and the man became a living being" (2:7). The animals were then created out of the same blood-colored soil: "Now the Lord God had formed out of the ground [*adamah*] all the beasts of the field and all the birds of the air" (2:19). Like many origin myths, the second Hebrew cosmogony recognizes, as an elemental condition of being, the consanguinity of living creatures. God's granting of dominion *(radah)* and Adam's naming of the animals are crucial points of differentiation, a supplementary response to the initial fact—the common origin, the shared capacity to bleed—of creaturely affinity.

While other species differ from humans in their behaviors and bodily forms, their essential likeness becomes vividly evident when the shared substance of life spills from the body. Blood bespeaks corporal vitality at the point of its vulnerability, life in its capacity to die. In Israelite society and throughout the ancient world, sacrificial practice follows from the consanguinity of human and animal, as is attested in stories of animal substitution like Isaac and the ram. In Leviticus, God identifies blood as the primary substance of sacrificial ritual: "For the life of a creature is in the blood, and I have given it to you to make atonement for yourselves on the altar; it is the blood that makes atonement for one's life" (17:11). William Burkert, in *Homo Necans,* sees in ritualized hunting practices and traditions of animal sacrifice a primal apprehension of shared corporeal vulnerability: "This similarity" of animal "with man was to be recognized in killing and slaughtering . . . most important of all, the warm running blood was the same."[7] Whether in the hunt or the sacrifice, the symbolic violence that sustains cultural authority derives from the innate human distress in witnessing blood pour from the ruptured body: "In the shock caused by the sight of flowing blood we clearly experience the remnant of a biological, life-preserving inhibition."[8] To break the skin, ceremonially, is to seize the line that distinguishes life from death for humans and other animals alike, giving symbolic form to the natural semiotics of red.

In *The Fable of the Bees* (1714), the political economist Bernard Mandeville considers the relation between creaturely consanguinity—this innate sympathy with other animals whose bodies, like ours, may be wounded, pierced, cleaved—and the dissimulation of violence in an emergent capitalist society:

> In such perfect animals as sheep and oxen, in whom the heart,
> the brain and nerves differ so little from ours, and in whom the
> separation of the spirits from the blood, the organs of sense, and
> consequently feeling itself, are the same as they are in human
> creatures; I can't imagine how a man not hardened in blood and
> massacre, is able to see a violent death, and the pangs of it, without
> concern. . . . Some people are not to be persuaded to taste of any
> creatures they have daily seen and been acquainted with, while
> they were alive; others extend their scruple no further than to
> their own poultry, and refuse to eat what they fed and took care of
> themselves; *yet all of them will feed heartily and without remorse on
> beef, mutton and fowls when they are bought in the market.* In this
> behavior, methinks, there appears something like a consciousness
> of guilt, it looks as if they endeavored to save themselves from the
> imputation of a crime (which they know sticks somewhere) *by*

removing the cause of it as far as they can from themselves; and I can discover in it some strong remains of primitive pity and innocence, which all the arbitrary power of custom, and the violence of luxury, have not yet been able to conquer.[9]

Mandeville points to our innate aversion to spilled blood, as what signifies what Jacques Derrida calls "the finitude that we share with animals, the mortality that belongs to the very finitude of life."[10] He also identifies the ways we overcome this recognition of consanguinity: in the justifying authority of custom and the emotional hardening of habit, but even more powerfully in the distanciation facilitated by the marketplace. Rather than ritualize violence, modern societies place it at a distance. The slaughterhouse replaces animal sacrifice, the sanctification of dominion through performative violence. Yet, as Mandeville suggests, the structural dislocations by which society hides its constitutive brutality are themselves a symptom of "primitive pity."

As Noëlie Vialles writes in her study of the abattoir, *Animal to Edible*, the industrial slaughter of animals "has become an invisible, exiled, almost clandestine activity," "condemned to an existence on the fringes of urban and rural society," like Cavel West, located on the outskirts of a small town in central Oregon.[11] Vialles dates this process to the early nineteenth century, but Mandeville's account of the gap between the slaughtering of animals and the selling of meat suggests a longer history. Technological modernization made slaughtering animals an increasingly sanitary, monitored, institutionalized, and en masse process. The premodern logic of ritual sacrifice, dependent on the act of bringing to visibility the dying animal's blood, was supplanted by an assembly-line process of "exsanguination." The transformation of the animal in the abattoir centers on the systematic process of debleeding, to produce meat: "bloodless flesh."[12] What must disappear from the animal to deanimate it and produce a substance fit for human consumption is its warm blood. The slaughterhouse itself is structured around managing blood, not only by washing, hosing, draining, and gathering excess blood for industrial use but also through its architectural divisions into "clean" and "dirty" areas, "where progress toward the 'clean' sector may be traced on the floor in terms of the gradual disappearance of bloodstains."[13]

The structural position of blood at the heart of the slaughterhouse's operations reveals the larger cultural repression necessary to the industrial production of meat. What must not be seen or acknowledged by the modern consumer is the death, the spilled blood, of the animal. If, as Vialles argues, "we demand an ellipses between animal and meat," the slaughterhouse oversees the production of this ellipses, the disappearance of the red blood of the living animal, the primary violence of its spilling dissimulated into regulated industrial process.[14] Blood becomes waste, sluiced down the drain, and the animal is transformed into meat—pork, bacon, ribs, steak—for the market. To make use of the animal as commodity, any semblance of a sympathetic recognition of its corporeal likeness must be overcome. In subsuming violence into industrial process, the slaughterhouse performs the cultural work of absolution: segregating the consumer from animal life, enabling him or her to enjoy, in innocence, the animal product like any other commodity. Of course, the suggestion of a "crime," written in blood, lurks in these very disavowals.

Red–Green Criticism:
Ecological Matter and the Commodity Form

While Americans value wild horses—which are themselves, ironically, a legacy of ecological imperialism—as charismatic embodiments of the freedom and beauty of the West, the global market recognizes their flesh as a potential commodity, a resource from which value may be extracted. As Mandeville observes, it is the "market" that oversees the transformation of living animals into saleable commodities, refiguring the affective relation between human and animal as an economic transaction between persons. What the slaughterhouse undertakes by design, the market accomplishes in its very structure: the effacement of the violence—abstraction, extraction, transformation—that occurs in producing the commodity. Such effacement occurs not on the level of ideology, in anthropocentric ideas of nature; it is immanent to the structural conditions in which ecological matter is transformed into commodities. A red-inflected green criticism would attend to the free market, under industrial capitalism and in its globalized forms, as the primary agent, the historical absent cause, that organizes human relations to nature in late modernity. We emphasize three aspects of this displacement: (1) the "real abstraction" of exchange,

(2) accumulation and global expansion, (3) and the changing of form that occurs in producing the commodity. It is an ontology of the commodity and not the object in general, we believe, that provides insight into the scenes of displacement, the "withdrawn core" unique to the commodity, that underlie the contemporary environmental crisis.

That ecocriticism has largely ignored the role of the market reflects its preoccupation with the encounter, conceptualized in idealist or ideological terms, between the thinking subject and the order of nature, from Andrew Marvell's pastoral "green thought in a green shade" to Timothy Morton's postmodern "ecological thought."[15] The historically consequential form of *thought* concerning the environment, however, transpires not in the individual subject's consciousness but in what Alfred Sohn-Rethel describes as the "real abstraction" of commodity exchange.[16] Mediated by money, commodity exchange makes equivalent labor, property, and natural resources, subjecting all to an abstract, quantitative valuation. The market is, *in effect,* always thinking about ecosystems and organisms, regarding them as sites of potential value and translating those quantifications into concrete activity. "It is the abstract logic that attaches to the creation and accumulation of social value," in the words of Neil Smith, "that determines the relation with nature under capitalism."[17] However individuals or societies regard the natural world, it is the market's valuation of ecological matter that is responsible for the most productive thinking about the global environment.

Fredric Jameson has often claimed that a defining characteristic of modernity is a breach between the global economic systems that determine experience and the perceptual or ideational content of that experience. While we may perceive ourselves to be enmeshed in a local, phenomenal environment, in reality our individual relation to nature is mediated by a global market, whose workings remain always at a distance. The market's driving tendency is not merely the reproduction of its conditions of production but ever-increasing accumulation of surplus value; in the words of Karl Marx, "capital is the endless and limitless drive to go beyond its limiting barrier."[18] Accumulation depends on expanding into new markets, discovering new sources of exploitation for profit, and extracting maximum value from whatever resources it can find. The market's thinking spans the biosphere, contemplating a global totality of resource extraction, productive development, circulation, and consumption. In this regard, all nature has come under the purview of development, a fact Marx recognized when he claimed that the "nature that preceded human history . . . today no longer exists anywhere."[19] The point is not that ecological and biogeo-chemical systems are no longer operative, but that the market has already valued their productions. What Rob Nixon calls "capitalism's innate ten-dency to abstract in order to extract"—its ability to detach an entity from its ecosystem and value it as resource for development—is intensified by a global market wherein, "to an almost occult degree, production has been disaggregated from consumption."[20] Geographic displacement is, today, the governing fact of ecological relations.

The abstract and speculative valuation of ecological matter determines the actual and ongoing production of nature as commodity. This material transformation involves a fundamental ontological displacement. Marx's account of the mystification that occurs in commodity exchange is well-known: the "social relation" among laborers is "presented to them" as a relation "between the products of their labour," leading to the fetishization of the commodity.[21] Marx identifies the imperceptibility of the commod-ity's concrete history as produced by human labor and the social relation implied in its exchange. There is, however, a further displacement gener-ated in commodity exchange: between matter and organisms, as they exist within the chemical, geological, and ecological systems from which they are extracted, and the commodity as it appears to the consumer. The material prehistory of ecological matter is elided along with the conditions of its production for exchange. Like the transformation of the animal that occurs in the slaughterhouse, the commodity's appearance on the market signals a twofold metamorphosis, an absolute changing of form, which erases both its ecological sources and its human production. This allows the con-sumer to partake, innocently, in the consumption of a commodity that appears unrelated either to the realm of social relations or to the ecosystem from which its matter was initially derived. What the commodity form mystifies, then, is not only the relation between consumer and laborer, the "social" relation Marx stresses, but also the relation of the consumer to the biological systems and organisms from which the commodity is extracted.

It is useful to distinguish this account of the production of ecological matter as commodity not only from models of green consciousness but also from the familiar thesis regarding the instrumental domination of nature, associated with Martin Heidegger and the Frankfurt school.[22] While the instrumentalization thesis identifies as a recognizable and localizable agent technology in its varied forms—the tool, the machine—mediating the human–nature (or subject–object) relation, we are stressing that the production of nature in modernity occurs at a remove. The beginning and the end of this production both manifest away from the site of active, visible intervention. Surplus capital in Belgium is invested in a slaughterhouse in Oregon, and at a later point, horse meat is purchased and consumed in Europe and Asia. It has been fully rendered, cleanly separated not only from the living horse but from the systems—ecological, political, and economic—in which the horse lived and died.

The chromatic intensity of contemporary life is itself structured by mystification. Even red is subject to the logic of the commodity. Allura Red AC, or Red 40, is the most commonly used synthetic dye approved by the Food and Drug Administration for food as well as cosmetics and pharmaceuticals. Allura Red is, not surprisingly, derived from the crucial commodity of industrial modernity. The bright red in Froot Loops and Gatorade is highly refined petroleum: long-ago decomposed organic matter, drilled, processed, and transported across global space. The effects of Allura Red go beyond vivifying the products of the industrial food system, repurposing a biological association of red with ripeness; there is significant research identifying the health risks of synthetic dyes, including increased hyperactivity in children. An alternative to Red 40 is natural red dye, such as the carmine that is also used widely in processed foods (including Cherry Coke) and cosmetics. Carmine dye derives from the cactus-eating cochineal beetle, *Dactylopius coccus,* of the American tropics. Its unparalleled crimson intensity made it a highly sought-after resource among the European powers in the eighteenth century (unsuccessful in breaking a Spanish monopoly, the British paid handsomely for the dye to color the uniforms of their soldiers), and it has in recent years come back into industrial production. In rare cases, carmine dye causes anaphylactic shock. A somewhat more common form of shock is the surprise of consumers, especially vegans and vegetarians, who discover that the red coloring in their Strawberry Frappuccino comes from the ground-up bodies of insects.

Red Sludge and Horse Blood

The unintended consequences of nature's commodification are mostly invisible, as cause and effect, origin and end come to be disaggregated in producing the commodity. How, then, to explain the alarming emergence of displaced red—horse blood passing into the waterways, red bees in Brooklyn soaked in Red 40 from a local maraschino cherry factory— which seems to expose, as symptom, the network of relations, at once productive and destructive, ordinarily hidden from view? Pascal Derde's account of the global circulatory loop that organically intertwines economic and ecological systems represses the violent beginnings and toxic ends of capital's production of nature. Blood seeping from the slaughterhouse wrests attention from this virtuous portrait of global capital's "ecosystem"— a fantasy of a perfectly efficient, waste-free, naturalistic capitalism echoed in contemporary discourses of green capitalism—to reintroduce the un- manageable excesses of its productive processes. The commodification of nature produces strange, spectral objects, integrated into neither ecologi- cal nor economic systems, objects that have neither the intrinsic value of a living being nor the exchange-value of a commodity: agricultural land denuded of fertility, waste and ruins, oceanic garbage patches, cancer clus- ters, carbon dioxide and methane in the atmosphere.

Waste is value's counterpart, the disavowed other of the commodity, and as such it must be identified and minimized or, ideally, itself found to contain value.[23] Animal rendering presents one such market for produc- ing surplus-value out of industrial waste. In her recent book of experimen- tal poetry, *The Cow,* Ariana Reines explores the mechanical, thermal, and chemical processes of industrial animal rendering, all of which transform waste into new sources of capital. Yet, as she writes, excess—viscera, blood, unusable flesh—lingers: "Something gets out from under the end."[24] Waste is the unproductive outcome of production, a by-product from which no value can be extracted. Sometimes this "something," like the blood in the Redmond water system, is reintroduced, accidentally, into a given regime of social or environmental visibility. Toxic red sludge from an alumina plant flooding towns in Hungary, killing nine people and hundreds of ani- mals. Red tides caused by rising sea temperatures and pollution. Dolphins, tortoises, and pelicans shrouded in spilled oil. Such instances graphically reveal the unpredictable ecological effects of capitalism's production of nature, presenting a powerful corrective to the fiction of a harmonious market cycle that coexists with natural ecosystems, each inevitable and governed by orderly laws.

Such stories make national, even international, headlines. Horrifying, revolting, they evoke collective fears of widespread ecological catastrophe and apocalyptic contamination. These accidents illuminate the material intimacy we share with the second nature of waste and the limits of its containability within a globalized industrial market. Julia Kristeva describes abject substances such as blood and refuse as "*show[ing] me* what I permanently thrust aside in order to live"; as such, the appearance of such forbidden matter is profoundly disturbing, intimating not only a temporary boundary breach but the larger frailty of the social, symbolic, and economic order.[25] Yet it is, finally, the very startling visibility of these incidents, their sudden emergence into collective consciousness, that allows them to be treated as aberrant. These instances of accidental breaching are represented as exceptional, prompting calls for greater governmental oversight of particular industries or prosecution of factory owners. Human error becomes a rationalizing explanation, pointing to specific failures of an otherwise functional system. And amid the swift cycles of contemporary media, these stories quickly recede from view. The symptom is treated—the sludge recedes, the blood disappears—and the overarching cause, the production of nature under late capitalism, remains everywhere and nowhere to be seen.

Fire: Illumination and Negation

Thus we turn to the symbolic nature, the *red* aspects, of ELF's activism. In the past three decades, radical environmental groups have, in the United States, offered a sustained and powerful form of resistance to the ecological violence of the free market and the state institutions that support it. This model of nonviolent civil disobedience, directed against capitalist development, is usually traced back to Edward Abbey's novel of 1975, *The Monkey Wrench Gang*, where a band of environmentalists, committing acts of ecotage in the American Southwest, are goaded to increasing radicalism by the Vietnam veteran George Washington Hayduke, who uses the pseudonym "Rudolf the Red." ELF described its actions as embodying "the burning rage of this dying planet,"[26] a return of the repressed, vivifying, through intentional symbolic action, the accidental breaches of capitalist production. The fires set by underground ELF activists—targeting SUV dealerships, ski resorts, condominium developments, logging companies, slaughterhouses, and research laboratories—offer the most visible sign of radical environmental resistance in the United States. More spectacular than tree spiking, more destructive than tree sitting, and more high profile than direct actions in unpopulated regions, ELF fires signify as consequential action and shadowy threat, as manifestation of "burning rage" and as promise of conflagrations to come. The "elves" themselves characterize these actions as *ecotage*, economic sabotage in the pursuit of ecological justice, intended to halt, however temporarily, the workings of a particular corporation. The success of the Cavel West arson in forcing the slaughterhouse's permanent closure is legendary in this regard.

These fires are less significant in their practical consequences than as symbolic action, red alerts that in drawing attention to themselves, draw attention to the commodification of nature continually underway. ELF communiqués point to this symbolic aim, to make visible the ecological violence on which globalized capitalism depends. Believing that "direct actions speak louder than words," the ELF follows in the long anarchist tradition that understands revolutionary resistance as performative.[27] The pedagogical dimension of these fires is underscored by ELF's insistence on publicizing its acts through communiqués that describe the techniques used to produce the fire, the justification for targeting a particular company, and the systemic critique that drives ELF's activism, which is directed at "the capitalist state and its symbols of propaganda."[28] ELF's tactics challenge the work of the market by mimicking its form. Unlike other modes of environmental activism, which depend on the bodily presence of activists sitting in trees or blocking roads, ELF's strategy of invisibility produces an abstract and delocalized agency, able to "strike when least expected," as an ELF communiqué claims.[29] A faceless, leaderless resistance movement without an organized agenda or preordained set of targets, ELF maintains that any individual "cell" can form spontaneously and take action in its name, so long as this action follows the movement's central principles. Each act signals the presence of an agential but decentralized antagonist to capitalism, which is, like the market itself, always thinking and planning, always potentially expanding in unknown directions.

It is, apparently, this classically "red" dimension of the activities of ELF and ALF that has led the US government to identify them with "ecoterrorism," a peculiar appellation given that none of the thousands of acts attributed to these groups have caused injury or death. The extreme caution exercised during the ecotages reflects one of ELF's central guidelines: the necessity of avoiding violence. ELF categorically distinguishes between the destruction of property and violence to living beings, a distinction that the government itself acknowledges in a profoundly revealing 2008 Department of Homeland Security report on ecoterrorism. Yet for the DHS, the destruction of property is itself understood to be violent and terror inducing.[30] The DHS document states that "the concept of direct action, as eco-terrorists practice it, is a euphemism for illegal *and violent* activities designed to halt the destruction of the environment and liberate animals."[31] It is not violent, according to this logic, to raze an old-growth forest; what happens in the slaughterhouse is not violence; yet destruction of private property is a violent activity. In so defining the violence of ecoterrorism, the state assumes as self-evident the same conceptualization of value as does the free market.

One remarkable quality of the DHS report on ecoterrorism is its explicit admission that these groups pose no practical threat to national security. Instead, ELF threatens to resist and reveal, in the amazingly apt words of the Department of Homeland Security, "the damaging encroachment of capitalist societies whose sole concern is profit regardless of any social or ecological costs or consequence."[32] The DHS worries that, given the reality of global warming and the government's lack of action, ELF's worldview is potentially contagious:

Perhaps the most constructive way to gauge the current and future strength of ecoterrorists is not to think in terms of actual numbers, but as a growing trend. The general perception that the planet is in peril, and the reluctance or even refusal of some parts of the U.S. government to acknowledge the damaging effects of global warming may increase the number of potential ecoterrorists. Individuals sympathetic to ecoterrorist philosophy or those generally concerned with the welfare of the environment, may become increasingly tempted to abandon traditional methods of environmental conservation and animal protection . . . and embrace militant tactics as a viable alternative.³³

Without a state apparatus designed to stop them, anyone "concerned with the welfare of the environment" might become an ecoterrorist, given the insufficiency of "traditional methods of environmental conservation" to save the imperiled planet. Looking ahead to a future of continued ecological destruction, the DHS fears a "growing trend" of radical, ecologically minded anticapitalist actions.

ELF's fiery protests intervene in a symbolic order, largely coextensive with the juridical order and the state, that sees private property as the locus of value and limits our historical ambitions to a future defined by the totalized capitalist world-system. Radical ecoactivism introduces a principle of uncertainty into the propulsive forward-thrust of capital accumulation and crisis. It signals a commitment to a different and unknown future. The willingness to act under the sign of red depends on a belief that nonaction is itself agential—that, as Blaise Pascal puts it in his description of the wager on God's existence, "you are already committed."³⁴ These conflagrations do not offer a glimpse of what such a future would look like, or what actions might bring it into existence. Instead, they signal the clearing away that provides an opening for new growth. At the same time, the fires embody the infectious potential of activism that so concerns the state's security apparatus. This potentiality, the spark passed from hand to hand to light a larger fire of protest, is a recurring symbol in the poetry of revolutionary action, as in Brenda Hillman's poem on the Occupy protests, "Types of Fire at the Strike": "Some carry fire in red shirts. / Some make sparks with their bikes. / Some bring boxes of burning words grown from roots / in the earth."³⁵

Apocalypse: The Anthropocene

Etymologically, the word *apocalypse* refers not only to a terminal event, a rupture in time's flow, but also to a moment of disclosure, an "unveiling" that prepares the world for judgment. It should come as no surprise that the Judeo-Christian apocalyptic imaginary is shaded deep, dark red. The total destruction of the Creation, before its refiguration in the "world to come," is known by its red auguries, a blood-red sky signaling the denouement of a story that begins in the blood-red soil. In "On the Morning of Christ's Nativity" (1645), John Milton captures the red presages alluded to in the Old and New Testaments:

With such a horrid clang
As on Mount Sinai rang,
While the red fire and smoldering clouds outbrake:
The aged Earth, aghast,
With terror of that blast,
Shall from the surface to the center shake,
When, at the world's last sessiòn,
The dreadful Judge in middle air shall spread his throne.[36]

Even more strikingly, given the thematics of this chapter, John of Patmos envisages the second horse of the apocalypse as red (the others are black, white, and pale): "When the Lamb opened the second seal, I heard the second living creature say, 'Come!' Then another horse came out, a fiery red one. Its rider was given power to take peace from the earth and to make men slay each other. To him was given a large sword" (Revelation 6:3–4). Through its metonymic association with the agents of transformation— the violent spilling of blood, a fire that burns the earth—red serves as the acute sign of apocalyptic revelation itself.

Since the 1960s, environmentalists have drawn on the rhetoric of apocalypse, anticipating the time when the ecological crisis will make itself unequivocally apparent, leading if not to redemption then at least to a final judgment.[37] While emphasizing the modern displacement of violence and crisis, in this chapter we too have drawn attention to the signs of the times: the disturbing reappearance of uncontainable waste, the fiery sparks of ecological resistance movements. Red returns yet, however insufficiently, at the edge of the symbolic order. This said, the defining material conditions of our historical present remain almost entirely unavailable to such disclosure. Of the mostly invisible by-products of industrial capitalism, the most consequential, if among the least conspicuous, are the greenhouse gases, primarily carbon dioxide and methane, produced in the combustion of fossil fuels. If waste is the disavowed other of the commodity, the atmospheric accumulation of greenhouse gases is the disavowed other of late modern capital accumulation. It is this recent, rapid transformation of the atmosphere's chemical composition—and thus, of the global climate—that has led geologists to define the emergence of a new geological epoch, the Anthropocene, the first in which a biological agent, human beings, shapes global geologic processes.[38] The "ecological rift"—in carbon dioxide concentrations in the atmosphere, but also in extinction rates, phosphorus transfer, ocean acidification, and land use—and its historical causes together amount to an ontological reordering of the economic, ecological, and biogeochemical conditions in which objects come into being. As has been widely noted, the temporal and geographic scale of this agency, our collective human capacity to transform the basic conditions of biological life, renders it unlocalizable. The paradigmatic instance of this displaced agency, unavailable to narrative representation, is the tipping point, where positive feedback loops related to forest dieback, permafrost methane release, and the ice-albedo effect generate—in some scenarios—"runaway" climate change, independent of human action.

If there is any concrete lesson from the two definitive crises of the present, the global economic contraction and human-forced global climate change, it is that liberal democratic nation-states are unequipped for the new ontological order of carbon-based global capitalism. Indeed, rather than respond to these grave emergencies, the US government expends its resources in hyperactive scrutiny and prosecution of those who seek to draw attention, under the sign of red, to the increasingly catastrophic work of the free market. We may take some ironic solace in the fact that the Department of Homeland Security, which surely knows more about these things than we do, responds with outsized vigilance to the scattered sparks of resistance. Perhaps the alignment of crisis and critique that would precipitate the transformation of a political order dedicated to the free market is closer than we imagine. The likelier alternative, from the vantage of the present, is that we will fail to apprehend modernity in its two "total" forms, global warming and global capitalism, as anything other than a red flickering, a slight disturbance at the edge of consciousness, unless or until this perceptual failure is pierced, by degrees or with sudden illumination, as the margins inexorably expand and the debris piles up, beneath fiery clouds and the smoldering sky.

Notes

1. Martha Mendoza, "From Symbol of American Frontier to Dinner," *Los Angeles Times,* January 5, 1997.

2. Quoted in Craig Rosebraugh, *Burning Rage of a Dying Planet* (Herndon, Va.: Lantern Books, 2004), 22–23.

3. Will Potter, *Green Is the New Red: An Insider's Account of a Social Movement under Siege* (San Francisco: City Lights, 2011), 65.

4. Charles Sanders Peirce, "What Is a Sign?," *The Essential Peirce: Selected Philosophical Writings,* vol. 2, ed. Nathan Houser et al. (Bloomington: Indiana University Press, 1992), 4.

5. Charles Sanders Peirce, "To Lady Welby," *Collected Papers of Charles Sanders Peirce,* vol. 8 (Cambridge, Mass.: Belknap Press of Harvard University Press, 1958), 221.

6. Herman Pleij, *Colors Demonic and Divine: Shades of Meaning in the Middle Ages and After* (New York: Columbia University Press, 2005), 17; Brent Berlin and Paul Kay, *Basic Color Terms: Their Universality and Evolution* (Berkeley: University of California Press, 1991).

7. William Burkert, *Homo Necans: An Anthropology of Ancient Greek Sacrificial Ritual and Myth,* trans. Peter Bing (Berkeley: University of California Press, 1983), 20.

8. Ibid., 21.

9. Bernard Mandeville, *The Fable of the Bees,* vol. 1 (1714; Indianapolis: Liberty Press, 1988), 137–38; our emphasis.

10. Jacques Derrida, *The Animal That Therefore I Am,* trans. Marie-Louis Mallet and David Wills (Bronx, N.Y.: Fordham University Press, 2008), 28.

11. Noëlie Vialles, *Animal to Edible,* trans. J. A. Underwood (Cambridge: Cambridge University Press, 1994), 5, 27.

12. Ibid., 73.

13. Ibid., 75.

14. Ibid., 5.

15. *Andrew Marvell: The Complete Poems,* ed. Elizabeth Story Donno (New York: Penguin Classics, 2005), 101; Timothy Morton, *The Ecological Thought* (Cambridge, Mass.: Harvard University Press, 2010).

16. "It is the action of exchange, and the action alone that is abstract. The consciousness and the action of the people part company in exchange and go different ways" (Alfred Sohn-Rethel, *Intellectual and Manual Labour: A Critique of Epistemology,* trans. Martin Sohn-Rethel [Atlantic Highlands, N.J.: Humanities Press, 1978], 26).

17. Neil Smith, *Uneven Development: Nature, Capital, and the Production of Space*, 3rd ed. (Athens: University of Georgia Press, 2008), 70.

18. Karl Marx, *Grundrisse: Foundations of the Critique of Political Economy*, trans. Martin Nicolaus (London: Penguin, 1973), 334.

19. Karl Marx and Friedrich Engels, *The German Ideology* (New York: International Publishers, 1970), 63.

20. Rob Nixon, *Slow Violence and the Environmentalism of the Poor* (Cambridge, Mass.: Harvard University Press, 2011), 41.

21. Karl Marx, *Capital: A Critique of Political Economy*, vol. 1, trans. Ben Fowkes (London: Penguin, 1990), 164–65.

22. Neil Smith observes that in the 1940s, Frankfurt school thinkers turned from the problem of the commodity—a "retreat from exchange-value"—toward an emphasis on the "instrumental" domination of nature (*Uneven Development*, 45).

23. Waste offers new markets for development, an example of the feedback loop of "disaster capitalism," described by Naomi Klein in *The Shock Doctrine* (New York: Picador, 2007), where the market discovers new sources of surplus-value in the very crises it generates. As John Bellamy Foster, Brett Clark, and Richard York note in *The Ecological Rift: Capitalism's War on the Earth* (New York: Monthly Review Press, 2010), "whole new industries and markets aimed at profiting on planetary destruction, such as the waste management industry and carbon trading, are being opened up" (70).

24. Ariana Reines, *The Cow* (New York: Fence Books, 2006), 80.

25. Julia Kristeva, *Powers of Horror: An Essay on Abjection*, trans. Leon Roudiez (New York: Columbia University Press, 1982), 3.

26. Potter, *Green Is the New Red*, 57.

27. "Direct Action Speaks Louder Than Words" is the title of an essay by ELF/ALF activist Rod Coronado, in *Terrorists or Freedom Fighters? Reflections on the Liberation of Animals*, ed. Steven Best and Anthony Nocella (Herndon, Va.: Lantern Books, 2004), 179.

28. Quoted in Paul Joosse, "Elves, Environmentalism, and 'Eco-Terror,'" *Crime, Media, Culture* 8, no. 75 (2012): 79.

29. Quoted in Leslie James Pickering, *Earth Liberation Front, 1997–2002* (Tempe, Ariz.: Arissa, 2007), 10.

30. Department of Homeland Security Universal Adversary Dynamic Threat Assessment, "Ecoterrorism: Environmental and Animal-Rights Activists in the United States," May 2008, 1, http://www.humanewatch.org/images/uploads/2008_DHS_ecoterrorism_threat_assessmentpdf. The existence of this document points to a peculiar fact of the ongoing post-9/11 "war on terror." Governmental resources ostensibly dedicated to fighting Islamic terrorism and national security

threats are instead being allocated to prevent the largely symbolic property damage of ecoradicals. "Terrorism is terrorism, no matter what the cause," stated FBI director Robert Mueller, tautologically, at the January 20, 2006, press briefing (quoted in Potter, *Green Is the New Red*, 64). Arrests and convictions of ELF members in 2005 and 2006 for various arsons, including the Cavel West fire—and the posttrial addition of "terrorist enhancement penalties" to their sentences—were touted as a major success by the Justice Department and the FBI, representing much-needed proof of their achievement in battling terrorism.

31. Department of Homeland Security, "Ecoterrorism, " 4; our emphasis.

32. Ibid.

33. Ibid., 11–12.

34. Blaise Pascal, *Pensées and Other Writings,* trans. Anthony Levi and Honor Levi (New York: Oxford University Press, 2008), 154. Michael Löwy writes that the "Marxist utopia of an authentic human community is of the order of a Pascalian wager: it is the engagement of individuals—or social groups—in an action that involves risk, the danger of failure, the hope of success, but to which one commits one's life" (*Fire Alarm: Reading Walter Benjamin's "On the Concept of History"* [London: Verso, 2005], 114).

35. Unpublished poem in manuscript, "Seasonal Work with Letters on Fire," which will complete Hillman's tetralogy of the elements.

36. "On the Morning of Christ's Nativity," in *The Norton Anthology of Poetry,* 5th ed. (New York: Norton, 2005), ll. 157–64.

37. Frederick Buell identifies environmental rhetoric with four features of "Judeo-Christian apocalyptic tradition": "sudden rupture with the past, presentation of a revelation, narration of a world-end and dramatization of a last judgment" ("A Short History of Environmental Apocalypse," in *Future Ethics: Climate Change and Apocalyptic Imagination,* ed. Stefan Skrimshire [London: Continuum, 2010], 15).

38. Paul Crutzen, "Geology of Mankind," *Nature,* January 3, 2002, 23.

Maroon

LOWELL DUCKERT

> Imagine dancing flames. As I write . . . I have before my eyes this
> crimson curtain that fluctuates, sends up great shoots, disappears,
> is fragmented, invades and illuminates space, only to die out,
> suddenly, in darkness. It is a complex and supple network, never
> in equilibrium—in other words, "existing"—striking and
> fluctuating swiftly in time, and having ill-defined edges.
>
> —MICHEL SERRES with BRUNO LATOUR,
> *Conversations on Science, Culture, and Time*

From Aurora, the Roman goddess of the dawn, comes aurora borealis
and aurora australis, winds of the north and south that speak of beginnings. I have never felt more attracted to a subject I have never seen. From
a scientific standpoint, my desire makes sense: auroras are places where
light and magnetism meet. Their colors are restless waves of charged particles; every flare catches something else and flickers anew. In a word, these
are luminous storms that *beacon*. "Beacon" comes from the Old English
béacn: a "sign" or "portent," a fire set on high to serve as a warning, signal, or celebration. "Beckon" *(bíecnan),* "to summon" or "to gesture," is a
close relative.[1] Perhaps the earliest English speakers, true boreals, experienced the beaconing powers of the aurora whenever they looked up into a
clear night sky and fixated on celestial flames. But what kind of structure
could I give to a signal that constantly signifies? For this chapter, I decided
to embrace the aurora's pull rather than uncurling its grasp. I traced the
diverse stories it tells instead of defining its voice. I imagined dancing
flames. And when the aurora beaconed, I tugged back at one of its energetic hues. Maroon is a color that *beacons* within the aurora: it invites
us into incendiary intimacies of violence and pleasure; it signals stories
of the past and lights potential futures to come; it sparks new relationships between humans and nonhumans that may ignite brighter ecological

communities for both. What follows is an *Arcticology* in and of maroon, an experiment in coexistence with a precarious world at the poles and everywhere in between. Now imagine, reader, drapes of deep reddish-brown unfurling before you:

The sky is firing . . .

Were you expecting the Robinson Crusoe of prismatic ecologies? I hope not. Look upon a desert isle for that sailor's least favorite color, the shade of the "lost" or "abandoned." Despite what it means to be "marooned," the color maroon is never alone. Look up instead; gaze into "darkness . . . buzzing with unseen activity."[2] You might be surprised to find undulating bands of maroon dancing above you. Auroras are astronomical collaborations, our universe aflame. In simplest terms, an aurora is powered by the sun, shaped by the magnetosphere, and colored by gases.[3] Charged particles from the sun (solar wind) collide with the earth's magnetic field; this plasma is funneled toward the poles where it contacts atmospheric gas at approximately sixty to two hundred miles up. Electrical discharges emit different colors depending on what speed of electron excites what. Atomic oxygen (O) produces the most common color—a greenish-whitish light—but above 150 miles or so O produces a dark-red color known as the red line. And when electrons are extremely active, thereby able to penetrate farther into the solar atmosphere, nitrogen molecules (N_2) create a maroonish glow at the bottom of the curtain.[4] Even if it fringes the lower and upper borders of the aurora, however, maroon is a site of intense activity rather than diminishment. Maroon lives up to its namesake: a late sixteenth-century word derived from the French *marron* ("chestnut"), maroon later meant "firework" because of the noise a chestnut makes when it bursts in the fire.[5] Though somewhat predictable—auroras intensify during sunspot cycles about every eleven years, for instance—erratic phenomena like solar flares affect auroral illumination. Both recognizable and mysterious, "the forces that dance in the polar dark are awe-inspiring—alien, uncontrollable, and immensely vigorous."[6] Maroon is fire (at) work, an event akin to cooperative conflagration.

The sky is firing . . .

Samuel Hearne was the first European to travel overland across Canada to the Arctic Ocean, but he is perhaps remembered best as the inspiration for

Samuel Taylor Coleridge's poem *The Rime of the Ancient Mariner* (1798). Born in 1745, Hearne joined the Hudson's Bay Company in 1766 and was stationed at the far-north outpost of Prince of Wales Fort in Churchill.[7] In 1769 he set out on his first of three voyages in search of the Northwest Passage and the legendary copper lodes along the Far-Off Metal River. With the help of the Chipewyan Dene and their leader Matonabbee—a close friend of Hearne's—he reached the Arctic Ocean on the third expedition of 1771–72, disproving the existence of both the Passage and the copper mines. Over the next several years, Hearne collated his notes and maps; established the first inland trading post at Cumberland House; became governor of the Prince of Wales Fort; and married the half-Indian daughter of the previous governor. When the French took the fort in 1782, he negotiated safe passage back to England. Though eager to finish his manuscript, he was even more eager to return to Churchill. Once there the following spring, however, he discovered that his wife had starved to death and that Matonabbee had hanged himself. Spiraling into alcoholism, Hearne made little progress on his narrative. He resigned his post in 1787 and, back in London, fell ill with dropsy. He signed a contract with a publisher in 1792 and died shortly thereafter. When *A Journey from Prince of Wales's Fort in Hudson's Bay to the Northern Ocean in the years 1769, 1770, 1771, 1772* finally appeared in print in 1795, it was enthusiastically received. Drafting a narrative of his Arctic adventures twenty years after the fact, Hearne must have felt terribly alone. His revisions meant revisiting the places and faces of those whom he had lost—or abandoned. Rime, rime, everywhere: no commercial success could possibly alleviate the pain of this ancient mariner.

The sky is firing . . .

Enter an alien beacon on its own trip. In the catalog of the landscape and its people found at the back of the *Journey,* Hearne takes a naturalist's approach to the aurora borealis. "The Northern Indians," he claims, "call the *Aurora Borealis,* Ed-Thin; that is, Deer."[8] When the lights are bright, deer are abundant in the atmosphere. But they have yet to "entertain hopes of tasting those celestial animals."[9] With his fur-trapping mind, Hearne translates the zoo-atmosphere into a realm fit for human consumption, for hunting and "tasting." Always skeptical of native knowledge, he researches the practical reasons behind the mythology of "Ed-Thin." He provides two theories in a footnote:

> Their ideas on this respect are founded on a principle one would not imagine. Experience has shewn them, that when a hairy deer-skin is briskly stroked with the hand in a dark night, it will emit many sparks of electrical fire, as the back of a cat will. The idea which the Southern Indians have of this meteor is equally romantic, though more pleasing, as they believe it to be the spirits of their departed friends dancing in the clouds; and when the *Aurora Borealis* is remarkably bright, at which time they vary most in colour, form, and situation, they say, their deceased friends are very merry.[10]

Hearne does not linger long on these auroral encounters. The possibility of the aurora as a living thing—able to "emit" sparks like a cat, or house the living spirits of the "departed"—is judged too "romantic." Hearne objectifies not only the aurora but also the natives' "principle" by footnoting both topics as afterthoughts in the final pages. There is little room for what Timothy Morton calls "ecorhapsody" here, even though the idea of the "Southern Indians" is "more pleasing" to Hearne.[11] Natural philosophy in this instance preserves the distance between the human subject and the alien outside world, despite Hearne's obvious intrigue with animalistic—even organic—explanations of "Ed-thin." We can almost feel the spark of "electrical fire" in his description of a "hairy deer-skin." (My own skin tingles; the fire catches.) Briefly excited, he turns away.

After Hearne's dismissal of indigenous beliefs, "one would not imagine" paying more attention to the northern lights. But what if one does? "Being much jaded" in a blizzard on his second voyage,[12] Hearne and Matonabbee dig a hole in the snow for shelter. After they finish, "the weather began to moderate, and the drift greatly to abate; so that the moon and the Aurora Borealis shone out with great splendor, and there appeared every symptom of the return of fine weather."[13] Hearne's gaze again seems fleeting. The beacon indeed "shone out," but it only illuminates "every symptom of the return of fine weather." Satisfied with his analysis, we sense him about to glance elsewhere. Yet recall that Hearne wrote his narrative nearly twenty years after the events, with full knowledge of the fates of those he loved. Writing the *Journey* proves that he could not turn away from the aurora—and that he did not want to. Like the aurora, the icescape undulates from danger to beauty, shelter to storms, "being much jaded" to being "with great splendor." If a meteor is an atmospheric body, the aurora as "meteor" is really an assemblage of multiple bodies in constant connection. Hearne might feel marooned in the blizzard, but he is never outside auroral "ideas" of collaboration no matter how "romantic." These foreign "ideas" about the lights display the "more pleasing" contacts human and nonhuman beings may make together: like the sparking touch of a hand on another's skin, like a polar landscape suffused with the light of moons and auroras "remarkably bright," like Hearne with his "departed" friend Matonabbee weathering a storm, like the living carrying on with the dead and "dancing in the clouds." The sky is firing even on a "dark night," and all types of bodies make and take the spark. Hearne's recollection might be a wish to "return" to better days, but it also reveals his desire for "fine weather" ahead. Though he cannot fully comprehend that the aurora's red line is really a thin one, bunkering down with other beings here in the snow signals our own potential for finer ecological futures. One can observe the beacons that show the way, just as Hearne did, in a volatile world. And be "merry" for it.

The sky is firing . . .

But could all this talk of auroral cascades be just a "silly notion," as ridiculous as the thought that fairies ("Nant-e-na") inhabit all the elements?[14] If so, realize what is at stake: Hearne could claim from firsthand experience that the dead could not dance. In July 1771 he witnessed another aurora borealis at the falls of the Far-Off Metal River. For reasons unclear to him, but to which he does not object, the Northern Indians despise the Eskimo. When five tents of the latter are seen on the river's west side, his companions thought solely on "how they might steal on the poor Esquimaux the ensuing night, and kill them all while asleep."[15] The Indians paint themselves for terrifying effect:

> Each painted the front of his target or shield; some with the figure
> of the Sun, others with that of the Moon, several with different

kinds of birds and beasts of prey, and many with the images of imaginary beings, which, according to their silly notions, are the inhabitants of the different elements, Earth, Sea, Air, etc.[16]

Symbols smeared in "accidental blotches" of "red and black."[17] Hearne could just as easily be describing the aurora borealis. These armed human bodies resemble the auroral streaks of maroon in the sky, those "celestial animals" Hearne derided "according to their silly notions."[18] The Indians attack in the middle of the night. Firing on the Eskimos on the other bank, the attackers ascend the top of a high hill "and standing all in a cluster, so as to form a solid circle, with their spears erect in the air, gave many shouts of victory, constantly clashing their spears against each other, and frequently calling out *tima! tima!* [Eskimo for "what cheer"] by way of derision."[19] Flashing spears of light high in the sky, and igniting the air with their gleaming guns, Hearne's circle is auroral ruination, a bloodthirsty beacon on a hill. Some Eskimos escape, but the Indians did all they could to "distress the poor creatures . . . who were standing on the shoal before mentioned, obliged to be woeful spectators of their great, or perhaps irreparable loss."[20] Now instead of seeing auroral "splendor," the Eskimos are forced to watch in horror as an aurora sweeps through their village. Approximately twenty men, women, and children are slaughtered while Hearne "stood neuter in the rear."[21] Hearne names this place "Bloody Fall" because so much blood stains the water.[22] What dancers awaited these Eskimo dead? What *tima*? Marauders painted in maroon paint the land red.

Over there is an old man slain by twenty men, so that "his whole body was like a cullender," a human being spouting his own bloody falls.[23] But here is one closer to Hearne: a young Eskimo girl about eighteen years old, struck in the side by a spear. She "twisted round my legs, so that it was with difficulty that I could disengage myself from her dying grasps."[24] As her pursuers approach her, he "solicited very hard for her life."[25] But to no avail: they stick two spears into her, pinning her to the ground. Ridiculing Hearne and the girl, they pay little attention to her shrieks and moans, even though she "was twining round their spears like an eel."[26] Hearne rebukes them, hoping they might dispatch her faster and put her out of her misery—or else he will do so himself. "The love of life . . . was so predominant," Hearne observes, that she tried to deflect this killing blow.[27] One assailant pierces her through the heart. This traumatic moment almost cannot be reiterated:

> It was with difficulty that I could refrain from tears; and I am confident that my features must have feelingly expressed how sincerely I was affected at the barbarous scene I then witnessed; even at this hour I cannot reflect on the transactions of that horrid day without shedding tears.[28]

What did this girl see in the night as the guns were blazing? "Twining" tighter and tighter around his body as well as the spears, she does not want to be deserted. Save me, she tells Hearne, the sky is on fire. But her "love of life" goes out. He may finally loosen her grip.

> There was that Eskimo girl
> at Bloody Fall, at your feet,
> . . . .
> and she twisted about them like
> an eel, dying, never to know.[29]

Though he departs from the dead at the falls, her memory is still wrapped around him, eel-like. Now is the time for his tears.

The sky is firing . . .

"Imagine dancing flames," Michel Serres says to Bruno Latour during one of their *Conversations*.[30] Latour is trying to comprehend Serres's "map of relationships,"[31] a philosophical method that traces relationships between things while creating new ones. For Serres, things exist through their alliances: "Relations spawn objects, beings and acts, not vice versa."[32] His is a map with "ill-defined" rather than sharp edges, a fluctuating and fragmented picture of reality quite different from the laminated easy-fold maps found on our dashboards. Every relation is an invention; every invention establishes new relations. A fluid map in flux—like a "crimson curtain that fluctuates."[33] Interesting, says Latour, but how do we get anywhere? "I don't make my abstractions starting from some *thing* or some *operation,* but *throughout* a relation, a rapport," answers Serres.[34] Relations create new routes; thus no map of relationships can ever be finished. So much depends on the *"throughout."* "Pre-position—what better name for those relations that precede any position?"[35] Human and nonhuman interrelations form networks that "sen[d] up great shoots" and thereby create new networks.[36] A map of endless positions—like "dancing flames" that flicker in the night.[37] Latour beckons: say more. As a "complex and supple network," this map views humans and nonhumans as ontologically inseparable and invites us to trace their "striking" collaborations "in time."[38] A map that "invades and illuminates space"—like an aurora.[39] Yes, I interject: I think I finally have it! This "dancing flam[e]" illuminates how humans and nonhumans forge new relations. This "crimson curtain" in the sky enfolds us with an ever-undulating world. Never marooned from things but always coimplicated with them (*pli* means "fold"), we are entwined with non/human beings on the move. What wrinkles of intimacy will be made?[40] Which directions will we take with the fiery and firing sky? Serres points to the map. Relation is everything, he says. "So—stand up, run, jump, move, dance!"[41]

The sky is firing . . .

Hearne is done surveying for the day; he folds up his unfinished map and puts it in his pocket. The governor of the fort ordered him to reconnoiter the land on his journeys and, with good judgment, to claim anything of value in the company's name. Hearne's journal and chart were indispensable for this mission. "I drew a Map on a large skin of parchment . . . and sketched all the West coast of the Bay on it, but left the interior parts blank, to be filled up during my Journey."[42] The blank space is meticulously filled in with information he records on separate pieces: his "daily courses and distance," natural landmarks like lakes and rivers, and knowledge gathered from the natives—"having corrected them by observations," of course.[43] Hearne's map must not be in disequilibrium; he allows for mistakes and diversions only so that they may be "corrected." This is a map with defined edges: as its "interior parts" are filled in, it will terminate at its borders, and no more connections will be made. Hardly erring or errant, Hearne stays the teleological course, follows his orders, and fills in the blanks. Native guides prevent him from wandering off course. Overall, Hearne's map of relationships rejects accidents, errors, and failures. When the wind knocks over his quadrant on the second journey, he begrudgingly returns, missing his chance to see himself and his journey "*throughout* a relation" with an object.[44] All points lead north by northwest: according to Hearne, the map is a puzzle that will eventually be solved. There cannot be any chance for this parchment to spark in the night like a "hairy deer-skin."[45]

No, his map shows a darker imprint: "I left the print of my feet in blood almost at every step I took."[46] Hearne was also instructed to "smoke [the] Calimut of Peace with their leaders, in order to establish a friendship with them [and] persuade them from going to war with each other."[47] As the Bloody Fall massacre makes clear, he failed in this regard. The "pre-position" is ethically charged.[48] Though "neuter" in the rear during the fight—which is still a choice—he had the opportunity to take a different position shortly beforehand. When a great number of Copper Indians join his party in July, they do so "with no other intent than to murder the Esquimaux."[49] The scheme is "universally approved by those people."[50] There is no reason for murder he can discern, and when he tries to persuade them against "putting their inhuman design into execution" he is called a coward.[51] Hearne faces a tough decision: if he leaves, he will be alone in an alien icescape. If he objects in defense of the harmless Eskimo, his companions will desert him. In the end, he saves himself by sticking with the group:

> I knew my personal safety depended in a great measure on the favourable opinion they entertained of me in this respect, I was obliged to change my tone, and replied, that I did not care if they rendered the name and the race of the Esquimaux extinct.[52]

His "change of tone" is so well approved, in fact, that he decides never to interfere again:

> It was the highest folly for an individual like me, and in my situation, to attempt to turn the current of a national prejudice which had subsisted between those two nations from the earliest periods, or at least as long as they had been acquainted with the existence of each other.[53]

How can Hearne allow a race to become "extinct" so easily? Easily: Hearne completes his survey after the massacre, erects a marker, and takes possession of the coast in the name of the Hudson's Bay Company. This ethical position begs other positions to take with humans and nonhumans: with copper, the Far-Off Metal River, "the race of the Esquimaux." His deplorable justification asks us how we can become better "acquainted with" coexistence. Presenting a choice between desertion and connectedness, however, is already a mistake: maroon beacons a world of inextricable enmeshment. Relations endlessly flame relations. Believing otherwise is a deadly notion: Hearne crosses paths with countless numbers of things that beckon at his bloody feet. But desertion is never an option, only a fantasy; ask Hearne if he has walked far enough away from the cries of the Eskimo girl to never hear them again. To make a map of the *Journey,* follow the trail of dead.

The sky is firing . . .

In contrast to Hearne's choice for "personal safety" that enables Indian–Eskimo violence, fleeing in the name of self-preservation can be a way to escape harm. "Maroon" could mean "a runaway slave" beginning in the late seventeenth century, derived from the French *marron* ("feral"), Spanish *cimarrón* ("fugitive" and "wild place"), and the community of escaped black slaves who settled in Suriname and the West Indies.[54] Hearne speaks of "cannibals" and "murderers" forced to wander from their communities and, presumably, form new ones elsewhere.[55] But perhaps the most fugitive character in the narrative is its desired object: the copper cache of the Far-Off Metal River. Writing the *Journey*'s introduction in hindsight, Hearne states that no man "ever found a bit of copper" in the region, proving "the improbability of putting their favourite scheme of mining into practice."[56] For all his toil and Eskimo blood spilled, he finds "an entire jumble of rocks and gravel" at the river's mouth.[57] He also finds a "strange tradition" among the Indians that links the violence recently done at Bloody Fall with the landscape's absence of copper:

> The first person who discovered those mines was a woman, and that she conducted them to the place for several years; but as she was the only woman in company, some of the men took such liberties with her as made her vow revenge on them; and she is said to have been a great conjurer. Accordingly when the men had loaded themselves with copper, and were going to return, she refused to accompany them, and said she would sit on the mine till she sunk into the ground, and that the copper should sink with her.[58]

When the men return the next year, she is waist high with less copper around her. The year after that, she has disappeared entirely and taken almost every bit of metal with her. Unlike the Eskimo girl winding herself around Hearne's body, these native and metallic bodies desire to be left alone, marooning themselves from men deeper into the earth. While it is not clear what "liberties" were taken with the woman, we may assume that Hearne means she was raped, establishing an uneasy connection between the miners' penetration of the land and her own unwilling sexual penetration. Although Hearne could not conceive of metallic agency ("Nant-e-na"), his anecdote depicts runaway metal withdrawing from his hands. It "sink[s] with her." Perhaps, just like the woman and the Eskimo girl, copper's "love of life . . . was so predominant" that it sought shelter in the bowels of the earth. Or perhaps it wanted to be found—it wished to escape one community to join another—only to be crushed underneath the weight of the conjuring human. We are never to know.

While hunting in January 1772, Hearne discovers "a young woman sitting alone" inside a hut.[59] According to him, she was a Western Dog-ribbed Indian, taken prisoner by Indians nearly two years before. Her captors had surprised her party in the night, killing everyone in the tent—her father, mother, and husband—leaving her and three other women alive. When her baby is found, it is killed on the spot: "The poor woman's relation of this shocking story, which she delivered in a very affecting manner, only excited laughter among the savages in my party."[60] The previous summer "she had eloped from [the Athapuscow], with an intent to return to her own country,"[61] but, becoming lost, built a hut to survive over the winter. Hearne cannot believe her healthy condition after all her travails. She is not "in want" but "one of the finest women, of a real Indian, that I have seen in any part of North America."[62] She is so attractive, however, that the men, many of them polygamous, fight over the right to wed her. She was "won and lost at wrestling" the entire evening.[63] Previously escaping enslavement to achieve a livable life, and now bound to an inextricable tug-of-war, what does this young marooner desire? If freedom, according to Latour, is relative to the number of "attachments" a given thing has with others, maroon invites us to consider a mode of ecological justice that not only investigates why fugitive things are on the run (whether copper or women) but also highlights their desires to join different constellations of relations.[64] Maroon lights up the commune.

The sky is firing . . .

Listen! Even though the sun barely rises in the polar winter, the sky above Hearne was ablaze on Christmas Eve, 1771. "The brilliancy of the Aurora Borealis" supplies him with enough light that he "could see to read a very small print."[65] But his sight is not the only sense stimulated that night. The aurora crackles: "I can positively affirm, that in still nights I have frequently heard them make a rustling and crackling noise, like the waving of a large flag in a fresh gale of wind."[66] He has not met any northern travelers who can say the same, but this audible dearth may "probably be owing to the want of perfect silence at the time they made their observations on those meteors."[67] Yet he has heard the noise in other places, which leads him to believe that "it is only for want of attention that it has not been heard in every part of the Northern hemisphere where they have been known to shine with any considerable degree of luster."[68] Hearne joins a long list of auroral auditors throughout history, including Canadian citizens who this year heard sounds like trumpets blaring in the sky.[69] Some theories have been suggested: the sound of ice crystals forming after exhalation;[70] radio waves from the upper atmosphere creating vibrations in piezo-electric materials (crystals susceptible to electromagnetic radiation) in rocks; or the hissing of static electricity.[71]

Respond! Hearne attunes us to the sound of the sky. There is another possibility within this soundscape ecology: to consider auroral sound not as a mystery to be solved but as an invitation to converse. Many indigenous cultures of the Arctic believe that the sound is made by the souls of the dead as they run across the heavens, playing soccer with a walrus skull.[72] While this puts the hearer in the position of receiving only, other legends claim that the aurora will vociferously interact with humans. One tradition believes that the noise is the voices of spirits trying to communicate with people on earth. "They should always be answered in a whispering voice."[73] Another holds that "one has only to whistle in return and the light will come nearer, out of curiosity."[74] The aurora's ability to participate in a lively conversation with the auditor grants it a life akin to "aerobiology" yet slightly different from it: (a) life less defined by airborne microbial communities (for instance) and more suggestive of nonorganic life.[75] An Eskimo tradition holds "that the aurora borealis is alive just as men and women are; for if you whistle at it, it crackles and comes nearer. But if you spit at it, it all runs together in the middle and forms another picture. It is just as if it understood people and did what they wanted it to do."[76] Hearne was right: it is not that the aurora does not make a sound, but that we are not very good listeners; it is our "want of attention" that stops our ears. Though personal (souls of departed family members) and anthropomorphic (souls of men and women), the whistling aurora is also an impersonal force: a nongendered and agentic "it" that possesses emotions and understands people.[77] The aurora might not always do what people want it to do, but it wants, and it waits for, "attention." Maroon can be an outspoken desire for intimacy, a yearning to be so close to things that only a whisper is needed in reply, a beacon that beckons us to join other voices colliding like electrons in the sky.

The sky is firing . . .

"The [rugby] ball," Serres tells Latour, "is the true subject of the game. It is like a tracker of the relations in the fluctuating collectivity around it."[78] For Serres, everything is on a level ontological playing field. The human athlete is not the primary subject of the game or even the sole player—the match would cease without the ball! Instead, we are to follow the relations as we would the action afield. Coincidently, the Eskimo word for "aurora" is *aksarnirq*, "ball player."[79] Take me up to the ballgame: an aurora is the luminous "ball" at the center of relations, a strange attractor of non/human collectives and actors at play. A maroon sky tends to attract specific relations, however. According to a circumpolar tradition shared by multiple indigenous cultures, an aurora represents the "souls of those who have died through loss of blood, childbirth, suicide, or through murder."[80] In Greenland it is called *alugsukat*: untimely births or children born in concealment.[81] According to the Chukchi people of Siberia, auroral strands are the ropes of suicides or the gory mess of dead infants who died during birth.[82] Other peoples believe them to be the souls of dead warriors continuing to fight. Deep reds only accentuated these ghastly meanings. Samis in Scandinavia and Russia refer to the aurora as *runtis-jammij*, "some who are killed by the use of iron" and who live in a large hall. When quarrels break out, they stab each other to death and the floors are stained dark red.[83] All in all, to be under a maroon sky means that something is bleeding, that the *oikos* ("household") of the sky-hall is dripping blood again, that the walrus skull is on a roll once more.

Because auroras at midlatitudes are extremely rare and typically tinted maroon (they must occur higher up in the atmosphere to be seen that far south), auroras in European history were fearful sights. Aristotle wrote in the *Meteorlogica* that "sometimes on a clear night a number of appearances can be seen taking shape in the sky, such as chasms, trenches, and blood-red colors."[84] For many premodern writers, auroras not only indicated violent activity in heaven but portended bad times ahead on earth as well. Pliny the Elder suggested that "there is no presage of woe more calamitous to the human race [than] a flame in the sky, which seems to descend to the earth on showers of blood."[85] Auroras could signify God's displeasure; almost a thousand pilgrims arrived in Paris to save their souls after a beacon appeared in 1583. The sky is on fire, and sinners will burn. Marching in formation like lances in the sky, an aurora's raylike structure often gave it a militaristic significance. Renaissance woodcuts illustrated the lights as clashing armies in the clouds. As above, so below: war in heaven, war on earth. Maroon conveyed these tints of danger and prognostication into the Enlightenment and beyond. Those who helped advance scientific knowledge of auroras in the eighteenth and nineteenth centuries were explorers who traveled to the icy ends of the earth, many looking for expeditions that never returned (like Sir John Franklin's, d. 1847). Herein lies the predicament: from a European perspective, auroras took place where human beings did not belong. The emergence of "maroon" as a verb from this period (1699) says it all: "to be lost or separated from one's companions."[86] You were irretrievably lost when beaconed by the light of maroon—a tradition that unfortunately persists.

The sky is firing . . .

Within several native belief systems, it is perilous to answer an aurora's beckoning. Eskimos in northern Canada call the lights the "dance of the dead,"[87] while the Dogrib people believe that their hero Ithenhiela sculpted the landscape of northwestern Canada and then rested in Sky Country. The lights are his fingers beckoning his people to come visit him far away.[88] A story among the Norwegian Lapps tells of a boy who sang to them; they began to flicker so wildly that he was incinerated.[89] Decapitation and abduction could result once the lights were summoned, and especially when goaded.[90] But additional dancers take the dance floor, too: boys dance

with the airy spirits down on earth;[91] the Eskimos of the lower Yukon
believe the lights to be the dancing souls of their favorite animals; for the
Finns, the "fire-fox" whisks snow into the air.[92] Thus if the aurora is a dance
to which both the living and the dead are invited, it is an open-ended one,
a "reciprocally structured interplay of human and nonhuman agency," to
cite Andrew Pickering, "*a dance of agency*."[93] An aurora is a kind of "man-
gling,"[94] a word that magnifies the potential for both singeing and singing with the light. The Chinese, Lakota Sioux, and Chuvash of central Asia
associate the lights with favorable childbirth; the Swedes believe they
increase the earth's fertility.[95] Dancing with the stars does not automatically result in death. An auroral "dance of agency" is one in which life and
death mangle up in maroon, where humans and nonhumans constantly
change partners and learn new steps to take. Just like partaking in the movement from a blizzard to "fine weather," in fact. By following the "splendor"
of spirits dancing above their foxhole, Hearne and Matonabbee prove to
be talented instructors.

The sky is firing . . .

Sometimes we can hear Hearne muttering in the darkness: agentic air is a
"silly notion."[96] Fetishistic mythologies of far-off folks are supposedly different from the scientific truths of today. Aristotle seconds: there is a "chasm"
(*chasmata*) between human and nonhuman, spectacle and spectator. And
unlike the earliest explorers, we can witness auroras nowadays with little
danger: be it in caravans of ecotourism or in controlled geophysics laboratories. Better yet, these fires in the sky do not seem to contribute to any
ecological crisis such as global warming. Why should auroras exist for anything but human enjoyment? Human-made auroras have been attempted,
and scientists have speculated about ways to harness its massive energy
output (in the millions of megawatts). The science fiction writer T. W.
Knox wrote in 1885 of "babies . . . reared on electricity" and "the world . . .
filled with giants nourished from the aurora."[97] During the winter of 2011–
12, many were "nourished" by a massive coronal ejection.[98] But if we resist
reading auroras solely in terms of human nutritional value—it is good for
the soul—we begin to see it in more collaborative ways. An aurora is a laboratory for us to gauge nonhuman agency: "Polar lights offer us a glimpse
into the complex workings of the plasma universe and provide us with a

natural laboratory in which it can be studied."[99] Like it or not, cultures are inextricably wrapped-up with auroras. *In medias maroon*: "The living world is 'wired in' to the auroral circuits," even during the day.[100] Magnetic storms interfere with radio transmissions, pipelines, power plants, and flight routes. Hydro Quebec's power grid shut down for nine hours in 1989 because of a geomagnetic storm.[101] Research suggests that biological functions—metabolism and sleep cycles, for instance—are affected by solar storms.[102] The bloody "chasm" need not be sutured, rewired, or relegated to native "ideas" (equivalent to mythology, for Hearne). The aurora illuminates a world that is always already "wired-in," where the human is not the motherboard but only one chip in an electrical network of complex interrelations. A beacon builds circuits—not breaks them. The true "silly notion" is to think any differently.[103]

The sky is firing . . .

John Muir cannot go to sleep. Bedded on two boulders in Alaska's Hugh Miller fjord in 1890, "magnificent upright bars of light in prismatic colors suddenly appeared," invading his solitary space.[104] He is overjoyed by these glad visitors: "How long these glad, eager soldiers of light held on their way I cannot tell; for sense of time was charmed out of mind and the blessed night circled away in measureless rejoicing enthusiasm."[105] The next day is tough going; fighting the ice packs of Glacier Bay, he is forced to retire close to his cabin. Before sundown he is treated to another display, this one not as "extravagant" as before. Yet he "lay awake watching."[106] Rejoining his party on the third night, Professor Reid calls out to him just before bed: "Muir, come look here. Here's something fine."[107] "I ran out in auroral excitement," Muir confides, "and sure enough here was another aurora."[108] Although Reid eventually leaves, Muir is never alone that night. He watches the "wonderful arch" for hours until it finally fades away.[109] Now he may sleep. But he is "too aurorally rich and happy" to do so.[110] Taking one last glance outside, his suspicions are confirmed: another aurora is coming. "Then losing all thoughts of sleep, I ran back to my cabin, carried out blankets and lay down on the moraine to keep watch until daybreak, that none of the sky wonders of the glorious night within reach of my eyes might be lost."[111] In the presence of these "restless electric auroral fairies,"[112] Muir becomes a body electric. His biorhythms speed up and slow down according to the auroras' "quivery step and time to music too fine for mortal ears."[113] Muir joins a disorienting dance of agency that must be shared: in writing, in beckoning, in laying awake and beside the wonders of heaven and earth. "Look here." Who is speaking? Muir is too aurorally excited to ask, "too aurorally rich" to say no.

The sky is firing . . .

The curtain falls on this chapter, but it does not mark an ending. If nothing about the aurora has flamed amazement so far, at least remember this: maroon is a color that infinitely beacons. Robert Falcon Scott died in an Antarctic blizzard in 1912 after losing the race to the South Pole. Writing about the southern lights in 1911 before his fatal expedition, he glimpsed "infinite suggestion in this phenomenon, and in that lies its charm."[114] As he considered entering this polar space of uncertainty, he described the aurora australis as ultimately unknowable: "Might not the inhabitants of some other world (Mars) controlling mighty forces thus surround our globe with fiery symbols, a golden writing which we have not the key to decipher?"[115] Scott betrays his anxieties, however: Mars, the god of war and the burned-red planet, sends forth his flames. For Scott, maroon is the color of either the conqueror or the conquered. But remember: maroon always beacons. So here is one more signal with which I leave you. A maroon ecology does not lift the curtain of relations to decipher a language or catalog its components but to shine on the folds of coexistence, and to find our shared, co-implicated, and more-than-human selves rolling around in ethereal undulations. Maroon is an invitation to leave the chasm between subject and object behind, to ask what is at stake when we forcibly unravel ourselves from things "twining round" us at all times.[116] Desertion is impossible in the light of auroral enmeshment. Maroon means that we never act alone, even in the darkest night when the "love of life" is "so predominant."[117] The key is to become so "aurorally rich and happy" that we must share our joy with other beings both seen and unseen[118]—a lost friend, a piece of copper, a snowdrift, a stranger at our feet. To feel the pull of things, and to beacon back:

The sky is firing . . .

"Come look here. Here's something fine."

Notes

Thanks to Jeffrey Jerome Cohen for the invitation to contribute to this volume, as well as his comments and suggestions.

1. *Oxford English Dictionary,* s.vv. "beacon" (n.), and "beckon" (v.).

2. Candace Savage, *Aurora: The Mysterious Northern Lights* (San Francisco: Sierra Club Books, 1995), 14.

3. Ibid.

4. Syun-Ichi Akasofu, *The Northern Lights: Secrets of the Aurora Borealis* (Anchorage: Alaska Northwest Books, 2009), 105–6.

5. *Oxford English Dictionary,* s.v. "maroon" (n.1; adj.1).

6. Savage, *Aurora,* 42.

7. The biographical information that follows is from Ken McGoogan, foreword to *A Journey to the Northern Ocean: The Adventures of Samuel Hearne,* by Samuel Hearne (Victoria: TouchWood Editions, 2007), ix–xxv. See also McGoogan, *Ancient Mariner: The Arctic Adventures of Samuel Hearne, the Sailor Who Inspired Coleridge's Masterpiece* (New York: Carroll and Graf, 2004).

8. Hearne, *Journey to the Northern Ocean,* 227.

9. Ibid.

10. Ibid., 234.

11. See Timothy Morton, *Ecology without Nature: Rethinking Environmental Aesthetics* (Cambridge, Mass.: Harvard University Press, 2007), 54–63.

12. Hearne, *Journey to the Northern Ocean,* 51.

13. Ibid.

14. Ibid., 227.

15. Ibid., 109.

16. Ibid.

17. Ibid., 110, 109.

18. Ibid., 227.

19. Ibid., 114.

20. Ibid., 116.

21. Ibid., 112.

22. Ibid., 118.

23. Ibid., 114.

24. Ibid., 112.

25. Ibid.

26. Ibid.

27. Ibid.

28. Ibid., 113.

29. John Newlove, "Samuel Hearne in Wintertime," Canadian Poetry Online, http://www.library.utoronto.ca/canpoetry/newlove/poem2.htm.

30. Michel Serres with Bruno Latour, *Conversations on Science, Culture, and Time,* trans. Roxanne Lapidus (Ann Arbor: University of Michigan Press, 1995), 105.

31. Ibid., 107.

32. Ibid.

33. Ibid., 105.

34. Ibid., 104.

35. Ibid., 105.

36. Ibid.

37. Ibid.

38. Ibid.

39. Ibid.

40. Credit goes to my friend Chelsea Estep-Armstrong, who came up with this phrase during a conversation we had on the banks of the Metolius River.

41. Serres and Latour, *Conversations,* 107.

42. Hearne, *Journey to the Northern Ocean,* 11–12.

43. Ibid.

44. Serres and Latour, *Conversations,* 104.

45. The maps I am promoting here, including Serres's, are Deleuzoguattarian in nature: "What distinguishes the map from the tracing is that it is entirely oriented toward an experimentation in contact with the real. The map does not reproduce an unconscious closed in upon itself; it constructs the unconscious." See Gilles Deleuze and Félix Guattari, *A Thousand Plateaus: Capitalism and Schizophrenia,* trans. Brian Massumi (Minneapolis: University of Minnesota Press, 1987), 12.

46. Hearne, *Journey to the Northern Ocean,* 128.

47. Ibid., 8.

48. Serres and Latour, *Conversations,* 105.

49. Hearne, *Journey to the Northern Ocean,* 86.

50. Ibid.

51. Ibid.

52. Ibid., 87.

53. Ibid.

54. *Oxford English Dictionary,* s.v. "maroon" (n.2; adj.2).

55. Hearne, *Journey to the Northern Ocean,* 36, 82.

56. Ibid., 2.

57. Ibid., 122.

58. Ibid., 131.

59. Ibid., 175.

60. Ibid., 178.

61. Ibid., 175.

62. Ibid., 176.

63. Ibid., 177.

64. "It was impossible before to connect an actor to what made it act, without being accused of 'dominating,' 'limiting,' or 'enslaving' it. This is no longer the case. The more *attachments* it has, the more it exists. And the more mediators there are the better" (Bruno Latour, *Reassembling the Social: An Introduction to Actor-Network-Theory* [Oxford: Oxford University Press, 2005], 217).

65. Hearne, *Journey to the Northern Ocean,* 152.

66. Ibid., 153.

67. Ibid., 152.

68. Ibid., 153.

69. A web search will yield plenty of results; I recommend CTV's investigation at North Battleford, Saskatchewan, available on YouTube: "Mainstream Reporting Strange Noises Heard around the World—Jan 26, 2012."

70. Robert H. Eather, *Majestic Lights: The Aurora in Science, History, and the Arts* (Washington, D.C.: American Geophysical Union, 1980), 159. Chapter 11 focuses specifically on auroral audibility (153–61).

71. Savage, *Aurora,* 53.

72. Akasofu, *Northern Lights,* 15.

73. Ibid.

74. Ibid., 16.

75. See Monika Bakke, ed., *The Life of Air: Dwelling, Communicating, Manipulating* (n.p.: Open Humanities Press, 2011), http://www.livingbooksaboutlife.org.

76. Akasofu, *Northern Lights,* 16.

77. For more on the notion of nonorganic life and the impersonal agency of the "it," see Jane Bennett, *Vibrant Matter: A Political Ecology of Things* (Durham, N.C.: Duke University Press, 2010), 52–61.

78. Serres and Latour, *Conversations,* 108.

79. Eather, *Majestic Lights,* 110.

80. Savage, *Aurora,* 33.

81. Eather, *Majestic Lights,* 110.

82. Savage, *Aurora,* 33.

83. Ibid., 37.

84. Eather, *Majestic Lights,* 38.

85. Ibid.

86. *Oxford English Dictionary,* s.v. "maroon" (v.).

87. Eather, *Majestic Lights,* 110.

88. Savage, *Aurora,* 32.

89. Ibid., 38.

90. Ibid., 40–41.

91. Akasofu, *Northern Lights,* 15–16.

92. Savage, *Aurora,* 25.

93. Andrew Pickering, preface to *The Mangle in Practice: Science, Society, Becoming,* ed. Andrew Pickering and Keith Guzik (Durham, N.C.: Duke University Press, 2008), vii.

94. Ibid.

95. Savage, *Aurora,* 28.

96. Hearne, *Journey to the Northern Ocean,* 227.

97. Savage, *Aurora,* 118.

98. Auroral titillation abounds on the web; for instance, see Rebecca J. Rosen, "The Sky Is on Fire! Your Complete Visual Guide to the Northern Lights," *Atlantic,* January 26, 2012, http://www.theatlantic.com/technology.

99. Savage, *Aurora,* 102.

100. Ibid., 130.

101. Ibid.

102. Ibid.

103. Ibid., 227.

104. John Muir, *Travels in Alaska* (New York: Modern Library, 2002), 236.

105. Ibid., 237.

106. Ibid.

107. Ibid.

108. Ibid.

109. Ibid.

110. Ibid., 238.

111. Ibid., 239.

112. Ibid.

113. Ibid.

114. Savage, *Aurora,* 79.

115. Ibid.

116. Ibid., 112.

117. Ibid.

118. Muir, *Travels in Alaska,* 238.

Pink

ROBERT MCRUER

In early 2012 a number of journalists and bloggers reported, with varying
levels of jocularity, that pink no longer existed. The spectrum of color
that appears in the sky when the sun shines onto moisture exists, but
pink (these stories suggested) does not, since it could be produced only
through a combination of red and violet, which are on opposite sides of
the rainbow.[1] Since the natural commingling of red and violet light is a
theoretical impossibility, pink in a certain sense is about as real as the
famous pink elephants Dumbo sees after he accidentally imbibes absinthe.
Of course, *Dumbo* really exists as a book, an animated film, and even a ride
at Walt Disney theme parks, and of course something is really happening
when, more generally, we tell stories of "seeing pink elephants" in an attempt
to account for the experience of drunken hallucinations. We might say,
then, that—jocularity aside—pink has a kind of existence; it obviously has
a textured narrative, social, and cultural existence. It is just that (so some
scientists say with a wink) pink's existence is not *exactly* natural.

Gay people, too, are not exactly natural. We have, after all, long been
described by social constructionist historians of sexuality as "a cultural
production no less than . . . table manners, health clubs, and abstract
expressionism." Gay and lesbian existence may feel as natural as the colors
on a rainbow flag look, but it is nonetheless evidence "of a previously
rehearsed and socially encoded ideological script."[2] There is, moreover, of
course nothing particularly natural about the *association* of gay people—
and gay men, in particular—with pink, even though (yet again) culturally,

socially, or narratively, it is an association that is obviously real and ready-to-hand. Natural or not, and in direct contradistinction to its apparent tendency to dissolve into thin air, pink is a color that "sticks," as Sara Ahmed might put it, to gay men and to the objects that we touch.

Given this paradox or logical impossibility (since I am conjuring up a queer substance that is both evaporative and viscous), Ahmed's theory of stickiness needs to be adapted somewhat when thinking pink in relation to gay men, which is what I aim to do in the first part of this chapter. Stickiness, in Ahmed's work (which refers to the ways that stereotypes or negative affects attach to certain bodies), generally impedes movement or is opposed to movement, whereas "pink" stuck to "gay" arguably tends, in the late twentieth and early twenty-first centuries, to accelerate movement (or, more properly, as I detail, circulation). For Ahmed, a "reading of what moves and what sticks in fear economies . . . differentiates between forms of mobility as well as different kinds of bodily enclosure, containment, or detainment."[3] In the current geopolitical order, Ahmed explains, fear, anxiety, and hate "stick" to figures such as the "asylum seeker" or "the international terrorist," and that stickiness both binds these different figures together as threats to the safety, order, and unity of the nation and justifies the expansion of state power to contain that threat: "The sticking together of the figure of the asylum seeker and the international terrorist . . . already evokes other figures (the burglar, the bogeyman)," and this figuration and stickiness materialize "those who are 'without home' as sources of 'our fear' and as reasons for new forms of border policing, whereby the future is always a threat posed by others who may pass by and pass their way into the community."[4] Fear economies depend on a structural racism and xenophobia, and thus if colors stick to the (threatening) future Ahmed invokes and critiques, they are generally dark: "fear . . . works to differentiate between white and black bodies."[5]

Pink, in contrast, is not only differently racialized but often actively welcomed as it crosses borders and passes into various communities; it would seem, in many locations, that fear economies and pink economies are directly opposed. As some gay travelers touch money, especially, it turns pink and works as a passport of sorts for tourist destinations where the metaphorical pink carpet is rolled out for those who would drop pink dollars, pink euros, or pink pounds as they pass through places like San

Francisco's Castro Street, Tel Aviv's Shenkin Street, London's Soho, or Mexico City's appropriately named Zona Rosa.[6] In what follows, I fill out this opposition between a stickiness that impedes and a stickiness that accelerates circulation; through an examination of the thoroughly cultural (and, as I argue, metropolitan) gay life of pink, I show how the two forms of stickiness are actually related and even, to a certain extent, dependent on each other.

Accelerative stickiness is a counterintuitive concept, yet of course in another sense that is what viscosity presents, something sticky (that clings) as well as lubricating (that makes things glide along). As well-lubricated bodies move through pink economies, my contention in the next section of this chapter is that these economies provide a context for the materialization of subject positions that can or would disavow what has been theorized most thoroughly by Stacy Alaimo as "trans-corporeality." Alaimo writes that "imagining human corporeality as trans-corporeality, in which the human is always intermeshed with the more-than-human world, underlines the extent to which the substance of the human is ultimately inseparable from 'the environment.'"[7] Transcorporeality, in all its dispersive adhesiveness (the sticky rhetoric oozes through everything I put forward here), becomes the pink elephant in the room in my argument. A metropolitan pink obscures the transcorporeal imaginations Alaimo invokes. But we are still stuck with the intermeshing and with the substance of the matter that Alaimo names, and transcorporeal imaginations are themselves sticky, if differently so.

Pink's tendency to obscure is paradoxical. If "obscure" means to dim, darken, or deprive of light, I am arguing that pink has the supranatural capacity to enact what has been enacted on it (it is supranatural in that what has been disappeared agentially exhibits a power to make other things disappear). The capacity to dim, darken, or deprive of light, however, is simultaneously a natural effect of oiliness. In the section that follows my whirlwind tour through pink economies, I turn to larger queer *critiques* of pink that demonstrate the slippery ways that this obscuring of transcorporeality and interdependence functions narratively in a specific location. I specify how pink is complicit with forms of border policing that would detain or enclose corporealized others to whom hate, fear, and anxiety stick; in a process that theorists and activists have begun to call "pinkwashing,"

pink colors over or refracts egregious forms of containment, exploitation, and bodily and environmental degradation. In the final section, more
speculatively and hopefully, I turn away from the global circulation of a
metropolitan pink to the queer and crip work of Eli Clare, which allows
me to gesture toward what I position as a minor, more sustainable pink, an
alternative pink imaginary that is, ultimately, transcorporeal.

Cruising Pink

The designers of Eau-Mo cologne for gay men, or "eau de toilette pour
gay"—a scent that comes in a bottle displaying "the elegance of a simple
contrast of forms and colours. Angles and curves, black and pink"—insist
that "the smell of things is the only unequivocal proof that the soul exists."[8]
The epithet "Homo!" does, of course, adhere to bodies in ways that impede movement. Hurled, for instance, at two men holding hands in the
street, "Homo!" originates in denigration and, truer to Ahmed's theory of
stickiness, fixes them in their place (and fists, sticks, or rocks can accompany the cry, making even more material its intention). Eau-Mo, however,
dreams of water (eau) and a flow without stickiness (or, again paradoxically, of a flow that will culminate in the stickiness of sex). As a sensual
pink mist descends over a warm pink background on the Eau-Mo website,
potential consumers of Eau-Mo are introduced to that watery flow, via
the cologne's "concept": "EAUMO smells like the first time. An endless
journey, a cold shower, an unmade bed. It smells of the man we are inside,
the man we'd like to be." As purchasers click through the "concept,"
"notes," and "design" of Eau-Mo, arriving eventually at the "shop" and "catalog" (where prominent hot pink buttons allow them to "Go to Product"
and "Buy Now"), images of the bottle and evocations of the cologne's
scent are supplemented by photos of brooding, smooth, buff, young, and
white male models. These are presumably photos of "the man we'd like
to be," and they are definitely—as "we" are schooled in compulsory desires
that will accompany us if we embark on this endless journey—photos of
the man we would like to have.

Without question, Michael Warner did not have Eau-Mo in mind in
1993 when he wrote that "post-Stonewall urban gay men reek of the commodity. We give off the smell of capitalism in rut, and therefore demand
of theory a more dialectical view of capitalism than many people have

imagination for."⁹ A consideration of Eau-Mo, however, might allow for the more dialectical view of capitalism Warner hopes for, if the contradictions stuck in the narratives around objects like it (i.e., objects that emerge from and travel through pink economies) are made clear and worked through, and if potential resolutions of those contradictions are becoming available.

There are several things to note about the pink narrative exemplified by Eau-Mo. First, the bodies in the (pink) mist are legible as minoritized gay bodies, and not only because "pour gay" is explicitly used to market the product. I am of course not making any claims about the sexuality of the anonymous models featured in the advertisement; I am, rather, asserting very simply that in late capitalism we have learned to associate readily certain gym-built male bodies, and the gazes that pass between them, with gayness. These advertisements, for better or worse, are *in part* an outcome of a long-standing gay liberationist emphasis on "visibility." It would be relatively easy to recoil from these minoritized bodies visibly emerging from the pink haze as easy signs of neoliberal capitalism's excesses, but to do so would neither encourage the more dialectical view Warner calls for nor be free of a certain homophobia.¹⁰

Second, nonetheless, both the bodies in the Eau-Mo advertisement and those hailed (or targeted) by it are homogenized. The men using Eau-Mo may speak English, French, and Spanish (the available languages for the website), but they are white, young, and able-bodied, and they clearly possess disposable income for not only designer fragrances (and, presumably, designer clothing, when they are dressed) but also gym memberships and (pink) tourism that brings with it the promise of erotic adventure—a promise that can be read relatively easily not only from the photos but also from the imagery of showers and unmade beds.

Third, in a very different sense from those whom Ahmed invokes, these men are "without home"; they are on an "endless journey" that could actually, at least partly, be read as a rejection of home (a location *from which* they may have been previously rejected). Put differently, one dominant story of gay identity and community formation over the past century places gay people, ostensibly alienated from their (often implicitly provincial) homes, on a journey to the metropole.¹¹ The story of gay tourism, in turn (the story of what Jasbir K. Puar terms the "circuits of queer mobility" that entice the gay male traveler), translates this original migration into a series of journeys between metropoles.[12] By the beginning of the twenty-first century, Judith Halberstam and other queer theorists were critiquing this rejection of home and migration to the big city as "metronormative," and positioning them as components of a larger "homonormativity." The imagined flight to the big city and rejection of the provinces, in other words, had become seemingly necessary components of gay identity formation and had become articulated by neoliberal capitalism to increasingly compulsory patterns of consumption that did nothing to challenge (and in fact upheld) larger structures of oppression.[13] It is because the consumers of Eau-Mo, or the men on these endless journeys more generally, are caught up in these larger historical narratives that I term the pink background through which they move a "metropolitan pink."

Fourth, understandable as this metropolitan pink might be (because it is still legible as having a connection to gay liberationist impulses or as a response to previous isolation and alienation), it is *unsustainable* in a number of ways that are relatively simple to point out because they apply to virtually all tourism originating in and marketed to the global North. Lionel Cantú, for example, notes that when Mexico is sold to tourists, including gay tourists, it is "not a Mexico of social inequality, economic turmoil, indigenous uprisings, and mass emigration."[14] It is also not a Mexico of eroding beaches, massive resorts that overuse water, endless sewage, toxic waste, and choking pollution.

The narrator of Carlos Fuentes's 1989 novel *Christopher Unborn,* writing from the streets of the fictionalized metropolis "Makesicko Seedy," describes the ambience of this other Mexico, literally opposing it to the Mexico desired by "gringo investors."[15] His dystopic vision can be usefully compared with the tourist utopias sold to travelers (explicitly sexualized utopias, in the pink economy). Musing on the transcorporeal question of what his unborn child will breathe when it is born, Fuentes's narrator declares:

The pulverized shit of three million human beings who have no latrines.

The pulverized excrement of ten million animals that defecate wherever they happen to be.

Eleven thousand tons per day of chemical waste.

The mortal breath of three million motors endlessly vomiting puffs of pure poison, black halitosis, buses, taxis, trucks, and private cars, all contributing their flatulence to the extinction of trees, lungs, throats, and eyes.[16]

Of course, the pulverized shit Fuentes writes about here, if literally carried to the eyes with which this passage ends, would cause swelling or infection of the membrane lining the eyelid—the painful condition commonly known as "pink eye." The contrasting description of Mexico for (gay) travelers, however, pulled from *Gay Mexico*, conjures up other pink eyes and gazes. Although focused not on Mexico City but rather coastal resort areas like Acapulco (which gets associated with terms like *Acapulcalypse* or *Kafkapulco* at various point in Fuentes's text),[17] the contrast could not be more striking: "The coastal regions all around the country are noted for their sexual ambience. Perhaps it's the heat but just about anywhere there's a beach and a city there's action, Acapulco, Cancún, Vallarta, Mazatlán, and Veracruz are all hot, and so are the men."[18]

Mexico City's tourism minister announced, after same-sex marriage was legalized in the federal district in 2009, "We will be a gay friendly city." When Argentina legalized same-sex marriage in 2010, the first couple married there was offered, by city officials, an all-expense-paid honeymoon to Mexico City. In the United States, Mexico City's efforts to woo gay honeymooners was even reported on CNN.[19] Yet Mexico is just one example of a tourist destination that is increasingly pink *at the same time* that it faces increasingly daunting problems of pollution, toxicity, and environmental degradation. Tourism, whether gay or not, tends to be bad for the environment. My larger point, however, is that the travelers targeted by pink economies are not encouraged to think, in Fuentes-like ways, about how their movements might be toxic for the planet. They are, moreover, encouraged not to think this in and through the apotheosis of their all-consuming, out and proud pink visibility. The selling of pink locations like Mexico, or the selling of locations like Mexico as pink, is premised on travelers *not* noticing pulverized shit and chemical waste.[20]

Pink economies, pink tourism, and pink products are thoroughly cultural in a few senses that I want to stress in concluding this section. First, as I emphasized at the outset, there is nothing particularly natural about the linkages between pink and gay identity; pink's capacity to set bodies in motion is due to its social and narrative existence. Second, and more importantly, it is cultural in a more problematic sense—merely cultural, we might say, in that it appears to be cordoned off from a more trans-corporeal understanding of the world. Alaimo repeatedly stresses in her work that the linguistic and cultural turns in critical theory, valuable as they have been for addressing a range of oppressions and hierarchizations, might also *block* an understanding of how material bodies are located in environments and interact with those environments in extradiscursive ways. My argument about pink is that it is particularly efficient for facili-tating the kinds of blockages Alaimo warns against. In other words, "gay bodies" and "pink economies" are cultural constructions and part of the complex story of late twentieth- and early twenty-first-century gay visi-bility. But acquiescing to that particular pink spectacle at this historical moment discourages a transcorporeal understanding of what happens as actual bodies interact with the environments through which they move.

Nonetheless, the minoritized bodies I have analyzed in this section, as part of the history of gay visibility, addressed real contradictions generated by heterosexism and homophobia, even as they have, over the past few decades, proved useful for capitalism. To continue in a more dialectical vein as Warner, suggests, however, that we can in turn move beyond the contradictions these narrativized bodies themselves generated as we move away from a metropolitan pink and toward a minor, more sustainable pink.

Critiquing Pink

Theorists have given a name—pinkwashing—to queer processes that ob-scure a more complex, interdependent (and, I argue, transcorporeal) under-standing of the world around us. And although pinkwashing can take place anywhere (the focus on "hot" action and men in *Gay Mexico*, for example, arguably pinkwashes global warming), the process is most associated with the state of Israel. For more than a decade, Israel has begun actively to think pink: to market the country, and specifically the city of Tel Aviv, as a gay-friendly tourist destination. The pink that state officials think is, not surprisingly, the metropolitan pink I have been analyzing. World Pride 2010 was held in Jerusalem, but it is Tel Aviv that is cast as the pink traveler's paradise. In a poll sponsored by American Airlines, Tel Aviv was named "Best of Gay Cities 2011." Visibly proud of the metropolitan area's queer distinctiveness as noted by American Airlines, Tel Aviv–Jaffa mayor Ron Huldai said, "Winning this competition constitutes an additional strengthening of the fact that Tel Aviv–Jaffa is a city that respects all people and allows everyone to live according to his/her own principles. Ours is a city in which everyone can be proud of who they are." Other city officials, including Yaniv Waizman, a city council member, stressed how the city has actively positioned itself as a (or, at least in 2011, the) capital of the pink economy; Waizman noted that five thousand gay tourists visited Tel Aviv during Gay Pride week alone.[21] The International Gay and Lesbian Travel Association held its annual symposium in Tel Aviv in October 2009; regarding this event, Shay Deutsch, a community spokesperson, said, "The advantage of such a convention is that it exposes to travel agencies all around the world what Tel Aviv has to offer to the gay population, and after such a convention, tourism blossoms in the hosting city.... Now just as we refer to Tel Aviv as the White City, we will also have Tel Aviv—the pink city.... Special packages for the gay community ... will include partying at Tel Aviv nightclubs, meetings with members of the community and more."[22]

"The community," however, is used here in a very specific way, and for the past decade queer activists inside Palestine, along with queer theorists in many locations, have termed what is happening in Israel *pinkwashing*. Pinkwashing consists of trumpeting the exceptional status of the Israeli state—not only because of its gay-friendly, open, and "democratic" policies but also because of how these antihomophobic policies supposedly contrast with the implicitly or explicitly antigay (and Islamic) surrounding locations, including the Palestinian territories occupied by Israel. Pinkwashing suggests, in other words, that Israel *uses* a pink story to color over an apartheid regime; the occupation of the Palestinian territories and the ongoing militarization of the region are refracted through a pink mist as real as the soul of Eau-Mo—that is, through a mist that in a certain sense is not real at all but that is nonetheless useful for directing attention to some stories while diverting attention from others. Pinkwashing thus obscures relations of domination and subordination between human beings (specifically, Israelis and Palestinians); moreover, it is narratively useful (yet again, and perhaps in even more pronounced ways than in my Mexico example) for disavowing transcorporeality.

In the United States, both Puar and Sarah Schulman have been at the forefront of theorizing pinkwashing, including in popularly disseminated venues. In an op-ed in the *New York Times,* for example, Schulman invokes gay subjects "without home" in her overview of pinkwashing, but remains attentive (in a more dialectical way) to how that potential condition need not shore up other systems of oppression. She argues:

> What makes lesbian, gay, bisexual and transgender people and their allies so susceptible to pinkwashing—and its corollary, the tendency among some white gay people to privilege their racial and religious identity, a phenomenon the theorist Jasbir K. Puar has called homonationalism—is the emotional legacy of homophobia. Most gay people have experienced oppression in profound ways— in the family; in distorted representations in popular culture; in systematic legal inequality that has only just begun to relent. Increasing gay rights have caused some people of good will to mistakenly judge how advanced a country is by how it responds to homosexuality.[23]

For Schulman, the pinkwashing message "is being articulated at the highest levels"; she notes that Prime Minister Benjamin Netanyahu told the US Congress that the Middle East is a region where "women are stoned, gays are hanged, and Christians are persecuted." This consistent theme works to construct Israel as exceptionally democratic and open (for business), but it does so, for Schulman and other critics, by "manipulate[ing] the hard-won gains of Israel's gay community . . . [and ignoring] the existence of Palestinian gay-rights organizations."[24] These include Aswat, Al Qaws, and Palestinian Queers for Boycott, Divestment and Sanctions.

For Puar, homonationalism refers to "the emergence of a national homosexuality" that is exceptional—a nation such as the United States, or Israel, is positioned as exceptionally advanced in relation to (gay) human rights *in contrast to* other places where homophobia, and "terrorism," are generated.[25] Homonationalism thus makes clear how the mobility of some (and, for the purposes of this chapter, the circulation of their pink currency) is related to the containment or detainment of others—for Ahmed or Puar, racialized others whose (supposedly excessively homophobic) corporealities are legible as "terrorist." Puar thus argues that the containment or elimination "of one population recedes [or is legitimized] as the securitization and valorization of another population triumphs in its shadow."[26]

The limited view of and for a pinkwashed Israel thus shuts down more complex views of the region—even, in Puar's analysis, of *tourism* in the region, given that pinkwashing subordinates (as homophobic and backward) a gay-friendly location like Beirut to the exceptional city of Tel Aviv.[27] It has not been a focus of these critiques, but the process of sticking pink to gay bodies and to gay cities like Tel Aviv shuts down not only a more interdependent analysis (of the relations between Israelis and Palestinians) but also a more transcorporeal analysis of the region. Occupation, arguably even more than tourism, is bad for the environment. Jad Isaac and Mohammed Ghanyem argue that although "its unique location at the crossroads of three continents has made Palestine an environmental melting pot for the flora and fauna of Africa, Asia, and Europe, this natural diversity has become an innocent bystander to the destructive practices of occupation."[28] Some of the practices Isaac and Ghanyem consider include the placement or relocation of Israeli industries in occupied areas, the unequal use of water resources (especially in tourist zones) that results in a depletion or drought in Palestinian regions, and the ongoing confiscation and subsequent overdevelopment of land. Overdevelopment leads to the uprooting of fruit trees (and consequent deforestation), soil erosion (and consequent desertification), and redirection of human and industrial waste toward poorer and undeveloped Palestinian areas (in addition to the general failure to contain pollution from Israeli factories inside the occupied zones, Isaac and Ghanyem particularly note the relocation of toxic waste from Israel to two locations in the northern West Bank).[29] There is obviously not a direct or active relation between the generalized invisibility of these practices of environmental degradation in Palestine and the pink visibility nurtured by the Israeli state; again, my argument is that pink visibility is in fact contingent on not noticing such relations. I want to suggest in my final section, however, that there *is* nonetheless an active relation between disidentifying with a metropolitan pink and thinking in more transcorporeal ways that would illuminate the connections between mobile bodies without homes and the larger environment.

Trans-forming Pink

Eli Clare's *Exile and Pride: Disability, Queerness, and Liberation* provides just such a disidentification. *Exile and Pride* presents autobiographical and theoretical reflections on such issues as the historical freak show, the visibility of disabled sexuality, and the need to tell a range of stories about queer and crip lives.[30] It also quite explicitly counterposes its local narrative—a part of which is titled "Losing Home"—to the narratives of metropolitan pink that I have outlined.[31] For this reason, I use *Exile and Pride* here to gesture toward a minor, more sustainable pink.[32]

Clare grew up among the forests and streams of rural Oregon: "Home for me is marked by Douglas fir and chinook salmon, south wind whipping the ocean into a fury of waves and surf. Marked by the aching knowledge of environmental destruction, the sad truth of that town founded on the genocide of Native peoples, the Tuni and Coquille, Talkemas and Latgawas."[33] Clare's description here already potentially marks another minor, almost ethereal, but nonetheless material pink. Although Clare explicitly names chinook salmon, a larger member of the various salmon species that populate the Pacific Northwest of the United States, there are more pink salmon than any other type. Pink salmon enter the rivers of the Puget Sound river system in Washington by the millions each year; the larger chinook salmon is more common in Clare's Oregon, although part of his project in general is to note the dwindling numbers of fish, trees, birds, and humans living harmoniously in the region. "Pink" will do as good as any color here to describe Clare's ecology beyond green, not only because salmon are a vital part of the complex local ecosystem he describes, but also because the book rereads and revalues human beings dismissed by others as "rednecks," but who, Clare argues, need to be understood in a complex, transcorporeal relation to the location. There are no easy answers in Clare's analysis of this small place; "I am the writer who wants to make sense," he insists as he searches for the words that will account for both the plight of working-class loggers whose livelihoods have disappeared as industries collapse (and logging executives nonetheless walked away with the capital) *and* the need to protect the trees, birds, and fish that live there.[34]

A key to understanding Clare's queer reflections on this location is his counterposition of it to urban locations and the spectacle of metropolitan pink economies that dazzles those locations. When Clare leaves home and arrives in the big city, he is appalled: "I am remembering the first time I went to OutWrite, a national queer writer's conference. From the moment I walked into the posh Boston hotel where the conference was being held, I gawked, staring unbelievingly at the chandeliers, shiny gold railings, ornate doors, in the same way I used to gawk at twenty-story buildings. . . . it leaves me feeling queer in the queer community."[35] Clare stresses in his overview of OutWrite that moving through metropolitan queer spaces explicitly entails not noticing or caring about other locations; the questions Clare faces from metronormative queers about his lost home move from incredulity to hilarity. Clare, in contrast, works toward the alliances "queers—urban and rural—need to create with straight rural people, the same folks urban people call rednecks, hicks, clods, and bigots. Building and supporting these alliances will entail many different kinds of organizing. At the heart of this work needs to be a struggle against economic injustice since most people—queer and straight—living in rural communities . . . are poor and working-class."[36] And building alliances to address these human needs always means, for Clare, thinking about them in relation to the larger environment. Clare's Oregon is a "minor" location, far from any metropole, but in Clare's writing he uses the home he has "lost" to generate a vision of more sustainable and transcorporeal relations.

Clare's vision has been re-presented in a portrait by Riva Lehrer (Figure 4.1). Lehrer uses a "collaborative method" for the series of paintings she calls Circle Stories. The disabled activists, academics, and artists represented in Circle Stories worked with Lehrer, from 1997 to 2003, in an "interview-based process" that, she says, aimed to "counter the coercive tradition of pictures of disabled people." Talking back to that tradition and with Lehrer, the figures in the Circle Stories series collectively generate new ways to comprehend disability, identity, and desire. "Our public mirrors," Lehrer insists, "have offered little but specimens, monsters, and freaks seen by the eye of normality."[37] Through collaboration, both Lehrer and the subjects she describes as "these people I'm falling in love with . . . this really amazing group of crips" access possibilities that normality cannot easily comprehend or accommodate.[38]

Figure 1. Circle Story #10. Portrait of Eli Clare, 2003, by Riva Lehrer.

Lehrer's portrait of Clare, in particular, not only counters in multiple ways the coercive and antidisabled traditions of representation Lehrer critiques but also provides a beautiful and colorful vision of Clare in transcorporeal interaction with the Oregon he loves. Completed in 2003, *Circle Story #10: Eli Clare* locates Clare in a forest or marsh; he is surrounded by growth—both old and new—and by generative decay. The forest floor is covered with living or formerly living things: twigs, branches, grass, and clover; dande-lions in full yellow bloom or gone to seed as white puffs. There are tufts of a few flowers that might be seen as pink, though whether they are "really" pink is less important than noting that all the minor colors here do not *obscure* (as a metropolitan pink does) but *illuminate* critically queer, crip, and environ-mentalist relations. A fish or fish fossil lies on the bank (read through *Exile and Pride,* this would be a salmon), while butterflies, beetles, or ladybugs crawl on the ground or hover just above it. A deer is discernible across the marsh or stream, which shimmers green, blue, and white, as though lit by the sun. Ancient trees with roots exposed hug the bank on both sides.

In the midst of all this, slightly off-center, Lehrer positions Clare. He is stooped, with one knee touching the ground. He wears glasses, hiking boots, shorts, and a light blue shirt; tattoos of frogs adorn his exposed leg in the foreground. A long-sleeve shirt or jacket (with a faint pink lining) has been discarded to the right of where Clare stoops, and shards of red hair, some of it braided, are strewn around the area. Most significantly or unexpectedly, a tree or sapling, rooted directly in front of Clare, winds upward into his clothing or body. Entering in the genital area (and thereby, albeit in an indeterminate way, evocative *of* genitalia), the sapling emerges from the top of Clare's shirt and from the sleeves. Its multiple branches are filled with soft red leaves. A focused or studied look on his face, Clare embraces the tree and—by extension and by merging—his own body.

Since Lehrer, Clare, and the others involved in the *Circle Stories* project are specifically rejecting univocal representations of disability, the painting of Clare necessarily lends itself to multiple interpretations. Neither cerebral palsy nor disability more generally are reduced here to the two-dimensionality characteristic of freakish or medicalized spectacles. If traditions for reading this extraordinary image are in fact available, they have been forged in the cultural movements in which Clare himself is rooted: trans, queer, crip, feminist, socialist, and environmentalist movements.

Two ways of reading, or critical literacies, strike me as especially pronounced in the painting. First, the idea that participants in such movements can represent *themselves* as engaged and critical readers of signs—as producers of meaning—is apparent. Clare's queer masculinity and his disability can be read as generative, not only because the sapling is literally sprouting from his particularized body (suggesting there are queer ways of being or living in harmony with the environment that are yet to be envisioned), but also because of how his gaze is focused. The glasses, a slightly furrowed brow, and a faint illumination from the left all combine to draw attention to Clare's thoughtful expression and to position him as an interpreter of the vibrant, ever-changing space in which he is located. His gaze might be registering the stages of an old-growth forest, monitoring the precariousness of fish life in the stream, or tracing the signs of the destructive flow of capital through this space—a flow that would homogenize (to its exchange-value) all the biodiversity in its path. The portrait, however, draws attention less to the specific object of his gaze than to the critical and interpretive subjectivity forged through progressive theory and activism.

Second, the idea that identity, culture, and space are processes, not products (or metropolitan commodities), is also legible here. The traditions Lehrer resists might proffer knowable "specimens," but the processes of composition and decomposition at work in her painting cannot be fixed. If transformation in this painting ceases, life ceases. The long hair on the ground might suggest, simply, that an old identity has been shed and a new (and more accurate) one assumed—butterfly not caterpillar, frog not tadpole. That singular reading, however, while important, would in many ways belie the complexity of the scene as a whole. From the dandelions blooming or going to seed to the dead fish feeding the grass and trees, the degeneration or decomposition of the old is as centralized in this portrait as the (ongoing) generation of the new. Even the hair on the ground itself is as much a beginning as an end; though not rapidly, the nitrogen and sulfur released from the decomposition of hair fertilize the plant life (and indeed, as an environmental activist in such a location, Clare would be unlikely to leave anything behind that would not decompose).

In the end, this chapter has been all about things that might not exist yet nonetheless quite materially stick, and trigger unexpected adhesions. Pink is absent from the spectrum of light but sticks to certain queer stories we tell ourselves. Pink economies and pink currency are not real yet generate a pink mist that obscures real, material relations. The tree impossibly or magically sprouting from Clare's body and clothing also does not exist yet evokes stories and materialities that might function differently from the dominant, metropolitan pink stories we have. Lehrer's transcorporeal, transgender, trans-formative image affirms the necessity of thinking beyond or outside the pink corners we have been painted into, generating in the process new and unexpected, yet material and sustainable, queer identities and relations.

Notes

1. These reports invariably directed readers back to a YouTube channel called "Minute Physics," which contains a series of animated video shorts, drawn by Henry Reich and intended to popularize physics by providing short and entertaining explanations of scientific facts. The animated short in question, "There is no Pink

Light," was featured in a range of reports in February and March 2012, generally under comical headlines such as "They Did It to Pluto, but Not to Pink! Please Not Pink!" or "Sorry girls, but the colour pink doesn't exist and is just a pigment of our imagination." See Robert Krulwich, "They Did It to Pluto," *Krulwich Wonders . . . An NPR Sciencey Blog*, March 2, 2012, http://www.npr.org/blogs/krul wich/2012/02/28/147590898/they-did-it-to-pluto-but-not-to-pink-please-not -pink; Daily Mail Reporter, "Sorry Girls," *Daily Mail Online*, March 9, 2012, http://www.dailymail.co.uk/sciencetech/article-2112339/Sorry-girls-colour -pink-doesnt-exist-just-pigment-imagination.html. The original can be found at "There Is No Pink Light," *Minute Physics*, October 16, 2011, http://www.youtube .com/watch?v=S9dqJRykoYM&list=PLED25F943F8D6081C&index=8&fea ture=plcp. My thanks to Jeffrey Cohen for bringing pink's removal from nature to my attention, and for his incisive editorial comments on earlier drafts of this chapter.

2. David M. Halperin, *One Hundred Years of Homosexuality and Other Essays on Greek Love* (New York: Routledge, 1990), 40. Halperin is referring to *both* homosexuality and heterosexuality in this quotation; for the purposes of my argument, I am highlighting here the gay and lesbian side of his social constructionist argument. Coincidentally, "hot pink"—which appeared in the original eight-stripe version of the gay rainbow flag designed by Gilbert Baker—was eventually removed, along with turquoise, and does not appear in the current six-stripe version.

3. Sara Ahmed, "Affective Economies," *Social Text* 79, no. 2 (2004): 128.

4. Ibid., 136.

5. Ibid., 126.

6. Mexico City's Zona Rosa (or Pink Zone)—filled with chic shops, restaurants, and bars—has been one of Mexico's main "zonas de tolerancia" and home to a gay population for some time. See Lionel Cantú, "*De Ambiente*: Queer Tourism and the Shifting Boundaries of Mexican Male Sexualities," *GLQ: A Journal of Lesbian and Gay Studies* 8, nos. 1–2 (2002): 145.

7. Stacy Alaimo, *Bodily Natures: Science, Environment, and the Material Self* (Bloomington: Indiana University Press, 2010).

8. "Eau-Mo: Style & Design," http://www.eau-mo.com/english/design.htm ?GETSTA=OFF (accessed May 6, 2102).

9. Michael Warner, introduction to *Fear of a Queer Planet: Queer Politics and Social Theory*, ed. Michael Warner (Minneapolis: University of Minnesota Press, 1993), xxxi.

10. I am drawing from Roderick Ferguson's work a discomfort with how certain subjects get cast as *mere* figurations. Ferguson examines, for instance, how the racialized sex worker gets cast as a queer sign of the excesses of capitalism. Such a figuration essentially silences and dismisses her, and blocks the possibility that

her subject position might itself generate new, critical imaginaries. See Roderick A. Ferguson, *Aberrations in Black: Toward a Queer of Color Critique* (Minneapolis: University of Minnesota Press, 2004), 9–10. I hope, as well, that the general trajectory of this chapter offers what Kevin Floyd terms "a return to the aspiration to totality that emerges from within the process of reification"—a process I am discerning in the Eau-Mo photographs. See Kevin Floyd, *The Reification of Desire: Toward a Queer Marxism* (Minneapolis: University of Minnesota Press, 2009), 194.

11. See Kath Weston, "Get Thee to a Big City: Sexual Imaginary and the Great Gay Migration," *GLQ: A Journal of Lesbian and Gay Studies* 2, no. 3 (1995): 253–77.

12. Jasbir K. Puar, "Circuits of Queer Mobility: Tourism, Travel, and Globalization," *GLQ: A Journal of Lesbian and Gay Studies* 8, nos. 1–2 (2002): 101–37.

13. Judith Halberstam, *In a Queer Time and Place: Transgender Bodies, Subcultural Lives* (New York: New York University Press, 2005), 36. See also Lisa Duggan, "The New Homonormativity: The Sexual Politics of Neoliberalism," in *Materializing Democracy: Toward a Revitalized Cultural Politics* (Durham, N.C.: Duke University Press, 2002), 175–94; Scott Herring, *Another Country: Queer Anti-Urbanism* (New York: New York University Press, 2010).

14. Cantú, *"De Ambiente,"* 139.

15. Carlos Fuentes, *Christopher Unborn,* trans. Alfred MacAdam and Carlos Fuentes (Champaign, Ill.: Dalkey Archive, 2005), 82.

16. Ibid., 81.

17. Ibid., 5, 222.

18. Quoted in Cantú, *"De Ambiente,"* 139.

19. Anna, "Mexico City Tourism Minister Says: 'We will be a gay friendly city," *Macha Mexico: A Lesbian Guide to Mexico City,* January 2, 2010, http://www.machamexico.com/2010/01/02/mexico-city-tourism-minister-says-we-will-be-a-gay-friendly-city/; "Free Mexico City Honeymoon for First Argentine Gay Newly-weds," *BBC News,* July 16, 2010, http://www.bbc.co.uk/news/world-latin-america-10658300; Catherine Shoichet, "Mexico City Woos Same-Sex Honeymooners," CNN.com, August 31, 2010, http://articles.cnn.com/2010-08-31/travel/mexico.same.sex.honeymoon_1_gay-marriage-law-gay-couples-gay-travelers?_s=PM:TRAVEL.

20. It is worth pointing out that products like the Eau-Mo fragrance are themselves toxic for many people. Increasingly, disability studies is encompassing a textured awareness of environmental illness or multiple chemical sensitivity (MCS). Alaimo, in fact, includes a chapter on this very issue in *Bodily Natures.* People with MCS react to a range of things but particularly to artificial scents, dyes, and coloring. Making the world more accessible for people with MCS would

actually mean shaping a greater transcorporeal awareness for everyone (Alaimo, *Bodily Natures,* 113–40). See also Mel Y. Chen, "Toxic Animacies, Inanimate Affections," *GLQ: A Journal of Lesbian and Gay Studies* 17, nos. 2–3 (2011): 265–86; Anna Mollow, "No Safe Space," *WSQ: Women's Studies Quarterly* 39, no. 1 (2011): 188–99. My thanks to Cindy Wu for encouraging me to include this point in my larger argument about pink toxicity.

21. Anthony Grant, "Think Pink! Tel Aviv Wins Best Gay City Poll," About .com, January 11, 2012, http://goisrael.about.com/b/2012/01/11/gaytlv-guide -pride.htm.

22. Danny Sadeh, "Tel Aviv—the Pink City," ynetnews.com, March 13, 2009, http://www.ynetnews.com/articles/0,7340,L-3685800,00.html. Tel Aviv is known as the White City because of hundreds of white, Bauhaus-inspired buildings built during the middle of the century.

23. Sarah Schulman, "Israel and 'Pinkwashing," *New York Times,* November 22, 2011, http://www.nytimes.com/2011/11/23/opinion/pinkwashing-and-israels -use-of-gays-as-a-messaging-tool.html.

24. Ibid.

25. Jasbir K. Puar, *Terrorist Assemblages: Homonationalism in Queer Times* (Durham, N.C.: Duke University Press, 2007), 2.

26. Ibid., 3.

27. Jasbir K. Puar, "'The Center Cannot Hold': The Flourishing of Queer Anti-Occupation Activism," *HuffPost Gay Voices* (blog), October 3, 2011, http://www.huffingtonpost.com/jasbir-k-puar/the-center-cannot-hold-th_b_9915 72.html.

28. Jad Isaac and Mohammad Ghanyem, "Environmental Degradation and the Israeli-Palestinian Conflict," 1, Applied Research Institute—Jerusalem (ARIJ)/ Society: Towards a Sustainable Palestine, http://www.arij.org/publications(2)/ papers/2003%20environmental%20degradation%20and%20the%20israeli-pales tinian%20conflict.pdf (accessed May 13, 2012).

29. Ibid., 16–25.

30. Eli Clare, *Exile and Pride: Disability, Queerness, and Liberation* (Cambridge, Mass.: South End). *Exile and Pride* locates Clare within lesbian communities and experiences, but between the first and second editions of *Exile and Pride,* Clare explicitly indicated a transition to the use of masculine pronouns, which I thus use here for discussing his work.

31. Ibid., 29.

32. I am thinking here, of course, of Gilles Deleuze and Félix Guattari's sense of "minor" literature: "It is a literature that produces an active solidarity in spite of skepticism; and if the writer is in the margins or completely outside his or her

fragile community, this situation allows the writer all the more possibility to express another possible community and to forge the means for another consciousness and another sensibility" (*Kafka: Towards a Minor Literature,* trans. Dana Polan [Minneapolis: University of Minnesota Press, 1986], 17).

33. Clare, *Exile and Pride,* 11.

34. Ibid., 21.

35. Ibid., 38, 39.

36. Ibid., 40.

37. Riva Lehrer, *Circle Stories, March 27, 2004–May 30, 2004* (Chicago: Gescheidle Gallery Exhibition Catalog, 2004), 5.

38. Quoted in *Self-Preservation: The Art of Riva Lehrer* (dir. Sharon Snyder; Brace Yourself Productions, 2004).

Orange

JULIAN YATES

The rainbow is a pure childlike image. In it color is wholly contour; for the person who sees with a child's eyes, it marks boundaries, is not a layer of something superimposed on matter, as it is for adults. The latter abstract from color, regarding it as a deceptive cloak for individual objects existing in time and space. Where color provides the contours, objects are not reduced to things but are constituted by an order consisting of an infinite range of nuances. Color is single, not as a lifeless thing and a rigid individuality but as a winged creature that flits from one form to the next. Children make soap bubbles. Similarly, games with painted sticks, sewing kits, decals, parlor games, even pull-out picturebooks, and, to a lesser extent, making objects by folding paper—all involve this view of color.

—WALTER BENJAMIN, "A Child's View of Color"

Waxing lyrical on the figure of the rainbow, bringing us back from the brink of an abstracting adulthood to a childhood in which color manifests as substance, Walter Benjamin posits something on the order of a prismatic materialism in these lines. Color morphs and moves. Insect- or angel-like, it "flits from one form to the next," rendering each lively if not alive. This undifferentiated relation to color as substance radicalizes perception. It ties color to the objects that play host to it such that the visual becomes tactile. Color becomes transitive or transactional. Color happens. It happens to you, through you.

For Benjamin, this orientation to color migrates to the gestures and habit world of children's toys and games. Fold the paper; place, press, and peel the decal; blow the bubble until its prismatic sheen pops; prance like a chicken; flit like a butterfly; allow a world to spill forth in foldout pages in your lap. And if you do, then know that you are taking on the colors of these objects or creatures and lending your body and voice to their forms in an ongoing becoming with the world. Benjamin wants this orientation to color to be primary. But in this brief unpublished thought-piece he is not able to say quite why, not sure what name to give to this phenomenology of color. He reaches therefore into the discourse of an uncertainly theological aesthetics and writes, "Color is something spiritual."[1] His words constitute color as primary; render it prior to calculation; insist that it comes prior to the sum of "intellectual cross-references" that stultifies the adult.

Almost immediately, this desire for firstness seems to turn sentimental: "children see with pure eyes"—"colorfulness does not stimulate the[ir] animal senses because the child's uncorrupted imaginative activity springs from the soul."[2] But such moves belie the way the figure of the child stands here with a cast of skilled mimetic operators, the insect and the plant, to insist on the tactile affect of color as a stimulus response. Aesthetics stands here, for Benjamin, as a discourse on sense perception, on the phenomenology of relations between variously animate objects. You are in the world; the world within you. By this color you are captured thus, so the flower says to the bee. Buzz. Buzz.

Years later, in "On the Mimetic Faculty" (1933), Benjamin will name this orientation the "powerful compulsion to become similar and to behave mimetically," in sympathy with an object.[3] And this insight stands surety for what becomes, in the *Passagenwerk,* an auto-archiving of consumer capital's broken or discarded goods become uncertainly temporal fossils, *things,* which, having lost the sum of their "cross-references," offer a perceptual jolt or "shock" to the viewer.[4]

Hovering at the edge of our vision, Benjamin's rainbow provides a rubric for modeling color by way of its contours, by way of the objects that host it in a built world. Here the phrase *built world* should be heard to include the reproductive technologies of plants; the camouflage rhetoric of insects; all manner of creaturely display; as well as the mineral efflorescence of rock formations.[5] Color phenomena qua color phenomena exist only by and in their apprehension by variously animate creatures. But the patterns that constitute them exist in and for themselves operating according to still other codes than we are able to perceive directly. It is to this elaborated world of stimulus response that Benjamin's sifting of the world of childhood for the substrates that bear color effects (paper, oils, watercolors, decals, books, sticks, etc.) belongs. Indeed, his sifting proposes what amounts to a type of prismatic grammatology that inventories all the forms that color phenomena take as they are hosted by this or that object in our visual field.

If the word *grammatology* augurs an overly linguistic model for thinking in ecological terms or for thinking color, recall that the word refers to a generalized question of coding and to the burden of telling "the history of life ... [or] differance" that is always also the story of the animal (human and not), of the machine, the plant. This story begins with the observation lethal to any metaphysics of presence that "life" emerges with the writing event of "'genetic inscription' and 'short programmatic chains regulating the behavior of the amoeba or the annelid up to the passage beyond alphabetic writing to the orders of the *logos* and of a certain *homo sapiens.*'"[6] Famously, for Jacques Derrida, this insight settles into what he terms a "cultural graphology" that attends to the workings of a "graphic code" and "the articulation of graphic forms and of diverse substances (materials: wood, wax, skin, stone, ink, metal, vegetable) or instruments (point, brush, etc, etc.)."[7] But it is worth remarking that from its inception this modeling of writing posits the *grammè* and the substrates that host it as something, after Donna Haraway, we might name a "multispecies" archive or impression. Grammatology takes as its object writing technologies that, however they change, remain coterminous with actor networks of variously manufactured plant, animal, and mineral remainders and the built world required to produce them.[8]

Such multispecies modeling of our writing machines suggests that we might broaden the notion of cultural graphology to inquire into the kinds of relays that form between differently animated beings and how those relays make possible certain kinds of worlds. Within such a modeling of the archive, color effects refer to a discontinuous, shifting world of sense impressions as perceived and hosted by perceptually competent actors. Color itself might best be modeled as a multispecies sensory process or network that generates biosemiotic-material effects that then take on a metaphorical life of their own as they are translated to different registers. Such metaphors prove reversible. The anthropomorphic experience of color conjoins with a zoomorphic becoming other than oneself—a prismatic biomimetic becoming, or, for the purposes of this chapter, a turning *"orange"* or *"orangey."*[9] Women who sold oranges in Restoration theaters in England, for example, were called "orange-women" or "orange-girls," rendering the color as hosted by the fruit mobile, stitching its presence into the visual field of Londoners.

Trace out the logic to Benjamin's rainbow; follow him into the habit world of children's games, and we begin to model that world as a prismatic archive—an archive of unstable, changing sense impressions as they were translated into other media. Within the parameters offered by this collection of essays, an *"orange* ecology" offers one orientation to this general, prismatic grammatology indexed to the historical coordinates and morphology of oranges. Choose another color, hosted by a different set of objects, and the story will shift, connect different historical moments, and involve different actors. This chapter is a small installment toward a book of *orangey* flowers or posies, then, a *florilegium,* perhaps, but only so long as we are willing to consider dead or withered flowers worth keeping alongside their poetic, flowering forms. For posies, like any gathering, recruit readers by translating the fact of life they record into a textual liveliness. The word *posy* designates occasional writing, writing tied to a spatiotemporal specificity—even as it may seek to transport us elsewhere in place or time.[10]

Such a *florilegium* offers little by way of consolation. Its own hue is almost entirely neutral or colorless. The gatherings it records may constitute dull routines or may generate spectacular surprises. But they remain partial, ephemeral, subject to dispersal. Like Benjamin's bubble that refracts light, posies come and go, change their hue, find themselves replaced by still other gatherings that host colors anew. The light changes. Time passes. And that passage registers differently according to the vagaries of our biosemiotic motors. An orange may change its color depending on its exposure to temperature. In the tropics, it is not *orange* at all but green. And as it decays, it turns other colors still (white, blue, black) as the polities of bacteria it hosts "flower." Still, my hopes are manifold. I hope that modeling a prismatic archive might produce an element of historical vertigo with regard to texts past that may lead us to see once again agentive pigments that have fled or faded. I hope also that by insisting on the phenomenon of color as the unreliable product of a joining of animal and world, I can argue for a conviviality or hospitality between deconstructive grammatology and the postcritical households founded on the work of the sociologist Bruno Latour and object-oriented ontology.

I begin before "orange," before the advent of the name that codifies the color, rendering it a sphere, a fruit, a *thing*. I go on to tell the story of "orange's" arrival and normalization in England; imagine its absence in one fictive future; its replacement by a different fruit and so color in another, and examine how the object-world rearranges itself to accommodate its absence. In each case, I argue that we learn lessons about the kinds of interventions thought possible at different historical moments in our writing machines, in our collective routines for making persons and worlds. As I show, the life and death of such things is a kind of dance, something on the order of the "ontological choreography" Charis Thompson sees as the process by which we comake ourselves and our worlds.[11]

Before "Orange" (1460)

"Richard of York," we know from the early twentieth-century rhyme–cum–mnemonic device, "gave battle in vain," but at the time of the Battle of Wakefield (1460), which he lost and at which he died, the word *orange* had only just entered the English language, and had only just come to designate the color phenomenon that occurs, in the visible spectrum, at a wavelength of about 585–620 nanometers. Without doubt Richard of York's supporters sang songs to remember a good many things. But when seeking to name the phenomenon we name "orange" they reached for an altogether different constellation of words to designate the range of tones and shades of things that hosted the color in their object world. White roses sported your allegiance to the House of York, distinguishing you from the red, red rose of the House of Lancaster, but if there were such a thing as an orange rose, it had yet, in English, to become "orange." The words *pome d'horange, oronge, orenge, orynge,* and *oringe,* designating the fruit, appear around 1400. But the extension of the word to include any color resembling the skin of an orange is not widely credited before the 1550s.[12] When met with the phenomenon, Richard of York and friends were not open-mouthed or mute. Hardly. They merely reached for different color words to describe the sun, a marigold, Herod's hair and beard.

Even the oranges that Hercules stole from the Garden of the Hesperides or which Venus gave to Hippomenes in order to beat Atalanta posed no problem, for they were not (and may never have been *orange* or, for that matter, oranges).[13] They remained *pomum aurantium,* golden apples, or, as rendered in neo-Latin, in homage to the citrus collections of Italian nobility, *Medici.*[14]

Codifying the practices of limners or portrait miniaturists in England, such as might once upon a time have painted Richard of York, in small, from life, Edward Norgate's *Miniatura or the Art of Limning* (ca. 1627–28) looks back over the techniques used to craft the jeweled worlds of fifteenth- and sixteenth-century English portrait miniatures. He synthesizes the techniques of his artisan forebears, Isaac Oliver, Nicholas Hilliard, Lavinia Teerlinc, and the color palettes of his time. "The names of the Severall Colours commonly used in Limning are these," he writes, "white," "yellow," "red," "green," "browne," "blew," "blacke."[15] These colors sport a host of medial hues, each of which has its own peculiar temperament according to the nature of the ingredients from which it is mixed. Yellow subsumes "Masticot, Yellow Oker, English Oker"; red, "Vermillion, Indian Lake, Red Lead." Each derives from a working of plant and mineral and insect ingredients, such that the limner had to do more than simply know her colors. She had to know their temperaments, their likes and dislikes, know which were "friends" and "foes." "English Oker," writes Norgate, "is a very good Colour and of very much use. . . . It is a friendly and familiar colour and needs little Art or other ingredient more."[16] But contrast this friendly color to the treacherous "Ceruse" (a white), which "will many times after it is wrought tarnish, starve and dye" and weeks after it is applied "become rusty reddish, or towards a dirty Colour."[17] Norgate goes on to describe a lengthy process by which ceruse might be rendered semistable by enlisting the aid of another, more friendly substance—the "hungry and spungie chalk," which will "suck out" all "the greasy and hurtfull quality of the Colour."

Less schematic in its organization, Hilliard's short *Treatise Concerning The Arte of Limning* (ca. 1600) codes this practical knowledge of the properties of different substances within an explicitly moral philosophical framework. For Hilliard, still the artisan, working hard for the gentrification of his art, the temperament of the limner proves as crucial as that of the ingredients. His advice to the would-be miniaturist sounds as though it derived from a careful reading of Benjamin's "On the Mimetic Faculty":

> the best waye and meanes to practice and ataine to skill in *Limning*, in a word befor I exhorted such to temperance, I meane sleepe not much, wacth not much, eat not much, sit not long, usse not violent excersize in sports, nor earnest recreation for you / but dancing or bowling, or little of either, / then the fierst and cheefest precepts which I give is cleanlynes, and therfor fittest for gentelmen, that the practicer of *Limning* be presizly pure and klenly in all his doings, as in grinding his coulers in place wher ther is neither dust nor smoake, the watter wel chossen or distilled most pure.[18]

The limner must curb her behaviors, practice temperance in all things so as to be able to temper the colors, manage the unmanageable liveliness or deadness of certain ingredients—learning which colors she can rely on, such as the friendly yellow ocher, and which require careful supervision, as in the fickle ceruse. In a historical moment when color fixity was the very emblem of scarcity value and pigments could turn fugitive and fade, the limner required a specialized knowledge of the etiquette of color, learning to pamper and flatter such substances that might provoke sympathetic color effects. In Latourian terms, we might suggest that here the limner must seek out friendly agencies, adapting her gestures in hopes of maintaining alliances that would keep color effects still.

Hilliard would have to wait for the ministrations of Henry Peacham's successively revised and enlarged *The Compleat Gentleman* (1622) for the ministrations of the limner to his or her ingredients to be accorded gentlemanly status.[19] But, eventually, his attentiveness or politeness to colors would lead to the inclusion of the art among pastimes deemed gentlemanly. In the enervated lexicon of the *Treatise,* however, such gentility manifests as an almost obsessive attention to the "fineness" and "purity" of the art. The word *pure* assumes a unique redundancy in the treatise as he seeks to name the quality of attention and behavior required of the limner in attending to the vagaries of colors whose qualities she inventories. The word *pure* comes to describe both the person of the limner and the materials he or she handles, purity becoming, in essence, a common property

or product in the making, to be proved by the effect of the finished miniature on the viewer. The limner's labor stands in reciprocal relation to the
final stability of color in the miniature. Her husbanding of the materials,
her artful handling of foes and reliance on friends, records a joint exercise
in making that understands poeisis as a cascade of competing agencies.[20]
One may neglect the friendly ocher, but on no account skimp on attention
to the ceruse. Keep the chalk dry until it is needed.

Hilliard's treatise and Norgate's *Miniatura* read like strange georgic
manuals, husbandry books, or participant-observation ethological studies
of the animal behavior of ingredients, all to obtain very particular qualities of color. Belonging to the long tradition of lapidaries that describe the
particular virtues (force or agency) of gemstones and minerals, both follow Aristotle's theory of substances, for which color was understood to be
contingent on physical variables.[21] As Bruce R. Smith summarizes, the
"color [red] happens only in the presence of fire or something like fire."[22]
Color manifests, then, as a form of affect or sympathy between materials
that "contain . . . something which is one and the same with the substance
in question." What matters for Aristotle and for the limner most is a color's
brightness, its saturation of a medium. For Hilliard and Norgate, this saturation, effected by differing processes in every case, leads to color fixity.
Such then was the essence of their skill—the art of keeping colors still by
cultivating or rerouting the desires of substances.

The salutary lesson of imagining a world before "orange," a world of
saffrons and ochers and yellows, lies not in a hard-line historical epistemology that would cry foul and insist that, there was, at that time, no such
color. The absence foregrounds instead the way the matter of "color"
yokes together questions of phenomenology (animal sense perception)
and ecology (the world writ large). For still today we have trouble keeping our colors straight and are unable, in their absence, to call up an exact
shade or hue with certainty. And, as I have shown with Norgate and
Hilliard, this problem of the unreliability or the drift to color reorients our
attention toward those kinds of practices and routines that keep phenomena still, regularize them, and with what order of politeness or hospitality
they do so.[23] It invites us also to attend to how certain operations are conserved, dropped, or redistributed into different discourses or disciplines
across historical periods.

Keyed to the rainbow as captured by Newtonian optics, the mnemonic "ROYGBIV" itself aims to keep something straight that is not, to manage the set of effects named "color" as they occur at the interface that is the human *sensorium*. Learn the rhyme, and one will remember the order of colors in the rainbow. Even as the mnemonic assumes a post-Aristotelian orientation to color, it retains, in shifted form, the order of labor that Hilliard and Norgate advertise via their husbanding of matter in limning. Both the rhyme and they speak to the translational or transactional properties of color effects, effects that today are managed via that strange, grown-up, ring-bound, folded-out-and-up book, *The Munsell Book of Color,* which allows us all to keep our colors straight, even in their absence.[24]

The Munsell Code assigns each color a number, and as Latour writes of the soil color guide version used in fieldwork by pedologists, "the number is a reference that is quickly understandable and reproducible by all the colorists in the world on condition that they . . . use the same code."[25] The book works through a "stupefying technical trick—the little holes that have been pierced above the shades of color," which enable you to align this or that colored something you have before you with its like and convert said something into its number referent. Such a book makes Latour almost as giddy as Benjamin contemplating the world of childhood toys—a world that understands the tactility and embodied understanding of color as a phenomenon. Indeed, the Munsell Code might be said to instrumentalize the media-specific orientation to color that Benjamin found in children's books and games. It suspends the "intellectual cross-references" of unreliable cognition so that we see with our fingers; see without seeing; touch without touching. The structure of reference so maintained keeps color still in and by its translation.

For us, the Munsell Code provides the key to a color stability underwritten by industrial production. It registers thereby the replacement of the moral philosophically coded labor and techniques of the limner who worked with substances by another order of techniques. But the very existence of the code as the bibliographical form of an elaborated infrastructure attests still to the deployment of labor and resources necessary to keep colors still. Once upon a time, the desire to keep colors still, to render their effects permanent, required the limner to embark on a quasi-mimetic sympathizing with her palette. Now, such embodied knowledge migrates to a book allied to a set of industrial practices and the adumbration of resources necessary to relaying colors on a global scale.

But let us return now to a moment just after the arrival of oranges and of *orange* in England, a world reordered by the mobility of a fruit that hosts the color and comes to give it its name.

"Oranges and Lemons" (ca. 1665)

"Say the bells of St. Clements." Maybe you learned this rhyme as a child or read it in a novel. Maybe you did not. Here is how it goes:

> You owe me five farthings,
> Say the bells of St. Martin's.
> When will you pay me?
> Say the bells of Old Bailey.
> When I grow rich,
> Say the bells of Shoreditch.
> When will that be?
> Say the bells of Stepney.
> I'm sure I don't know.
> Says the great bell at Bow.

Then it all gets a bit frightening: "Here comes a candle to light you to bed. / Here comes a chopper to chop off your head. / Chop, chop, chip, *chop*!"[26] The rhyme choreographs a street game in which two children "determine in secret which of them shall be an 'orange' and which a 'lemon'; they then form an arch by joining hands, and sing the song while the others in a line troop underneath." When the rhyme approaches its gruesome finale, marked by the rising tempo, the two children repeat "Chip chop, chip chop," and "on the last chop they bring their arms down around whichever child is at that moment passing under the arch. The captured player is asked privately whether he [or she] will be an 'orange' or a 'lemon' and then joins the team of the said 'orange' or 'lemon.'"[27] Typically, the game ends in a tug-of-war between the two arbitrarily composed teams, leading to a victory for either "oranges" or "lemons."

The rhyme's text can be traced no farther back than the eighteenth century. It appears, in a slightly different form, in *Tom Thumb's Pretty Song Book* (1744), though there was a square for eight dance called "oringes and lemons" recorded in the third edition of Playford's *Dancing Master* (1665)—but the text of this dance, if there was one, is not preserved.[28] According to Peg, a character in Edward Ravenscroft's play *The London Cuckolds* (1682), which takes a postfire 1666 London as its scene, "oranges and lemons" is but "one of a great many things [they cry] in London."[29] This is as far as the written record permits us to travel back into the rhyme's origins, but it attests to the fact that by 1665 orange was a word you might expect to hear as you walk down the street in London. Generically, the rhyme belongs to that group of verses that recall what bells *say*, and such rhymes were marketed to parents as "artificial memory" devices for children in the eighteenth and nineteenth centuries.[30] The text of the rhyme itself is subject to vigorous debate among local historians and antiquarians today who lay claim to phrases from it for different churches that they wish to make more of a landmark. (The rivals are St. Clement's Dane in the Strand and St. Clement's in Eastcheap, which boasts a Sir Christopher Wren–designed postfire interior.)

Oranges began to arrive in London from Spain and Portugal at the beginning of the fifteenth century. They arrived in March or April, staying good until December. They were not outrageously expensive but neither were they cheap, and they were sold in theaters, on the street, and in bulk for the Inns of Court and well-to-do houses. Seasonally, then, waves of orange entered the country, *orange* coming to punctuate market stalls, dinner tables, finding its way into the hands and mouths of Londoners. As with any imported commodity, the key to the fruit's naturalization stemmed from the import of the concomitant skill and knowledge of their use (values).[31] Oranges were not always an edible, finding themselves pressed into use as medicinal items, fashion statement, cleanser, and invisible ink.[32] To extend our picture of London, we might imagine, its built world further littered with small piles of orange rind, rind that might be discarded, composted, or recycled for other uses such as in the pomanders sported by the well-to-do, or by Jesuit priests held prisoner in the Tower of London, who cut and pieced them into rosaries, having saved their juice for ink in secret writing.[33] As these leftovers aged and oxidized, their color would shift, deepen, bleach, and blacken.

Oranges would never be successfully cultivated in England, and so the fruit remained an exotic, a foreigner whose elaborated use-values might be extolled by some or vilified by others depending on the vagaries of political allegiance, national identity, and religion. The vector attaching to the fruit's appearance every season meant that when apprehended systemically as a commodity, the fruit and the trees became subject to economic criticism given the reciprocal flow of capital out of the country on which their re/appearance depended. The price of all that orange was a commensurate absence of gold and silver that went abroad. Likewise, oranges especially were uncertainly coded according to their Spanish and Catholic origins. Still, oranges remained the object of desire, veneration, and even addiction. In the *Paston Letters* we learn that "Dame Elizaet Calthorp is a fayir lady and longyth for orangis, thow she is not with child."[34] And famously, in "Employment 2," George Herbert exclaims, "Oh that I were an Orenge-tree, / That busie plant! / Then should I ever laden be, / And never want / Some fruit for him that dressed me," inducting the peculiarity of the orange tree's ability to flower and fruit at the same time into his attempts to craft prosthetic prayer machines.[35]

If it seems that I have drifted from the color to the fruit, then that essentially is the point I wish to make. The word *orange* designates a multiplicity, a sheaf of multitemporal references, and an accrued metaphorology that it is only partly possible to connect back to past transports and transfers of properties between persons and fruit and color. Each instance of the word exceeds its immediate referent to sport still other associations and possibilities depending on how and by whom it is received. Orange stands as a threading together of multiple, incompatible meanings that very precisely do not cohere to form a whole. And this insight, I argue, is the ecological import that we may derive from modeling the color effect "orange" in relation to the elaborated object world that hosts it. Such a prismatic archive forces us to be content with charting multiple, asynchronous chronologies, partial foldings of space, subject to revision, and so places us in a plural relation to things past and present. Methodologically, it will prove best not to subject the color or the fruit to a simple chronology or geography. For color, like any complicated phenomenon, reveals itself to be a multiplicity, a knot in motion that connects different times and places in a structure of only apparent simultaneity. And so, at almost every moment, my orange ecology waxes in and out of being, revealing itself to be merely one orientation to a generalized prismatic archive.

"Oranges and Lemons" serves as a fitting emblem or jingle for this process. The rhyme itself exists as a multiply authored, multitemporal, inhuman archaeology, accreting references to differently timed peals of bells, landmarks, and half-remembered, half-forgotten "events." These different elements coexist only as the rhyme is sung or in the children's performance of the rhyme as they occupy a city street and arbitrarily become "oranges" and "lemons." Indeed, the work of antiquarians and local historians today who wish to disambiguate the lines and provide them with a stable historical referent stands as the reciprocal fetish work necessary to posit the supposed labors, lives, and deaths lived by previous generations of Londoners as they intersected with oranges and orange. The endeavor may prove beguiling, inviting us to hallucinate a past or to catch traces of otherwise undocumented lives as we imagine this or that boy or girl, on the very edge of our vision, unloading oranges from a barge on the Thames wharf. For such are the diversions offered by the archive fever enabled by the rhyme, by the catachresis of bells saying things, bells that momentarily possess those who sing, those with ears to hear and tongues with which to vocalize the peal. For, by our singing, the rhyme seems to render us mute as we are sung by phrases past.[36] The cries of London come again. "Chip. Chop."

Heard this way, the rhyme reveals the tropic or rhetorical work of certain language games in producing events, in establishing and maintaining routines, of keeping the built world built, even as its buildings disappear. And while it may fund an order of archive fever, the rhyme has within it everything we need to recognize that, in ecological terms, language arts, metaphor, rhetoric remain key relays within a political struggle for citizenship, and for imagining alternate futures. The rhyme produces different orders of group belonging, marking your relationship to London (did you know it already?); your relation to your peer group (will you be an orange or a lemon?); and your relationship, once upon a time, to a neighborhood, whose streets you lay claim to as a play-space. "Oranges and lemons" figures a proactive, forward-looking mimesis that makes a world by its recycling of remainders. It is a machine, in small, for writing a certain kind of world—a contested world. If you can lay claim to it or part of it today, you may be able to direct tourist traffic to your landmark, sell a few more postcards and tea things; mend your roof. And under certain circumstances, the mere fact of singing it, badly, of giving your voice over to bells you have never and may not now hear, might matter, might strive to do something.

Clocks Not Bells (1949)

"It was a bright cold day in April, and the clocks were striking thirteen."[37] Against these clocks whose striking announces the altered routines and disavowed past of George Orwell's *1984*, Winston Smith is taken momentarily by a rhyme he hears and that he begins to hum, trying his best to lend his voice to bells he cannot remember hearing, perhaps has never heard. He is alive to the way the Party implants false histories, and so he trolls around, acting on a note to self in his diary that "if there is hope . . . it lies in the proles."[38] He slums; eavesdrops on the cries of London; tries to talk to people; fails. He finds himself seized with "helplessness" when he questions an old man about the past—"the old man's memory was nothing but a rubbish-heap of details."[39] Still, Winston comes to sift the rubbish for this or that stray object that he finds "beautiful." The words *beautiful* and *rubbish* circulate through the novel until they eventually connect, and Winston owns that fact that he is on a quest for what he names "beautiful rubbish."[40] He is embarked, as it were, on a becoming antiquarian, a becoming collector—trawling the remains of London for stray objects whose forms, whose fragmentary archives, somehow activate something in him that he does not quite know how to name. We join him as he considers renting a room from the old man we later learn is named Mr. Charrington, a room, Winston gasps, with "no telescreen."[41]

Mr. Charrington asks if Winston is interested in old prints and beckons him to join him in front of an old picture. Winston

> came across to examine the picture. It was a steel engraving of an oval building with rectangular windows, and a small tower in front. There was a railing running round the building, and at the rear end there was what appeared to be a statue. Winston gazed at it for some moments. It seemed vaguely familiar, though he did not remember the statue.[42]

"I know that building," says Winston. "It's in the middle of the street outside the Palace of Justice." "That's right. Outside the Law Courts," adds the old man. "It was a Church at one time. St. Clement's Dane, it's name was." "He smiled apologetically, as though conscious of saying something slightly ridiculous, he added 'Oranges and Lemons' say the Bells of St. Clements." "What's that?" asks Winston—who does not get it, who does not know the rhyme. "Oh, 'Oranges and lemons' say the Bells of St. Clements. That was a rhyme we had when I was a little boy . . . it was kind of a dance."[43] Mr. Charrington sings it over, but cannot remember the last line.

Winston looks around at the scene in the print but is unable to date the buildings, unable to make sense of the overlapping of medieval, renaissance, and modern forms and painfully aware that "anything that might throw light upon the past had been systematically altered" by the reigning regime. The old man proceeds to go through the rhyme or most of it and to describe the churches to which it refers in detail. It all washes over Winston, and he cannot quite process what he has heard. At the end of their meeting, Winston does not buy the picture, but he is haunted by the rhyme. "It was curious," he remarks to himself,

> but when you said it to yourself you had the illusion of actually hearing bells, the bells of a lost London that still existed somewhere or other, disguised or forgotten. From one ghostly steeple after another he seemed to hear them pealing forth. Yet so far as he could remember he had never in real life heard church bells singing.[44]

In a moment sometimes held to ridicule for its sentimentality, the rhyme's linguistic materiality captures Winston and transports him not into the past but into what he calls a "lost London"—that exists but which may never be located. This affective or druglike hit of transport, this fever that comes by the blocked immersion in a lost series of objects, leads him to continue in what he names "his pursuit of beautiful rubbish," his idiotic desire to rent the room, buy the engraving of St. Clement's Dane, and carry it home concealed under his jacket. On the way, he starts to hum "oranges and lemons" to an improvised tune—not quite his own, perhaps, but some partial mimesis of Mr. Charrington's rendition.[45] The moment is shattered by the appearance of the glaring woman from the Department of Fiction walking down the street—and Winston "was too paralyzed to move."[46]

As the novel progresses, the rhyme "oranges and lemons" reappears at key points allied to an encrypted past that might set all free. Julia, Winston's lover, betrayer, and the woman he betrays, knows part of the rhyme (her grandfather taught it to her) and even remembers seeing oranges even as she cannot quite keep them or their color straight—"they're a kind of round yellow fruit with a thick skin."[47] Winston recalls a lemon—"so sour that it set your teeth on edge"—and he takes their sharing of partial knowledge as "two halves of a countersign." All comes to founder, however, on the fact that O'Brien, Winston's interrogator, knows the rhyme in toto, including the last line, "'When I grow rich,' say the bells of Shoreditch,"[48] which empties the rhyme of any escape or reactualizing possibility, signaling also that the fragments of the past, all its "beautiful rubbish," might be deployed by the state to keep tabs on and eventually to ensnare those who stray.

In the end, "oranges and lemons" stands in contrast to or is countered by the compromised lyric of another nursery rhyme—"under the spreading chestnut tree," revised by the telescreen, and intoned by a lobotomized Julia, "I sold you and you sold me."[49] There is nothing stable or safe about the aesthetic, the novel seems to say, about the technologies of writing, quite the reverse; whoever controls the sites of articulation, such as the telescreen, the clocks, or the bells, will write the end of the story. Winston's antiquarian rebellion and turning collector of lost forms augurs no escape even as it might offer consolation. "Beautiful rubbish," it turns out, was merely one further mode of the state's biopolitical articulation and profiling of its citizens—part of its gathering less of biometric than bioaesthetic data. The bleak beauty of the novel is that it offers no alternative. Colors die. Pigments fade. We do not know what they were like exactly. Still, as Mr. Charrington tells Winston in passing, "Oranges and lemons" was "a kind of a dance." Winston's collecting of "beautiful rubbish," of forms and objects that sit mutely still, might yet have within it, idling, in abeyance, the kinematics of a dance still to come. Indeed, such collecting and inventorying as I perform in this chapter would prove defensible only for as long as we allow our subjects to keep turning, dancing, moving—allowing oranges and *orange* to play out as tropes, and so to surprise us.

So, what might happen if the dance were to stall? What if the actors that hosted *orange* disappeared? What if the color and the fruit were recoded, cordoned off as a biohazard, designating less an orange ecology than a citrusy crime scene? What if there was only one orange in the world—an orange on which the world turned in parody of the great solar eye?

An Orange out of Season (1997)

In *The Tropic of Orange* (1997), Karen Tei Yamashita imagines just such a world. The novel begins in Mazatlán, where there exists an orange grown on a tree transplanted from California. It figures a hybrid; the problematic of the deracinated immigrant become emigrant. "The tree was a sorry one," we learn, "and so was the orange. . . . it was an orange that should not have been."[50] Attached to this "aberrant orange—not to be picked" is a "line— finer than the thread of a spiderweb—pull[ing]" on it "with delicate taut- ness."[51] This line connects the orange to the Tropic of Cancer. One day the orange falls from the tree and rolls "to a neutral place between owner- ship and the highway,"[52] where it is picked up by Arcangel, a magical realist, angel-trickster-performance artist let go from some Gabriel García Márquez story.[53] He is on his way north across the border with a post-NAFTA Cal- ifornia friendlier to pairs of Nikes than theoretically free persons, and he takes the orange with him, causing space and time to collapse, as Mexico and the United States fold on each other. People's TVs go all wonky. They get more and fewer channels. Spanish replaces English; English, Spanish. The cries of the city as broadcast by the news radio in place of bells and clocks get stuck, looped in endless repetitions. Time collapses to an instant.

Meanwhile, a consignment of lethal cocaine-concealing "death oranges," "spiked oranges,"[54] produced by a team of Brazilian drug dealers, wreck the world market for oranges—which are now too lethal a food item to consider eating. Arcangel's orange becomes a hot commodity; finds itself singularized as a piece of "beautiful rubbish"; worth a fortune, perhaps, if it is one of the cocaine-bombs, or maybe, even, simply as an orange, for its *orange*. One of these bombs goes off, causing a SigAlert of epic pro- portions on the 10 freeway, turning it into a city where the homeless set up camp in a utopian cessation of happening. The novel merely describes and establishes the situation, builds several worlds (in small) via its paral- lel and sometimes intersecting character-bound narratives—seven in all, unfolding over seven days. It ends with a knock-down, drag-out, Sunday, glam-wrestling contest between Arcangel and the cyborg SUPERNAFTA while the LAPD storm the 10 freeway to restore their brand of order.

The novel's climax comes when Bobby Ngu, who's "Chinese from Singa- pore with a Vietnam name speaking like a Mexican living in Koreatown" and who peppers his sentences with "That's it,"[55] stumbles late onto the wrestling match in search of Sol, his son, and Rafaela, his wife, who is in the ring. Bobby does not know about the orange. And Rafaela's yelling at him to cut it—"Cut what?"[56]—"Cut it now!" Rafaela feeds the orange to a dying Arcangel, and the line that was attached to it flies free. Bobby holds on to it—"Dude's skinny, but he's an Atlas."[57] Despairing of all these "lines"— "tied fast to them"[58]—Bobby "lets the lines slither around his wrists, past his palms, through his fingers. Let's go. Go figure. Embrace. That's it." The novel's final words are a cry of the city, the tagline of one character. Bobby knows no more than he knows, lacks access to the whole. "That's it."

Yamashita's novel proffers an interesting future, a future hard to read, for it collapses to an apocalyptic orange event that seems to inaugurate or to admit that there is nothing more to be had than a perpetual instant or a series of disconnected moments that it is the "life" and "death" of finite beings to connect. When the elaborated networks of industrial capitalism that ensure that oranges and *orange* keep showing up in all the expected places find themselves challenged by the dangerous recoding of oranges, they effortlessly substitute passion fruit as the breakfast beverage of choice. "Talk Show [host] Tiffany" does not "miss a beat: 'That's right. Passion fruit is all the rage. Minute Made is selling it under the name, *Passion*™. Make the change now. *Passion*™.'"[59] Overnight, purple becomes the new *orange*— rewriting the visual field that we saw get built in England in the sixteenth and seventeenth centuries. Everything and nothing changes; juice glasses flush purple instead of orange. These networks prove less resilient to metaphysical or aesthetic attack, however, by the one remaining orange in California, the "aberrant," inedible, unusable, or purely aesthetic "un-seasonal" orange, which says "no" to any use-value. The collisions, the careering dance moves, and tableaux it produces as it comes north choreograph less a series of utopian cessations than a disorienting rewiring of expectations and experiences that produce the possibility that something might happen differently, today, tomorrow, now, or already has.

Shame, then, that it is just in our heads. Shame that line that connects to the orange is visible only to a few—but that proves to be precisely the consolation. Bobby acts without knowing, trusting those in whom he has trust. Thus Atlas no longer shoulders the world. He puts down the globe. Partial, fragmentary knowledge is all you will get, and still you must act, the novel seems to say, without assurances. Welcome to what Ursula K.

Heise calls Yamashita's "junkyard ecology," in which freeways that annihilate distance and pit driver against driver or carpool become sites of possible cosmopolitical joining, and the world remains available to be read.[60] Such instantaneous, time-bound occupations of place sponsor the possibility of a hospitable and polite commons, a common becoming, in which car horns become musical instruments and freeways communities—which they already are. In whose "beautiful rubbish" shall you trust to find the wherewithal to transform lines that bind us to deadly presents into nodes of becoming otherwise? "That's it."

In ending my experiment with a prismatic grammatology that would own the dropped connection between deconstruction and actor network theory with Yamashita's novel, the temptation, fairly obviously, is to disappear into Bobby's tagline and write, "That's it." You are on your own. This book of flowers wilts. The last posy unravels. But there is another cry to be had from Bobby that resonates even more closely with the prismatic grammatology I have attempted: "Go figure?" Perhaps we may hear in his words both a question and an affirmative call for the figures we have to keep turning, dancing, troping. More than anything, the prismatic factoring of a green ecology into ecologies of many shades and hues foregrounds the way ecology refers to a practice of writing and making, a figural enterprise that understands the way forms of language and forms of life are coextensive. One important strand of cosmopolitical thinking will involve attending to and altering the figural routines by which worlds remain the same or move differently. Hence my desire to retain a sense of the figural dimension to *things*, to color effects, and the objects that host them, objects in all their creaturely density. "Go figure!"

Notes

1. Walter Benjamin, *Selected Writings,* vol. 1, ed. Michael W. Jennings (Cambridge, Mass.: Belknap Press of Harvard University Press, 2002), 50.

2. Ibid., 51.

3. Walter Benjamin, *Selected Writings,* vol. 2, pt. 2, ed. Michael W. Jennings (Cambridge, Mass.: Belknap Press of Harvard University Press, 2005), 720.

4. Walter Benjamin, *The Arcades Project,* trans. Howard Eiland and Kevin McLaughlin (Cambridge, Mass.: Belknap Press of Harvard University Press, 2002).

5. On the representational possibilities to be found in rock formations by human observers that exceed human agency in their making, see Roger Caillois,

The Writing of Stones, trans. Barbara Bray (Charlottesville: University Press of Virginia, 1985). See especially his discussions of a series of limestones from Tuscany whose forms elicit from him the words "Castle" and "Portrait" (85–104). I am grateful to Jeffrey Jerome Cohen for this reference.

6. Jacques Derrida, *Of Grammatology,* trans. Gayatri Chakravorty Spivak (Baltimore, Md.: Johns Hopkins University Press, 1974), 84. In modeling Benjamin in relation to the figure of Derrida's "general or generative text," I follow Samuel Weber, "Streets, Squares, Theaters: A City on the Move—Walter Benjamin's Paris," in *Benjamin's-abilities* (Cambridge, Mass.: Harvard University Press, 2008), 227–39.

7. Derrida, *Of Grammatology,* 87.

8. On "multispecies," see Donna Haraway, *When Species Meet* (Minneapolis: University of Minnesota Press, 2008). On actor networks, see *Actor Network Theory and After,* ed. John Law and John Hassard (Oxford: Blackwell/*Sociological Review,* 1999) as well as the numerous writings of the sociologist Bruno Latour. My aim is not to assimilate grammatology to the sociological models of actor network theory but to own its parasitic orientation to texts and systems and to offer it as complementary to the more optative models actor network theory and Latour tend to favor. The importance of deconstructive critique, I argue, derives from the orientation it provides toward acts of making and manufacture, attempts to intervene in the "built world" and consequences that derive from them. Here I follow Cary Wolfe's rezoning of deconstruction in relation to systems theory as outlined in his introduction to Michel Serres, *The Parasite,* trans. Lawrence R. Schehr (Minneapolis: University of Minnesota Press), xi–xxviii, and in *What Is Posthumanism?* (Minneapolis: University of Minnesota Press, 2010), xi–xxxiv.

9. On the exchange of properties between person and object by their joining, see Bruno Latour, *Aramis; or, the Love of Technology,* trans. Catherine Porter (Cambridge, Mass.: Harvard University Press, 1993). Whimsically, I hope not unjustifiably, I maintain the distinction between the fruit and the color throughout this chapter, by writing "orange" and "*orange,*" respectively.

10. Juliet Fleming, *Graffiti and the Writing Arts of Early Modern England* (Philadelphia: University of Pennsylvania Press, 2001), 10.

11. Charis Thompson, *Making Parents: The Ontological Choreography of Reproductive Technologies* (Cambridge, Mass.: MIT Press, 2005), especially 8–11.

12. *Oxford English Dictionary,* s.v. "orange," http://www.oed.com/view/Entry/132163?rskey=VeajGY&result1&isAdvanced=false (accessed July 17, 2013); *Middle English Dictionary* (Ann Arbor: University of Michigan Press, 1998), s.v. "orange."

13. See Arthur Golding's rendering of the story of Atalanta in *Ovid's Metamorphoses, The Arthur Golding Translation [1567]*, ed. John Frederick Nims (Philadelphia: Paul Dry Books, 2000).

14. Samuel Tolkofsky, *Hesperides: A History of the Use and Culture of Citrus Fruits* (London: J. Bale and Sons and Currow, 1938), 168–70. Pierre Laszlo's *Citrus: A History* (Chicago: University of Chicago Press, 2007) covers much of the same ground.

15. Edward Norgate, *Miniatura or the Art of Limning*, ed. Jeffrey M. Muller and Jim Murrell (New Haven, Conn.: Yale University Press, 1997), 59.

16. Ibid., 63.

17. Ibid., 59–60.

18. *Nicholas Hilliard's The Art of Limning*, ed. Arthur Kinney and Linda Bradley Salamon (Boston: Northeastern University Press, 1983), 21.

19. Henry Peacham, *The Art of Drawing with a Pen, and limning with water colours* (London, 1606) and *The Compleat Gentleman* (London, 1622). Peacham publishes numerous revised editions of his *Compleat Gentleman,* enlarging the sections on drawing and painting and so ennobling these activities.

20. On this model of poeisis, see Bruno Latour, *Pandora's Hope: Essays on the Reality of Science Studies* (Cambridge, Mass.: Harvard University Press, 1999), 281.

21. On the efficacy of gemstones and minerals in this tradition, see Valerie Allen, "Mineral Virtue," in *Animal, Vegetable, Mineral: Ethics and Objects,* ed. Jeffrey Jerome Cohen (Brooklyn: Oliphaunt Books, 2012), 123–52; and Kellie Robertson, "Exemplary Rocks," in *Animal, Vegetable, Mineral,* 91–121.

22. Aristotle, *De Anima,* 418.b.14–20. Quoted in Bruce R. Smith, *The Key of Green: Passion and Perception in Renaissance Culture* (Chicago: University of Chicago Press, 2009), 58. Aristotle's color spectrum included the following: "black | gray | deep blue | leek-green | violet | crimson | yellow | white"; see John Gage, *Color and Culture: Practice and Meaning from Antiquity to Abstraction* (Berkeley: University of California Press, 1993), 12–13.

23. On the ethical and political functions of politeness in scientific and ecological practice, see Isabelle Stengers, *Cosmopolitics I,* trans. Robert Bononno (Minneapolis: University of Minnesota Press, 2010).

24. Jim Long, *The Munsell Book of Color,* 3rd ed. (New York: Fairchild Publications, 2011); and *Munsell® Soil Color Book,* rev. ed. (Grand Rapids, Mich.: Munsell Color, 2012).

25. Latour, *Pandora's Hope,* 59.

26. *The Oxford Dictionary of Nursery Rhymes,* 2nd ed., ed. Iona Opie and Peter Opie (Oxford: Oxford University Press, 1997), 398.

27. Ibid.

28. Nurse Lovechild, *Tom Thumb's Pretty Song Book* (1744; rpt. Glasgow: Lumsden and Sons, 1813), 24. On Playford's *Dancing Master* (1665), see Opie and Opie, *Oxford Dictionary of Nursery Rhymes,* 399.

29. Edward Ravenscroft, *The London Cuckolds* (1682). Additional street cries for golden, ripe, and fine oranges are recorded in Charles Hindley, *A History of the Cries of London* (London: Reeves and Turner, 1881).

30. See Hindley, *History of the Cries of London,* frontispiece.

31. On this point, see Arjun Appadurai, "Introduction: Commodities and the Politics of Value," in *The Social Life of Things: Commodities in Cultural Perspective* (Cambridge: Cambridge University Press, 1986), 41–42.

32. Cardinal Wolsey was posthumously described twinned with an orange (pomander) he carried to ward off evil smells in George Cavendish, *The Life and Death of Cardinal Wolsey,* ed. Richard S. Sylvester and Davis P. Harding (1557; rpt. New Haven, Conn.: Yale University Press, 1962), 25. On oranges as stain remover, see Leonard Mascall, *Of Spots and Stains* (London, 1588), A3r.

33. The Jesuit priest John Gerard describes how he escaped from the Tower of London, mending his body from bouts of torture by making rosaries of orange rind and communicating via letters written in invisible ink in *The Autobiography of a Hunted Priest,* trans. Philip Caraman (New York: Pellegrini and Cudhay), 116–27.

34. John Gardiner, ed., *The Paston Letters* (London, 1904), 66.

35. On Herbert's prosthetic poetics, see David Glimp, "Figuring Belief: George Herbert's Devotional Creatures," in Judith H. Anderson and Joan Pong Linton, eds., *Go Figure: Energies, Forms, and Institutions in the Early Modern World* (New York: Fordham University Press, 2011), 112–31.

36. On the allure of the archive, see Jacques Derrida, *Archive Fever: A Freudian Impression,* trans. Eric Prenowitz (Chicago: University of Chicago Press, 1996).

37. George Orwell, *1984,* in vol. 9 of *The Complete Works of George Orwell,* ed. Peter Davison (London: Secker and Warburg, 1984), 3.

38. Ibid., 85.

39. Ibid., 95.

40. Ibid., 104.

41. Ibid., 100.

42. Ibid., 101.

43. Ibid., 102.

44. Ibid., 103.

45. Ibid., 104.

46. Ibid.

47. Ibid., 153.

48. Ibid., 186.

49. Ibid., 307.

50. Karen Tei Yamashita, *The Tropic of Orange* (Minneapolis: Coffee House, 1997), 11.

51. Ibid., 12.

52. Ibid., 13.

53. Ibid., 71.

54. Ibid., 139–40.

55. Ibid., 15.

56. Ibid., 267.

57. Ibid.

58. Ibid., 268.

59. Ibid., 141.

60. Ursula K. Heise, *Sense of Place and Sense of Planet: The Environmental Imagination of the Global* (Oxford: Oxford University Press, 2008), 201.

Gold

GRAHAM HARMAN

In the late 1990s I coined the phrase "object-oriented philosophy."[1] By the time of this writing (May 2012), the term had gained widespread international usage.[2] The two basic principles of my object-oriented approach are as follows: (1) objects have genuine reality at many different scales, not just the smallest, and (2) objects withdraw from all types of relation, whether those of human knowledge or of inanimate causal impact. In short, objects exist at many different levels of complexity, and they are always a hidden surplus deeper than any of the relations into which they might enter. The rest of object-oriented philosophy follows from these two points.

The first point tells us that objects should not automatically be "undermined" or reduced to a tiniest layer of particles, fields, or mathematical structures from which everything else is built. It may be correct to undermine "morning star" and "evening star" by showing that the two are different appearances of Venus. Louis Pasteur was largely right in claiming that a plethora of nineteenth-century hygiene rules could be reduced to just one rule: prevent the spread of microbes.[3] Yet it does not follow from these successful underminings that everything at intermediate scales must be undermined via reduction to its smaller components, so that everything would be ground up into nothing but subatomic powder. There is no good reason to assume in advance that electrons are more real than water, aluminum chairs, or the Pizza Hut corporation.

The second point tells us that objects should not automatically be "overmined," or reduced upward to their appearance in human consciousness or their environmental effects. Admittedly, it seems to be the case that "witchcraft" is a nonexistent unifying cause for a number of unrelated accidental effects and that there is no such entity as Poseidon that links horses, earthquakes, and the sea. Paranoid conspiracy theories can be successfully overmined by showing that no connection exists between the CIA, the Masons, the Egyptian military, and the man across the street who watches my every move through binoculars. Yet from these victorious overminings it does not follow that there are never any hidden causes linking the various appearances in the world. The cosmos is made of objects, not "bundles of qualities" and "family resemblances," as too many all-knowing critics of metaphysics like to believe.

This essay follows the fortunes of one specific object that is both widely prized and universally known: gold. I examine the long history of gold from cosmic eons predating humans and consider various structural features of gold that arise from its chemical properties without being reducible to them. After considering examples of the effect of gold on humans, who are dazzled by its splendor, corrupted by its value, and made cruel through their ravenous hunt for the metal, I observe gold in its interactions with bacteria, governments, collapsing stars, geothermal currents, and mountain streams. Since the great value of gold entails that it is rarely discarded, the total human storehouse of gold continues to expand while losing very little, making gold the great unifier of all the generations in human history. But while gold represents a vast sum of "congealed human labor,"[4] it also has countless properties that humans had no role in producing, but which force human labor into definite channels. For this reason, today's Hegelian Marxists miss the point whenever they claim that object-oriented philosophy is a form of "commodity fetishism."[5] Marx's claim was that *value* is congealed human labor, not that *reality itself* is generated by such labor. In this way, gold refutes the metaphysically idealist brand of Marxism that has so little promise as the future of the political Left, while the realist tenets of object-oriented philosophy are shown to have nothing to do with "fetishism." Humans lose their place as the metaphysical core of the universe in object-oriented thought, but only because *no* object is allowed to occupy that core, including the inanimate sort. Instead, all objects are equally decentered, equally converted into just one object among others. Gold, trees, neutrons, cats, and humans have different properties and varying life spans, but none is more or less an object than any other.

From Supernovas to the Ganges

In the coldness of outer space, clouds of hydrogen gas sometimes become so dense that nuclear reactions occur. Through the work of gravity, some of these clouds collapse to form stars. Stars are the great furnaces of the universe, fusing hydrogen with its single proton into helium, which has two protons. Small stars produce insufficient energy to generate elements heavier than helium. Even our own star, the sun, goes only as far as the production of carbon (element 6). But when larger stars have exhausted their typical hydrogen fuel, they begin a daring ascent of the periodic table, producing ever-weightier elements until eventually reaching a point of crisis. Imagine an aged red giant star pushing atomic fusion as far as nickel with its twenty-eight protons. The nickel will undergo radioactive decay back downward into cobalt (element 27) and then iron (element 26), in the hardy and durable form of isotope iron-56. From this point onward, additional reactions absorb heat rather than produce it, and the star's energy begins to dwindle. The star collapses into its growing iron core, and suddenly explodes. This explosion is a supernova, which generates enough energy to outshine entire galaxies. The first few seconds of a supernova harbor enough power to produce elements heavier than iron, all the way up to uranium (element 92), the last of the elements able to exist stably in nature. A gaseous nebula spreads outward from the exploding star, sweeping heavy waste elements along a shockwave through empty space. Among these transferric wastes is gold (element 79), the hero of our story.[6]

Some 4.5 billion years ago, our solar system was nothing but a vague molecular cloud. Part of this cloud collapsed through the force of gravity. Our sun began to form at the center of this cloud, surrounded by a disclike swirl of gases that eventually gave birth to the planets.[7] Initially there were dozens of minor planetoids, which collided and merged over time until gradually giving rise to the current official solar system of eight planets and their myriad moons. During the accretion of the earth, heavier metals sank to the center of our planet. This parade of sinking elements was dominated by iron—the same iron that was responsible for the supernova explosion that destroyed its original parent star. As plebeian iron sank into the planetary core, it was accompanied by its more dazzling metallic sisters, such as platinum and gold. In this way the earth's original supply of gold was concentrated at the inner planetary core, more than three thousand miles from even our low-lying sea-level cities. This primeval terrestrial gold lies far beyond reach of the mining conglomerates whose infernal pacts with the devil have brought them no deeper than two or three miles beneath the earth's crust. Having lost its original supply of gold, the earth's surface had to receive it from a foreign source. This happened nearly 4 billion years ago, during the so-called terminal bombardment of the earth and moon by asteroids, and by other objects that invaded the solar system because of internal gravitational changes.[8] In short, all the gold enjoyed and exploited by humans today came from the dangerous invaders that slammed long ago into the planet's recently cooled surface. It is now known that some bacteria lead to the coalescence of gold in an effort at self-defense from the metal, leaving it behind in clumps as a kind of microbial waste product.[9] Whether such bacteria played an extensive role in forming veins and nuggets of the metal is unclear. But we know that in nature gold can be found either alone in freestanding form, in the gold–silver alloy known as electrum, or in an amalgam with swift and toxic mercury.

Underground gold can be dissolved by extreme pressure and heat, and the resulting fluids (often containing quartz) stream up through faults in the earth, especially those faults that separate two different types of rock. As temperature and pressure decrease, the gold hardens into veins.[10] These veins can be eroded and washed down ridges and mountains. As a result, the streams of the world bear dust and nuggets of gold, and this may have been the first human contact with metal—despite Jean-Jacques Rousseau's hypothesis that this happened when early humans witnessed liquid ore streaming from volcanoes.[11] Even the seas of our planet bear gold in trace amounts. Gold is not hard to work with, being both soft and malleable, and thus it is not surprising to find remarkable cases of goldsmithing at a relatively early date. In 1972 electrical workers in the Black Sea port of Varna, Bulgaria, made an astonishing discovery of elaborate gold objects approximately 6,500 years old.[12] In the Bronze Age period, there were centers of golden wealth in such locations as modern-day Ireland.[13] The abundant gold of ancient Egypt is proverbial. Gold appears throughout the Bible, in both positive and negative senses. The first mention comes early at Genesis 2:11–12: "The name of the first [river] is the Pishon. It is the one that flowed around the whole land of Havilah, where there is gold. And the gold of that land is good." The first negative reference to the metal comes from the famous episode at Exodus 32:2–3: "So all the people took off the rings of gold that were in their ears and brought them to Aaron. And he received the gold from their hand and fashioned it with a graving tool and made a golden calf. And they said, 'These are your gods, O Israel, who brought you up out of the land of Egypt!'" Christianity took contempt for the metal another step farther, but in a way that emphasized its preciousness all the more. At 1 Peter 1:7, we read: "so that the tested genuineness of your faith—more precious than gold that perishes though it is tested by fire—may be found to result in praise and glory and honor at the revelation of Jesus Christ." The Greeks and Romans were rampant in their thirst for gold, as reflected in the parable of King Midas. In the civilization of India, the ancient northern settlements of Harappa and Mohenjo-Daro (located in present-day Pakistan) have been traced to the Kolar gold fields deep in the southern sun of Karnataka.[14] Later, the Spanish conquistadors were haunted by dreams of El Dorado, the legendary city of gold. The Americans of the 1840s, hunting a less delusional but equally bellicose gold, rushed westward into a California recently seized from Mexico as spoils of war.

We saw that the original gold of the earth sank irretrievably into the planetary core and had to be replaced by extraterrestrial gold from asteroid debris. This new gold of the surface has remained so precious throughout human history that only a tiny portion has been lost, or deployed in nonrecyclable uses such as highly miniaturized electronics. The World Gold Council estimates that a grand total of 166,000 tons of gold have been mined throughout human history,[15] a small-sounding figure equaled by the annual world sum of textile waste, or the yearly American consumption of batteries. It is said that these 166,000 tons of gold would form a cube only sixty feet on each side—smaller than many apartment buildings. Yet this small and glittering golden cube would be valued at nearly ten trillion dollars, enough to rebuild all housing units in the United States if a great disaster were to destroy them all.[16] But if gold no longer sinks downward through a now-solidified earth, it slides laterally across the planet instead, concentrating in some places more than others. In the United States, two such locations have especial prominence. The first is the well-known United States Bullion Depository at Fort Knox, Kentucky, with its 5,046 tons of gold, equal to more than 2.5 percent of all the gold mined in human history. But even on American soil, the romantic Fort Knox is overshadowed by the bureaucratic Federal Reserve Bank of New York, which holds 7,716 tons of gold, or nearly 4 percent of humanity's historical stock of the metal. Yet even these staggering repositories of a superpower are eclipsed by the common households of India, which have amassed an astonishing 11 percent of all gold ever mined.[17] Just as gravity sucks gold to the center of the earth, power diverts it to American fortifications while tradition draws it to Indian homes.

Color and Chemistry

Just as three-dimensional landmasses cannot be projected accurately onto the flat surface of a map, neither can the hue of gold be depicted as a solid color. A flat color of this sort misses the characteristic sparkle of the metal, which results from variations in angle between the light source and the gold's surface. For this reason, to give the aesthetic impression of gold, paint must either be enhanced with glitter or with gold itself (as in the case of religious painting).[18] Most metals are white or silvery in appearance, but gold, like copper, reflects red and yellow more than they do other colors.[19] Here Albert Einstein makes a surprising appearance in our story, since the color of gold is due to effects of relativity.[20] For various reasons, electrons move especially close to the speed of light in the case of gold. As a result, the ratio of the relativistic radius of valence electrons to their nonrelativistic radius reaches an absolute minimum for gold (only platinum, element 78, is even close). This helps explain the unusually strong absorption of blue and violet light by gold, and hence their absence from gold's resulting color. It also makes gold much smaller in size than an equivalent amount of silver, and increases the interactivity of gold molecules with each other—a phenomenon named "aurophilic attraction" by the venerable Munich chemist Hubert Schmidbaur (b. 1934).

The philosopher Saul Kripke holds that the name of anything continues to point rigidly at that thing even if all the properties we initially ascribe to it turn out to be utterly false. Kripke uses the color of gold as one of his most important examples: "Kant (someone just pointed out to me) gives the example of 'gold is a yellow metal,' which seems to me an extraordinary one, because it's something that I think can turn out to be false."[21] Kripke imagines gold as appearing green under some other planet's differing light without gold thereby ceasing to be gold. Yet we hardly need to visit another planet to explore these variations in color. Even on the earth, gold nano-particles are red when viewed in direct light, and a brownish-orange in reflected light, but on aggregation they become blue—a fact that finds medical application in the new hepatitis C test of Hassan Azzazy and his team at the American University in Cairo.[22] There are also nanoshells, which not only offer promise as treatments for cancer but in the case of gold can also be varied in thickness to yield colors such as purple, blue, or green. The infamous substance iron pyrite—also known as iron disulfide, or "fool's gold"—gives us further reason not to identify gold with any agglomeration of surface qualities. Far from being a good example of an obvious tautological truth, "gold is a yellow metal" turns out to be false indeed. At nanoscale, gold also exchanges its chemical role as inert and metallic for the more dramatic status of chemical catalyst and semiconductor.[23]

The philosopher Manuel DeLanda emphasizes that gold should not be identified so readily with individual atoms of gold, since it has different scales or layers, each with its own characteristic features:

much as between individual cells and the individual organs which compose them there are several intermediate structures bridging the two scales (tissues, organs, organ systems) so between individual atoms of gold and an individual bulk piece of solid material there are intermediately scaled structures that bridge the micro and macro scales: individual atoms form crystals; individual crystals form small grains; individual small grains form larger grains, and so on. Both crystals and grains of different sizes are individuated following specific causal processes, and the properties of an individual bulk sample emerge from the causal interactions between these intermediate structures. There are some properties of gold, such as having a specific melting point, for example, which by definition do not belong to individual gold atoms since single atoms do not melt. Although individual gold crystals may be said to melt, in reality it takes a population of crystals with a minimum critical size (a so-called "microcluster") for the melting point of the bulk sample to emerge. Moreover, the properties of a bulk sample do not emerge all at once at a given critical scale but appear one at a time at different scales.[24]

Gold is obviously classified as a metal, and metals are recognizable even by children. What most children do not realize is that metals make up a full 96 of the 118 elements in the periodic table. Atoms of metal easily lose electrons, and with the loss of these negatively charged particles the atoms become positively charged ions. Metals can be viewed as positive ions surrounded by a swarm of free electrons with which they form bonds. This vast number of free electrons explains why metals conduct electricity so easily, and also why many of them (though not gold) rust because of interaction with atmospheric oxygen. Metals also tend to be ductile, malleable, and lustrous.

Unlike the soft and reactive alkali metals (sodium and potassium are the best known of this group), the so-called transition metals have a partly filled D-shell, making them relatively unreactive and therefore more stable but also more magnetic. This transition group constitutes a gang of at least thirty-five elements, including gold and most of the other substances readily identified as metallic: titanium, iron, nickel, copper, silver, tungsten, and platinum. But zinc and mercury are much-debated borderline cases that may prove to belong instead with lead, tin, and aluminum among the so-called posttransition metals. Gold also belongs to the Group 11 elements, so named because they are found in the eleventh column of the periodic table. Of this group of six elements, three are nonradioactive: copper, silver, and gold. These are known informally as the "coinage metals," since all are soft enough to be stamped with images but hard enough to resist wear through decades of use. The only Group 11 elements not used in coins are the rare earth gadolinium (found in nature only in the form of fluorescent salts) and the radioactive elements curium and roentgenium, far too hazardous to be used as coins. The nonreactivity of gold with other elements is what ensures that so much of it occurs in freestanding form around the earth. Yet gold, like platinum but unlike titanium, is dissolved by aqua regia, a potent mixture of nitric and hydrochloric acids. The Hungarian chemist George de Hevesy succeeded in hiding the Nobel Prize medallions of James Franck and Max von Laue from the Nazis by dissolving them in aqua regia, preserving them until after the war when the metal was recast.[25] Gold also dissolves in cyanide, that beloved potion of cult leaders and fallen tyrants. Alchemists were not wrong to think that lead could be changed into gold. Rather than simple tabletop chemicals, high-energy physics is needed to remove the necessary three protons from lead (element 82) and change it into gold (element 79). While this has been accomplished at least twice by physics, the cost of the process far eclipses the value of the resulting gold.

Humans do not just stare in wonder at the beauty of gold, nor do we only kill each other to seize it. We also eat and drink it. This practice has a long history, especially in the Middle Ages, under the assumption that anything so beautiful must also be especially healthy. Both the United States and the European Union permit the use of gold in food products. But though gold has earned praise in the confectionary industry for its "non-allergenic properties,"[26] it was in fact named 2001 Allergen of the Year by the American Contact Dermatitis Society,[27] with women increasingly likely to suffer from an allergy to the metal. Gold is also consumed in liquefied form: the liqueur known as Danziger Goldwasser has been brewed in Gdansk, Poland, since 1598. Enjoyed by such dignitaries as Catherine the Great, the brew is injected with perfectly visible flakes of twenty-two-karat gold.[28] Yet the nonreactivity of gold not only makes it tasteless and harmless to those who devour it but also deprives the metal of all nutritional value. Emitted from the body after consumption in one way or another, it ends up in the earth once again, eventually to be recycled in mountain veins by hydrothermal currents millions of years after humans have vanished from the cosmos. Yet gold can assist in nutrition in indirect ways, as when used in nanoparticle form to help in maturing young sorghum plants, or to assist in detecting microbial pathogens.[29]

Politics and Ecology

Initially the Lydians in Asia Minor used coins made of electrum, the common silver–gold alloy. But toward 550 BCE, under the reign of the wealthy Croesus, the Lydians introduced pure silver and gold coins, in what is said to have been the first bimetallic coinage system in the world. When Croesus was captured by the Persians, the practice spread eastward. Two centuries later Philip II of Macedon, father of Alexander the Great, minted gold coins in honor of his personal triumph in chariot racing; this was one of the first known cases of propaganda coinage. His son Alexander later seized and coined the fallow stocks of Persian treasury gold, setting a fixed exchange rate of ten pieces of silver per one piece of gold. In Rome there

was endless political struggle over gold, with Augustus Caesar introducing pure gold coinage, Nero soon debasing the metal, and later emperors
trying and failing to use gold as a hedge against inflation. But Constantine
introduced the gold *solidus* coin, which remained in use for the staggering period of seven centuries after his death. New gold coins came into
use throughout the Middle Ages. In 1450 Europe suffered from a shortage
of gold, but was rescued by the Portuguese, who imported new supplies
of the metal via Ghana and Mali. Yet these new supplies only decreased
the value of gold while empowering silver, leading to a boom in European silver mines. In the sixteenth century Spain shipped abundant New
World gold back to Europe, first by robbing the Aztecs and Incas, then by
establishing mines of its own. The plundered Native Americans had been
more charmingly practical, often using cocoa beans as currency alongside
gold dust. The Incas possessed large quantities of gold and silver but used
none of it as money, which was absent from their social system. In 1599
the value of pepper briefly exceeded that of gold, because of the success of
the Dutch in dominating the pepper market. In the seventeenth century
British goldsmiths begin to accept valuables for safekeeping, beginning
their slow evolution into bankers; goldsmiths' deposit slips would later
transform into paper currency. In 1699 one hundred years after the height
of the Dutch pepper monopoly, Sir Isaac Newton became England's master of the mint. The psychotic Newton took perverse delight in hanging
counterfeiters, but also shifted the major output of the mint from silver
coins to gold. In post-Revolutionary America, silver and gold were the
only permissible legal tender. Britain established a gold standard in 1816
and introduced the gold sovereign coin. The American gold rush of 1848
produced enough gold to put an effective end to the bimetallic standard
of United States currency. The discovery of gold in Australia in 1851 vastly
increased world supplies of the metal. In 1865 France, Italy, Belgium, and
Switzerland formed a largely forgotten Latin Monetary Union, in which
gold and silver coins from any of these countries were valid in the others.
In 1871 newly unified Germany adopted the gold standard. Japan made
the same move just before 1900. But shortly thereafter, in 1931, Britain
and most of the Commonwealth abandoned gold in a move away from
classical economics, leaving France and the United States briefly in possession of 75 percent of world supplies. In 1971, with American gold reserves

dwindling, President Richard Nixon ended the convertibility of the dollar into gold, paving the way for American withdrawal from the gold standard altogether in the oil embargo year of 1973.[30]

Gold can be mined harmlessly in small quantities through romantic gold rush techniques such as panning and sluice-boxing, activities still available at numerous tourist sites. But when pursued at industrial scale, gold mining is an enterprise filled with personal and environmental hazard. Though cyanide is usually linked with mass or high-profile suicides, the main purpose of this fearful chemical is to assist in dissolving gold and silver during the mining process. The toxic effects on the environment are inevitable, even when the cyanide occurs in low concentrations. It is of course little better when mercury is amalgamated with gold as a means of extracting it, since once this is done the mercury must be boiled away, creating dangerous vapors. An estimated 11 percent of atmospheric mercury in the United States is the result of gold mining (though this admittedly pales before the 40 percent of mercury vapors generated by coal-fired power plants). Finally, gold mining poisons the environment through the simple proximity of gold to dangerous heavy metals that are pulverized along with the gold ore and left behind as groundwater-tainting rubble.

As of 2010 the world's leading gold producer was China, followed by Australia and the United States. But over the previous century, South Africa had been King of Gold, though the politically tense former outlaw nation has now slipped into fourth place globally. But South Africa still boasts the world's deepest gold mine, more than two miles underground: "Not surprisingly, conditions at its depths are hellish. The commute down takes more than an hour. The rock itself can reach 140 degrees Fahrenheit and occasionally explodes."[31] The massive mine shaft elevators move up to 120 miners using cables up to 10,000 feet long. The walls of the mine must be sprayed with concrete-steel mixtures to prevent them from bulging and bursting. Ventilation fans are gigantic, as required by the sweltering temperatures at a depth far greater than any human was meant to visit. My friend the journalist Graeme Wood of the *Atlantic* reports on the mine as follows: "I have actually been to the deepest part of it, which is absolutely Dantesque in its horror. The heat is like summer in Sharjah. It's dark, and since the space is so tight that you must wriggle on your belly, your sweat quickly mingles with dirt and covers you with a filthy salty mud-slime. To move from place to place a man your size or mine must crawl through spaces so tight that you could barely lift your head to see the boot soles of the person crawling ahead of you."[32]

The reward for the builders of this underground hell is the ability to spend $550 per ounce to retrieve the gold while selling it for $1,300. The owner of the dismal mine is AngloGold Ashanti, a new hybrid name for a company that in 2004 merged AngloGold and the Ashanti Goldfields Corporation, a conglomerate approved by the High Court of Ghana but based in Johannesburg. As one might expect of a juggernaut mining operation, AngloGold Ashanti has earned little praise from observers of corporate ethics. In fact, Human Rights Watch issued a 159-page report titled "The Curse of Gold,"[33] accusing the company's Congo operations of paying off warlords infamous for large-scale atrocities.[34] The antipoverty group War on Want reports ominously from Colombia of "murders of trade union and community leaders who oppose the company's activities in the region."[35] Singled out by Greenpeace as the "Most Irresponsible Company in the World," AngloGold Ashanti is even more reviled by GhanaWeb Business News, which calls it "the World's Most Evil Company."[36] At the Davos ceremony where this backhanded honor was announced, AngloGold critic Daniel Owusu Koranteng "told of mining waste that contaminates rivers and wells from which entire villages must drink." Beyond this, "local residents particularly at the Obuasi mine, were occasionally tortured at the mining firm's guard house; some cases resulted in deaths." And even worse, "some of the violations included the use of Guard Dogs to chew suspects who trespass on the company's concession. . . . In some cases, suspects were shot by a combined team of the AGC security, the police and the military." In one specific case, "Awudu Mohammed . . . was shot by a security team made up of the security of AngloGold Ashanti and police on 20th June 2005 resulting in his intestines gushing out. Even at the point when he was in a critical condition, the security team used their boots to hit his head several times."[37] The gold in your teeth and your rings may have been mined in ancient Egypt or Bulgaria, or it may have been the product of recent South African apartheid. Either way, it is likely that blood was shed and throats were slashed to produce, refine, or acquire it at some stage in its history. Yet that gold will sparkle in the courts of the queens of Mars, Europa, and Titan long after the suffering miners of earth have turned to dust.

Conclusion

We have followed gold in its remarkable career from the primordial eons of the universe to social and political effects as recent as the past eight thousand years. Too exotic to be produced by the Big Bang or the normal life cycle of stars, gold is a relative latecomer generated only in stellar explosions. It lingered in prestellar clouds and landed on earth during the planet's formation, only to sink to oblivion in the planetary core. Gold then returned to earth during its bombardment by asteroids, scattered across the planet's now-hardened surface in the form of dust. Through the work of bacteria and geothermal circulation it was concentrated in veins, and later released as nuggets in streams and mountainous regions. With the rise of humans, gold enjoyed a new career because of its aesthetic allure and practical utility for our complicated species. Gold has been shaped into religious artifacts and used to depict the haloes of saints in Italian churches. As a nonradioactive Group 11 element, along with copper and silver, it has provided a basis for coinage—soft enough to serve as a receptacle for the images of the vain and the proud, yet durable enough to endure across the millennia. Eaten and drunk by the curious, filling the teeth of dental patients, and enhancing the works of microcircuitry, gold has used its efficiency and luster to capture the hearts of Bronze Age, medieval, and modern artisans.

Abandoned by Keynesians and Richard Nixon as the ultimate standard of currency, gold lives on as decorative jewelry and in the nostalgic reveries of conservative economists. Gold drove the conquistadors to their doom and filled California with those wild visionaries who even now set American trends and produce the movies that dominate the dreams of the globe. Gold drifts horizontally across the earth, toward the treasure houses of empires or the polytheistic households of India graced with swastika, crescent, and cross. It bewitches the security apparatus of darkest Africa, with its guard dogs, beatings, shootings, and exploited miners. Gold summons the cyanide just as pine trees call down the lightning. It is released from the earth in the company of toxic metals that poison the streams and destroy frogs, birds, and indigenous peoples. Gold forms the rings and necklaces given to your truest love; it commemorates your weddings, your scientific breakthroughs, your Olympic champions, your remembrance of whatever happened fifty years ago. It is the king of your dreams and the alibi of your noble lies.

At the start of this chapter, I said that object-oriented philosophy is governed by two basic principles: (1) objects have genuine reality at many different scales, not just the smallest, and (2) objects withdraw from all types of relation, whether those of human knowledge or of inanimate causal impact. Gold has helped us to reinforce these two points. As DeLanda noted in the passage above, not all statements about gold are statements about atoms of gold, and not all higher-level properties of gold emerge at the same higher scale. Instead, gold displays new properties as we reach larger and larger aggregates of the metal. It changes its color, its melting point, its conductivity, and its status as a chemical catalyst, depending on the amount or conditions of the gold of which we speak. When deposited on a cooling planet, the role of gold is to sink to the core. Nor is there any reason to limit our discussion to various scales of the *nonhuman* world. At various human scales, gold also displays shifting properties. In a Bulgarian village it can form simple artifacts. In Pharaonic Egypt it can be shaped into sarcophagi that move from tombs to museums to international cargo containers as they age. Later it becomes dental filling. Still later, it turns into a luxury beverage or microcircuitry. Eventually it becomes an attractor for cyanide and mercury vapor and thus for human disease, not to mention an attractor for hazardous wage slavery in Colombia, Congo, and Ghana. But we cannot say that these higher-level properties of gold are any less real than the basic properties of gold atoms, since the features of these atoms emerge in turn from even darker depths of the physical world. Smallness and simplicity are not what constitute reality.

But neither should anyone claim that these new properties of gold exist *only* in their effects on humans and other entities. Gold is not merely a series of effects or events that lack a unified underlying agent. The lustrous and ductile element 79 may be refined and priced through the congealing of human labor, but it cannot be *generated* by such labor—only a supernova can build it. Humans cannot find gold when and where they wish, but must expend countless efforts searching in mountain veins and spilling cyanide in the ground in order to coax out small amounts of gold. Nor is gold reducible to our sufferings in producing it, since it will retain its value for humans long after the victims of gold have disappeared. We cannot do as we wish, but gold makes us do as it wishes. Even the beauty of gold is not entirely in the eye of the beholder, since the physics of relativity already anoints gold and platinum as special through the distorted radii of their valence electrons. And finally, we cannot say that gold is reducible to its environmental effects on other inanimate beings. Gold reflects different wavelengths of light when found in nanoparticle form than when grouped into veins, chunks, nuggets, or on the surface of a green-lit planet called Kripke. These effects of the gold are real, but they are not dependent on the entities with which they interact. Gold nanoparticles need photons to be red, but the photons are not free to make them red, blue, or white at random; nor is this gold exhausted by these photons, since it has properties not dreamed of by what merely makes it red. Like every object, gold takes on different forms at different scales of interaction and always has secrets in store for whatever tries to exhaust it. Immanuel Kant's example of an obvious philosophical truth, "gold is a yellow metal," should have been reformulated as "gold is an inscrutable object existing at countless layers of reality simultaneously."

Notes

1. As far as I can tell from my computer files, I first began using the term *object-oriented philosophy* in late 1997. On page 93 of *Towards Speculative Realism: Essays and Lectures* (Winchester, U.K.: Zero Books, 2010), I stated that the first occurrence of the term in my writings was in a September 11, 1999, conference paper at Brunel University, Uxbridge, United Kingdom. But it was then pointed out, to my surprise, that "object-oriented philosophy" already occurs in the March 1999 PhD thesis version of my debut book, *Tool-Being: Heidegger and the Metaphysics of Objects* (Chicago: Open Court, 2002), and further searches of computer files then showed that I was using the phrase at least as early as the end of 1997.

2. For a concise overview of the principles of object-oriented philosophy, see *The Quadruple Object* (Winchester, U.K.: Zero Books, 2011). In France, the surprising object-oriented turn was spearheaded by Tristan Garcia's impressive *Forme et objet: Un traité des choses* (Paris: PUF, 2011).

3. See the first half of Bruno Latour, *The Pasteurization of France,* trans. C. Porter (Cambridge, Mass.: Harvard University Press, 1988).

4. Karl Marx, *Das Kapital* (Washington, D.C.: Regnery, 2009).

5. See Wesley Phillips, "The Future of Speculation?," *Cosmos and History* 8.1 (2012): 298, http://www.cosmosandhistory.org/index.php/journal/ article/ viewFile/259/444.

6. An oft-cited introduction to the topic of nuclear fusion in stars is Rudolf Kippenhahn, Alfred Weigert, and Achim Weiss, *Stellar Structure and Evolution* (New York: Springer, 2012).

7. Frank Crary, "The Origin of the Solar System," http://nineplanets.org/origin.html (accessed May 15, 2012).

8. Laila Battison, "Meteorites Delivered Gold to Earth," *BBC News,* September 8, 2011, http://www.bbc.co.uk/news/science-environment-14827624.

9. Shanta Barley, "There's Gold in Them There Modified Bacteria," *New Scientist,* October 5, 2009. http://www.newscientist.com/article/dn17915-theres -gold-in-them-there-modified-bacteria.html.

10. Chris Ralph, "The Geology of Coarse Gold Formation," http://www.nuggetshooter.com/articles/CRGeologyofcoarsegoldformation.html.

11. Jean-Jacques Rousseau, *Basic Political Writings* (Indianapolis: Hackett, 1987), 61, 66.

12. "Varna—World's First Gold, Ancient Secrets—Pointe-à-Callière, Montréal Museum of Archaeology and History," http://pacmusee.qc.ca/en/exhibitions/ varna-worlds-first-gold-ancient-secrets (accessed May 15, 2012).

13. "Bronze Age Gold. Ulster Musem—National Museums Northern Ireland," http://www.nmni.com/um/Collections/Archaeology/Bronze-Age/Bronze-Age -Gold (accessed May 15, 2012).

14. John Marshall, *Mohenjo-Daro and the Indus Civilization* (London: Arthur Probsthain, 1931), 30.

15. "FAQ's—Investment—World Gold Council," http://www.gold.org/investment/why_how_and_where/faqs/ (accessed May 15, 2012).

16. RonK of Seattle, "How Much Is Ten Trillion Dollars, Really?," http://www .dailykos.net/archives/002779.html (accessed May 15, 2012).

17. "Association: India Gold Reserves in the World 11%," http://www.thehaveninqatar.com/2011/09/association-india-gold-reserves-in-the-world-11/ (accessed May 15, 2012).

18. "Gold (color)," http://en.wikipedia.org/wiki/Gold_(color) (accessed May 15, 2012).

19. "What Causes the Colors of Metals like Gold?," http://www.webexhibits .org/causesofcolor/9.html (accessed May 15, 2012).

20. The go-to source for specialists is Pekka Pyykkö, *Relativistic Theory of Atoms and Molecules,* 3 vols. (New York: Springer, 2001). But a good summary is also available in "The Chemistry of Gold by M. Concepción Gomez, an excerpt from *Modern Supermolecular Gold Chemistry: Gold-Metal Interactions and Applications,* ed. A Laguna (Weinhem, Germany: Wiley-VCH Verlag, 2008), http://www .wiley-vch.de/books/sample/3527320296_c01.pdf.

21. Saul Kripke, *Naming and Necessity* (Cambridge, Mass.: Harvard University Press, 1980), 39.

22. Hazem Zohny, "Nanoscale Gold to Help Diagnose HCV Infection," http://www.nature.com/nmiddleeast/2011/110304/full/nmiddleeast.2011.27 .html (accessed May 15, 2012).

23. "Nanogold Does Not Glitter, but Its Future Looks Bright," *Science Daily,* http://www.sciencedaily.com/releases/2004/04/040428062059.htm (accessed May 15, 2012).

24. Manuel DeLanda, *Intensive Science and Virtual Philosophy* (London: Continuum, 2002), 40.

25. "George de Hevesy and Aqua Regia," http://thestrayworld.com/2011/05/29/george-de-hevesy-and-aqua-regia/ (accessed May 15, 2012).

26. "Edible Gold," http://www.delafee.com/index.php?cPath=48_57&page=ediblegold (accessed May 15, 2012).

27. "History of Allergen of the Year," http://www.contactderm.org/i4a/pages/index.cfm?pageid=3467 (accessed May 15, 2012).

28. "Gdansk's Goldwasser: Alchemical Elixir," http://www.gdansk-life.com/poland/goldwasser (accessed May 15, 2012).

29. Li-Yun Lin et al., "Acceleration of Maturity of Young Sorghum (Kaoliang) Spirits by Linking Nanogold Photocatalyzed Process to Conventional Biological Aging—a Kinetic Approach," *Food Bioprocess Technology* 1, no. 3 (2008): 234–45; S. Susmel, G. G. Guilbaut, and C. K. O'Sullivan, "Demonstration of Labelless Detection of Food Pathogens Using Electrochemical Redox Probe and Screen Printed Gold Electrodes," *Biosensors and Bioelectronics* 18, no. 7 (2003): 881–89.

30. Roy Davies and Glyn Davies, "A Comparative Chronology of Money: Monetary History from Ancient Times to the Present Day," http://economics.about.com/gi/o.htm?zi=1/XJ&zTi=1&sdn=economics&cdn=education&tm=20&f=10&su=p284.13.342.ip_&tt=2&bt=0&bts=0&zu=http%3A//www.ex.ac.uk/%7ERDavies/arian/amser/chrono.html.

31. Nick Wadhams, "Digging for Riches in the World's Deepest Gold Mine," *Wired,* http://www.wired.com/magazine/2011/02/ st_ultradeepmines/ (accessed February 28, 2011).

32. Graeme Wood, pers. comm., May 15, 2012.

33. Human Rights Watch report, "The Curse of Gold," http://www.hrw.org/reports/2005/06/01/curse-gold-0 (accessed May 15, 2012).

34. "D. R. Congo: Gold Fuels Massive Human Rights Atrocities," http://www.hrw.org/news/2005/06/01/dr-congo-gold-fuels-massive-human-rights-atrocities (accessed June 2, 2005).

35. "The 100 Most Powerful Women: #7 Cynthia Carroll, Chief Executive, Anglo American, U.K.," http://www.forbes.com/lists/2007/11/biz-07women_Cynthia-Carroll_4PVY.html (accessed May 15, 2012).

36. "AngloGold Is World's Most Evil Company," *GhanaWeb*, January 30, 2011, http://www.ghanaweb.com/GhanaHomePage/NewsArchive/artikel.php?ID=202199.

37. Ibid.

Chartreuse

ALLAN STOEKL

Light Green, Dark Green: Spectrum Disorder

The Carthusian monks are an ancient and venerable order, founded by St. Bruno in 1084, at what is still today their main abbey, the Grande Chartreuse in the Chartreuse Mountains, Jura, France—just to the north of Voiron. The site was chosen for its (at the time) profound isolation: it was known as the "desert of the mountains" because of its utter remoteness.[1] Indeed the order, as conceived by St. Bruno, was meant to accomplish what might seem impossible: to fuse hermetic life with the communal life of an established and official monastic discipline. The sanctity and rigor of the desert fathers would be melded with the established discipline of a religious organization. The site's remoteness would make possible the hermetic isolation, while the communal buildings would enable the monks to live and, most importantly, worship together.[2]

In their small cells, the monks spend their days praying in solitude; in the chapel, from 11:45 p.m. to 2:30 a.m. they chant the Night Vigil of Matins and Lauds, unaccompanied by musical instruments, each monk hidden from the view of others by wooden partitions. From 2:30 a.m. to 7:15, sleep; then private prayer until 8. This is followed by more prayers (Little Office of Our Lady) to 8:15, then Mass (which is repeated in the cell, since each monk is also a priest). After Mass, until 11:15, "the Carthusian Father devotes himself in his cell to spiritual exercises, prayer, reading and absorbing the Scriptures in *lectio divina*. No special methods of prayer are laid down: each monk is free to follow the path from which he expects to reap most fruit."[3] The Little Office of Our Lady at 11:15; then lunch at 11:30, delivered by a brother (one of the nonordained monks who provide for the needs of those who have taken the solemn vows), passed through an opening in the wall.[4]

And so it goes, with more prayer and quiet meditation, followed by vespers, and other carefully prescribed prayers, until bed at 8 p.m. (until 11:30 p.m., when the next day commences).

One is struck, when considering the lives of the Carthusians, above all by the absolute regularity and formulaic nature of the life of the "Solemn" monk (an ordained Carthusian who has taken his final vows). Only on Mondays are the monks to eat together, and to go out on short, pre-planned walks, each man talking with one other, until, after fifteen minutes, he moves in the line to be able to speak with another (all this under the direction of one of the monks).[5] Even recreation, in other words, is highly formalized and regulated. To say this, of course, is not to criticize the rules of the order; they are what they are, and have been, for over nine hundred years. Moreover, the monks live what we would call a "sustainable" life—in the earliest days, they were completely self-sustaining in their mountain retreat. They, and the brothers who made their lives possible, were "green" in the sense that the mountains they lived in were green: unlike the desert fathers, who were often fed in their caves or on their pillars by followers, devotees, bringing nourishment from afar, the Carthusians were completely shut off and sustained by the fertility of their desert.[6] For just as the Carthusians live a profound paradox—the hermetic community—they live in the paradox of a green and flourishing desolate waste. Abandoning society for the desert, they live together in a fragrant and rich mountain ecology, through the variations of summer, fall, winter, and spring: rain, wind, snow, and ice.[7]

But how can one *live* as a Carthusian? It is not enough to say that one must "believe in God"—that is obvious, but what, in a life like this, does belief mean, how is it lived? Of course the monks value their privacy, and so we are not in a position to ask them. But we can observe one thing: that the order is exclusive to a great degree because of its rigor. Fully 90–95 percent of novices drop out before final vows.[8] A life of solitude, with virtually no contact with others outside of the early morning chanting and the later morning Mass, and even that with no conversation, no looking, and then

with many hours alone in a cell pursuing one's private spiritual practices—
all this is extremely difficult. Nancy Klein Maguire, whose excellent book
An Infinity of Little Hours charts the trials of five novices in their attempt to
live the Carthusian life, has this to say of one of them:

> The noonday demon came and went, but when he was present,
> Dom Philip felt as if he would never leave. Dom Philip kept
> conversing with God, but was anyone listening? He wasn't sure:
> he felt parched. But he took comfort, as did the other monks, in
> the belief that the harder life got, the more you were progressing
> to God.[9]

This is after Dom Philip has spent a good bit of time in his cell, alone of
course, trying "to solve the riddle of the Trinity."[10] Failing in this, he gives
up reading . . .

Needless to say, the problem Dom Philip faces, as do many of the other
novices, is that he is trying to conform to a prescribed life that he finds,
in the end, intolerable. What does one do, alone, in the cell? Meditate on
theological mysteries, convinced that by doing so one can work out the
truth? Read and reread the same manuscripts? Copy over the same manuscripts? Make small wooden objects with the lathe in the cell? This is
clearly a life—a holy life, to be sure—that one can either sustain, or not.
No adaptation to it for easily comprehensible reasons—one does not want
to let down one's family, for example, or admit to them, or to one's friends,
that one has failed—will be sufficient to enable one to stay in an order this
rigorous.[11] In fact, in Maguire's account one of the monks literally wastes
away and is at the point of total physical collapse when he finally with-
draws from the monastery.[12]

It is clear that one either sustains, and is sustained by, this life, or not. It
is clear that one cannot, for whatever reason, force oneself to adapt to it.
Rather it can be argued that the life was formulated to allow certain individuals to live a spiritual existence. Sustainability and rigor are no doubt
linked—one does not survive indefinitely in the desert of the mountains
without a precise order, but likewise one can survive in the order only with
a precise need for order. It is an order strangely without order as well—a hermetic communitarian life whose hermeticism is both rigorously defined and

laid out, yet is open to individual activity ("No special methods of prayer are laid down") within the carefully circumscribed domain of structured prayer. Enclosure both within a space and within a procedure; openness to tailor that procedure to individual orientation and—dare one say it?—desire.

Perhaps this is the secret of the Carthusians' long-term sustainability (nine hundred years and counting), and of sustainability in the larger sense: radical freedom arising from carefully elaborated self-restraint.

Who would demand such a claustrophobic, rigorous, even perhaps rigid, yet free—abyssal, to the failed novices—set of practices? I would argue that the rigor of the Carthusian monastery is ideally suited to a person with autism, or Asperger's syndrome.

Temple Grandin, an authority on autism who is autistic herself, in her book *The Way I See It: A Personal Look at Autism and Asperger's,* has this to say about the rigidity of the autistic person:

> Rigidity in both behavior and thinking is a major characteristic
> of people with autism and Asperger's. They have difficulty
> understanding the concept that sometimes it is okay to break a
> rule. I heard about a case where an autistic boy had a severe injury
> but he did not leave his bus stop to get help.[13]

Grandin notes: "Children and adults on the autism spectrum are concrete, literal thinkers. Ideas that can't be understood through logic or that involve emotions and social relationships are difficult for us to grasp, and even more difficult to incorporate into our daily lives."[14] Grandin stresses that there are different kinds of ASD (autism spectrum disorder) thinkers: those who are visual, those who are musically and mathematically oriented, and those who are verbal logic thinkers.[15] In the case of verbal logic thinkers, Grandin writes: "These children love lists and numbers. Often they will memorize bus timetables and events in history. Interest areas often include history, geography, weather or sports statistics."[16]

If ASD people have a tendency to favor repetitive activities, and are often fascinated by repetition in the world (the movement of machines or the processes of mathematics or logic), they have, nevertheless, great difficulty grasping and reproducing the subtleties of unspoken social interactions. Grandin notes that as an autistic person her forte is intellectual complexity, not social complexity; her "emotions are all in the present."[17] ASD people often are extremely sensitive physically: to sound, to light, to the feeling of certain clothes.[18] Further, and most interesting, is the fact that they often have difficulty generalizing: they may think in details to such an extent that two objects "neurotypicals" would characterize with the same name do not seem the same at all:

> Dr. de Clercq described a boy who was using the toilet properly at home but would not use it at school. He would only use the toilet if the seat was black, a detail that had meaning to him but did not aid in forming the concept of *toilets*. For him, a toilet with a white seat was not recognized as a toilet.[19]

Jill Boucher in her book on autism writes of a "superior low-level processing as the most likely cause of a bias toward local as opposed to global processing."[20] But Grandin would probably add that if this processing is "local" in its intensity—in other words, those with ASD shy away from global statements and focus on very particular tasks and actions, rigorously repeated—at the same time it presents a certain valid perception that others, "neurotypicals," may miss. It certainly need not be "low-level." No doubt de Clerc's patient saw the truth of "toilets"—that indeed toilets with black seats are not the same as those with white seats. Even though this boy saw what might be called the truth, he had to learn, and eventually did learn, that a certain discounting was necessary: he came to conform to a rigorous external structure—language—ignoring its arbitrariness, even mendacity, while relying on its comforting aspect: that following its conventions, which (unlike other people) he had to explicitly learn, could make life easier and more productive. Grandin makes a strong case that people "on the spectrum" are as essential to society as neurotypicals:

> There is no black-and-white dividing line between computer nerds or geeks or [those with] Asperger's or high-functioning autism. And there will always be friction between the techies and the suits. The suits are the highly social people who rise to the top and become managers. However, they would have nothing to sell and no business to run if they lost all their techies.[21]

Given this, one cannot strictly speak of "disability" of those with ASD: they have certain needs, but can certainly make contributions to society every bit as important as the contribution of others. The two general types of individuals—techies and suits—need each other, and probably always have.

Thus the idea that many members of religious orders have all along been "on the spectrum" should not seem controversial. The church, too, has depended on the neurotypical-ASD interaction. John Gillibrand, an Anglican priest and author of a book considering the theological implications of ASD, writes:

> One could imagine that for a person with autism the high levels of structure within the daily monastic regime, the provision within that daily routine of productive work alongside the removal of the constant need to communicate with others could prove highly beneficial.[22]

The Carthusian order could therefore be characterized as an organization devoted to enabling ASD individuals to live, and flourish, in a social setting tailored to their needs. Their work—prayer, and the reading and copying of sacred texts—is as essential to the church as the work of "techies" is to a modern corporation. But I would argue that ASD is deeply coded not only within the Catholic Church but within modern philosophy as well: in the Kantian theory of the sublime, and in the theory of "deep ecology" that can be seen to derive from it. Further, the gap between deep ecology and a more superficial ecology—between dark and light green—may not be as profound as one might think.[23] Autism and its fellow traveler, the Kantian sublime, are integral to a philosophy of nature and of subjectivity within it; it was among the monks in the mountains a thousand years ago, and, in a different but still recognizable version, it still is today, among environmentalists and philosophers of ecology.

What is the link between autism and the sublime? We might recall that in Kant the sublime is not so much "in" the object—the waterfalls, the volcanoes, the galaxies that dwarf the individual—as in the reaction to "natural" (mathematical, dynamical) immensity or power on the part of the subject. Kant situates the sublime in the mind: "instead of the object it is rather the cast of the mind in appreciating it that we have to estimate as sublime."[24] And we should recall that it is not merely the mind but the means of the mind that leads to the pleasure of sublimity: Kant cites the movement by which eventually we arrive at the size of galaxies, and even the cosmos itself, through the derivation of "proportionately greater units."[25]

> The systematic division of the cosmos . . . represents our imagination in all its boundlessness, and with it nature, as sinking into insignificance before the ideas of reason, once their adequate presentation is attempted.[26]

Thus there is a final "pleasure . . . to find every standard of sensibility falling short of the ideas of reason."[27]

Thus we can say that Kant affirms the feeling of the sublime as situated in the subject rather than the object, and that the pleasure of the sublime—since the sublime entails a subjective "cast of mind"—is tied (rather than to a simple feeling of being overwhelmed ["sensibility"]) to a rational procedure involving, at least in the case of the mathematical sublime, *computation.*

I would argue that this is an autistic model of sublime pleasure: what the subject revels in, in its own stupendous magnitude, is its ability to compute. Its ability to make all the details, all the particles that can stand in for other particles, fit together. The sublime self is a techie self. Much like Grandin's techies, Kant's engage in an activity whereby reactions that might lead to a larger group or social experience—the awe-inspired group dance before the grandeur of the Grand Canyon, for example, or a night vigil under the spread of the Milky Way—are replaced by the putatively more genuine sublime of a cool rational and calculating activity, one that can be carried out by a trained expert alone in his or her room, working with measurements, scales, and (nowadays) computers. One does have the sense that by shifting the sublime from object to subject Kant manages to deritualize the sublime, taking it away from what inevitably are awestruck groups reacting to the immensity of their environment, and giving it to the self-pleasuring of the self-effacing individual expert.

We are not so far from the Carthusians as it might first seem. They of course live in community—as do we all—but their community life is solitary, and it is above all technical: they are the technicians of prayer, hewing carefully to the prescribed chants and recitations of the given day. True, for the most part they are not mathematicians, but their religion stresses the formal procedures out of which a faith can develop on an individual level. We are not that far from Blaise Pascal here, for whom the sublime of the infinitely great and small was terrifying, but who found relief and transcendence, and prescribed relief for others, in the carrying out of abstract religious duties: the sign of the cross, holy water, no doubt regular attendance at Mass. Pascal the great mathematician melded with Pascal the great religious thinker in his recognition of the "disproportion of man"—between two infinities—and the prescribing of ritual.[28] Kant goes Pascal one better only in that he proposes individualized mathematical rituals—the determination of what the sizes of the immensities are through abstract rituals of computation—to replace the ancient ritual of belief. But it is hardly surprising that Pascal himself was one of the greatest mathematicians in history and, dare one say—given his seclusion, seeming misanthropy, and single-minded contemplation/calculation—on "the spectrum."

One thinks of ASDs as well in Frances Ferguson's characterization of the sublime as not only a validation of one's own individuality but a validation of one's individuality as an absolute: as absolute freedom.[29] Just as ASDs in many instances dislike the unforeseen and the unforeseeable, and prefer the rigors of repetition, the Kantian sublime subjectivity, according to Ferguson, "comes increasingly to seem like a repudiation of all accidents."[30] Death comes to seem the ultimate sublime act, because it is the ultimate act of control: one's subjective will conquering what is most uncertain: one's own death. Ferguson writes:

> Thus when Schiller describes suicide, taking one's own death into one's hands, as the inevitable outcome of the logic of the sublime, he is of course right: the outcome of the subject's search for self-determination is not the achievement of absolute freedom in positive form but rather the achievement of a freedom from the conditions of existence by means of one's nonexistence.[31]

In the same way, the affirmation of sublime subjectivity for Ferguson is apocalyptic, in the sense that an affirmation of apocalypse entails "[thinking] the unthinkable and [existing] in one's own nonexistence."[32] One can certainly see (as did Friedrich Nietzsche) a version of willed nonexistence in monastic self-sacrifice, but today a radical self-sacrifice does not end at the monastery doors. Ferguson's essay dates from 1984, the era of the last, great fear of Cold War nuclear holocaust. But this hardly dates it; if the great obsession of the early eighties was the Bomb, nowadays ecological collapse—global warming, resource depletion, the complete destruction of a livable environment—is the paramount concern. And the role of the sublime—the spectrum of the Kantian autistic sublime—has not changed. Take, for example, the philosophy of deep ecology. Dark green. But what is dark green? If we turn to Arne Naess, the leading philosopher of this shade of the spectrum, we realize that it entails, precisely, the self-effacement of "man" with an affirmation of the overwhelming power of "his" technical, and calculating, abilities. In fact the pleasure of a restored environment for Naess will be part and parcel of a world where this ecological plenitude is enjoyed because of, and from the perspective of, the technical mastery of human inputs and outputs. In other words, the experience of the environ-ment and the calculation of the ecological footprint that allows humans to thrive in that environment will be one and the same, and inseparable from the retreat, if not the total extinction, of the human.

Naess condemns "shallow ecology" because its "central objectives," along with "[fighting] against pollution and resource depletion," are "the health and affluence of people in the developed countries."[33] But does the deep ecology alternative represent a turning away from the empire of the human, and of human subjectivity? On the contrary: one could argue that in Naess's future the human, in its technical mastery, will be all the stronger—totally dominant in fact—by virtue of its very withdrawal. Naess and George Sessions write: "The flourishing of human life and cultures is compatible with a substantial decrease of the human population. The flourishing of nonhuman life requires such a decrease."[34]

One imagines, as the Earth First! movement (influenced by "deep ecol-ogy") often does as well, a nature cleansed of Man, once again pristine, or tending in that direction. We will act against our own "interests," and in-stead of always affirming and facilitating human communities—no matter where and how numerous they might be—we will actually reduce or elim-inate them, if it is in the better interest of the "nonhuman world" as well as the human. But to imagine, and affirm, the world of the nonhuman is paradoxically to depend all the more on the calculating reason of the techie subjectivity. Naess and Sessions continue: "Policies must therefore be changed. These policies affect basic economic, technological, and ideological structures. The resulting state of affairs will be deeply different from the present."[35]

At this point one has the sense of coming full circle: "shallow ecology" as well put man at the center. But man was at the center there only in a superficial way, a "light green" way. It was human survival that was in question, but the easy human survival of more or less Western consumerist lifestyles, which would be ameliorated and made less lethal by an awareness of, and moderation of, the ecological footprint, tied perhaps to making manufacturing and distribution techniques more efficient as a way to increase profitability. The dark green alternative scorns this complacent emphasis on survival as usual and stresses the extirpation of the human as a tactic for larger ecological health—and survival. But that extirpation itself is dependent on a higher technical expertise and certainty; if it were not, it would appear most sinister. It is apocalypse against apocalypse: against what Naess implies is the light green apocalypse of business as usual with a little less waste leading inevitably to planetary die-off of humans *and* nonhumans, we have the affirmation of an apocalypse in which humans are evicted to make a larger survival possible. But note in the latter case that this eviction is inseparable from the exercise of a technical reason ("These policies affect basic economic, technological, and ideological structures"), which is all the stronger—is omnipotent—for its affirmation of the mortality, the radical separability, of the merely human. The sublime of apocalypse is now firmly situated in the "ideas of reason" of those capable of calculating sufficiently the indefinite survival of all species, in their current (or rather imagined, ideal) mix.

Both light and dark green, then, presuppose a precise calculation of externalized costs, the technical determination of the true cost of things, usually obscured in capitalist (and light green) economics: the ultimate power of the human lies not in the clear-cutting of forests or the amping up of the heat and violence of global climate systems—what gives us a more thorough *frisson* than contemplating the sublime dynamics of a nature whose inestimable, infinite violence is a product of mystified technical reason?— but in the power of reason to calculate all the inputs and outputs so that our carbon footprints can be effectively reduced, to that magic number, "one planet."[36] Worth stressing here is that to be totally calculable the earth's systems must be reformulated as finite. The calculable entails the measurable, which in turn entails eliminating the infinite, that is, all that cannot be reduced to a single number that goes into a formula. This is one thing that Kant did not seem to include in his theory of the sublime: that the infinite is not in fact reducible to simple calculation, that when measuring the size of the universe, for example, reason hits a limit and is left only with a nonknowledge of numbers and things (and hence Pascal, with his trembling before the two infinities, the infinitely large and the infinitely small, threatens to return).[37]

Thus in figuring external cost, which is really what the ecological footprint calculations are all about, we have to know everything: all the various carbon expenditures (for example) that go into the production of an article, or the carrying out of a human activity. All the things I buy, all the miles I drive, can be carefully calculated in terms of both monetary expenditure, and, behind that, energetic expenditure. Once I have determined that I know the true cost, I can reduce my expenditures accordingly. In the same way, once we have determined the real costs of the destruction of the Amazon we can stop it, reverse the damage, get all the people causing the problems in this fragile environment out of there. The pleasure, the satisfaction, will lie in the knowledge not only that we have "saved the earth" but that we have saved, and affirmed, the power of our technical reason, and subjectivity, affirming them precisely in the absence, the desert so to speak, of the human. In our very narrowly circumscribed sphere, in the death of the human as an overweening power on earth, we revel in our ultimate and sublime power.

It seems that we have come a long way from our Carthusians. They are still there in their monasteries, doing what they have always done, and they could not care less about what we do and say. They certainly are not concerned (at least as an order) with deep ecology; their theology is deep enough as it is.[38] They are on the spectrum—the autistic spectrum (at least some of them, probably), but also the spectrum of light green, deep green, and the sublime—they are God's techies, those who affirm the total technico-theological solution (prayer) to humanity's problems (or problem: damnation).

I want to stress that to recognize the autistic sublime—of deep (and related shallow) ecology, of the "techies" and the Carthusians, is not to pathologize it but, on the contrary, to recognize, in the calculating reason of its sustainability, its *necessity,* and thus affirm it. Technico-ecological reason, the dark green–light green spectrum disorder, provides us "suits" with the recognition of the withdrawal (or extinction) of the human, in the very affirmation of the human. Technical reason, in calculation, maybe even in prayer, may be a hope, for survival in and beyond apocalypse. But how do we arrive at that reason? And is its sublime the only game in town? Might there be another sublime, even another autism, that is inseparable from it? That is, in a sense, logically prior to it?

The Carthusians, through their liqueur, may point the way to this other sublime, to another relation to apocalypse, to another hue in the autistic-ecological spectrum: the color chartreuse.

Chartreuse: Disorder of the Spectrum

The Chartreuse is the mountainous area where the Grande Chartreuse is located. The Grande Chartreuse is the "Charterhouse" of the Carthusian order. Chartreuse, the liquor, has been produced by the monks of the Chartreuse, off and on in the midst of much drama (persecutions, expulsions), since 1737; its formula, secret to this day (known only by two monks), dates from 1605. The resulting liqueur, made from herbs found in the mountains around the Grande Chartreuse, is, of course, Chartreuse. This greenish (or yellowish) liqueur provides, through metonymy, the name for the green-yellow (or yellow-green) color, chartreuse, we recall with such fondness from our parents', or grandparents', 1950s living-room decor.[39] The Chartreuse elixir is described in this way on the official Chartreuse website:

> The Herbal Elixir de la Grande-Chartreuse
> Made by the Chartreuse Monks [sic] since 1737 according to the instructions set out in the secret manuscript given to them by Maréchal d'Estrées in 1605.
> The Herbal Elixir gets its unique flavour from 130 medicinal and aromatic plants and flowers. It is a cordial, a liqueur and a very effective tonic.

Ingredients : alcohol, sugar, plants and flowers.

Alcohol content : 69% (138° proof US)

Presentation : in a small bottle, itself placed in a wooden case which protects it from the light and makes sure it keeps perfectly.

Use: a few drops on a lump of sugar, straight, or in a little sugared water, as an infusion.[40]

Ah, that little bottle, with a kind of drip-spout—you take your Chartreuse with a spoon, like medicine.[41] (When it was introduced it was "used" as an infusion, for health: a "very effective tonic," whatever that means.) Pretty powerful stuff coming from those ascetic-autistic monks. Sixty-nine percent, that suggestive number, will get your head spinning, or at least confuse you a bit about what it was that hit you. And it comes in its own nice little cell, a "wooden case." Nowadays the elixir's younger siblings, Chartreuse Green (chartreuse-green in color) and Chartreuse Yellow (chartreuse-yellow in color) are apéritifs, and go well in all sorts of mixed drinks (according to the website).

So what is Chartreuse? The region? The order? (A Carthusian monk, in French, is a Chartreux. A Carthusian nun—and there is a convent—would be a Chartreuse.) The drink? (Which drink?) The color? All of the above, of course. But what is the color? Green? Yellow? Both? Neither? What I want to stress here is that Chartreuse functions as a metonym; each term is a "part" for a "whole," supposedly referring back to a "whole" referent, but really, when you look for that "whole," it is rather elusive. Your head starts to spin. Certainly the monastery, the Grande Chartreuse, is "in" the Chartreuse (the mountainous area). So it is part of it, in that sense. But the "desert of the mountains" is in itself not all that religious. They are green, to be sure (at least the part that is not rock colored), and everything on the metonymic spectrum I have just mentioned is part of that greenness, but they are also a desert, and deserts are not green. But the desert thing is a metaphor—or is it? And the drink, Chartreuse, is not all that religious either, though it is made by religious people (monks), at least two of them anyway (with a lot of help from layworkers), and the profits from its sale go to help the order. And the color, sort of green, sort of yellow, but tending toward the green, is also never fully identifiable as a part, because if there is a chartreuse that tends toward green, that "stands for" the color of

Chartreuse (the aperitif), it could do so only as long as that aperitif is green(ish) (ah, these nuances)—but there is also a yellow Chartreuse, and thus there is also a chartreuse color that looks more yellow than green.[42] Chartreuse the color is therefore double, each side a metonym of the other—or a metonym of itself (as double).[43] And then of course there is also the elixir, and a series of other Chartreuse drinks—there are even Chartreuse-filled candies. Confusing.

So we have a "spectrum disorder," not only of the color spectrum but of the spectrum of language as well. "Part for the whole" would seem to characterize, if nothing else does, the word *Chartreuse* (or *chartreuse*). But what is the whole? And where do we situate its parts? Where do we look for the whole? We are deep in what I would call the autism of language, not "disabled" language, or as Roman Jakobson would call it, "aphasic" language, but just language-language: the language where words are metonyms, but in their particularity, their fragmentation, enable us to lose sight of a whole.[44] A whole that in any case does not "exist." We think of the case of the autistic boy who did not realize that a toilet with a white seat was a toilet, since the only toilet he knew had a black seat. But what if the "toilet" itself, like Chartreuse (whatever that is) is a "whole" that allows us to forget only the decisive differences between things? What if there is an infinity of small things, a million little pieces, which can be linked only through deceptive figures of speech? This is the thesis of Nietzsche's famous essay "On Truth and Lie in a Nonmoral Sense."[45] And here we are back in the sublime: we stagger in our "disproportion," like Pascal, before the infinity of figures, within it, all those figures truthful but worthless in their particularity, and worthless in their generality as well, and realize that a "truthful" language would recognize only the vacuity of the whole: it is true, but it is not there, meaningless in its mendacious universality. Like Chartreuse.[46] There is no Kant to rescue us from this disproportion, to give form to the formless: where is the reason that will save us, the mathematical proportion that will allow us to create a coherent order of meaning, and master it? The autistic boy is, in the end, right: a toilet with a black seat is not at all the same thing as one with a white seat. To confuse the two is to lie— perhaps creating a useful lie, but a lie nonetheless. The word *toilet* causes us to forget more than it causes us to remember. Each thing is quite different, and the putative whole of which it is a part is illusory (but useful).

Without credence in the lie, the mastery of calculating reason is gone, and so is the mastery of sublime human (technical) agency.

And Chartreuse? That elixir has a real kick to it. It is details like that, that overwhelm everything. You get kind of confused. Uh . . . is that kick on a metonymic chain, a spectrum, with chaying and pranting—I mean praying and chanting? Kind of. Colors on the spectrum are linked metonymically, if you think of it. Each has a part of the next, can sort of stand for the next in line. To be a "kind of" the next color, the next shade. To be a color is to be on the spectrum, and to be on the spectrum is to be partly similar to the colors next in line. Red, red-orange, orange, orange-yellow, yellow, yellow-green—chartreuse—and so on. Chartreuse? Where exactly does it go, since it is double? Part of one color, part of another. Green, kind of. Yellow, kind of. Green-yellow, yellow-green, kind of. Not on the spectrum (we do not learn ROYCCGBIV) but still on it . . .[47]

A toilet, kind of. That "kind of" wrecks everything. We want a toilet to be a toilet, green to be green, then we could run the numbers, do the math, come up with the totality—but there are only shades, resonances, textures, timbres, sometimes too loud, incomparable qualities . . . Suddenly white is supposed to be black, light green may not really be all that different from dark green, one toilet seat's as good as another, "there's no difference." OK, fine, sure. But "chartreuse" is just a metonym for nothing left to lose.[48] We can cobble things together—meanings, objects, drinks—but they are always just metonyms on the way to the infinity of the spectrum, the overwhelming spectrum (overwhelming in its post-Kantian sublimity), an infinity that has little use for the rigor of our self-confident reason. How do I keep from noticing the color of the toilet seat?[49] Chartreuse is, then, among other things, a drink. It is quite material, quite delicious (if you like that kind of thing), quite intoxicating. It has a history. The Chartreuse (the "Grande," the monastery) was broken up during the French Revolution, and the secret of the formula of Chartreuse (the drink, or at least one of the drinks) got out. An M. Liotard, obviously not a monk, got hold of the formula. We learn from the Chartreuse website:

> In 1810, when the Emperor Napoleon ordered all the "secret" recipes of medicines to be sent to the Ministry of the Interior, Monsieur Liotard duly followed the law and submitted the

manuscript. It was returned to him marked "Refused." Refused as
not considered "secret," already well known.

When Monsieur Liotard died, his heirs returned the manuscript to the
Chartreuse monks who had returned to their monastery in 1816.[50]

The formula's secret was not a secret on at least one occasion (note the
scare quotes around "secret"): M. Liotard at least learned it, even though
he never did anything with it (he never distilled Chartreuse). The authorities considered it "not a secret." Chartreuse, in other words, was open
to the world all along, at least according to the authorities (who should
have known), open to reformulation, metonymization, bricolage, by others,
nontotalized in its "secret" totality.

Another Lyotard, Jean-François—maybe a relative?—recasts the sublime in light of a post-Kantian aesthetics. For this Lyotard, the mind's
integrity is suspended, if only for a moment, by a materiality that cannot
be reappropriated by the movement of an overarching reason. Materiality
unmoors from subjectivity, in other words, and the position of a human-
centered sublime—the sublime of human ratiocinative power—slips back
to a recalcitrant materiality. This is the postsublime of a materiality of the
spectrum, of the loss of the integrity of things through their incorporation
in a totality of the human. Lyotard writes:

> Within the tiny space occupied by a note or a color in the sound-
> or color-continuum, which corresponds to the identity-card for the
> note or the color, timbre or nuance introduce a sort of infinity, the
> indeterminacy of the harmonics within the frame determined by
> this identity. . . .
>   From this aspect of matter, one must say that it must be
> immaterial. Immaterial if it is envisaged under the regime of
> receptivity or intelligence. . . . The matter I'm talking about is
> "immaterial," an-objectable, because it can only "take place" or find
> its occasion at the price of suspending these active powers of the
> mind. . . . [This is] a mindless state of mind, which is required of
> mind not for matter to be perceived or conceived, given or grasped,
> but *so that there be* some something. And I use "matter" to designate
> this "*that there is*," this *quod*, because this presence in the absence of

the active mind is and is never other than timbre, tone, nuance in
one or other of the dispositions of sensibility.[51]

The spectrum of matter is disrupted, rendered formless, in its nuances;
Lyotard is doing nothing other than resituating the postsublime back "in"
matter itself, away from the mind—where it was for Kant. Lyotard's "mind-
less state of mind" is the affirmation of an active matter ("so that there be
some something") that escapes the dominion of the mind: a formlessness
situated in the nuances, the infinity of differences on the spectrum. What
Lyotard calls "sensibility" might be nothing more than that formlessness.
The infinity in question, I would argue, is the metonymic multiplicity of a
matter, all those "suggestive," nongraspable nuances that resist submission
on a hierarchy to an ultimate referent; it is on the contrary the an-hierarchic,
the anarchistic spectrum-fragment that "is" not only a sublime matter but
a generative matter presencing, but not reducible to, the very stuff that the
mind thinks it "knows" (all those toilets and colors . . .) and thinks it is
capable of rationally ordering.

Lyotard is talking about the *agency* of matter, and this active matter by
its very situation on and out of the spectrum resists easy quantification.[52]
Chartreuse is the color of a sustainability based not on the precise quantification of external costs—which is quite impossible, even if necessary[53]—
but on the recognition that externalities, like Lyotard's nuanced matter,
like the metonymic delirium of the spectrum, are generated in the very
impossibility of their calculation. What, for example, is the external cost
of the burial of casks of nuclear waste in the desert for ten thousand years?
How can one ever tally all the carbon inputs that go to make up even the
simplest commodity? The calculation of the ecological footprint, like the
characterization of the toilet, is a lie, a useful lie no doubt (and sometimes—like the lie concerning the toilet), but one whose light green–dark
green certitude sets reason up on a Kantian pedestal it can no longer fully
claim. Matter is not, alas, a straightforwardly quantifiable element, entirely
graspable through totalizing and totalized formulas, maintained in secret
and solitude by techie-experts.

It is a necessary but deluded hubris that claims to know the cost of
dangerous waste in the distant future.[54] The cost to whom, in what economy, what civilization? By recognizing the delirium of metonymy—the

delirium of the spectrum—the drunken Chartreuse-fueled dance of post-sustainability, matter reasserts itself as a post-technic postsublime, shows its agency ("that there is") in a way that resists, that threatens, the empire of human reason. Having done so, what is left of the human—the post-human—is free to consider the nuances of a (of all?) matter that can never be "thrown away," that can never fit into easy categories, either as trash or as definitively calculated external cost.

There may be two autisms, then—in metonymic relation? Two of an infinity of shades on the spectrum? One is the techie, so useful, so Kantian-sublime. The other is the metonymic, which is both generated out of, and gives the lie to, the techie. This second autism—inseparable from a doubled, nuance-sublime—somehow opens the possibility of matter ("that there is"), opens the possibility as well of all distinctions, of all spectrums. Chartreuse (representing here, through metonymy, the drunken movement of metonymy) acts on us, acts on the monks: in its concrete and unassimilable detail it is the force of a sacred, of another kind of ritual. Another kind of prayer?

On a rare occasion the monks leave the monastery for a daylong explore. On their return, a surprise:

> On this special day, the brothers left a four-ounce bottle of 110-proof green Chartreuse in the monks' hatches with a summer supper of sardines on toast and a salad. Dom Ignatius enjoyed feeling the diminutive cork against his forefinger and the convex bottom of the glass bottle in the palm of his hand.[55]

Notes

1. Un Chartreux, *La Grande Chartreuse* (Grenoble: Auguste Côte, 1882), 2, 7.

2. Ibid., 30–32.

3. Robin Bruce Lockhart, *Halfway to Heaven: The Hidden Life of the Carthusians* (Kalamazoo, Mich.: Cistercian Publications, 1999), 59.

4. Generally, all members of the Carthusian order who have taken their final vows are called "monks." There is, however, quite frankly a caste system in the order (as there is in the Trappist order [James Bianco, *Voices of Silence: Lives of the Trappists Today* (New York: Anchor Books, 1992), 136–39]): one group of monks, those whom I generally refer to in this chapter as "monks," and who spend most of their time either in choir or in their cells, are "fathers"—that is, ordained

priests. Thus they can go to Mass, and later on the same day say Mass in their own cells. On the other hand, the "brothers," also members of the order, are not ordained. These brothers, often in earlier times illiterate, did (and do) the basic work of cooking, farming, haircutting, tailoring of habits, and so on. The brothers are identifiable by their beards. Maguire throughout her book (see note 5, below) refers to the father-monks as "Solemns," in that they have taken the final (solemn) vows. When I use the term *monks* here, it is to refer to these Solemns. In its description of the two monks responsible for the mixing of the 130 herbs that go to make Chartreuse, the distillery website notes that one is a father (Dom Benoît) and one is a brother (Brother Jean-Jacques). It thus seems that, today at least, there are Solemns who occupy themselves with tasks other than prayer in the cell (http://www.chartreuse.fr/how-chartreuse-is-made-today;article;66;uk.html [accessed May 23, 2012]).

5. Nancy Klein Maguire, *An Infinity of Little Hours: Five Young Men and Their Trial of Faith in the Western World's Most Austere Monastic Order* (New York: Public Affairs, 2006), 81–82.

6. Today the Carthusian order is "sustained" financially through the sales of Chartreuse liqueur, whose production is supervised by several monks. In earlier days, they made money by iron mining, and smelting, with wood from the mountains, converted to charcoal, fueling the process. They also sold and felled particularly straight trees for use as ship's masts. For all their withdrawal from the world, then, the monks from the earliest days have also been economically integrated in it. See http://www.chartreuse.fr/economic-activities;article;42;uk.html (accessed May 24, 2012).

7. This is shown very beautifully in the film *Into Great Silence* (dir. Philip Gröning; 2007). Do not watch this film, however, expecting to learn much, or hear much from, the Solemns; the majority of the monks shown in action are actually either novices or brothers. It will take more than a movie to get the "Solemn" monks to talk!

8. Maguire notes that, at the Parkminster Charterhouse in England, of twenty novices in 1960, by 1965 only two remained. Of these two, one went on to take the final vows (*Infinity of Little Hours,* 206).

9. Maguire, *Infinity of Little Hours,* 163.

10. Ibid., 162.

11. Dom Damian—in lay life Chuck—eventually returns to the United States from Parkminster Charterhouse with his father. Maguire writes: "He [Chuck] had left the States a hero and now, a twenty-five year old man, he could not return without his father" (*Infinity of Little Hours,* 205–6).

12. Ibid., 202–3.

13. Temple Grandin, *The Way I See It: A Personal Look at Autism and Asperger's* (Arlington, Tex.: Future Horizons, 2008), 37.

14. Ibid., 143.

15. Ibid., 15–17.

16. Ibid., 17.

17. Ibid., 148.

18. Ibid., 77.

19. Ibid., 199–200.

20. Jill Boucher, *The Autistic Spectrum: Characteristics, Causes, and Practical Issues* (Los Angeles: Sage, 2009), 195.

21. Grandin, *Way I See It,* 224.

22. John Gillibrand, *Disabled Church—Disabled Society: The Implications of Autism for Philosophy, Theology, and Politics* (London: Jessica Kingsley, 2010), 67.

23. Immanuel Kant, *Critique of Judgement,* trans. James Creed Meredith (Chicago: Encyclopedia Britannica, 1990).

24. Ibid., 500.

25. Ibid., 501.

26. Ibid.

27. Ibid.

28. Blaise Pascal, *Pensées sur la religion et quelques autres sujets,* ed. Louis Lafuma (Paris: Delmas, 1960). In the Lafuma edition, section 199, Pascal writes: "Notre intelligence tient dans l'ordre des choses intelligibles le même rang que notre corps dans l'étendue de la nature" (the mind for Pascal is not somehow superior to the physical realm, but parallel to it [it is as out of proportion to the two infinities—of great and small—as the human body is]).

29. Frances Ferguson, "The Nuclear Sublime," *Diacritics* 14, no. 2 (1984): 4–10.

30. Ibid., 6.

31. Ibid.

32. Ibid., 7.

33. Arne Naess, "The Shallow and the Deep, Long-Range Ecology Movement: A Summary," in *The Deep Ecology Movement: An Introductory Anthology,* ed. Alan Drengson and Yuichi Inoue (Berkeley: North Atlantic Books, 1995), 3.

34. Arne Naess and George Sessions, "Platform Principles of the Deep Ecology Movement," in *The Deep Ecology Movement: An Introductory Anthology,* ed. Alan Drengson and Yuichi Inoue (Berkeley: North Atlantic Books, 1995), 49.

35. Ibid., 50.

36. Famously, the typical American consumes resources at a rate that, if it were generalized throughout the world, would require six planets to provide for all inhabitants (Mathis Wackernagel and William E. Rees, *Our Ecological Footprint:*

Reducing Human Impact on the Earth [Gabriola Island, B.C.: New Society Books, 1996]). Fully accounting for all the external (energetic) costs of our individual consumption, as these two authors recommend, will in principle help us understand how to calibrate (and downsize) our personal consumption to the scale of only one "planet." Thus Wackernagel and Rees's book is concerned primarily with indicating how the reader can calculate, based on various precise measurements, his or her "footprint."

37. Of course in all this one can argue that Pascal and Kant are also manifesting ASD symptoms—identifying authors as autistic is (too) easy (and fun), but it can also produce some interesting insights. See Julie Brown, *Writers on the Spectrum: How Autism and Asperger Syndrome Have Influenced Literary Writing* (London: Jessica Kingsley, 2010).

38. The Carthusians would probably leave such concerns to the Jesuits, or the Dominicans.

39. Metonymy rules in the case of Chartreuse (or chartreuse), because metonymy most often indicates two objects, constituting a whole, separate but associated. This might include cause for effect, thing for location, location for thing, and so on. On metaphor, metonymy, and synecdoche, see Paul Ricoeur, *The Rule of Metaphor: Multi-Disciplinary Studies in the Creation of Meaning,* trans. Robert Czerny (London: Routledge and Kegan Paul, 1978), 55–59. Thus Chartreuse (the drink) is a metonym for Chartreuse (the location), and so on. But one could just as easily reverse this and say that the location is a metonym for the drink. The typical use of "green" for ecology is an obvious case of metonymy, a physical to moral link, where the color of an object (e.g., a leaf) comes to stand for a moral stance or a morally charged discourse ("ecology," "conservation").

40. http://www.chartreuse.fr/elixir-vegetal;fiche;5;uk.html (accessed May 23, 2012).

41. One irony of the spectrum of chartreuse colors is that the actual color of the Chartreuse elixir (the "original" Chartreuse) is not chartreuse at all but . . . dark green.

42. See the Wikipedia entry for the color "chartreuse": Chartreuse green-yellow is called for some reason "web color"—though it is more or less the color of the (green) Chartreuse—and yellow-green chartreuse is called "traditional," even though yellow Chartreuse (the aperitif) was first produced more than one hundred years after green Chartreuse (http://en.wikipedia.org/wiki/Chartreuse [accessed May 24, 2012]).

43. I am using *metonym* in its most general sense here—one could see the relations of colors (and toilets, in the white seat–black seat problem) technically as synecdoches of each other, if one assumes that the "part for whole" relation is

synecdochic rather than metonymic. Since one can never definitively separate one color from another, each arbitrarily defined color will represent part of another ("next to it," in contiguous relation), "stand for it," in a sense. But synecdoche is often seen as a subcategory of metonymy, and for a good reason: thing for location (for example), is both metonymic (relation of things that are completely separate, one standing for the other conceptually) *and* synecdochic (part for whole). Chartreuse liqueur and the monastery of the Grande Chartreuse are certainly separate things, but one can find the liqueur if one goes into the monastery—it is part of it, the larger "whole" (for the moment, at least, until a monk consumes it).

44. Recall that for Jakobson, aphasia tending toward metonymy was associated with the literary genre of realism: the overburdening of metonymic detail was both a symptom of a speech disorder and the defining feature of the descriptive axis of prose. See Roman Jakobson, "Two Aspects of Language and Two Types of Aphasic Disturbances," in *On Language*, ed. Linda Waugh and Monique Monville-Burston (Cambridge, Mass.: Harvard University Press, 1990), 115–33.

45. Friedrich Nietzsche, "On Truth and Lie in a Nonmoral Sense," in *Philosophy and Truth: Selections from Nietzsche's Notebooks of the Early 1870s*, ed. and trans. Daniel Breazeale (Atlantic Highlands, N.J.: Humanities, 1979), 79–91.

46. Un Chartreux in *La Grande Chartreuse* informs us (31) that the name of the Chartreuse mountains was taken from St. Pierre-de-Chartrousse and/or Chartrosse (the original spelling[s]). But he does not tell us where St. Pierre got its first Chartrousse (and/or Chartrosse) from; yet more metonyms trail off into the mountain haze.

47. For David Batchelor, in his brilliant book *Chromophobia*, the strangely nameless (to him, anyway) color between yellow and green is emblematic—a metonymy—of the impossibility of "holding the entire disorganized and antagonistic mass" of a given color in the "prim cage" of a word (*Chromophobia* [London: Reaktion Books, 2000], 91–92). It is almost as if Batchelor refuses to recognize that there is already a word, *chartreuse*, a metonym, for this (doubled, multiple) color, and for the failure of the coherent figures and figuration of the spectrum. He prefers mystery, or unknowing, or not-knowing, to the ritual-autistic-sublime history of the word (and perhaps he is right: a word trailing off into metonymic infinity points to its self-erasure). My thanks to Jeffrey Cohen for calling my attention to Batchelor's book.

48. Just as "green" is one metonym—among many—for conservation.

49. Of course the boy who associated the toilet seat for the toilet was the victim of a metonymy disorder—he was confusing the part (the color of the seat) for the whole (the toilet). A delirium of metonymy (or synecdoche, if you want to be a stickler) that was also "true": a black-seated toilet is not a white-seated one.

50. http://www.chartreuse.fr/history-of-the-liqueurs;article;40;uk.html (accessed May 23, 2012).

51. Jean-François Lyotard, *The Inhuman*, trans. Geoffrey Bennington and Rachel Bowlby (Stanford, Calif.: Stanford University Press, 1991), 140.

52. On the agency of matter, see above all the superb book by Jane Bennett, *Vibrant Matter: A Political Ecology of Things* (Durham, N.C.: Duke University Press, 2010). Cary Wolfe, for his part, in his book *What Is Posthumanism?*, has linked autism—and he cites Grandin—to a "multidimensionality that cannot be calculated" (*What Is Posthumanism?* [Minneapolis: University of Minnesota Press, 2010], 142). Perhaps eventually one could link the sublime of externalities to an autism of ethical acts beyond (or below) any concern for a calculable reciprocity.

53. Balking before this duality is no more necessary than refusing the fact that autism, a "disability," is nevertheless an access to *both* a technical sublime of calculation and a material postsublime of incalculable externalities (in the infinite proliferation of metonymies).

54. I write "necessary" because the only alternative to the techie calculation of the "carbon footprint" is a world of naive refusal of the material consequences of overconsumption in all its dimensions: one thinks of global warming deniers, and so on. There may be a need, however, given the fundamental limitation of the ecological-autistic-sublime that I have indicated, to recognize the necessity of carbon footprint calculation as an *aftereffect* of a larger "tendency to expend," one that fully affirms the delirium—and desire—of a recalcitrant metonymic, and postsustainable, world. On this, see Allan Stoekl, *Bataille's Peak: Energy, Religion, Postsustainability* (Minneapolis: University of Minnesota Press, 2007). I write "deluded" because the belief (and it is a belief, more than anything else) that rigorous sustainability calculation, presupposing a closed system, a "restrained economy" of inputs and outputs, is sufficient in and of itself to resolve the current "ecological crisis" is bound to be mistaken.

55. Maguire, *Infinity of Little Hours*, 96.

Greener

VIN NARDIZZI

The linguistic stem of my title is now a vital "keyword on the order of 'gender,' 'sexuality,' 'nation,' 'race,' and 'ethnicity'—words that dominated looking, listening, reading, and critical thinking during the last third of the twentieth century."[1] Green has reached this status in the twenty-first century because it is a "totemic color for popular environmentalism as well as for ecocritical inquiry,"[2] and it remains the recognizable hue of nature's beauty.[3] To wit, I teach students excerpts from *The Green Studies Reader: From Romanticism to Ecocriticism* (2000) and *Green Shakespeare* (2006); I could readjust my daily habits with the help of *365 Ways to Live Green: Your Everyday Guide to Saving the Environment* (2008); and I visited the Greenpeace booth on Earth Day 2012 in Vancouver, British Columbia, which, according to Mayor Gregor Robertson, aspires by 2020 to be "the greenest city in the world."[4] In its many guises, then, popular environmentalism (from Earth Day booths to how-to guides for saving the planet) and certain strands of literary ecocriticism offer "green hope" for a future (or a back to the future) in which "a healthy relationship between human beings and the natural world" obtains, usually within the confines of a normative family structure.[5] We can go farther and regard ecodiscourses and practices that wash their advertising campaigns in a green sheen as symptomatic of "Savanna syndrome," a model in sociobiology that posits that members of *Homo sapiens* have "remade the wooded landscapes of Europe and North America in the image of East Africa" because they prefer to dwell in verdant spaces resembling the short-grass savanna where their ancestors evolved.[6]

According to such logic, green articulates a genetic fantasy dreamed by white privilege.[7]

My title, of course, intensifies the rubric green. I do so to mark a distinction from its usages in the ecodiscourses and practices sampled above. The intensification, however, does not call us to imagine and to implement ever more sustainable living habits, whether at the personal, the institutional, the national, or the global level. For as a number of ecocritics have demonstrated, in both scientific and popular literatures, sustainability—that sweet spot of equilibrium that many of us hope will be achieved for the sake of the planet's health—is actually a "vague,"[8] "wildly optimistic,"[9] and "diluted"[10] "pipe dream" of "green pastures"[11] that capitalism has generated to sustain its own development and to safeguard its own hegemony.[12] So invasive and pervasive are sustainability's tendrils, as Stacy Alaimo observes, they have "smoothly co-opted and institutionalized" "environmentalism as a social movement."[13] Sustainability's official badge is green, and in our cultural moment this badge functions as shorthand for environmentalism's goals. In contrast, as this chapter's discussion of ecoapocalyptic science fiction details, *greener* encompasses for me the dire ecological conditions and the unsustainable inequities that motivate and are further produced by attempts to stimulate "green" economies on a global scale. However well meaning, such attempts can also contribute to and trigger unexpected ecological catastrophe. I am calling the tint of such catastrophe "greener."

My direct inspiration for theorizing greener is Ward Moore's long-forgotten midcentury American novel *Greener Than You Think* (1947).[14] I came across a synopsis of it in Mike Davis's *Ecology of Fear,* which on its back cover describes Los Angeles "as a Book of the Apocalypse theme park." In Davis's summary, the "novel is about the lawn that ate Hollywood. It is, by turns, the funniest and the most frightening Los Angeles disaster book ever written."[15] This one-liner about the lawn that the novel figures as an "omnivorous" "invader," "occupier and colonizer," captures Moore's send-up of "suburban vanity" and "lawnconscious[ness]."[16] With my interest piqued, I discovered in *Greener Than You Think* that the grass's polyvalent status as allegory—from the movie industry's stranglehold on Hollywood, to suburban sprawl, mob mentality, communist infiltration, and capitalism—is calculated to satirize in absurdist terms some of the postwar era's staple cultural fears and hallmarks. Yet unlike other works of fiction

(John Wyndham's *Day of the Triffids* [1951], John Christopher's *Death of Grass* [1956], and Thomas M. Disch's *Genocides* [1965]) and films (Christian Nyby's *The Thing from Another World* [1951], Don Siegel's *Invasion of the Body Snatchers* [1956], and Roger Corman's *The Little Shop of Horrors* [1960]) about alien, monstrous, or man-eating plants that I consulted, Moore's *Greener Than You Think* traces more explicitly the terrible and far-reaching effect of an ecoerror. For the fertilizer mistakenly applied to the lawn was intended for primary use in a global project of sustainable food production, and the distortions wrought on the grass's biology metamorphose *the* American sign of Savanna syndrome—the well-trimmed lawn—into sinister vegetation that exiles human beings across the globe from homes and homelands alike. In Moore's novel, then, the promise of what would be later dubbed the "Green Revolution," a series of global agricultural initiatives begun in the 1940s that sought to reduce starvation rates and attendant political instability by increasing crop yields so that the world's food supply would meet the new demands placed on it by population growth,[17] is fodder for a Hollywood B movie that Moore casts in prose. This horror is shot, as it were, in greener, not black-and-white, tones.

Although the mutations of the vegetation and their large-scale eco-effects in *Greener Than You Think* are my main concerns, I am, like Moore, a creature given to allegorizing the grass. Thus, by way of conclusion, I revisit and reconfigure the relation that the novel establishes between the grass's rapacious growth and monopoly capitalism to reflect briefly on events in New York City's Zuccotti Park in 2011, where protesters demonstrating against unsustainable economic and environmental policies were sprayed with chemicals and treated as so many grassroots out of place. They and their allies across the world amassed and continue to amass in order to agitate, in Rob Nixon's formulation, against "voracious" neoliberal "emissaries who have no respect for limits and no sustainable, inclusive vision of what it means, long-term, to belong."[18] In the cultural imagination, they have come into view as protesting "plants."

The Metamorphic Lawn

At the start of *Greener Than You Think,* our unreliable and unlikable first-person narrator Albert Weener, a salesman in need of dental work and suffering from an "unfortunate skin condition," answers an advertisement for employment that "J S Francis" has placed in the local newspaper.[19] Albert arrives at "an outdated, rundown apartment in the wrong part of Holly-wood," surprised to discover himself in the presence of a person of the "wrong gender," Josephine Spencer Francis.[20] In her kitchen, which "appar-ently was office and laboratory also," Josephine thinks that she hires Albert to demonstrate to farmers in the San Fernando Valley the effects of the industrial fertilizer that she has invented, which she brands "Metamor-phizer."[21] When combined in "proper proportion to the irrigating water,"[22] this concoction, according to Josephine, "will change the basic structure of any plant inoculated with it": "Plants will be capable of making use of any-thing within reach. . . . Rocks, quartz, decomposed granite—anything."[23] The product's name thus encapsulates its biochemical novelty: the treated crop transforms all mineral matter into "free nitrogen" and opens the pos-sibility of making the "whole world . . . teem with abundance."[24] For Josephine, such novelty articulates a fantasy of global plenty, while for the plants, in Michael Pollan's terms, the fertilizer could be imagined as an acceleration of a "remarkably clever strategy: getting us to move and think for them" (the "edible grasses") and "incit[ing] humans to cut down vast forests to make more room for them." Agriculture, as Pollan elaborates in *The Botany of Desire,* may well be "something the grasses did to people as a way to conquer the trees," but in Moore's novel the fertilizer re-forms "the basic structure" of the plant's desire. Metamorphosed, the grass, which is said to have an "insatiable appetite," now conquers "anything."[25] This is an ominous proposition indeed.

In light of his disdain for his employer, it is no surprise that Albert pays little heed to Josephine's instructions about industrial farming. He wants to turn a quick buck and tells her that she has the wrong customer in mind. "I know something about marketing a product," he lectures. "Yours should be sold to householders for their lawns."[26] He even ad-libs an uninspiring jingle to persuade her: "No manures, fuss, cuss, or muss. One shot of the Meta—one shot of Francis' Amazing Discovery and your lawn springs to new life."[27] Josephine is indeed interested in turning a profit, but only enough to "further experiment" on the Metamorphizer,[28] a detail about the fertilizer's possible limitations that clues us in to the eco-mayhem that Albert will trigger when he ignores his charge. But she also figures her product as a panacea for the world's insufficient food supply, a common ecoanxiety and node of humanitarian interest during the post-war period: "No more usedup areas, no more frantic scrabbling for the few bits of naturally rich ground, no more struggle to get artificial fertilizers to wornout soil in the face of ignorance and poverty."[29] At another point in the novel, she elaborates her aims:

> I want no more backward countries; no more famines in India or China; no more dustbowls; no more wars, depressions, hungry children. For this I produced the Metamorphizer—to make not two blades of grass grow where one sprouted before, but whole fields flourish where only rocks and sandpiles lay.[30]

In the face of dearth, war, and poverty, she does not advocate reducing the world's population, as some scientists and popular nonfiction ecowriters do today.[31] Instead, her plan would adjust the planet's carrying capacity by increasing metamorphically—perhaps exponentially—food output. Her mantra of "no more" thus articulates a desire that links "green" economy and political stability. But ecocolonialism also undergirds her philanthropic impulse, and it becomes literalized in the novel's depiction of the grass's lethal and monocultural march across South America, Australia, Asia, Africa, and Europe, where it finally invades England, the birthplace of the modern American lawn.[32]

Although the outset of the Metamorphizer's career is more local than is its end, the lawn on which it is first applied is, fittingly, the historical product of ecological invasion. Albert's one—and only—customer is Mrs. Dinkman, the owner of the "most miserable lawn" on the block. Pump in hand, looking as if he were an "invading Martian," he approaches her forlorn patch of Bermuda grass (*Cynodon dactylon*), a "portmanteau biota" that is native to Africa and that Alfred W. Crosby describes as "one of the most irrepressible tropical weeds."[33] But in concert with Los Angeles's dry and hot summers, the Dinkmans have repressed this invasive species. Albert observes that their lawn is "yellow, the dirty, grayish yellow of moldy straw; and bald, scuffed spots immodestly exposed the cracked, parched earth beneath. . . . Where the grass had gone to seed there were patches of muddy purple, patches which enhanced rather than relieved the diseased color of the whole and emphasized the dying air of the yard."

There is discernible green in this band of drab coloring, but it is "faint" and confined to the creepers near the untidy flowerbeds.[34] After Albert "squirt[s] a fine mist" of undiluted Metamorphizer on the lawn,[35] he returns the next day to discover it fully "translated":

> There wasnt a single bare spot visible in the whole lush, healthy expanse. And it was green. . . . Not just here and there, but over every inch of soft, undulating surface; a pale applegreen where the blades waved to expose its underparts and a rich, dazzling emerald on top. Even the runners, sinuously encroaching upon the sidewalk, were deeply virescent.[36]

Albert waxes poetic at the sight of the lawn, but Mrs. Dinkman does not share his sense of wonder. Now that her lawn is verdant, she requires "*lawn order,*" which is Lydia Davis's wickedly punning phrase for a mown lawn.[37] It will take a scythe to cut through the grass doused with a solution intended for industrial farming;[38] both the neighborhood "jimdandy" and its "powermower" fail to tame it.[39] The resilience of the metamorphized Bermuda grass is a sign that the dream of Savanna syndrome is turning into a nightmare on the front yard.

The scythe's victory against the superfertilized lawn is short-lived, of course. Albert visits the Dinkmans' property the next day to discover the grass's outrageous rebound. "Bold and insolent, it had repaired the hacked-out areas and risen to such a height that, except for a narrow strip at the top, all the windows of the Dinkmans house were smothered."[40] It had also enveloped the garage, "sprawl[ing]" across the architecture "kittenishly, its deceptive softness faintly suggesting fur; at once playful and destructive."[41] The image of the stand-alone home choked by the sinister kin of kudzu, the invasive and exotic species of climbing plant that has transformed landscapes throughout the southern United States, provides a wry commentary on the symbolic status of the American lawn.[42] As Timothy Morton observes, this green patch of Americana is a fresh-air carpet that "chiastically invert[s] inside into outside." It is, he continues, a tactile emblem of the owner's "republican openness and externalized intimacy."[43] In Albert's view, the Dinkmans' unfertilized lawn is indeed carpetlike, but hardly steeped in such venerable traditions: "Over the walk, interwoven stolons had been felted down into a ragged mat, repellant alike to foot and eye."[44] Having been ill tended by the Dinkmans, sprayed with Metamorphizer, and then shorn, the Bermuda grass scrambles the lawn ideal on the second day. It behaves as if it were a hirsute botanical creature—a pelted lawn (*pelouse*)—trying to force its way back into the house, attempting to roll up the exterior rug and shove it inside through the front windows.[45] The ideal lawn's manicured relation between intimacy and hospitality has thus been irrecoverably disturbed; now there is only grass, and it is uninhabitable.

Having eaten the Dinkmans out of house and home, the lawn also sprawls in a promiscuous manner. The front lawns of American suburbia tend not to have fences, for the erection of such bounds undermines the civic openness that Morton describes. As the state of their lawn on the previous day intimates, the Dinkmans do not display this virtue in their lawn care, which is likely why a row of "chesthigh hedges" once separated their lot from their neighbor's. I employ the past tense because, upon arriving to the Dinkmans' upholstered home, Albert notices that the grass has "overwhelm[ed] [the hedges] in the night" and "invaded the neat, civilized plots behind, blurring sharply cut edges, curiously investigating flowerbeds, barbarously strangling shapely bushes."[46] The grass is an intrusive, uncivil species that attacks the idea of private property insofar as the grass overruns its borders. More radically, the grass also shows no respect for public property. It has moved into the streets, encroaching on the "cement sidewalk," and has made "demands on curbing and gutter"; it will later turn the sidewalk around the Dinkman property into "an enormous green woolly rug."[47] As the arduousness and the ultimate failure of the previous day's endeavors to trim the lawn indicate, curbing this "riot of vegetation" will prove no easy task.[48] By the close of the novel's third section, "one solid mass of green devilgrass"—another more ominous-sounding name for Bermuda grass—holds "undisputed possession of nearly all Southern California."[49] The homogeneous mob of grass renders cities and counties a no-man's land, transforming SoCal into a giant unwelcome mat.

As a local radio announcer informs his listeners, the grass spilling out of the Dinkmans' lawn is "alive and coming at you. It's alive. It's alive."[50] Our on-the-scene correspondent records here the novel's debt to horror film: he channels the language of Colin Clive in James Whale's adaptation of *Frankenstein* (1931). But the quotation sets up a comparison that is not quite exact. Whereas the mad scientist's galvanized creature is a new-fangled entity, pieced together from the fabric of many dead bodies, the novel's vegetable body—even when it was the Dinkmans' "dying" lawn—is not dead. The attack on regimes of property that the Metamorphizer energizes thus draws its force from the inoculated grass's capacity to stimulate virtually unchecked growth in matter that is already alive. In Aristotelian terms, the fertilizer enhances the animating property that defines the life of plants, the vegetative soul. Since classical times, this soul's faculty was thought to govern growth, nutrition, and reproduction in plants and in all higher-order earthly creatures;[51] by such premodern taxonomic logic, plants exemplify bare life.[52] Structurally altered by chemicals, *Greener Than You Think*'s grass now "grow[s]," like Andrew Marvell's "vegetable love," "vaster than empires," but more quickly.[53] Its Aristotelian essence has been amplified and magnified to the extent that its desire (in Pollan's sense) for territory becomes newly and lethally visible to human eyes.

Such geographic expansion, as *Greener Than You Think*'s radioman further reports, "actually" enables witnesses to "see [the grass] move."[54] Defined in Aristotelian terms, plants move, of course: they grow and decay and change states, but it is difficult to detect their minute activities without the aid of stop-motion technology. The gigantism of *Greener Than You Think*'s vegetation corrects for this incapacity in the human visual field and leaves onlookers groping for language to describe the voracious entity that they are watching. The radioman mixes creaturely similes, telling listeners that "creepers run out in front and crawl ahead like thousands of little green snakes" and "travel forward like an army of worms."[55] Albert piles up a series of participles to capture how the "thing moved": it "kept on moving; not in one place, but in thousands; not in one direction, but toward all points of the compass. It writhed and twisted in nightmarish unease, expanding, extending, increasing; spreading, spreading, spreading."[56] He later recalls having observed the grass move as if it were a "green glacier crawling down the sidestreets and over the low roofs of the shops to pour like a cascade upon the busy artery." The "tendrils" of this formation were "splaying out over the sidewalks, choking the roadways, climbing walls, finding vulnerable chinks in masonry, bunching themselves inside apertures and bursting out, carrying with them fragments of their momentary prison as they pursued their ruthless course."[57] Whereas the radioman sees in the grass an anthropomorphized company of invading bugs or clump of snakes, Albert figures the grass as a soulless glacial mass that obliterates all material bodies (brick, concrete, and presumably other fabrics, from glass to flesh) that impede its path and then sweeps up their shattered pieces in its relentless flow.[58] By Albert's account, then, a deep freeze of sorts has descended on Los Angeles to mark the onset of the Greener Age.

The grass's unintelligible and inhuman kinesis differs sharply with the class of man-eating plant—Wyndham's triffid—that has come to overshadow its botanical cousins in the sci-fi tradition Robert Macfarlane dubs the "floral apocalypse."[59] Approximating human locomotion, triffids ambulate on three "legs" as if they were disabled human beings: "When it 'walked' it moved rather like a man on crutches. Two of the blunt 'legs' slid forward, then the whole thing lurched as the rear one drew almost level with them, then the two in front slid forward again."[60] In contrast, Moore's "Green Horror" is a form of life exiling human characters who discover in the grass no morphological resemblance, no correspondence in mobility, and no confirmation of anthropocentric narcissism.[61] Perhaps surprisingly, it takes the authorities in the novel some time to drop the bomb on this "thing."

Atomic Grass!

The "outlawed atomicbomb" had indeed been deliberated as an option for curbing the lawn's metastasizing growth earlier in *Greener Than You Think,* but a salt barrier proved to be a less "terrible" solution.[62] The saline band, however, "tamed" the grass for only two years.[63] As reports of grass patches appearing outside the brine ring begin to circulate in the media, the bomb reenters public discourse as the "weapon" that will be the "end of the grass."[64] To the delight of San Franciscans, the Commission to Combat Dangerous Vegetation selects Long Beach, California, for ground zero. Ten days after what Albert describes as a "little bomb—hardly more than a toy, a plaything, the very smallest practicable"—detonates, the grass reacts vividly. The periphery of grass around the crater "turned a brilliant orange," and the grass "just beyond the orange . . . was still more brilliant. It writhed and spumed upward in great clumps, culminating in enormous, overhanging caps inevitably suggesting the mushroomcloud of the bomb." One week later, after the nuked grass has ceased mimicking the bomb's distinctive plume and its dazzling brightness, it turns a "green unknown in living plant before; a glassy, translucent green, the green of a cathedral window in the moonlight." The mass then "burst[s] into bloom," generating "purple flowers . . . redviolet, brilliant and clear," and discharges into the sky a "cloud bearing the germ of the inoculated grass."[65] In short order, the grass reseeds the blasted area, and its "exotic growth" reminds Albert of the "flowers which came up to hide some of London's scars after the blitz and the lush plantlife observed in Hiroshima."[66] Although the mass of evocative vegetation soon loses its nuclear brilliance and although its "mutants"—the germs projected into the air—ultimately prove "sterile,"[67] the atomic grass nonetheless continues to spread unabated across North America over the course of the novel. The bomb, in short, was not the "end of the grass." As Josephine cautions the public during a newspaper interview, it will be difficult to ascertain if future changes in the grass's behavior and structure stem from radiation exposure.[68]

In targeting Long Beach, a site of intense anxiety about civil defense and further submarine strikes after the bombing of Pearl Harbor,[69] in refiguring that possible wartime scenario so that the American military attacks this precise spot during peacetime, and in designating this detonation as the trigger for war with the Soviet Union, *Greener Than You Think* melds its satire on suburban sprawl and lawn care with a counterfactual foray into Cold War history.[70] I have little space to rehearse all the twists of this plotline, except to note that the Americans temporarily celebrate the grass as a "National Park" when it absorbs members of an invading Soviet army who trek across its top on snowshoes.[71] Although the grass has been lethal to "anything," including human beings, from the start—a Los Angelino commits suicide by walking through its outer fringe, and it consumes a stuntman journalist—it is unclear whether the Green Horror's capacity to feed on the Red Army is a radioactive "aftereffect."[72] The persistent association in US popular culture between nuclear testing and the unleashing of mutant creatures, especially insects and lizards, on an unwitting public adds strength to the suggestion that radiation is responsible, in some discursive measure, for the postatomic appetite of this "army of worms" and "green snakes." Some of the novel's scientists even "predict" a future scenario often imagined in a subgenre of 1950s sci-fi cinema, the "big bug" film: "Man, they said, could not adapt himself to the Grass—this was proved to the hilt by the tragedy of the Russian armies in the Last War—but insects had."[73] According to eyewitness reports, the creatures "living in and below the Grass" are indeed thriving. They are "growing ever larger and more numerous. Expeditions had found worms the size of snakes and bugs big as birds, happy in their environment."[74] Are the members of this nonanthropomorphic, radioactive ecology—gigantic worms, bugs, and even the mass of snakelike and wormlike grass—as eager to prey on human flesh as their celluloid cousins are in *The Beast from 20,000 Fathoms* (1953), *Gojira* (1954), and *Them!* (1954)? Since the grass's expansion triggers global migration as well as poverty, sickness, starvation, and cannibalism, there are plenty of vulnerable bodies and rotting corpses for both the vegetation and the gargantuan critters that it harbors to consume. By magnifying the size of these creatures, *Greener Than You Think* puts to delicious effect an unsettling and simple fact of life: decompositional agents have always fed on—and inside—human bodies.[75] Changes in vegetable and animal scale thus propel the novel toward the end of the Anthropocene, a disanthropic fate aided and abetted by the unforeseeable effects of nuclear fallout.[76]

In conjuring the annihilation of human civilization and in locating its source in the misapplication of synthetic agents—first the fertilizer and then the bomb—on vegetation, the novel anticipates by fifteen years the rhetoric of Rachel Carson's *Silent Spring* (1962), which stands as the urtext of the modern "green" movement in the United States.[77] To trace and forecast the lethal effects of releasing herbicides and insecticides on plants, animals, and unsuspecting human beings, Carson peppers her text "with imagery borrowed from military holocaust reportage: weaponry, killing, victimage, extermination, corpses, massacre, conquest."[78] More specifically, she employs the trope of nuclear bombing—not only testing—in a way consonant with its use in *Greener Than You Think*.[79] In a chapter called "Indiscriminately from the Skies," for example, Carson figures the "mass-spraying campaigns" deployed against fire ants and gypsy moths—both of which, incidentally, are invasive species—as "all-out chemical war[s]" supervised by US authorities on American soil. Indeed, these blitzes prove a repurposing of midcentury militarism: according to Carson, "surplus planes" from World War II were retrofit to dust rural and urban areas with "poisons."[80]

Drawn by Lois and Louis Darling, the ink-and-paper illustration that accompanies "Indiscriminately from the Skies" further links chemical spraying to aerial bombardment (Figure 1). Sketched from above, as if providing readers with a bird's-eye view, it depicts an aircraft flying over a suburban block that features, among other wholesome activities, children playing catch in a field, a mother pushing a stroller on the sidewalk, and of course a man mowing a lawn. The single-propeller craft has already crossed the book's gutter and is about to exit. Behind it trails at least three long blank streaks, which represent the discharge of its chemical cargo, probably pesticides; these white bands erase and visually obliterate the houses and trees below. As Carson details in "Indiscriminately from the Skies," such attacks, especially those targeting the fire ant in the southern United States, were carried out under a misleading banner—the protection of agricultural health and production—since there was little evidence proving the harmful effects of the ants on crops.[81] Both Moore's Metamorphizer and the killing agents that Carson exposes in *Silent Spring* thus allege to control and foster agricultural fertility, but they do so from opposite directions. I argue that in each case the misapplication of chemical compounds is also responsible for creating "greener"—that is, dangerous, even lethal—ecoconditions for all creatures, great and small.

Yet the concluding chapter of *Silent Spring,* "The Other Road," sounds a chord of optimism amid the bleakness. In its catalog of "new, imaginative, and creative approaches to the problem of sharing our earth with other creatures,"[82] the chapter, which alludes in its title to Robert Frost's poem,

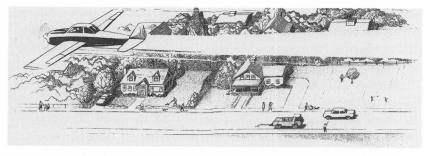

Figure 1. Drawing by Lois and Louis Darling, from *Silent Spring* by Rachel Carson. Copyright 1962 by Rachel L. Carson, renewed 1990 by Roger Christie. Reprinted by permission of Houghton Mifflin Harcourt Publishing Company. All rights reserved.

proposes that the grass is indeed greener—in its proverbial sense—on the other side. From the release of sterilized male insects into habitats as population restraints, to the reduction of pests through "new biotic control[s]," Carson promotes a regime of insect biopolitics that, in her formulation, is more humane than chemical warfare because it takes into consideration "living populations and all their pressures and counter-pressures."[83] Despite Carson's ecocentric rhetoric of "sharing our earth with other creatures," the practices that she surveys in this final chapter work to resolve "the problem" of cohabitation on earth to humanity's distinct advantage: "Only by taking account of such life forces and by cautiously seeking to guide them into channels favorable to ourselves can we hope to achieve a reasonable accommodation between the insect hordes and ourselves."[84] Carson's proposals for fashioning this state of "reasonable accommodation," which I would gloss as a point of equilibrium, confirm Stacy Alaimo's observation that anthropocentrism has historically tended to structure the discourses of sustainability.[85] The figure who selects the other road in Carson is, after all, "We," "the people."[86]

There is no such programmatic optimism for humanity at the close of *Greener Than You Think*. On its last page, the stolons of the "very green" grass have colonized the ship on which Albert, Josephine, and a crew of lab technicians have boarded when it overtakes England, the novel's final terrestrial frontier. The grass's onboard advance compels Albert to seal a "manuscript"—the first-person account of the grass's history that is *Greener Than You Think*—"into the casket which floats" and seems to prevent the scientists from implementing the counteragent for the fertilizer that they may (or may not) have just perfected. Although the casket contains a kernel of Pandora-like hope for human beings insofar as our reading the novel presupposes humanity's continuance, Albert's repetition of the phrase "There can be no question of that" (the "indubitable success" of the do-or-die experiment),[87] nonetheless casts scientific enterprise—theirs and maybe ours—as a sinking ship. The novel may afford us, its readers, the opportunity to reboot, but have—or will—we?

Grassroots

Albert Weener is a member of the 1 percent, and not only because, as our narrator, he is necessarily left standing as the sprawling novel careens towards ecoapocalypse. By the novel's end, he is also the planet's most powerful capitalist and political insider. His rise to fortune is as improbable as the fulfillment of the American dream. After he unleashes the super-fertilized lawn on Los Angeles, Albert finds employment as a freelance and then contract celebrity columnist. Fulfilling a long-held desire, he purchases stock in Consolidated Pemmican and Allied Concentrates.[88] With the grass fenced in temporarily by the salt band, the financial markets recover, and Albert learns that he has purchased more shares of this company than there are in existence. He refuses hush money, insisting instead on taking possession of Pemmican's ramshackle "plant," which is located "somewhere in New Jersey."[89] Having moved to the Garden State, Albert begins to play—and to win—a more global game of Monopoly. The novel's spoof of the board game's Rich Uncle Pennybags, the famous monocled and top-hatted figure modeled on J. P. Morgan,[90] lands himself a military contract and, by the close of the war with Russia, "had fourteen factories, stretching like a string of lustrous pearls from Quebec down to Montevideo, and . . . was negotiating to open new branches in Europe and the Far East."[91] After having cornered the market on nearly all goods from food to steel, Albert takes up cozy residence in England, where he demolishes an Elizabethan manor and builds there anew, in the California style.[92] The self-made man thus buys himself status as member of the leisure class while bankrupting and starving the peoples of the world and "kill[ing] civilization."[93] As the grass expands in size, so too do Albert's empire of plants and his pile of green dollar bills. By this logic, the all-consuming grass proves to be a counterpart to the unfettered growth of monopoly capitalism.

Yet it is equally possible to comprehend the creepers and tendrils of this "riot of vegetation" as terrorizing Albert (with massive collateral damage) all the way to the "great and ample bungalow" he built in the English countryside as retribution for his ruthless business practices,[94] which first manifested in his decision to mistreat the Dinkmans' lawn. This reallegorization posits the grass as an unremitting force gathered to counteract—indeed to root out—capitalism. While I was thumbing through the novel again, the grass suggested itself to me as a precursor of the protesters who demonstrated in 2011 against more modern versions of Albert's multinational corporation. In the estimation of David Graeber, the social anthropologist credited with coining the phrase "We are the 99 percent," no social justice movement prior to Occupy Wall Street (OWS) has "grow[n] so startlingly quickly."[95] Near Ground Zero, the epicenter of this nominally horizontal—that is, nonhierarchical—movement is Zuccotti Park, which protesters dubbed Liberty Park (or Square).[96] Such naming is an act that stakes problematical possession,[97] and the movement's assemblage of participants, from anarchists, environmental activists, students, unemployed and underemployed workers to the homeless and disenfranchised, occupied public space owned by Canada's Brookfield Office Properties; its participants did so by camping under Liberty's canopy of honey-locust trees.[98] In running a food kitchen, operating sanitation details, offering medical services, and establishing a communications center and library, OWS protesters articulated "Grassroots Practices for Global Change."[99] In Michael Marder's apt formulation, they enacted a plantlike resistance, a "kind of lingering, being in a place on an ongoing basis, bodily occupying it, being physically there," "exposed to the elements."[100] In effect, they translated the park's slabs of granite into their own "turf."[101]

In newspaper and journalistic accounts of OWS, protesters have been imagined as vegetation that spread across this turf and that, in Joanna Slater's telling phrase, "spawned offshoots" across the globe.[102] In the most lyrical moment of her essay on OWS, Rebecca Solnit also imagines the movement in botanical terms. Evoking both the Prague Spring and the non-violence of 1960s flower power, she proposes that "flowers seem like the right image for this uprising led by the young, those who have been most crushed by the new economic order, and who bloom by rebelling and rebel by blooming."[103] For their part, the New York City Department of Sanitation and the New York Police Department construed the situation differently. They instituted "lawn order," treating OWS protesters as if they were weeds (or insectlike pests), subjecting them in November 2011 to pepper spray and forcibly removing them from the premises; law enforcement officials treated protesters at UC Irvine, UC Berkeley, and Oakland in similarly violent ways.[104] During the spring months of 2012, the "political plant[s]" did not rebloom en masse in the Park,[105] but they continued to camp (or clump together) in pockets along Wall Street. In the lead-up to the OWS movement's one-year anniversary, a group of protesters marched out of Zuccotti Park and into Lower Manhattan, as if they were a mass of agitating annuals.[106]

We could take the vegetable metaphors for describing the force of OWS too far, and maybe I have. But we cannot fail to recognize that OWS unleashed into public discourse a vital rhetoric of political protest and resistance. The American Dialect Society, for example, selected *occupy* as 2011's "Word of the Year."[107] Indeed, this hashtagged buzzword, which encapsulates an argument against the persistence of the status quo, might well prove to be an effective counteragent to the optimism of "green," which itself has co-opted the popular environmental movement. For OWS to "occupy green," the movement will need (at least) to rearticulate online and in other forums its formal relation to "Sustainability projects," those cotravelers of "green" that do not assist in "Building a New World" but rather function as capitalist code for more of the same.[108] Around OWS's one-year anniversary date, such rearticulation seems to be occurring in entries on the Adbusters website known as "Tactical Briefings." Whereas "Tactical Briefing #38" celebrates the fact that "Occupy" is "morphing into" something else,[109] "Tactical Briefing #37" affords more concrete information about this metamorphosis: "the Zuccotti encampment model might have passed its heyday, but the spirit of Occupy is still very much alive . . . evolving and inspiring, expanding our understanding of the possible, exploding our political imagination." "Tactical Briefing #37" goes on to describe OWS's former model of protest: "Before S17 [September 17, 2011] we relied on the same dinosaur paradigm of the dusty old left. We looked backward for inspiration instead of forward. With Occupy we jumped over that old dead goat. Now it's time to leap fresh again." And it imagines a new model: "Occupy began as a primal scream against the monied corruption of our democracy . . . but after a year of struggling against an unrepentant corporatocracy, our goals are now deeper, our dreams are now wilder. We see a common thread emerging—a blue-green-black hybrid politics—that unites and elevates our movement." Tellingly, the "green" of this "hybrid politics" constitutes a "deep green front," in which "we institute a binding international accord on climate change, pursue a worldwide de-growth economic agenda funded by a Robin Hood Tax and establish an across the board true cost market regime in which the price of every product tells the ecological truth."[110] By this account, an "evolving" OWS is, like Moore's grass, "expanding, extending, increasing; spreading, spreading, spreading," a nightmare to those who want it stamped out. Since Moore's novel demonstrates that there is no getting ahead of such movement, no predicting where it will go next or when, I stop here, knowing full well that ever-changing conditions on the ground cast my ecothoughts about OWS as already belated.[111]

Notes

For their conversations and recommendations, I thank Chris Chia, Jeffrey Cohen, Marty Favor, Deanna Kreisel, Gordon Mackie, Gregory Mackie, Scott MacKenzie, Dory Nason, Britt Rusert, Karl Steel, Will Stockton, Tiffany Werth, Derek Woods, and Mike Zeitlin.

1. Bruce R. Smith, *The Key of Green: Passion and Perception in Renaissance Culture* (Chicago: University of Chicago Press, 2009), 1.

2. Dan Brayton, "Shakespeare and the Global Ocean," in *Ecocritical Shakespeare*, ed. Lynne Bruckner and Dan Brayton (Farnham, U.K.: Ashgate, 2011), 173.

3. On "light greens" as hues "most appropriated to beauty," see Edmund Burke, "A Philosophical Inquiry into the Origins of Our Ideas of the Sublime and the Beautiful," in *The Portable Edmund Burke,* ed. Isaac Kramnick (New York: Penguin, 1999), 81.

4. For the mayor's statement, see http://vancouver.ca/greencapital/index .htm.

5. Steve Mentz, "Shakespeare's Beach House, or The Green and the Blue in *Macbeth*," *Shakespeare Studies* 39 (2011): 90. I thank Sylvan Goldberg for sharing with me his unpublished manuscript, "Queering the Lawn: Performing Place in the Front Yard," which critiques the "green" normativities of American lawn culture.

6. On the savanna theory, see Michael Pollan, "Why Mow? The Case against Lawns," in Fritz Haeg, *Edible Estates: Attack on the Front Lawn* (New York: Metropolis Books, 2008), 30.

7. On the neglected and undertheorized place of race in US environmental discourse, see Britt M. Rusert, "Black Nature: The Question of Race in the Age of Ecology," *Polygraph* 22 (2010): 149–66.

8. John P. O'Grady, "How Sustainable Is the Idea of Sustainability?," *ISLE* 10, no. 1 (2003): 1.

9. Dan Brayton, "Writ in Water: *Far Tortuga* and the Crisis of the Marine Environment," *PMLA* 127, no. 3 (2012): 565.

10. Lynn Keller, "Beyond Imagining, Imagining Beyond," *PMLA* 127, no. 3 (2012): 579.

11. Steve Mentz, "After Sustainability," *PMLA* 127, no. 3 (2012): 586, 591.

12. On the relation between environmentalism and capitalism, see Timothy Morton, "Ecology after Capitalism," *Polygraph* 22 (2010): 49–50.

13. Stacy Alaimo, "Sustainable This, Sustainable That: New Materialisms, Post-humanism, and Unknown Futures," *PMLA* 127, no. 3 (2012): 559.

14. On Moore's career and the place of *Greener Than You Think* in it, see Sara Oswald, "Ward Moore," in *Twentieth-Century American Science Fiction Writers*, pt. 2, ed. David Cowart and Thomas L. Wymer (Detroit: Gale, 1981), 34–36.

15. Mike Davis, *Ecology of Fear: Los Angeles and the Imagination of Disaster* (New York: Vintage, 1999), 318–19.

16. Ward Moore, *Greener Than You Think* (New York: William Sloane Associates, 1947), 29, 217, 5, 8. Throughout this chapter, I do not amend the high modernist compound words of our narrator.

17. See John H. Perkins, *Geopolitics and the Green Revolution: Wheat, Genes, and the Cold War* (New York: Oxford University Press, 1997).

18. Rob Nixon, "Neoliberalism, Genre, and 'The Tragedy of the Commons,'" *PMLA* 127, no. 3 (2012): 598.

19. Moore, *Greener Than You Think*, 9, 2.

20. Ibid., 1, 2.

21. Ibid., 2.

22. Ibid., 6.

23. Ibid., 2–3.

24. Ibid., 25, 4. On the production of synthetic nitrogen during the early twentieth century for use as crop fertilizers, see Vaclav Smil, *Enriching the Earth: Fritz Haber, Carl Bosch, and the Transformation of World Food Production* (Cambridge, Mass.: MIT Press, 2000). *Greener Than You Think*'s scientist takes the production of nitrogen out of the laboratory and places it in the fields, where the grass can make "do-it-yourself" nutrients.

25. Michael Pollan, *The Botany of Desire: A Plant's-Eye View of the World* (New York: Random House, 2001), xx–xxi; Moore, *Greener Than You Think*, 29.

26. Moore, *Greener Than You Think*, 5.

27. Ibid.

28. Ibid., 3.

29. Ibid.

30. Ibid., 6.

31. See James Lovelock, *The Revenge of Gaia: Earth's Climate Crisis and the Fate of Humanity* (New York: Basic Books, 2006), 140–43; and Alan Weisman, *The World without Us* (Toronto: HarperCollins, 2007), 272–73.

32. On the relation between invasive species, especially "weeds," and colonialism, see Alfred W. Crosby, *Ecological Imperialism: The Biological Expansion of Europe, 900–1900* (New York: Cambridge University Press, 2006), 145–70. On more modern forms of ecocolonialism, see Vandana Shiva, *Biopiracy: The Plunder*

of Nature and Knowledge (Toronto: Between The Lines, 1997). On the importation of lawn aesthetic from England to the United States, see Virginia Scott Jenkins, *The Lawn: A History of an American Obsession* (Washington, D.C.: Smithsonian Institution Press, 1994), 13–15; and Timothy Morton, *Ecology without Nature: Rethinking Environmental Aesthetics* (Cambridge, Mass.: Harvard University Press, 2007), 89–90.

33. Moore, *Greener Than You Think,* 9; Crosby, *Ecological Imperialism,* 150, 162.

34. Moore, *Greener Than You Think,* 9–10.

35. Ibid., 11.

36. Ibid., 14.

37. Lydia Davis, "A Mown Lawn," in *Samuel Johnson Is Indignant* (New York: Picador, 2001), 2.

38. Moore, *Greener Than You Think,* 31.

39. Ibid., 23, 26.

40. Ibid., 36.

41. Ibid., 37.

42. For a superb account of lawn history in the United States, see Georges Teyssot, "The American Lawn: Surface of Everyday Life," in *The American Lawn,* ed. Georges Teyssot (New York: Princeton Architectural Press, 1999), 1–39.

43. Timothy Morton, "Wordsworth Digs the Lawn," *European Romantic Review* 15, no. 2 (2004): 321.

44. Moore, *Greener Than You Think,* 10.

45. On the etymological and popular links between lawn and hair, see Teyssot, "American Lawn," 5–6.

46. Moore, *Greener Than You Think,* 37.

47. Ibid., 37, 50.

48. Ibid., 51.

49. Ibid., 105, 155.

50. Ibid., 53.

51. For a concise discussion of this Aristotelian logic, see Katharine Park, "The Organic Soul," in *The Cambridge History of Renaissance Philosophy,* ed. C. B. Schmitt, Quentin Skinner, Eckhard Kessler, and Jill Kraye (Cambridge: Cambridge University Press, 1988), 464–84. On Aristotle's place in more modern plant studies, see Michael Marder, "Is Plant Liberation on the Menu?," *New York Times Online,* May 8, 2012, http://opinionator.blogs.nytimes.com/2012/05/08/is-plant-liberation-on-the-menu/. On more modern studies of "vegetable growth," see also Timothy Morton, *The Ecological Thought* (Cambridge, Mass.: Harvard University Press, 2010), 68.

52. On the link between bare life and Aristotle's vegetative soul, see Giorgio Agamben, *The Open: Man and Animal,* trans. Kevin Attell (Stanford, Calif.: Stanford University Press, 2004), 15.

53. I cite, by line number, Andrew Marvell, "To His Coy Mistress," in *Andrew Marvell: The Complete Poems,* ed. Elizabeth Story Donno (Harmondsworth, U.K.: Penguin, 1981), ll. 11–12.

54. Moore, *Greener Than You Think,* 53.

55. Ibid.

56. Ibid., 59.

57. Ibid., 100.

58. For a fabulous account of glacial ontology and affects, see Lowell Duckert, "Glacier," *postmedieval* 4, no. 1 (2013): 68–79.

59. Robert Macfarlane, introduction to John Christopher, *The Death of Grass* (London: Penguin, 2009), vii.

60. John Wyndham, *The Day of the Triffids* (New York: Modern Library, 2003), 27.

61. Moore, *Greener Than You Think,* 102.

62. Ibid., 138.

63. Ibid., 160.

64. Ibid., 138, 168.

65. Ibid., 170–73.

66. Ibid., 173.

67. Ibid.

68. Ibid., 169.

69. On the perception of Los Angeles's vulnerability to submarine attack and to the establishment of heightened "security" measures, including the internment of Japanese Americans in the wake of Pearl Harbor, see John Buntin, *L.A. Noir: The Struggle for the Soul of America's Most Seductive City* (New York: Harmony Books, 2009), 95–96.

70. Moore's most-celebrated novel, *Bring the Jubilee* (1953), is a time-traveling counterfactual history of the Battle of Gettysburg. On this novel, see Fred Bilson, "The Colonialists' Fear of Colonisation and the Alternate Worlds of Ward Moore, Philip K. Dick, and Keith Roberts," *Foundation* 34, no. 94 (2005): 50–63; and Mike Davis, "Ward Moore's Freedom Ride," *Science Fiction Studies* 38, no. 3 (2011): 385–92.

71. Moore, *Greener Than You Think,* 200.

72. Ibid., 102, 119, 172.

73. Ibid., 333.

74. Ibid., 311.

75. On these decompositional agents in premodern contexts, see Ian MacInnes, "The Politic Worm: Invertebrate Life in the Early Modern English Body," in *The Indistinct Human in Renaissance Literature*, ed. Jean E. Feerick and Vin Nardizzi (New York: Palgrave, 2012), 253–73; and Karl Steel, "Abyss: Everything Is Food," *postmedieval* 4, no. 1 (2013): 93–104.

76. On this phenomenon in modernist and environmental art, see Greg Garrard, "Worlds without Us: Some Types of Disanthropy" *SubStance* 41, no. 1 (2012): 40–60.

77. For an account of Carson's primary status in modern American environmentalism, see Craig Waddell, "The Reception of *Silent Spring*: An Introduction," in *And No Birds Sing: Rhetorical Analyses of Rachel Carson's* Silent Spring, ed. Craig Waddell (Carbondale: Southern Illinois University Press, 2000), 1–3.

78. Lawrence Buell, *The Environmental Imagination: Thoreau, Nature Writing, and the Formation of American Culture* (Cambridge, Mass.: Harvard University Press, 1995), 293.

79. On the relation between *Silent Spring* and Cold War popular culture, see Ralph H. Lutts, "Chemical Fallout: *Silent Spring,* Radioactive Fallout, and the Environmental Movement"; and Cheryll Glotfelty, "Cold War, *Silent Spring*: The Trope of War in Modern Environmentalism," both of which are included in Waddell, *And No Birds Sing*, 17–41 and 157–73, respectively. On Carson's environmentalism and Cold War "monster" films, see Joshua David Bellin, "Us or *Them!*: *Silent Spring* and the 'Big Bug' Films of the 1950s," *Extrapolation* 50, no. 1 (2009): 145–68.

80. Rachel Carson, *Silent Spring* (Boston: Houghton Mifflin, 1962), 156, 158, 155. On the popular depiction of insects—the Japanese beetle, for instance—as foreign agents invading American lawns, see Beatriz Colomina, "The Lawn at War: 1941–1961," in Teyssot, *American Lawn*, 138–41.

81. Carson, *Silent Spring*, 163.

82. Ibid., 296.

83. Ibid., 288, 296.

84. Ibid., 296.

85. Alaimo, "Sustainable This, Sustainable That," 562.

86. Carson, *Silent Spring*, 277, 3. Carson's use of the first-person plural pronoun reconfigures here the culprit that she holds responsible in *Silent Spring*'s sci-fi-inflected opening chapter, "A Fable for Tomorrow," for its postapocalyptic landscape: "The people had done it to themselves" (3). On Carson's place in the sci-fi tradition, see M. Jimmie Killingsworth and Jacqueline S. Palmer, "*Silent Spring* and Science Fiction: An Essay in the History and Rhetoric of Narrative," in Waddell, *And No Birds Sing*, 174–204.

87. Moore, *Greener Than You Think,* 358.

88. Ibid., 137–38.

89. Ibid., 153.

90. On the artistic history of Rich Uncle Pennybags, see Philip E. Orbanes, *Monopoly®: The World's Most Famous Game and How It Got That Way* (Philadelphia: Da Capo, 2007), 76–77.

91. Moore, *Greener Than You Think,* 202.

92. Ibid., 280–81.

93. Ibid., 295.

94. Ibid., 281.

95. David Graeber, "Occupy Wall Street's Anarchist Roots," in *The Occupy Handbook,* ed. Janet Byrne (New York: Back Bay Books, 2012), 147.

96. I gleaned many details about the OWS movement from Mattathias Schwartz, "Pre-Occupied," *New Yorker,* November 28, 2011, 28–35; and George Packer, "All the Angry People," *New Yorker,* December 5, 2011, 32–38.

97. For a critique of OWS from the perspective of indigenous property rights, see the video project *The 1491s Occupy Wall Street,* which the Native American sketch comedy group known as The 1491s posted to YouTube on November 26, 2011.

98. On Zuccotti Park's complex property status, see the blog entry "# Liberty Square /// The Spatial Issues at Stake with Occupy Wall Street: Considering the Privately Owned Public Spaces," *Funambulist,* October 12, 2011; and Joanna Slater, "The Comeback of Occupy Wall Street," *Globe and Mail Online,* September 14, 2012.

99. This gloss for the movement's project appears on #HowToOccupy, which can be accessed through the website, http://howtooccupy.org/.

100. Michael Marder, "Resist Like a Plant! On the Vegetal Life of Political Movements," *Peace Studies Journal* 5, no. 1 (2012): 25, 26.

101. Jeff Sharlet, "Inside Occupy Wall Street," *Rolling Stone Online,* November 10, 2011, http://www.rollingstone.com/politics/news/occupy-wall-street-welcome -to-the-occupation-20111110.

102. Slater, "Comeback of Occupy Wall Street."

103. Rebecca Solnit, "Civil Society at Ground Zero," in Byrne, *Occupy Handbook,* 296. Solnit has in mind Alexander Dubček's prediction about the resiliency of the Prague Spring: "You can crush the flowers, but you can't stop the spring."

104. For an account of these incidents, see Zoe Corneli, "Inquiries on Violence at Occupy Protests Move Slowly," *New York Times Online,* March 16, 2012, http:// www.nytimes.com/2012/03/16/us/inquiries-on-violence-at-occupy-protests -move-slowly.html.

105. Marder, "Resist Like a Plant!," 28.

106. For a great account of these events and the mainstream media's reception of them, see Allison Kilkenny, "More Than 180 Arrested on Occupy Wall Street's First Anniversary," *Nation Online,* September 18, 2012, http://www.nation.com/blog/170001/more-than-180-arrested-occupy-wallstreets-first-anniversary.

107. Michael Greenberg, "On the Meaning of Occupation," in Byrne, *Occupy Handbook,* 265.

108. Under the rubric "Building a New World" on #HowToOccupy, there are tabbed subheadings for "Sustainability projects" and "Ecology." These are the two rubrics with the most number of articles, eleven and twelve, respectively. The most recent update to these categories is December 3, 2011, a sign perhaps that they have lost their traction.

109. I borrow phrasing from the full title of "Tactical Briefing #38," "What is Occupy morphing into?," which can be accessed on the website for *Adbusters,* http://www.adbusters.org/blogs/adbusters-blog/tactical-briefing-38.html.

110. Tactical Briefing #37," "S17 anniversary: Where do we stand?," http://www.adbusters.org/blogs/adbusters-blog/s17-one-year-anniversary.html. A "Robin Hood Tax," according to the website http://robinhoodtax.org/, is a "tax on the financial sector [that] has the power to raise hundreds of billions every year to provide funding for jobs to kickstart the economy and get America back on its feet. It could help save the social safety net in the United States and around the world."

111. On OWS's unpredictable life, see Kilkenny, "More Than 180 Arrested."

Beige

WILL STOCKTON

B eige is the average color. If all the light in the universe, from all its known galaxy systems, were mixed together, what results would look like a latte.[1] The universe used to be bluer, but stars turn red as they age. As the age of star production moves toward its end, which is also perhaps a new beginning for the matter utilized in that production, the universe fills with the detritus of exploded stars, the waste of the former systems of the world.

Prompted by this astrophysical fact, but hardly limited to astrophysics or to astronomical systems, a beige ecocriticism takes as its subject apocalyptic eruptions within, encounters between, and condensations of the systems of the world. It tracks these eruptions, encounters, and condensations by focusing on the creation of products coded as waste; it studies the end of the world—but also, more hopefully, the creation of new worlds— that this waste encodes. Unlike a green ecology, it focuses not on conservation and sustainability but on destruction and re-creation: on recycling that does not simply preserve the environment. As a "neutral" color like white, however, it also mingles well with many other colors—especially, for my purposes here, the colors of human waste products: yellow and brown, both colors into which beige can shade.

Beige shades, too, in pink, or queer, directions. Thus a beige ecocriticism shares Catriona Mortimer-Sandilands and Bruce Erickson's goal of "developing a sexual politics that more clearly includes considerations of the natural world and its biosocial constitution, and an environmental politics that demonstrates an understanding of the ways in which sexual relations organize and influence both the material world of nature and our perceptions, experiences, and constructions of that world."[2] The age of star production will come to an end with no concern whatsoever for human life or sexual politics, but as practiced here, a beige ecocriticism remains anthropocentric to the extent that it focuses on how humans sexually inhabit a natural world that includes stars, planets, plants, animals, and all forms of being both animate and inanimate that contribute to the construction of the "environment." Inhabiting this world are humans who subscribe to social, philosophical, and theological mandates about what is natural, as well as humans who are sometimes abjected as waste from the category of humanity, including nonwhites, perverts, the homeless, and the insane. Also inhabiting this world are the microorganisms—the viruses and bacteria—that affect sexual relations between humans and provoke transformations in the places and spaces they inhabit. Apocalyptic (world-ending and world-changing) events in this natural world cue a beige ecocriticism. The queerness of this ecocriticism lies in turn in its antiheteronormative insistence that sex, itself a potentially apocalyptic act, is always a social, environmental act, too, not merely a private and personal one.

In its stubborn hope for a "brighter" future after the end of the star systems that the universe's redshift predicts, beige ecocriticism resists the antisocial turn against futurity in queer studies. This turn locates queerness, in Lee Edelman's words from *No Future*, "in the negativity opposed to every form of social viability."[3] Yet the social and environmental dimensions of sex imbue it with the possibility to enable ways of living that evade Edelman's totalizing equation of social viability with the abjection of the queer. Sex facilitates queer, "futuristic" ways of being social that a beige ecocriticism maps within the extant systems of the world. As it does so, beige ecocriticism also resists a tendency within ecocriticism to reduce apocalyptic tropes to divisive tools of Armageddon romance narratives. Apocalypticism often provides, as Greg Gerrard writes, "an emotionally charged frame of reference within which complex, long-term issues are reduced to monocausal crises involving conflicts between recognizably opposed groups."[4] Edelman's polemic uses just such a frame to oppose queerness and the social, but a beige ecocriticism focuses instead on apocalypses that reflect the multiplicity and coexistence of the systems of the

world and the complexity of their interactions. It focuses on the conjunc-
tions of ends and beginnings, reminding us that almost everything is star
stuff—that we are all, in a sense, waste products. (All elements heavier
than hydrogen and helium are cooked in the nuclear furnace of stars. All
elements heavier than lead are created in the violence of supernova explosions.) Rather than share in what José Esteban Muñoz terms a "romance
with the negative," a beige ecocriticism allies itself instead with a queer
criticism that, like Muñoz's own, will not turn loose of the future.[5] The
future in which a beige ecocriticism invests is not the static, perpetually
deferred future of heterosociality, a future figured in the image of the child
and subject to Edelman's devastating critique. The queer future of beige
investment follows an apocalypse that does arrive: a future forged in the
combination and reconstruction of refuse elements from the systems of
the world.

As an exercise in beige ecocriticism that takes as its object of analysis
the novel that also fuels its theorization, this essay explores the apocalyptic
work of future-forging in Samuel Delany's *The Mad Man* (1994, revised
and expanded in 2002). To use Mortimer-Sandilands and Erikson's metaphor, *The Mad Man*—which shows no interest in the color beige per se,
but which readily lends itself to thinking simultaneously about brown, yellow, pink, and white—traces out threads in the biosocial fabric into which
certain sexual practices involving urological and scatological waste, homeless and nonwhite bodies, are woven. Queer pasts, presents, and futures
form, within the novel, against the discourses of sexual health and normality that knit together heterosexist ecologies—a word that slides into
economies—and sometimes incorporate "healthy" homosexual lives, which
are ostensibly monogamous and therefore "safe." *The Mad Man's* pornographic representations of "insane" gay sex apocalyptically *reveal* (from
the Greek *apokalyptein:* to uncover, disclose) how these discourses sim-
plify intricate patterns in the biosocial fabric and distort the map of the
sexual landscape that we negotiate, often unconsciously, all the time.
These revelations produce, in the novel, particular critical effects, including a quasi-utopian critique of economies of sexual scarcity, the development of an approach to sexual risk that does not partake of the illogic of
phobias, and a reconceptualization of the institution of the home and its
ecology (from the Greek *oikos:* home, house, dwelling place, habitation)

against heteronormative models of domesticity. Collectively, however, these revelations pull apocalypticism out of the ethical waste bin, using it to trope the world-altering consequences of what Michel Foucault calls the *bios philosophicus:* "the animality of being human, renewed as a challenge, practiced as an exercise—and thrown in the face of others as a scandal."[6] In *The Mad Man,* the *bios philosophicus* reorganizes "perceptions, experiences, and constructions" of the natural world. As a beige way of life, it reclaims the color itself from the popular perception of beige's mundane safety.

Pornapocalypse Now!

Foucault's definition of the *bios philosophicus* provides an epigraph for Delany's generically eclectic *The Mad Man,* the protagonist of which is a gay, black, philosophy graduate student named John Marr, who lives in New York City throughout the 1980s and early 1990s. As a green graduate student, Marr plans to write a Hegelian tome called *The Systems of the World,* which will put "psychology, history, reality, and metaphysics . . . once and for all into their grandly ordered relation."[7] A year of schooling disabuses him of this ambition toward totalization, however, and soon afterward his white adviser introduces him to the work of the young Korean American philosopher Timothy Hasler, whose murder in 1973, in a hustler bar called the Pit, Marr proceeds to investigate. In this academic-cum-mystery-cum-philosophical-cum-pornographic novel that emphasizes the dynamic, transformative, and sometimes catastrophic interrelations of the systems of the world, Marr, like Hasler, lives the *bios philosophicus,* recounting his numerous sexual encounters with New York City's homeless and detailing the effects of the AIDS outbreak on attitudes about and places for public sex.

Translating philosophy from the academy to the streets of New York City, from the writings of white men to the lived lives of the nonwhite, and from the high jargon of professional journals to the lowest and most intentionally salacious of genres, *The Mad Man* aims at a mode of pornography narratively akin to the cosmic latte's computational mixing of all color in the universe: a coming together of the systems of the world. Delany describes the book in his prefatory disclaimer as "a pornotopic fantasy: a set of people, places, and relations among them that have never happened and never could happen for any number of surely self-evident reasons."[8] "'Pornotopia,'" he further explains in an interview, "is not 'the good sexual place.' (That would be 'Upornotopia' or 'Europornotopia.') It's simply *the* 'sexual place'—the place where all can become (apocalyptically) sexual."[9] Pulled from Delany's parentheses, pornotopic apocalypticism—or what I call *pornapocalypticism*—proves crucial to Guy Davidson's provocative and nuanced effort to use Delany's novel to rehabilitate utopianism not as an imagination of homogeneity and stasis (a imagination Delany has himself described as tyrannical) but as a "'future-oriented' potential within eros" that works to ameliorate tensions within a stratified capitalist society.[10] Pornapocalypticism repeatedly tropes sexual desires for partners across barriers of class and race especially, facilitating an imaginative project of social remodeling in which these barriers are lowered and transgressed, though not necessarily dismantled entirely.

Pornotopia, Davidson emphasizes, is a place of sexual imagination—a point Delany's disclaimer makes, and which Delany has made elsewhere again in rejecting realist interpretations of *The Mad Man*.[11] We can none-theless gain some material and ecological purchase on the relationship between the fictitious and the real, and the effect of pornapocalyptic desire on specific locations in the biosocial fabric, if we understand pornotopias as versions of Foucault's heterotopias. In Foucault's words, heterotopias are "counter-sites, a kind of effectively enacted utopia in which the real sites, all the other real sites that can be found within the culture, are simulta-neously represented, contested, and inverted."[12] The systems of the world and their detritus mingle in these sites. Delany's career-long interest in het-erotopias, which is most explicit in his 1976 science-fiction novel *Trouble on Triton: An Ambiguous Heterotopia,* lies principally in what Foucault calls "heterotopias of deviation: those in which individuals whose behavior is deviant in relation to the required mean or norm are placed." These sites include "rest homes and psychiatric hospitals, and of course prisons," as well as porn theaters and gay bars.[13] These last two sites figure highly in *The Mad Man,* one of the former as a site of revelation about sexual risk taking, and one of the latter, the Pit, as a site governed by an economics of sex overthrown in a long, climactic orgy that takes place in Marr's apart-ment. Because the Pit, as a kind of effectively enacted utopia, exists within and in relation to capitalist assumptions about the scarcity of resources for which people must compete, violence erupts from the clash between the utopian promise of easy and available pleasure and the "real" lack of resources to supply that pleasure. The apocalyptic devastation of Marr's apartment, in contrast, results from an anticapitalist mode of queer world-making that eschews these economics of sexual scarcity.[14]

As "the hard-core hustling bar" among "the ecological deployment of bars along the Strip,"[15] the Pit sits at the narrative center of both Marr's and Hasler's efforts to live the *bios philosophicus*. Hasler dies, as does Marr's friend Crazy Joey, in this bar whose biosocial fabric is one subject of Hasler's careful ecological meditation. As Marr quickly deduces, a set of informal rules easily separates and identifies sellers for buyers: the johns sit at the bar, the hustlers along the wall, each group divided by the floor. The exceptions to the rules—a hustler and a john out of place, an unidentifiable person—are nonetheless significant ecologically. In the novel's terminology, they showcase "Hasler structures": roughly, a system "seen as a reduction of unsystematic data," or more precisely, the "more or less violent, more or less efficient, more or less powerful attempt to tame . . . the always more or less chaotic asystematicity that is actual language as it pervades and constitutes the world."[16] The systematizing rules that spatially arrange hustlers and johns do not secure the relationships between what may appear at first like a cosmic latte of bodies. Rather, these rules reduce from an ever-present latte, from a continuous generation of "exceptions." Not only do all systems of the world produce detritus; this detritus, these exceptions, provides raw material for the construction, the reduction, of these systems.

This systematizing reduction can be, as Marr says, "more or less violent." Hasler dies in this place that offers its patrons, as one puts it, the opportunity "to pursue our clean and costly pleasures."[17] Patrons of the Pit assume the relative scarcity of beautiful boys. The hustlers available on a given night, and their rates, determine the pleasure patrons can find, and patrons pay for these pleasures because of their correlative assumption that free sex, even if it were available, is more sordid. As the bartender tells Marr, "The thing that makes this whole place possible is a belief that sex—the kind of sex that gets sold here—is scarce. Because it's scarce, it's valuable. And because it's valuable, it goes for good prices."[18] Hasler died, Marr learns, by stepping in front of a knife meant for his lover, Mad Man

Mike, who flashed his cock around the bar and offered himself to a john for free. A hustler, "roaring like a crazy man," saw this offer as a threat of wasted, economically unproductive sex, a threat to a fantasy he was monetarily invested in protecting.[19] Seventeen years later, the night of the orgy in Marr's apartment, Crazy Joey dies making a similar offer. Both Guy Davidson and William Haver have rightly argued that these murders result from the clash of economies of pleasure and monetary production.[20] Yet this clash happens only because of the latter economy's assumption of sexual scarcity. "Mad men" offer pleasure for free, pornapocalyptically upending the economy of scarcity that organizes the ecology of the bar. In doing so, mad men prompt another kind of "crazy" reaction by hustlers trying to protect this economy in which they produce sex as a costly commodity.

Pornapocalypticism does not reduce to this deadly clash of systems, however. Delany works instead toward what he identifies as "a more rigorous and productive sense of the apocalyptic"—one that resists simple us versus them antagonisms—by recalibrating the very terms of "production" through the novel's establishment of alternative economies that reject the assumption of sexual scarcity even as they reference it.[21] One such economy organizes relations among the group of white, black, and Latino men with whom Marr becomes sexually involved. The leader of this group is Hasler's former lover, Mad Man Mike, a "light-skinned"—somewhere between yellow, pink, and brown—black man.[22] Mad Man Mike and these other men, Crazy Joey among them, have developed a sexual trade system in which everyone costs exactly one penny. This trade system pornotopically references most obviously the slave trade in black bodies. At the same time, the penny trade references a system of sexual buying and selling within a capitalist economy that ascribes no worth to the homeless. It mirrors the sex trade in such a way that everyone acquires an equal, minimal worth. As Davidson notes, it "both parodies and undermines the system of monetary exchange that governs places such as the Pit and the city more generally."[23] The nominal transaction flaunts the terms of this exchange through its radical democratization of bare minimum worth. One result of this economic revolution is an ecological revolution in the space of Marr's apartment. The orgy that takes place there and spans parts 4 and 5 of the novel—titled, respectively, "The Place of Excrement" and "The Mirrors of

Night"—charts out a reflective, pornotopic ecology that eroticizes rather than simply dispenses with waste: a system of piss drinking and shit eating as men are traded between one another for a coin with the head of the Great Emancipator on one side.

This aesthetically assaulting, alternatively repulsive and erotically stimulating, orgy evinces a more rigorous and productive sense of the apocalyptic in which various kinds of waste products are put to a newly productive use outside the economies of monetary profit that assume a competition for scarce resources. This erotic enlistment of material forms of negativity thus differentiates itself, as an ecological action, from an environmentalism promoting capitalism's own ability to enlist waste again in the production of profit. As Mary Catherine Foltz observes, "'Rubbish' or excrement in Delany's account does not re-enter a market nor is it 're-cycled' through waterways and treatment centers; he [Marr] enjoys what is freely disposed of by others and becomes exemplary of a contemporary subject, a gleaner, who lives off the excess of others."[24] This pornapocalyptically produced ecology develops only in relation to capitalism, yet its anticapitalist mode of relationality consists in its simultaneous repudiation of the profit motive. When Leaky, Marr's eventual long-term, white lover, acquires all the pennies during the orgy, "the Mad Man, by fiat, simply redistribute[s] the wealth as absolutely and autocratically as Marx himself might have done."[25] This redistribution is itself an apocalyptic resetting of the system, but the system actually solicits the shock because its goal is not profit through exploitation but the production of pleasure and friendship through equitable exchange. These different objectives serve, in the end, to distinguish Delany's pornapocalypse from that imagined by the Marquis de Sade. As Marr observes, "The same thing that seems so abhorrent in Sade, when it actually occurs among people of good will . . . is as reassuring as a smile or a warm hand on your shoulder, or a sharp, friendly smack on the ass."[26]

Cruising Pornotopia, or the
Science (Fiction) of Risk Management

But what about the health risks of all this sex? Of drinking piss, as Marr enjoys, and eating shit, as his friend Tony enjoys? Of such beige—brown and yellow—ingestions? In what ways does a more rigorous and productive sense of the apocalyptic relate to the realities of risk—to the fact that sex can be a vehicle not only for epidemiological but also, more broadly, ecological disaster? The second of Delany's disclaimers states,

> *The Mad Man* is not a book about "safe sex." Rather, it is specifically a book about various sexual acts whose status as vectors of HIV contagion we have no hard-edged knowledge of because the monitored studies that would give statistical portraits of the relation between such acts and seroconversion (from HIV- to HIV+) have not been done.[27]

As the novel nonetheless demonstrates, governing discourses of safe sex and public sanitation exaggerate known biological dangers in the name of realizing sex-negative and homophobic objectives. These discourses militate against contact with "dirty" people in "dirty" places. Marr imagines a mother, for instance, who has told her children that they can catch "'diseases' from sitting on a public toilet seat."[28] These children will likely

> never know that 60 percent of shit is harmless bacterial mulch and that the other 40 percent is even more harmless fibers. Likely they'll never know that urine is all-but-distilled water, with some urolic acid in it, which some of those bacteria, in an oxygen-rich atmosphere, eventually turn into antiseptic ammonia—which, yes, is caustic to imbibe after a day or three.[29]

Drinking urine and eating shit are not without health risks, but campaigns against "dirt" generally exaggerate risks that are, for some, worth taking.

Jeffery Allen Tucker and Reed Woodhouse have both argued that, despite its disclaimer, *The Mad Man* is a novel about negotiating sexual risk.[30] The novel opens by locating itself in the wake of the AIDS pandemic: "I do not have AIDS. I am surprised that I don't. I have had sex with men weekly, sometimes daily—without condoms—since my teens, though true, it's been overwhelmingly . . . no, more accurately, it's been—since 1980— all oral, not anal."[31] Woodhouse notes that these sentences echo those Harold Brodkey wrote in a 1993 *New Yorker* essay: "I have AIDS. I am surprised that I do."[32] Brodkey's surprise stems from the fact that he messed around with men in the 1960s and 1970s, before AIDS arrived to wreak havoc on New York City's urban ecology. "What one hears in Delany's sentence," Woodhouse concludes, "is the sound of a gauntlet being thrown down, for he wants to completely reverse the story Brodkey tells: the story, that is, of an 'innocent victim' who may have played around a *little* but very *long ago* and certainly not doing *those things*." John Marr is a "guilty victor" who "*has* done all those things (though not, it is true, unprotected anal intercourse) and has yet survived."[33] I would add that Delany's presentation of Marr as a "guilty victor" meditating on the relationship between sex acts and seroconversion additionally locates *The Mad Man* in an apocalyptic world ravaged by AIDS. Filled with meticulous descriptions of the heterotopias in which Marr satisfies his desires for gay sex, *The Mad Man* is a science-fiction novel in another guise. It is a novel about the *social* science of risk management, a novel about living and loving in the same environment, in the same political and economic climate, with a deadly microorganism that motivates both genocidal homophobia and, among queers themselves, judgmental attitudes about "unsafe" sex practices.

Rather than militate against risk taking, *The Mad Man* suggests that living "productively" within the AIDS pandemic affecting urban environments like New York City requires the development of ecologies organized around values other than profit.[34] One such value is goodwill, which, to put the point simply, tends to make human life more pleasant. Delany has elsewhere written about the personal and social importance of pleasure that results from interpersonal contact motivated by goodwill, often for another's sexual needs. In *Times Square Red, Times Square Blue*, he memorializes the late porn theaters in Times Square as sites enabling a more "rewarding, productive, and pleasant" life within "a current mode of capitalism" that discourages interclass contact.[35] The theaters number among the heterotopian institutions that have helped urban gays—rich, poor, white, black, Asian, Latino, young, old, abled, and disabled—overcome the sexual scarcity problem besetting rural areas.[36] Some of these contact relationships are momentary, and some become long-term friendships and partnerships—but, Delany insists, all contacts *are* relationships, and intimate ones at that.[37] They are also productive relationships, if productivity is understood in social, emotional, and intellectual, rather than simply monetary, terms. In Marr's words, the "camaraderie" he experiences with the people he meets in the theaters is "disturbing" only because "there is no economy that reconciles my actions around them with my emotional responses to them, as well as my intellectual convictions about who they are as political/ethical beings."[38] There is no economy, in other words, that reconciles Marr's own sense of these people's worth and attractiveness with their social status outside the theaters as worthless and filthy.

Imbuing with apocalyptic potential this friction between economic value and the valuations of sexual desire, *The Mad Man*, like *Times Square Red, Times Square Blue*, underscores the distinction between utopias and dually heterotopian and pornotopian institutions in ways that map onto the distinction between a camaraderie of homogeneous subjects and a camaraderie of subjects positioned very differently in social, political, and economic hierarchies. These pornotopian and heterotopian institutions, which offer condensed contestations and reflections of the "real world," thereby offer an erotic twist on the concept of universalism that colors them beige qua the universal average. As Darieck Scott demonstrates in his account of the novel's erotics of abjection, mad men do not desire the eradication of difference. Rather, they fetishize difference in ways that reflect and work through the trauma of real-world discrimination by gaining power over discrimination in erotic situations where partners are motivated not by animus but instead by goodwill.[39] Marr likes being called a nigger by the men he is blowing. Leaky, who grew up on a farm on the border of West Virginia and Maryland, likes being called stupid, and he wears a dog collar to signify Marr's ownership of him. Drinking piss and eating shit, consuming the waste of another, is also repeatedly troped in the novel as an eroticizing of one's own "lowness." Positions of domination and subordination can switch quickly, and self-degradation can itself function as a mode of domination. After drinking Tony's piss in a cellar, for instance, Marr orders Tony, in a passage I quote at length as characteristic of this drama of reversal, to eat his shit, which Tony dug out of Marr's ass:

> That's fresh nigger shit. You ask fifty guys what the lowest thing
> in the world is. They'll tell you, it's a cocksucker. Ask them
> what's lower than a cocksucker, and they'll tell you it's a nigger
> cocksucker—right? And that's a nigger cocksucker's *shit*—that
> *you're* gonna eat! You'd eat a nigger cocksucker's shit—which makes
> you the fucking lowest scumbag around, right? Well, see, not only is

it a nigger scumbag shit, man. It's a nigger cocksucker who was
sucking on *your* fucking dick, drinking *your* fucking piss! That
means it's gonna be even *lower*—and the only way you could be
lower than that, dog, is if you ate my fuckin' shit. Scarfed it all
down. In front of the fuckin' nigger himself." I put my arm around
his back and squeezed the far helmet of his hard shoulder. "Then
you'll be so fuckin' low that if you rang the goddamn nigger's
doorbell and he answered it, the door would swing right over your
head—you'd be that low! Go on, you fuckin' homeless shit-eatin'
scumbag—.[40]

Marr's gesture of squeezing Tony's shoulder is a crucial reminder of the
goodwill motivating this erotic race to the bottom where each partner is
turned on by his own lowness with respect to the other. In the erotic conjunction of bodies and ingestion of piss and shit, in this act of world making out of bodily waste and waste bodies, each partner revels in his own
lowness and, simultaneously, in his difference from the other: Marr is a
"nigger cocksucker," and Tony is a "homeless shit-eatin' scumbag." As the
color I am using to trope these experiences of self-debasement—these
experiences of self-"marring"—beige does not denote the end of difference in utopian equalization. It tropes the "hot" concentration of difference continuously in evidence in the attention drawn throughout the novel
toward racial identity, skin tone, sexual identity (or lack thereof), erotic
preferences, class positioning, hygiene, and sanity.

This heterotopian maintenance of difference as the basis for erotic
contact proves crucial to the novel's development of a more-nuanced, ecological approach to apocalypticism. Marr's first revelation—"as close as I,
personally, will probably ever get to a mystical experience"[41]—comes
while cruising the Variety Photoplays Theatre in the mid-1980s. He enters
the theater, "doubtless, like half the men there, terrified of AIDS," but he
leaves without "any fear of the disease."[42] In that afternoon, he realizes that
there is no guarantee against acquiring AIDS. To live is to live with risk, with
the impossibility of possessing a perfect knowledge that would dissolve
the difference, in this case the unknown HIV status, of each new partner.
In Marr's words, "It is the realization that one is gambling, and gambling
on one's own—rather than seeking some possible certain knowledge, some

knowledgeable belief in how intelligent or idiotic the chances are—that obliterates the terror."[43] Marr does not stop cruising, and life after his revelation is not without threat: people who cruise still "move through life fully and continually oppressed by the suspicion/conviction" that they already have AIDS.[44] Yet more comfortable with the difference of the other, the sero-status enigma that each new partner presents, Marr does become a more content cruiser. As Delany explains, the apocalypse is "a symbol of the end of things but also . . . for the beginning of things."[45] For Marr, this revelation is the beginning of a more comfortable, more bearable way of being in the world, of living with the risk of dying.

In the absence of good data about which acts carry what seroconversion risks, Marr does take some precautions to protect himself: "I don't suck within three hours of brushing my teeth in the morning; and I don't brush my teeth within six hours of sucking."[46] But uninterested as he is in sustaining life at *all* costs, he is not entirely risk averse. He rejects the techniques of the activist groups that tour the bars and baths: "Their particular option—condoms, no fluid exchanges—while I feel it is just as valid *as* mine, is not mine."[47] The novel, through Marr, endorses different, idiosyncratic ways to negotiate this ecology of risk, collectively irreducible to a single prescription. At the same time, the response of the City Fathers to the outbreak of AIDS has far less to do with containing its transmission than with quelling the sex panic surrounding gay heterotopias. They simply close down the bars and the baths. Marr condemns this response as nothing less than "a murderous act by the city—not because of anything necessarily to be learned from the 'Safe Sex' demonstrations about AIDS, but because it drives tens of thousands of gay men from a fairly protected environment out into far more dangerous venues, where robbery, murder, and general queer-bashing are common."[48] The safe-sex demonstrations bring attention to the public sex already transpiring in these sites, but sustaining gay men's lives is nowhere on the City Fathers' agenda. Like the homeless, gay men are the city's dehumanized refuse, its disposable bodies. *The Mad Man* protests this act of apocalyptic genocide by revealing the ecological complexity—the intricate relationships between people and spaces and diseases—within heterotopias that can enable more pleasant and "healthy" ways of living. As Marr explains, "I don't think anyone can really understand what AIDS means in the gay male community until she or he has some understanding of the field and function—the range, the mechanics—of the sexual landscape AIDS has entered into."[49] Yet the City Fathers do not seek this understanding. They remain willfully ignorant of "both the camaraderie and good will that exists in so much of it," and the "barriers to social communication" that carve up these spaces as well.[50] They know nothing of these sites' formal and informal behavioral and information-sharing systems. And thus they are responsible for an enormous ecological disaster: the murder of thousands of gay people, and the transformation of New York City into an environment less safe for, and less welcoming to, queers. An environment, in a word, sanitized.

Home/less

People who frequent the theaters and other queer heterotopias have no home, no *oikos,* within the homophobic and sex-negative discourses of sexual health and sanity that the City Fathers deploy. Within the beige ecologies that *The Mad Man*'s oppositional discourses construct, the connections among homosexuality, homelessness, and waste are therefore, as Foucault says, "simultaneously represented, contested, and inverted." Early in the novel, Marr marvels at the discursive conjunction of "bums, hoboes, derelicts, and winos" into "'the homeless,'" as the city consolidates into a nest of "homes."[51] Despite having his own apartment in the city, Marr too feels, in a sense, homeless: "Home" is "that distant and ephemeral institution that, once on Christmas, once on Mother's Day, and once on my father's birthday . . . I would take the Ferry across to Staten Island to visit."[52] The final, more rigorous and productive sense of the apocalyptic that I would like to track pertains to the ecological renovation of the home that takes place through the novel's efforts to theorize more pleasant ways of living in a sex-negative environment.

This renovation takes the form of innovation and reinvention through pornapocalyptic destruction. During the orgy, Marr's apartment is utterly defiled with piss and shit. Later that night, Mad Man Mike further destroys the apartment when grieving the death of Crazy Joey, who was stabbed in the Pit. This defilement and destruction invert what Foucault identifies as the rituals of purification that certain heterotopias provide, but defilement and destruction also purify the apartment in such a way that it becomes Marr and Leaky's home.[53] The new lovers clean the apartment and divide the space to support their social life and Marr's burgeoning academic career. They put stripping around the bedroom door to segregate the smell of urine from dinner guests. In a moment of postcoital satisfaction during the orgy, Marr wonders whether "this" is the "'home'" that Leaky is "trying to reach" by telling Marr incestuous, homoerotic, urine-soaked stories about being raised on a farm by his father and his father's black friend.[54] The scare quotes around *home* suggest the term's "possibly imaginary status," as Davidson notes in his consideration of home's utopian potential.[55] But imagination shapes social reality. The institution of the home is reimagined in this postcoital moment and in the life, the future, that Marr and Leaky subsequently build together.

This purification is also ritualistic, as it replays an almost identical series of events that takes place seventeen years earlier in Hasler's apartment, directly below Marr's 1990s one. Hasler is stabbed to death in the Pit after an orgy that Mad Man Mike arranges. The person who afterward enters Hasler's apartment describes it as "a sty . . . a shambles, an abattoir." Piles of clothes had been "urinated on and defecated on—repeatedly," and shit had been "smeared over the walls."[56] *Ekpyrosis*—Hereclitus's word in *On Nature* for world-consuming conflagration—had also "been written in shit, twice on the walls and once on the inside of a window."[57] (Marr uses Joey's shit to write the same word on a broken piece of mirror—the mirror being Foucault's figure for the place between utopia and heterotopia.)[58] After hearing this description of Hasler's apartment, Marr dreams of a flying, clawed monster—the novel's figure for desire itself—that defiles Hasler's apartment in an "apocalypse of piss and shit."[59] The dream imagines the destruction of the home that Hasler, had his life not been cut short, might have continued to share with the Mad Man, much as Marr will share his with Leaky. In the novel's apocalyptic logic, the apartment has to be defiled before it can become a home to the formerly homeless. It has to be "purified" of the very notions of cleanliness and sanity that structure normative domesticity before it can become a suitable home for those who, troped as waste, eroticize waste.

As an ecological disaster novel, *The Mad Man* lays waste to familiar tropes of the home as productive of a clean, economically successful, heterosexual citizenry, but it then reinvents these tropes to suit the lives of those who would deploy them differently. Marr's apartment becomes a home for the homeless, including Marr himself, who works temp jobs until, at the end of the novel, he graduates and becomes both an adjunct professor and a paralegal. Delany has indicated that the novel offers an academic as well as a sexual exposé: "It's a novel that allegorizes—if you want to read it that way—the situation our contemporary graduate students (who, in most major universities, teach 50 percent or more of our university classes) have to endure to survive."[60] Many of these students, especially in the humanities, do not land tenure-track jobs; they are the detritus of a university system that churns through cheap labor. The novel does not explicitly dwell on this churning; the academic allegory works instead through the novel's larger interests in the production of economic, social, and physical waste. Questions about academic labor nonetheless frame a narrative whose protagonist "wastes" a decade in New York while he tries, in fits and starts, to work on a dissertation about another graduate student who also never received his doctorate. Marr's work at the temp agency allegorizes the transient status of academics who work to find and define a home within a labor market organized to deny it to them.

This apocalyptic pattern of tropological destruction and re-creation repeats at the novel's end when Marr and Leaky visit the farm on which Leaky grew up. The sexual ecology of this farm maps onto neither of the dominant ecologies of rural queerness. It is neither the sexually repressive environment from which young queers long to escape nor the green, bucolic, pastoral space of queer liberty. This farm is a heterotopian space in which American racial oppression and the discourses of mental health and sexual innocence are refracted in pornographic scenes featuring Leaky, his white father Billy (a.k.a. Ol' Fuck), Billy's best friend Big Nigg, and Big Nigg's little, hunchbacked, toothless brother Blacky. (In brief, Blacky likes sucking cock and drinking piss, and Ol' Fuck, Big Nigg, and Leaky like getting their cocks sucked and pissing down Blacky's throat.) These scenes comically cinch Darieck Scott's argument that "Delany's characters render hyperbolic racialized roles and emphasize domination; and in doing so they insist on the relation of white-top/black-bottom BDSM play to the history of conquest, subjugation, and violence that instantiated the roles and established the terms and modes of domination."[61] At the same time, Marr's education in rural queerness consists of an ecological lesson in sexual diversity, or the coexistent systems of the world. When he and Marr first meet, Leaky takes strong exception to Marr's suggestion that Leaky's childhood was sexually abusive. For Leaky, this suggestion refuses the reality that his family is "good people" who love each other.[62] The suggestion also misses the narrative point, for it attempts to graft an imagination of pastoral innocence onto an ecology that instead produces hyperbolic, parodic versions of the rural pervert. "Nigger," Leaky explains, "some weird things go on, up in those mountains."[63] Reducing these "weird things" to sexual abuse blankets the mirror the farm holds up to the racial and sexual systems of the world.

The systems of the world collide again as Marr wonders whether urban queer conversations about marriage rights have any traction in "this eccentric American margin."[64] When he asks Billy and Blacky if they would ever marry, Blacky demurs, claiming that Billy "fucks too many women." Billy adds that he and Big Nigg have been married since they were kids in reform school. "I don't mean we ever had no sex or nothin'," he qualifies. "I mean sex for *real*, Nigg and me. Sure, we *shared* enough of it—like with ol' Blacky here."[65] Later that night, Leaky explains to Marr, "Ain't everybody *ready* for your kind of Gay Liberation shit, little guy. They got their own ways of doin' it—and they ain't *all* bad, neither."[66] Marr himself feels little ownership over "Gay Liberation shit," for as a black gay man with highly nonnormative object choices, his own sexual desires find little representation there. Yet during his visit, Marr learns, as he does many times throughout the novel, that different ways of "doin' it"—that is, living and living-with, being viable and social, counting and not counting certain acts as sex—are not necessarily less valid, ethically speaking, if all involved act out of goodwill and without causing harm. As Marr tells Billy on the drive back to the bus station, "You're trying to do the same thing everybody else I know is. To live life right for the way you want it."[67]

The Mad Man refracts the pastoral heterotopia of the farm in the many scenes set in New York City parks. Historically these parks were constructed to offer city dwellers a rural respite from the moral chaos of urban life. They were, in Mortimer-Sandilands and Erickson's words, "places for the cultivation of morally upstanding citizens . . . and sites of regulated sexual contact, in which courting heterosexual couples could 'tryst' in an open space that was both morally uplifting and, given its visibility, highly disciplined."[68] The ironic reclamation of the parks by cruising gay men has subsequently effected a "democratization of natural space, in which different communities can experience the park in their own ways."[69] While some people play sports, go jogging, and take walks, as well as engage in heterosexual and homosexual courtship, others have sex in the bushes. The former groups do not necessarily see the latter, as Marr learns from a homeless man called Pop, who claims he learned this bit of wisdom from "this chink kid"—someone like a young Hasler—who sucked him off. "There's two kinds of people in the world," Pop explains. "There's baseball players. And there's cocksuckers. An' most of the time the baseball players don't even *see* the cocksuckers."[70] This blindness suggests moral blindness to the sight of the homeless and homosexuals, but it also suggests the mutual enjoyment of a natural space experienced simultaneously and differently by different groups of people.

The farm, the parks, the bars, the theaters, and Marr's apartment all serve as sites in the novel for elaborating its ecological argument for the coexistence of multiple forms of sociality—many of them negotiated between beings vulnerable to abjection from the category of the human. Marr and Leaky's visit, near the novel's end, to Mad Man Mike's two-room, makeshift quarters above an abandoned track tunnel underscores this multiplicity through Mike's "antisocial," binary reduction of it. Mike lives among "cardboard, canvas, and newspaper dwellings. Some had roofs. Some didn't. Some were just . . . coffins people could crawl into."[71] In this waste of stuff, of shelters manufactured out of other people's trash, Mike remembers Hasler's death and what he has learned about those more "hard-edged" systems of the world:

> "See, I learned it costs too much. To do that shit, out *there* where
> you are. Here it costs you a penny. Out there. . ." Mike's hand went
> up to rub the scar showing between his shirt rags. ". . . it costs you
> your fuckin' life!"[72]

Mike prefers it "here," in the relative space of queer liberty where the costs of pleasure are negligible and pleasure is abundant. I nonetheless want to suggest that Mike also overdraws the distinction between "here" and "there," disallowing the apocalyptic reconfiguration of social space that Marr and Leaky, border crossers and mess makers both, simultaneously evince is possible, and which Mike himself helped facilitate in the orgy and its aftermath.

The last we hear of Mike, Leaky says that he and Mike "piss and shit on a white feller" over in the park, and Leaky got his dick sucked, but not as well as Marr sucks it: "[Marr's] just about got me house broke."[73] The term *house* denotes a system, an ecology, of domesticity that now includes two people, one of them a person and pet (a collared dog), previously excluded from its borders—two people whose own sexual practices, Davidson notes, "it makes sense here to call *undomesticated*."[74] The permanence of this particular inclusion, this happy ending, and the future of Marr and Leaky's relationship, is in no way guaranteed, however. Marr predicts that his and Leaky's relationship "is doomed to continue,"[75] but this oxymoronically pleasant "doom" is still subject, as the tragic deaths of Hasler and Joey suggest, to the contingencies inherent in living the *bios philosophicus.* In developing a more rigorous and productive sense of the apocalyptic, the novel has provided queers with the possibility for a better future— even a domestic future, if such a future is what one wants—but it has not guaranteed structural stasis. The systems of the world continue, inevitably, to interact. Here *and* there, messes will be made.

Notes

For their help on this essay, I am grateful to Samuel R. Delany, Jeffrey J. Cohen, Matt Mackenzie, and Vin Nardizzi.

1. Ivan K. Baldry, Karl Glazebrook et al., "The 2dF Galaxy Redshift Survey: Constraints on Cosmic Star Formation History from the Cosmic Spectrum," *Astrophysical Journal* 569, no. 2 (2002): 582–94.

2. Catriona Mortimer-Sandilands and Bruce Erickson, "Introduction: A Genealogy of Queer Ecologies," in *Queer Ecologies: Sex, Nature, Politics,* ed. Mortimer-Sandilands and Erickson (Bloomington: Indiana University Press, 2010), 5. In my materialist deployment, which insists on a connection between queerness and the particular bodies denigrated and labeled queer, a queer ecology is queer only insofar as its subject is antiheteronormative sex and sexual expression. Compare Timothy Morton's much more sweeping homologization of queerness and antifoundationalism in "Queer Ecology," *PMLA* 125, no. 2 (2010): 273–82.

3. Lee Edelman, *No Future: Queer Theory and the Death Drive* (Durham, N.C.: Duke University Press, 2004), 9. Not all antisocial queer theory similarly rejects futurity. On alternative modes of queer sociality, see especially Judith Halberstam,

In a Queer Time and Place: Transgender Bodies, Subcultural Lives (New York: New York University Press, 2005) and *The Queer Art of Failure* (Durham, N.C.: Duke University Press, 2011); Tim Dean, *Unlimited Intimacy: Reflections on the Subculture of Barebacking* (Chicago: University of Chicago Press, 2009); and José Esteban Muñoz, *Cruising Utopia: The Then and There of Queer Futurity* (New York: New York University Press, 2009).

4. Greg Gerrard, *Ecocriticism* (New York: Routledge, 2004), 105. I do not mean to imply, apocalyptically, that ecocriticism or critical theory has been entirely hostile to apocalypticism. Slavoj Žižek also seizes on the ethical potentials of apocalypticism in *Living in the End Times* (New York: Verso, 2010), for instance, "One should keep an open mind towards new possibilities, bearing in mind that 'nature' is a contingent multi-faceted mechanism in which catastrophe can lead to unexpectedly positive results" (351). Sensitive to the fact that apocalyptic discourse has been enlisted to justify an extraordinary amount of violence, Richard Dellamora also argues that apocalyptic desire can "motivate the pursuit of social renovation" for the oppressed (*Apocalyptic Overtures: Sexual Politics and the Sense of an Ending* [New Brunswick, N.J.: Rutgers University Press, 1994], 26).

5. Muñoz, *Cruising Utopia*, 12.

6. I cite the translation provided in the epigraph to *The Mad Man* (Rutherford, N.J.: Voyant, 2002). A slightly different English translation can be found in Michel Foucault, *The Courage of Truth (The Government of Self and Others II): Lectures at the Collège de France 1983–1984,* ed. Frédéric Gros, trans. Graham Burchell (New York: Palgrave Macmillan, 2011), 265.

7. Delany, *Mad Man*, 8.

8. Ibid., ix.

9. Samuel Delany, *Shorter Views: Queer Thoughts and the Politics of the Paraliterary* (Hanover, N.H.: University Press of New England, 1999), 133.

10. Guy Davidson, "Apocalypse and Utopia in Samuel Delany's *The Mad Man*," *Journal of Modern Literature* 32, no. 1 (2008): 14. Davidson is citing Ernst Bloch as cited by Fredric Jameson in *Archaeologies of the Future: The Desire Called Utopia and Other Science-Fictions* (London: Verso, 2005), 2. (Bloch's utopianism also informs Muñoz's.) Davidson's rehabilitation of apocalypticism also owes much to Richard Dellamora's *Apocalyptic Overtures.*

11. Davidson, "Apocalypse and Utopia," 17; Delany, *Shorter Views,* 133.

12. Michel Foucault, "Of Other Spaces," *Diacritics* 16, no. 1 (1986): 24.

13. Ibid., 25.

14. I borrow the phrase *world making* from Lauren Berlant and Michael Warner, "Sex in Public," *Critical Inquiry* 24, no. 2 (1998): 558.

15. Delany, *Mad Man,* 120.

16. Ibid., 307.

17. Ibid., 424.

18. Ibid., 313.

19. Ibid., 417.

20. Davidson, "Apocalypse and Utopia," 26; and William Haver, "Of Mad Men Who Practice Invention to the Brink of Intelligibility," in *Queer Theory in Education,* ed. William F. Pinar (Mahwah, N.J.: Lawrence Erlbaum Associates, 1998), 360–61.

21. Delany, *Shorter Views,* 132.

22. Delany, *Mad Man,* 367.

23. Davidson, "Apocalypse and Utopia," 26.

24. Mary Catherine Foltz, "The Excremental Ethics of Samuel R. Delany," *SubStance* 37, no. 2 (2008): 54.

25. Delany, *Mad Man,* 391.

26. Ibid., 391.

27. Ibid., ix.

28. Ibid., 481.

29. Ibid., 481–82.

30. Jeffrey Allen Tucker, "A Revolution from Within: Paraliterature as AIDS Activism," in *A Sense of Wonder: Samuel R. Delany, Race, Identity, and Difference* (Middletown, Conn.: Wesleyan University Press, 2004), 230–75; and Reed Woodhouse, *Unlimited Embrace: A Canon of Gay Fiction, 1945–1995* (Amherst: University of Massachusetts Press, 1998), 212–21.

31. Delany, *Mad Man,* 5.

32. Harold Brodkey, "Personal History: To My Readers," *New Yorker,* June 21, 1993, 80–82.

33. Woodhouse, *Unlimited Embrace,* 213.

34. And how much more humane is this suggestion from the conservative one to settle down, marry, and raise children that Gabriel Rotello offers in *Sexual Ecology: AIDS and the Destiny of Gay Men* (New York: Dutton, 1998).

35. Samuel R. Delany, *Times Square Red, Times Square Blue* (New York: New York University Press, 2001), 111. See also Dianne Chisholm, *Queer Constellations: Subcultural Space in the Wake of the City* (Minneapolis: University of Minnesota Press, 2004), 1–9.

36. Delany, *Times Square Red, Times Square Blue,* 196.

37. Ibid., 40.

38. Delany, *Mad Man,* 127.

39. Darieck Scott, *Extravagant Abjection: Blackness, Power, and Sexuality in the African American Literary Imagination* (New York: New York University Press, 2010), 204–56. See also Philip Brian Harper, "'Take Me Home': Location, Identity, Transnational Exchange," *Callaloo* 23, no. 1 (2000): 461–78.

40. Delany, *Mad Man,* 286–87.

41. Ibid., 142.

42. Ibid., 152.

43. Ibid., 156. This is Marr's most concise explanation of his revelation, here in a letter to his friend Sam, to whom he is more largely trying to reveal the details of his gay life. He otherwise has pronounced difficulty communicating this revelation and worries that "to push my revelations on other people" risks "slip[ping] across that iffy border that separates the revelation from what, yes, I call madness" (*Mad Man,* 157). Davidson associates this slippage between revelation and madness with apocalyptic mysticism ("Apocalypse and Utopia," 21).

44. Ibid., 155. In other words, the end is here and has already passed. On the proleptic temporality of apocalypticism, see also Garrard, *Ecocriticism,* 86; and Morton, *Ecology without Nature,* 28.

45. Delany, *Shorter Views,* 131.

46. Delany, *Mad Man,* 155.

47. Ibid., 159.

48. Ibid.

49. Ibid., 158.

50. Ibid.

51. Ibid., 81.

52. Ibid.

53. Foucault, "Of Other Spaces," 26.

54. Delany, *Mad Man,* 345.

55. Davidson, "Apocalypse and Utopia," 22.

56. Delany, *Mad Man,* 269.

57. Ibid., 270.

58. Foucault, "Of Other Spaces," 24.

59. Delany, *Mad Man,* 277.

60. Delany, *Shorter Views,* 213.

61. Scott, *Extravagant Abjection,* 241.

62. Delany, *Mad Man,* 331.

63. Ibid.

64. Ibid., 466.

65. Ibid.

66. Ibid., 468.

67. Ibid., 473.

68. Mortimer-Sandilands and Erickson, "Introduction," 18.

69. Ibid., 26. On this particular reclamation, see also George Chauncey, *Gay New York: Gender, Urban Culture, and the Making of the Gay Male World, 1890–1940* (New York: Basic Books, 1995), 180–84.

70. Delany, *Mad Man,* 51.

71. Ibid., 443.

72. Ibid., 450.

73. Ibid., 485.

74. Davidson, "Apocalypse and Utopia," 16.

75. Delany, *Mad Man,* 468.

Brown

STEVE MENTZ

Smelly, rancid, and impure, it is no one's favorite color. We need brown but do not like looking at it. It is a color you cannot cover up, that will not go away. At the end of a long afternoon finger-painting with the kids, it is what is left, sprawling across the page. A color you cannot see through, brown captures a connecting opacity at the heart of ecological thinking. It comes at us from both sides of our world, the living and the dead. Brown marks the fertile soil that plants consume and the fecal waste that animals reject. Thinking brown pushes us into hybrid spaces that span living and nonliving matter, aesthetic values and biological drives. Plunging into this color challenges many ecological and theoretical models, including ancient anthropocentric fantasies, green pastoral recuperations, and even today's expanded universes of object-oriented philosophical and literary ontologies. Brown is the color of intimate and uncomfortable contact between human bodies and the nonhuman world. Drawing brown out requires extracting sense from stinking goo. This chapter follows three different brown threads: first, dry sand, which marks and unmarks boundaries; second, wet swamp, into which we do not want to sink; and last, the once-living shit that bodies excrete into the world around them. Literary brown remnants trace paths across organic and inorganic spaces, demonstrating a hybridity that frustrates order-making systems. To be ecological is to be brown, disturbingly.

This chapter's three browns seep out from three canonical literary texts: Edmund Spenser's *Amoretti* 75 ("One day I wrote her name upon the

194 Steve Mentz

strand"), the Slough of Despond in John Bunyan's *Pilgrim's Progress,* and a tantalizingly oblique vision of excretory transformation in Shakespeare's *Antony and Cleopatra.* These three examples help reconceptualize the relationship between human experience and nonhuman matter. These texts emphasize the mutual porousness of bodies and environments, in part because of distinctively premodern understandings of how human corporeality interacts with the nonhuman world, as recently explored by Gail Kern Paster among others.[1] Along with this literal mixing of bodies and their environs, early modern English poetry provides allegorical structures in which physical properties acquire symbolic meanings; to be brown on Spenser's beach, in Bunyan's "Miry Slow," or with Shakespeare's crocodile combines physical and intellectual registers. These spaces fill in the hybridity that Stacy Alaimo has recently called "trans-corporeality, in which the human is always mixed with the more-than-human world."[2] My emphasis on brown as a combination color, blending the red of fire with biotic green, extends Alaimo's theoretical frame into the literary past while emphasizing sloppy discomfort. Brown mixtures, whether sand, swamp, or shit, repel human interactions. We go there, but not to stay. Brown blends liquid and solid, washing the inhuman fluidity of blue oceans into the purported stability of green land. It is the color on which all agricultural societies, which is to say, all human societies, depend, no matter how green our environmental fantasies. Down in the muck, life is a brown business.

But at the same time I cannot help remembering that it is not possible to talk about brown, stinking *bios*-fragments without being overcome by our culture's most insistently social brown, human skin color. This racialized brown stains my metaphors, so that it is difficult to argue that brown is the color of shit, excess, and revulsion without courting racist codes. This chapter wants to bracket race and explore brown as an organic–inorganic borderlands, a swampy terrain of hybridity and exchange. But brown logic proclaims that all things mix together, the ones you want and the ones you try to reject, living bodies and dead matter and pernicious cultural fantasies. To be brown is to be human; there is no nonbrowned strain of human pigmentation. Rear-guard paranoid fantasies of whiteness like Edgar Allan Poe's *Narrative of Arthur Gordon Pym* must give way to an aesthetics of impurity. We need to learn to see our human world as does the narrator of Mat Johnson's recent novel *Pym,* which retells and inverts Poe.

At the novel's end, on an imaginary Antarctic coast, he recognizes our brown globe: "On the shore all I could discern was a collection of brown people, and this, of course, is a planet on which such are the majority."[3] The brown of race is not exactly this chapter's brown, but its mixture feels right.

As a blended color, brown invites textual and stylistic variety. Brown mixtures are not smooth; they contain lumps of matter, undissolved quotations, little pieces of stray undigested things. Moving from sand to swamp to shit descends deeper into brown discomfort while moving closer to our own bodies. At the end we find brown not at the aesthetic edge of the world ocean but by staring at our digestive system's just-barely former contents. Each section of this chapter textualizes brown hybridity through disruptions, including unattached quotations and autobiographical excurses. Sand, which accumulates unlike particles in such vast numbers that they appear to be alike, marks its interruptions with a dash: —. Swamp, which hides interruptions beneath the water, encircles them with parentheses: (). Shit, which is itself an interruption, a small bit of living matter extracted from the body and expelled into the world, calls attention to its internal breaks with three asterisks: ***. Together these modes, — () ***, mark the incessant mixing and remixing that makes brown brown. If the goal of ecological thinking is, in Timothy Morton's phrase, to "love the nonhuman," squalid brown mixtures represent blended things that are hard to love but also important not to ignore.[4]

The Dry Brown: Sand

Beaches are meeting places, borders, and models of change. Standing on the sand locates human bodies near oceanic immensity, but beaches are also, as Greg Dening has explored, privileged sites of transcultural encounters.[5] "Writing the beach" is Dening's phrase for making sense of the encounters that define this space. Sand, despite its many colors, represents two strains of ecological brown: it consists of a near-infinity of particles always touching each other, and its forms constantly change their structures. All holiday beachcombers know that the footprint you leave at low tide will not last. Sand between your toes squishes impermanence.

Poetic promises of immortality have a vexed relationship with sandy flux, as one of the Renaissance's most famous love sonnets shows. Edmund

Spenser's *Amoretti* 75 juxtaposes the fleeting presence of a beloved's name
on the sand and the eternal record of verse:

> I wrote her name upon the strand,
> But came the waves and washed it a way:
> Agayne I wrote it with a second hand,
> But came the tyde, and made my paynes his pray.
> Vayne man, sayd she, that doest in vaine assay,
> A mortall thing so to immortalize.
> For I my selfe shall lyke to this decay,
> And eek my name bee wiped out lykewize.
> Not so, (quod I) let baser things devize
> To dy in dust, but you shall live by fame:
> My verse your vertues rare shall eternize,
> And in the hevens wryte your glorious name,
> Where whenas death shall all the world subdew,
> Our love shall live, and later life renew.[6]

Sand is love's enemy, as impermanence challenges poetic and theological
clarity. The ecological point lurking within the poem, however, is less about
the putative success of poetic eterniz-ing and more about human blending
with the inorganic world. The two unequal halves of the sonnet represent
different stances in relation to sand-framed disruption. The poet and his
beloved—unlike many Renaissance love poems, we know the name of the
addressee, Spenser's soon-to-be wife Elizabeth Boyle—struggle against
brown knowledge but invent ways to reconcile with it.

The opening octet establishes the challenge that sand poses to poetic
forms and human emotions. These eight lines divide into two quatrains;
the poet speaks four lines about losing the beloved's written name, and
then she responds in her own voice emphasizing "decay."[7] First, the ocean
re-marks the strand, replacing "her name" with emptiness.[8] Brown sand
and blue ocean together disperse language, washing the name "a way"
and later making it "his pray."[9] Spenser's manipulation of flexible Elizabethan spelling emphasizes the overlap between prey as devour and pray
as prayer.[10] The ocean, ancient symbol of divine power, consumes the
poet's words and partly transforms them into a divine appeal.[11] At first the

narrator can register the flooding of his written word only as loss; when the name is washed away, he writes "with a second hand."[12] At this point sand remains only a substrate, not a source of meaning in itself.

The correcting voice of the beloved in the second quatrain forces a brown mixing of living and dead bodies. These lines shift the poem from beach to charnel house, so that oceanic washing modulates into fleshy decay. The key accusation, repeated twice in the same line, albeit in different spellings, is vanity: the poet is a "vayne man" for attempting to write on the sand, and writing is a "vaine assay."[13] In brown terms, the distance from beach to corpse is short. In English latitudes, sand is mostly silicon, but it contains the carapaces of myriads of once-living creatures, especially shellfish and, in tropical regions, coral. Like loamy soil, inorganic sand overflows with biotic remnants. The washed-clean strand occupies the same mixed brown materiality as the decayed corpse. The beloved insists that neither "my selve" nor "my name" can persist on the beach,[14] but the essentially physical connection between written name and living body subjects both to dissolution. Neither bodies nor names last in this mixed and mixing space.

> Almost to its farthest reaches
> The sea is a simple thing, reiterant wave upon wave.
> But in nature
> The simplest things cannot be broached without formalities
> without bowing and scraping
>
> —FRANCIS PONGE, "Sea Shores"

Spenser's poem builds "formalities," to adapt Francis Ponge's term, so that it can escape what its opening quatrain describes as the all-dissolving sea. Seeking in the idiom of sixteenth-century love poetry what the twentieth-century Caribbean poet Édouard Glissant, in his essay "The Black Beach," calls a "valid language for Chaos," the sonnet reaches for fame.[15] "My verse your vertues rare shall eternize,"[16] insists the poet, and the stumbling alliteration of verse/vertues, the awkward Latinized verb "eternize," and the slightly unusual adjective-after-noun word order of "vertues rare" all suggest that immortality might not be as smooth as it sounds. "Rare" appears where it does to preserve the iambic rhythm, and Spenser's poem exploits the slight tension between the line's rhythmic consistency and syntactic awkwardness. Like the works of modern sea-poets including Ponge and Glissant, Spenser's sonnet puts familiar poetic structures in touch with beachy hybridity. For all three poets, the brown beach-world corrodes but does not quite dissolve poetic immortality. Reaching for eternal fame was a familiar poetic trope for Renaissance sonneteers, as for their models Ovid and Petrarch, but on the beach it becomes impossible to believe in a world that does not change.

The "desavaging" of beaches came at a price.

—JEAN-DIDIER URBAIN, *At the Beach*

—*I remember where I was the first time I realized that the beach is not just the skin of the shore, not simply an extension of land's kingdom. That was the morning when I first realized beaches were brown antennae, retractable and sensitive, reaching down into blue vastness. I learned that beaches don't stay on land in Windy Bay, Alaska, in August 1989. I was living on board the* Optimus Prime, *a 185-foot fishing vessel named for a Transformer and playing host, that summer, to a couple dozen Athabascan natives from English Bay, a collection of commercial crab fisherman from Alaska and the Pacific Northwest, and one wayward college graduate. During the days we'd hit the beaches with shovels to bag up the slop of the* Exxon Valdez. *The gritty sand smelled like the inside of an auto repair shop. Viscous tar clung to rocks, gravel, our hands, and our clothes. The clear plastic bags grew slowly brown and full, day by day. But one week in August, late-summer weather trapped us on the boat for a few days, and when the storm passed the beach was gone. Nothing left but bare rocky coast. Happens every year, the locals said. Storms claw the beach down into the sea, taking the shore back to bare rock. It'll be back in April. This lost beach doubles the discontinuity of Spenser's poem: not only won't writing on the strand last, neither will the strand itself. Sand belongs to ocean as well as earth. We can't, in the end, desavage these places, no matter how many vacation days we spend lolling in the sun.—*

∽

Spenser, as much as any English Renaissance poet, straddles embodied change and eternal truth. His *Epithalamion*, the wedding poem that was published with the *Amoretti*, concludes with a famous paradox about poetry's desire to fix motion in place, so that the poem, and possibly also the combined *Amoretti and Epithalamion* volume, makes up "for short time an endlesse moniment."[17] The play between "short" and "endlesse" increases the ambiguity of "moniment," which flexibly indicates both a brief moment and an enduring monument. To be short and endless, moment and monument represents Spenser's poetics of the ineffable. Similarly, *Amoretti* 75's concluding couplet suggests a brown middle way between decay and eternity. The rhyme between "subdew" and "renew" draws together opposing movements in a familiar paradoxical pattern. But the poem's narrative of renewal is not simply an oscillation between life and death, or land and sea. Rather, it is a three-stage intermixture of desire and materiality: first death subdues the world, next "love" maintains itself through poetry, and last "life" begins again.[18] The biographical subtext of the *Amoretti* implies the biological continuity of childbirth for the happy couple at some "later" time,[19] but the churn of these lines insists on mixing up everything: sexual reproduction, apocalyptic regeneration, even an implied poetics of compost and recycling. From a dry strand, the poem imagines a wet future. To "renew" in this context means to return not to the eternity that the beloved has rejected but to brown ecological mixture.[20]

The Wet Brown: Swamp

The problem with brown mixtures including the one to which Spenser's poem leads is that we can get stuck in them. What looks like dry strand has a tendency to bog. Any attempt to imagine a brown ecology must confront swamp, its disorienting pull and voyage-stopping suction. Swamps are obstacles and also, for those who live near them, sources of food, fuel, and other biotic matter. For a brown ecologist, swamp contains the world.

An essential literary touchstone for swamp-thinking is John Bunyan's Slough of Despond in *Pilgrim's Progress* (1678), which uses swamp to represent worldly failure and alienation from the divine. The Slough is an early obstacle on the allegorical journey of Christian toward the holy City. The marshland represents sin and the world's decay, and its mire separates Christian from neighbor Pliable, who briefly joins the journey but cannot make it to the far side of the swamp: "And with that [Pliable] gave a desperate struggle or two, and got out of the Mire, on that side of the Slow which was near to his own House."[21] Remaining in the Slow—Bunyan, like Spenser, employs symbolically flexible spelling—represents Christian's struggle with despair.[22] The traveler requires Help's aid to leave the brown Mire, and this allegorical figure provides an explanation of the mudscape:

> This *Miry slow,* is such a place as cannot be mended: It is the descent whither the scum and filth that attends conviction for sin doth continually run, and therefore is it called the *Slow of Dispond*: for still as the sinner is awakened by his lost condition, there ariseth in his soul many fears, and doubts, and discouraging apprehensions, which all of them get together, and settle in this place: And this is the reason of the badness of this ground.[23]

The Slough cannot be repaired or drained, despite the presence of "certain good and substantial steps" throughout it,[24] which Bunyan's marginal note links to Gospel promises. Wet brown represents spiritual errancy that clings and hinders the forward-progressing soul. Like all allegorists, Bunyan asks to be taken literally: crossing the mudscape means travail in spiritual and physical senses. Help's allegorical reading focuses on swamp's flow, "for sin doth continually run." Being in the brown thus represents a fork—Pliable turns back, Christian goes on—and a squishy encumbrance, physical evidence of sin.

> Where land meets the sea in the Mississippi River Delta, down at the bottom of the Louisiana boot, the term "coastline" doesn't really apply. There is no line. There are only the dashed pen strokes of the barrier islands, a dozen or so thin beachheads, and beyond, a porous system of open bays, canals, salt and brackish marshes, and freshwater swamps running inland for twenty-five to a hundred miles.
>
> —BRUCE BARCOTT, "Forlorn in the Bayou"

Bunyan's narrative also provides an eschatological reading of the Slough, in which muddy sin will not endure. Unlike Spenser's celebration of embeddedness and fertile regeneration, Bunyan looks forward to a time after time. Help explains that the Slough, though constantly renewed by sin, will not last, that the King's laborers have been working on its amendment "for above this sixteen hundred years."[25] God's mercy becomes analogous to a land reclamation policy that will, at end times, drain the swamp. Help further explains why over sixteen hundred years of Gospel promises have not yet drained the Slough: there is too much sin flooding down that mighty Mississippi: "*Here* hath ben swallowed up, at least, Twenty Thousand Cart Loads; yea Millions of wholesome Instructions, that have at all seasons been brought from all places of the Kings Dominions; (and they that can tell, say, they are the best Materials to make good ground of the place,) If so be, it might have been mended, but it is the *Slow of Dispond* still."[26] The drainage project Help imagines would convert brown swamp into rich soil, extending in a spiritual dimension the seventeenth-century project of salvaging agricultural land from English Fens, as recorded by Bunyan's contemporary William Dugdale.[27] If swamp embodies the fallen world, fen-draining represents salvation.

> I wish for, and practice, the dispossession of the world.
>
> —MICHEL SERRES, *Malfeasance: Appropriation through Pollution?*

(I sometimes tell people that in October 2010 I traveled to Cocodrie on the coastline of Louisiana, southwest of New Orleans, to see the aftermath of the BP/Deepwater Horizon oil spill.[28] But that is not quite right: I went there, but found no line and no real coast. It is a brownscape and watery borderlands, in which everything solid slowly oozes. I do not think of W. H. Auden as a poet of the American South, but his lines were sloshing about in my head all week:

. . . the silent dissolution of the sea
Which misuses nothing because it values nothing.[29]

The human struggle down in the Delta is worldlier than the narratives in Bunyan's or Auden's poems, but it is the same brown Mire. Delta dwellers are stuck in the brown of between—between the needs of the Mississippi River itself, which wants to jump its Army Corps of Engineers banks and shift its main current west toward the Atchafalaya Delta; between the needs of the oil and gas industries, who service their off-shore rigs and take in international cargo at Port Furchon, a delta town that is almost surrounded by open water; between the needs of fishermen both commercial and sport; and between the diverse needs of Cajun people whose land is reverting to open water.³⁰ The swampy brown marks a constant exchange between dry and wet, land and sea. Today in southern Louisiana, land is disappearing. It is sinking into the sea, marshy wetlands dissolving into open water at a rate of roughly a football field per day.³¹ You can see the saltwater encroachment on the drive down to Cocodrie, where the road is lined with trailer homes, hurriedly jacked-up ten feet on stilts made out of telephone poles after the insurance companies changed their flood requirements post-Katrina. Now the once-yards of these houses, which the locals call "camps" because they are built for hunting and fishing trips, are open ponds and wet bayou. Only the raised bed of the state highway knifes straight through the bog. The oil companies have publicly committed to maintaining Port Furchon as a functioning port even when it becomes, after another decade or two, an isolated island.)³²

～

In *Pilgrim's Progress*, supernatural guides lead Christian toward a mire-free vision. At the end of the first part of the narrative, after he has seen the Gates to the holy City, he wakes "and behold it was a Dream."³³ The dream allegory never drains the Slough of Despond, but rather envisions the supernatural labor necessary to do so. All ecosystems ask to be read as allegories. All brown spaces must be dispossessed. It is not clear what is going to happen at the mouth of the Mississippi.

The Once-Living Brown: Shit

Shakespeare's *Antony and Cleopatra* is the most beautiful play ever written in English. We literature professors do not often make aesthetic pronouncements these days, but there it is. I will add a pungent kicker: this play's beauty has everything to do with shit.

～

*** I've been searching for years for a lost quotation about the metaphysics of shit. I used to know it, or I think I did. I had hoped to find it for this essay, but I have not. It is a phrase from the Argentine novelist and poet Julio Cortázar, maybe the best and certainly the most stylistically outrageous writer of the Boom generation that surged out of Latin America in the 1960s. It is probably somewhere inside the vast labyrinth of Rayuela (Hopscotch), *his 1963 masterpiece, but maybe it is someplace else. It is an aside—Cortázar loves asides,*

and Rayuela *structures itself through digressions—in which the narrator describes the metaphysical wonder of looking down into the toilet bowl: "How could I," he thinks, "possibly have made that?" Shit here represents the miracle of the physical world, the shocking createdness of real things. The world as it is, staring up at you, undeniable proof of your body's fetid entanglement with matter. Someday I will reread that novel, and the others, plus the collections of short stories, essays, poems, and experimental pieces, searching for that brown nugget. I do not expect to find it, though I am pretty sure it is there. The physical and metaphysical mystery lies in shit's not-quite reappearance, in our unwillingness to look again even when we know it is there. Read only once, before flushing.* ***

∽

Antony and Cleopatra's fascination with fertility, "Nilus slime," and hybridization are well-established in modern criticism. A recent essay by Edward J. Geisweidt has uncovered a specifically excremental poetics in the play, focusing on the "shard" of a metaphorical beetle, which refers to its own, and possibly a cow's, dung.[34] Shakespeare's play, Geisweidt notes, engages a then-familiar understanding of the Nile as a source of both excrement and biotic life; the Nile Delta, like the Mississippi Delta, embodies brown *bios*. To extend this reading, I focus on a moment in the play that is often taken to refer to the transmigration of souls, Mark Antony's description of an Egyptian crocodile. By suggesting that this image blends Pythagorean transformation with physical excrement, I argue that the play's beauty resembles the flower on the dunghill. The play's organic fertilizer fuels an aesthetic that, like Egypt's queen, is "with Phoebus' amorous pinches black / And wrinkled deep in time."[35] From brown shit, we get Cleopatra.[36]

Like his dark-skinned "serpent of old Nile,"[37] Antony's description of a real crocodile characterizes the play's brown ecological ferment: "It is shaped, sir, like itself, and it is as broad as it hath breadth. It is just so high as it is, and moved with its own organs. It lives by that which nourisheth it, and the elements once out of it, it transmigrates."[38] This passage stymies itself with illegible surfaces. The crocodile cannot be described because it is only and always itself, and the running gag of Antony's subsequent dialogue with the drunk Lepidus—it is of its own color, its tears are wet, and so on—extends this pattern. But closer attention to the strange creature reveals a steady descriptive movement from outside—shape, breadth, height—to inside: organs, nourishment, "elements." As Antony's words draw us into the croc's belly, we follow down, through, and out. The key term, *transmigrates,* is Pythagorean, and editors note that Shakespeare often recalls the Greek philosopher's theory of souls.[39] But it is not only souls that exit bodies, especially not when you are following the alimentary trail from mouth to stomach and so downward.

I do not expect my shitty reading of this line to convince all the Shakespeareans who read this book, but the closeness of Pythagorean transmigration to the physical products of digestion represents exactly the sort of aesthetic gambit this play loves. The "it" of the final phrase ambiguously spans both the crocodile's soul, headed for a new body, and the excrement that has been moving through its digestive tract. The image unites the circulation of souls and the progress of dinner. It is this combination of the rarefied and disgusting that makes this play my final literary example of brown ecology. *Antony and Cleopatra,* to an extent unusual even for Shakespeare, insists on the mutual implication of opposites. Men and women, Rome and Egypt, land and sea, loyalty and treachery, mother's milk and adder's poison—all these and more opposed things entwine each other, as generations of critics have shown. The "it" that transmigrates may only rhyme with "shit," a word that does not appear in Shakespeare, but the passage plays on our desire to see inside living things. Cleopatra herself often gets described through her appetite, as well as the appetites she stimulates in Roman men. In her "salad days" with "broad-fronted Caesar" she was "morsel for a monarch."[40] As eater and food, she represents brown hybridity. "Other women cloy / The appetites they feed," Enobarbus rhapsodizes, "but she makes hungry / Where most she satisfies."[41] These familiar lines, like the description of the crocodile, allude to digestion as well as aesthetic performance. Her "infinite variety" spans Pythagorean and excremental meanings.[42] The "vilest things"—shit itself—"become themselves in her."[43] Unlike Bunyan's Christian, she is happy in the brown.

Antony's wavering devotion refuses the brown as brown. To love Cleopatra not despite her fickleness, greed, and always shifting strategic sense but because of these wayward qualities would entail a self-abnegation alien to the Roman general. His on-again commitment to his Isis of brown gives rise to the occasional hubristic rhetorical gleam—"Let Rome in Tiber melt, and the wide arch / Of the ranged empire fall!"[44]—but he is looking high, not low. He is the dolphin to her crocodile.[45] For Roman heroes, elements are primarily for transmigration.

〜

Shakespeare was not the only English writer to make poetry out of brown elements. But for the real shit-eating, we need to turn to Thomas Pynchon's fictional depiction of early 1940s Germany, where Brigadier Ernest Pudding, a World War I veteran, encounters Katje Borgesius, Queen of the Night. In a brutal depiction of transcorporeal enmeshment, she controls him by making him eat her feces:

> The stink of shit floods his nose, gathering him, surrounding. It is the smell of Passchendaele, of the Salient. Mixed with mud, and the putrefaction of corpses, it was the sovereign smell of their first meeting, and her emblem. The turd slides into his mouth, down to his gullet. He gags, but bravely clamps his teeth shut. Bread that would only have floated in porcelain waters somewhere, unseen, untasted—risen now and baked in the bitter intestinal Oven to bread we know, bread that's light as domestic comfort, secret as death in bed. . . . Spasms in his throat continue. The pain is terrific. With his tongue he mashes shit against the roof of his mouth and begins to chew, thickly now, the only sound in the room.[46]

Coprophagia is rare in literature, and it seems possible that scenes like this may have prevented the Pulitzer board from agreeing to award its prize in 1973, when *Gravity's Rainbow* was unanimously selected by the fiction committee. Shit eating represents the end point of loving brown. This devotion may not be healthy—we learn three hundred pages later that Pudding dies from "a massive E. coli infection"[47]—but it connects the German soldier to a darkly resistant strain of Pynchonian rebellion. Pudding's ghost returns late in the novel, "a member of the Counterforce."[48] His presence sparks a grotesquely hilarious antidinner, featuring alliterative dishes from snot soup to hemorrhoid hash.[49] This brown enmeshment helps Pynchon's Everyman, Seaman Bodine, imagine that it may be possible to escape the war.[50]

> We should no longer be the masters and possessors of nature. The
> new contract has become a rental agreement. . . . May this *cosmocracy*
> come soon.
>
> —MICHEL SERRES, *Malfeasance:*
> *Appropriation through Pollution?*

Pynchon's escape through revulsion sits oddly beside *Antony and Cleo-*
patra's aesthetic marvels. The play's beauty, however, as I have shown,
depends on its closeness to excrement. If we read the play only through its
"cloth-of-gold of tissue" opulence,[51] we miss the brown beneath. Recover-
ing that biotic brown, the brown of the Mississippi Delta and Cleopatra's
skin as well as the fetid mixing and recombining of living and dead things,
allows this play to guide us toward an ecological order beyond green harmonies. As Michel Serres writes, pollution has become our global norm;
the mixing of human and nonhuman wastes and products has built a world
in which things cannot be distinguished from each other: "Our effluents
are inextricably blended. *We can no longer enclose a piece of land. . . .* We
haunt a topological space without distances."[52] In this world-blend, Serres's "rental agreement," his refusal to possess any land, resembles brown
ecological thinking. We cannot own the brown stuff even though it is
ours and so remains. In this hybrid world, all encounters, joinings, and dis-
persals are temporary. We cannot go away, and we cannot connect forever
either.

Conclusion: In a Brown Study

It is a melancholy color. The *Oxford English Dictionary* says brown studies
have been sad places since Gilbert Walker's first recorded use of the phrase
in *A Manifest Detection of Diceplay* (1552). In the summer I swim every
day in the brown saltwater of Long Island Sound, where the color dissolves up from a muddy bottom, but like most people I prefer the clear
blue. I once claimed this swimming for blue cultural studies, but it is really
quite brown.[53] Brown ecology describes a melancholy insight, that the living can never escape mixture with the nonliving, and that human beings,
as individuals and global populations, cannot leave our waste behind. Like
the shit-soul of the Egyptian crocodile, it constantly transmigrates—and
so do we.

If nature is to matter, we need more potent, more complex
understandings of materiality.

—STACY ALAIMO, *Bodily Natures:*
Science, Environment, and the Material Self

I propose brown as a color for transcorporeality because it signals toward
both living potential and dead excess. The nonhuman world engages our
bodies constantly, in processes of exchange, digestion, excretion, and friction. This blending challenges happy green fictions and anthropocentric
visions of power. Humans cannot escape entanglement in the brown soup
of the world, and whatever beauty we find remains deeply sunk in the mire.
A brown ecology responds to Alaimo's desire for "more potent, [and] more
complex" visions of materiality by refusing boundaries. The world crosses
into and out of ourselves. In adding the crocodile's bivalent transmigration
to transcorporeality, I signal both a desire to include ancient understandings of spiritual exchange in contemporary ecodiscourses and an attempt
to reconsider daily bodily processes. Brown fluids and solids surround us;
we cannot live without touching them.

Few cultural ecologists will dispute this emphasis on entanglement
and incomplete estrangement, but brown's hybridizing force can also push
against a tendency in recent philosophies to describe objects through
separation. Ian Bogost writes, "A fundamental separation between objects
is fundamental to OOO," or "object-oriented ontology."[54] The repeated
word *fundamental* emphasizes the distances between things, what Graham
Harman calls the inability of objects to "touch one another fully."[55] While
Bogost, Harman, and the other scholars associated with OOO, including Timothy Morton, devise ingenious schemes through which separate
objects interact with each other—"vicarious causation" is Harman's phrase,
"strange strangers" one of Morton's—thinking brown suggests that separation itself may be problematic. What if the question is not how do essentially alien objects interact with each other over the vastness of subjective
experience? but, instead, how do essentially connected beings reconcile
a felt experience of separation with the awareness that there is no final separation? All objects, or "units" in Bogost's alternative term,[56] might have
difficulty fully distinguishing themselves from the brown interchange of
life and nonlife.

The problem with dissolving the separate object, as doubtless these philosophers have considered, is that a world without distinctions quickly becomes a world in which nothing new happens. Nonetheless, I think that a soupy brown challenge to the separation of objects can help contribute to OOO-thinking, not least because it might refine the practice of making and interpreting lists. Litanies, called "Latour litanies" after the French philosopher, mark the object-oriented style. As Bogost notes, lists are attractive because of their nonteleological nature: "Lists offer an antidote to the obsession with Deleuzean becoming" by counterproposing "distinction instead of flow."[57] Bogost overstates literary culture's addiction to coherence and "traditional narrative" when he suggests that lists operate as an antiliterature, an "abandonment of anthropocentric narrative coherence in favor of worldly detail."[58] Experimental literary projects such as *Gravity's Rainbow* trace intricate patterns of semicoherence, refusing both the full patterning that characterizes Bogost's traditional novel and the full chaos of the random. This interplay of connection and disruption, I submit, underlies all literary practices, including Spenser's sonnet, Bunyan's allegory, and Shakespeare's play. Literary forms revel in partial internal inconsistencies. Even Bogost's computer-generated list-maker, the *Latour Litanizer,*[59] in practice operates through the human reader's frustrated desire to make sense out of all juxtapositions, to overcome through interpretation the apparent separation of objects in the list. Reading machine-generated lists resembles reading experimental fiction: it displays not failures of coherence but instead moments of recognition that interpretive success is always fleeting, partial, and to some extent illusory.

To blend the philosophical desire for separation with a literary focus on incomplete connection, I propose a partial distinction between two kinds of lists: Latour Litanies and Borges Catalogs. The first takes its inspiration from Latour and appears in the works of Bogost, Harman, and others; this type operates through the full distinction of each item listed. I suspect that only computers can really create unconnected lists, though human authors often approximate them. The second kind of list, to which I might have appended the term *literary* had not the letter "l" already been taken by the philosophers, derives from Borges's famous imaginary Chinese encyclopedia, the *Heavenly Emporium of Benevolent Knowledge:*

It is written that animals are divided into (a) those that belong to the emperor; (b) embalmed ones; (c) those that are trained; (d) suckling pigs; (e) mermaids; (f) fabulous ones; (g) stray dogs; (h) those that are included in this classification; (i) those that tremble as if they were mad; (j) innumerable ones; (k) those drawn with a very fine camel's hair brush; (l) etcetera; (m) those that have just broken the flower vase; (n) those that at a distance resemble flies.[60]

This enigmatic list, celebrated by Michel Foucault in *The Order of Things,* resembles the Latour Litany as Bogost describes it.[61] But the crucial feature of Borges's list is that it is not random, though it almost appears to be so. Its categories trace a mosaic of partial connection and imperfect separation, together making up a human response to universal disorder. The short essay within which this excerpt appears, "John Wilkins' Analytical Language" (1942), describes several alternative categorizing systems, including the catalog of the Bibliographical Institute of Brussels and the artificial language of the seventeenth-century English philosopher John Wilkins.[62] Borges's key point contrasts Wilkins's invented language with the Chinese encyclopedia. Wilkins's system is total and philosophically coherent: "Every letter is meaningful, as those of the Holy Scriptures were for the Kabbalists."[63] In an OOO sense, each symbol or object is fully separate. The thought-exploding feature of the *Heavenly Emporium* puts this coherence into crisis; it is confusing and frustrating to categorize the world in the multiple manners this list proposes. Wilkins builds Latour Litanies that recall Bogost's Litanizer; the *Heavenly Emporium* creates a self-fracturing Borges Catalog that appears random but is not so. Wilkins's synthetic desire resonates with the stated aims of the philosophers who define themselves as speculative realists.[64] The *Heavenly Emporium*'s broken literary logic muddles both unity and separation in favor of contradiction, internal tension, and the play of paradox.

My concluding claim is that brown ecology is the ecology of the *Heavenly Emporium.* All things connect and cannot escape into separation, and in the face of soupy, smelly, brown existence human intelligences struggle to grasp fleeting separations and imperfect categorizations. "There is,"

Borges's essay observes, "no classification of the universe that is not arbitrary and speculative"; in fact it may be that "there is no universe in the organic, unifying sense of that ambitious word."[65] Which is to say: we do not know what brown is, but we are in it. Most of us, I estimate, fit comfortably into about half of the encyclopedia's categories. Brown ecology asks for membership in all of them at once.

Notes

1. For a collection of essays building on Paster's work, see Mary Floyd-Wilson and Garrett Sullivan, *Embodiment and Environment in Early Modern England* (London: Palgrave, 2007).

2. Stacy Alaimo, *Bodily Natures: Science, Environment, and the Material Self* (Bloomington: University of Indiana Press, 2010), 2.

3. Mat Johnson, *Pym: A Novel* (New York: Spiegel & Grau, 2010), 322.

4. Timothy Morton, *The Ecological Thought* (Cambridge, Mass.: Harvard University Press, 2010).

5. Greg Dening, *Beach Crossings: Voyaging across Time, Cultures, and Self* (Philadelphia: University of Pennsylvania Press, 2004).

6. Edmund Spenser, *The Yale Edition of the Shorter Poems of Edmund Spenser,* ed. William Oram, Einar Bjorvand et al. (New Haven, Conn.: Yale University Press, 1989), 645.

7. Ibid., l. 7.

8. Ibid., l. 1.

9. Ibid., ll. 2, 4.

10. I assume in this reading that the printed text follows Spenser's intentions. Published in 1595 by William Ponsonby, a well-known publisher, Spenser's *Amoretti and Epithalamion* appears to be an authorized text.

11. For more on oceanic ecologies, see Steve Mentz, *At the Bottom of Shakespeare's Ocean* (London: Continuum, 2009).

12. Spenser, *Shorter Poems,* l. 3.

13. Ibid., l. 5.

14. Ibid., ll. 7, 8.

15. Édouard Glissant, *Poetics of Relation,* trans. Betsy Wing (Minneapolis: University of Minnesota Press, 1997), 123.

16. Spenser, *Shorter Poems,* l. 11.

17. Spenser, *Shorter Poems,* 679.

18. Spenser, *Shorter Poems,* l. 14.

19. Ibid.

20. Ibid.

21. John Bunyan, *Pilgrim's Progress,* ed. W. R. Owens (Oxford: Oxford University Press, 2008), 16.

22. W. R. Owens, the Oxford Classics editor, cites passages in Bunyan's spiritual autobiography, *Grace Abounding to the Chief of Sinners* (1666) at this point in *Pilgrim's Progress.*

23. Ibid., 17.

24. Ibid.

25. Ibid.

26. Ibid.

27. William Dugdale, *History of Imbanking and Drayning of Divers Fens and Marshes* (London, 1662).

28. I thank Jim Carlton and the Williams-Mystic Maritime Studies Program for hosting me on this trip.

29. W. H. Auden, *The Sea and the Mirror: A Commentary on Shakespeare's "The Tempest,"* ed. Arthur Kirsch (Princeton, N.J.: Princeton University Press, 2003), 5.

30. For a scientific survey, see John Day et al., *Answering Ten Fundamental Questions about the Mississippi River Delta: A Report by the Mississippi Delta Science and Engineering Special Team* (Baton Rouge, La.: Mississippi River Delta Science and Engineering, 2012).

31. See Elizabeth Kolbert, "Southern Louisiana Is Sinking," *New Yorker,* February 27, 2006.

32. For earlier articulations of this point and related Louisiana 2010 commentary, see my blog, http://www.stevementz.com/dissolution/.

33. Bunyan, *Pilgrim's Progress,* 154.

34. Edward J. Geisweidt, "'The Nobleness of Life': Spontaneous Generation and Excremental Life in *Antony and Cleopatra,*" in *Ecocritical Shakespeare,* ed. Lynne Bruckner and Dan Brayton (Aldershot: Ashgate, 2011), 99.

35. William Shakespeare, *Antony and Cleopatra,* ed. John Wilders (London: Arden, 2005), 1.5.29–30.

36. On swampy generation in this play, see Gabriel Egan, *Green Shakespeare: From Ecopolitics to Ecocriticism* (London: Routledge, 2006), 112–15.

37. Shakespeare, *Antony and Cleopatra,* 1.5.25.

38. Ibid., 2.7.42–46.

39. See, for example, Rosalind in *As You Like It,* who was an Irish rat in "Pythagoras' time" (3.2.176–77).

40. Shakespeare, *Antony and Cleopatra,* 1.5.76, 1.5.30, 1.5.33.

41. Ibid., 2.2.246–48.

42. Ibid., 2.2.246.

43. Ibid., 2.2.248, 2.2.249.

44. Ibid., 1.1.34–35.

45. On Antony as dolphin, see Steve Mentz, "Half-Fish, Half-Flesh: Dolphins, Humans, and the Early Modern Ocean," in *The Indistinct Human,* ed. Jean Feerick and Vin Nardizzi (London: Palgrave, 2012), 29–46.

46. Thomas Pynchon, *Gravity's Rainbow* (New York: Penguin, 1973).

47. Ibid., 533.

48. Ibid., 715.

49. Ibid., 715–17.

50. Without getting too deep into Pynchonian weeds, I note that characters named Bodine crop up recurrently; Pig Bodine is a major figure in *V.* (1963); his ancestor, Fender-Belly Bodine, appears in *Mason & Dixon* (1997); O.I.C Bodine appears in *Against the Day* (2006). Why no Bodines show up in *Inherent Vice* (2009) is still open for debate.

51. Shakespeare, *Antony and Cleopatra,* 2.2.209.

52. Michel Serres, *Malfeasance: Appropriation through Pollution?* (Stanford, Calif.: Stanford University Press), 67.

53. See Mentz, *At the Bottom,* 100.

54. Ian Bogost, *Alien Phenomenology, or What It's Like to Be a Thing* (Minneapolis: University of Minnesota Press, 2012), 123.

55. Graham Harman, "On Vicarious Causation," *Collapse: Journal of Philosophical Research and Development* 2 (2007): 187–221, http://urbanomic.com/pub_collapse2.php.

56. Bogost, *Alien Phenomenology,* 27.

57. Ibid., 40.

58. Ibid., 40, 41–42.

59. Ibid., 94–96.

60. Jorge Luis Borges, "John Wilkins' Analytical Language," in *Selected Non-Fictions,* ed. and trans. Eliot Wineberger (New York: Viking, 1999), 231.

61. Michel Foucault, *The Order of Things: An Archeology of the Human Sciences* (New York: Vintage, 1994), xv.

62. Borges, "John Wilkins's Analytical Language," 231.

63. Ibid., 230. Readers of Borges will note parallels with "Funes el memorioso" and "Tlön, Uqbar, Orbis Tertius."

64. Borges notably uses the term *speculative* ("John Wilkins' Analytical Language," 229) to characterize Wilkins.

65. Borges, "John Wilkins' Analytical Language," 231.

Blue

EILEEN A. JOY

Our Plight

This chapter is an attempt, and perhaps a failed one, to think about depression as a shared creative endeavor, as a transcorporeal blue (and blues) ecology[1] that would bind humans, nonhumans, and stormy weather together in what Tim Ingold has called a meshwork, where "beings do not propel themselves across a ready-made world but rather issue forth through a world-in-formation, along the lines of their relationships."[2] In this enmeshment of the "strange strangers" of Timothy Morton's dark ecology, "the only way out is down" and art's "ambiguous, vague qualities will help us to think things that remain difficult to put into words."[3] It may be, as Morton has also argued, that while "personhood" is real, nevertheless, "both the surface and the depth of our being are ambiguous and illusory." And "still weirder, this illusion might have actual effects."[4] I want to see if it might be possible to cultivate this paradoxical interface (lit. "between faces") between illusion and effects,[5] especially with regard to feeling blue, a condition I believe is a form of a deeply empathic enmeshment with a world that suffers its own sea changes and that can never be seen as separate from the so-called individuals who supposedly only populate ("people") it. I want to ask further, with Spencer Reece, "Weather. Weather. How's the weather? / When [we] speak of the weather is it because [we] cannot speak of [our] days spent in the / nuthouse?"[6]

Is depression, sadness, melancholy—feeling blue—always only taking place within the interior spaces of individually bounded forms of sentience

and physiology, or is it *in the world* somehow, a type of weather or atmosphere, with the becoming-mad of the human mind only one of its many
effects (a form of attunement to the world's melancholy)? Could a more
heightened and consciously attuned sense of the emanations and radio signals of blue sensations, feelings, and climates enable constructive interpersonal, social, and other blue collaborations that might lead to valuable
modes of better advancing "into / the sense of the weather, the lesson of /
the weather"?[7] Here there is no environment, only fluid space (from tears
to rain to oceans and everything in between), and in Ingold's formulation
(following Andy Clark) everything *leaks*.[8] Themes of exile, and of moving through and inhabiting *furnished* and *unfurnished* worlds (where life is
played out on the either hostile or hospitable surfaces of the earth's crust),[9]
although powerfully attractive in Western cultural narratives, break down
under the pressure of the fact that everything is always already an "intimate
register of wind and weather."[10] As Phreddy Wischusen writes, in a letter to
his estranged mother, who when he was a child loved him with such a desperate and frightening neediness that he felt almost destroyed by it,

> I hope even if you can't feel it, even if it tastes too different, even if
> you can't live in it, you will enjoy knowing that far from your shores
> your love is falling like rain on empty streets, on forests and green
> fields, on friends of mine with silly hair-dos and filthy skirts. And
> though I sometimes fear the waves, I will always look for myself and
> all that is good beyond my terrestrial frontiers.[11]

As Ingold argues, and Wischusen intuits in a more poetic register, wherever "there is life and habitation, the interfacial separation of substance
and medium is disrupted to give way to mutual permeability and binding."[12] We must risk drowning ourselves in these watery *temperaments* of
the world, and as Steve Mentz urges, when we resurface "back to air and
light, we [will] sing what we can and sell the rest, remembering what we
can't salvage."[13]

The weather I concern myself with here will be stormy, postapocalyptic, riven with the rime of hail and frost, cold and frozen, but also sun-
bleached and lit by fires along the shoreline . . . and the persons, fictional,
lost at sea, shipwrecked, cast adrift, drowning, beached, going mad with

melancholy and grief, all enmeshed together on a blue planet that is itself adrift in space which is also always drifting, always expanding. Through brief readings of two Old English elegies, *Seafarer* and *Wanderer,* and the novel *Wittgenstein's Mistress* by David Markson, this chapter attempts to trace the *affective* relations between the "strange strangers" of postapocalyptic, oceanic landscapes in order to think (and write) my way toward a blue ecological aesthetic that might take better account of our world as both empty (void) and full (intimately crowded), and more *bearably* sad. This will also be to take seriously Lisa Robertson's plea for poetics as a "delusional space" par excellence, where the weather becomes our "wild fantasy. It seizes us. Together our faces tilt upwards." And if "each forecast is a fiction," then we "prefer to add to that fiction alternate delusions—a delusionary politics that describes current conditions as it poses futurities."[14] Thus we must go weathering and also deterritorialize ourselves, seeing each other and the world as an atmospheric multiplicity, just as Rhoda does in Virginia Woolf's novel *The Waves,* looking "far away" over the heads of her friends "to a hollow where the many-backed steep hills come down like the birds' wings folded. There on the short, firm turf, are bushes, dark leaved, and against their darkness . . . a shape, white, but not of stone, moving, perhaps alive. But it is not you, it is not you, it is not you; not Perceval, Susan, Jinny, Neville or Louis," yet "these pilgrimages, these moments of departure, start always in your presence."[15] Here we also see the "lines" of which Ingold has become such a sensitive cartographer: "Life will not be confined within bounded forms but rather threads its way through the world along the myriad lines of its relations. . . . Thus wherever anything lives the infrastructure of the occupied world is taking up or wearing away, ceaselessly eroded by the disorderly groping of inhabitants, both human and non-human, as they reincorporate and rearrange its crumbling fragments into their own ways of life."[16] It is to crumbling, especially—crumbling persons, crumbling worlds—that I want to attend to here.

But first, a caution: I do not approach the subject of depression blithely or without a deep understanding of the ravages that depression has wrought in individual persons (and families), who will possibly gain no hope or remedy from the poetry and other art of catastrophe, or from the idea of a creative collective endeavor to share in their oceanic sorrows. I am not a psychiatrist, or a psychologist, or even a skilled practitioner of psycho-analytic critique.[17] I also grew up in a family ravaged by mental illness, which was a source of deep shame, strife, general anxieties that went on for years, and ultimately, a willful forgetting and disavowal of our shared suffering. There is a sense (or a reality) in which the person who is de-pressed, manic, and suicidal is in a place beyond affection and beyond assistance—everyone gropes around in the dark, and in the case of my family, where those who were ill refused to stick with the professional (and pharmaceutical) help they needed, there are ongoing events of encroach-ing blackness, breakdowns, and rescue attempts, and then everyone drifts away from each other and enters, by months and years, into long-distance telephonic relationships that devolve into empty, detached politeness with occasional bursts of rampant, spontaneous affection. There is still love and co-implication, but the reality of the persons, once intimate and close, fades into the remote distance. It all feels like a failure of love wrought by an inscrutable family chemistry, or to put it more poetically by way of Edward Mullany's poem, "A Suicide in the Family": "The doorbell rings. Or a mountain / speaks to a mountain // in a language only mountains understand."[18]

But all ecology commences from family and home, or the *oikos*.

This is not to be maudlin or confessional for confession's sake, but to say, again, that I do not offer in this chapter either a diagnosis or a remedy for clinical depression in human subjects; rather, as a literary scholar, I want to think about certain sites in literary texts that are saturated or charged with lonely, watery, and blue affects that also, paradoxically, offer openings toward more capacious modes of interlinear ecological entangle-ments (reading and writing, with salt in our eyes, between the lines of our enmeshment with everything), where we might allow ourselves to be traversed by others' emotions, by the weather, which traversals might then become a valuable form of aesthetic (if sad) solidarity. And our shared uncertainty will figure, "not as terror, but as erotic collective being."[19] I consider this thought (and feeling) experiment important because I am increasingly appalled by the political discourses so predominant today, especially on the conservative right, where everyone is made to feel as if everything that happens to them is simply *their,* and not *our,* predicament, not our concern, and where becoming an individual, as Zygmunt Bauman has argued, is not a choice, or even a communal endeavor, but a *fate*.[20] Here we might turn premodernist-etymologist and remind ourselves that the word *plight*, from the Old Frisian, Middle Dutch, and Middle Low German *plicht*, means "care" or "responsibility," also "community" and "obligation," and is also related to the Old English *pleoh* ("danger," "hurt," "risk") and *pleon* ("to risk the loss of," "expose to danger"), which is also related to the Latin *pliter* (from which we get "plait"): "to fold," "to pleat," which is to say, again, that everyone else's plight, which is to say *their* "danger," is also *our* danger.

The world can be insane sometimes, places can be insane, and some people are more sensitive to that fact—think of the heroine of Michelangelo Antonioni's 1964 film *Red Desert*, Giuliana (played by Monica Vitti), who wanders aimlessly through the polluted landscapes of Ravenna, Italy, where her husband manages the petrochemical plant, and where only she, suffering from feelings of anxiety and dreams of drowning in quicksand, seems to understand how sick the landscape is, and wants to flee from it, saying at one point, "I can't look at the sea for long or I lose interest in what's happening on land."[21] Although Antonioni claimed that he was not necessarily making a film about one woman's neurosis induced by an inhuman industrial landscape—indeed, he claimed that "the line and curves of factories and their chimneys can be more beautiful than the outline of trees," and there are some people who just "can't manage, perhaps because they are too tied to ways of life that are now out of date"[22]—nevertheless, similar to Carol White (played by Julianne Moore), the protagonist of Todd Haynes's enviro-horror film *Safe* (1995), who is hypersensitive to the chemicals that are rampant throughout the suburbs of Los Angeles and who feels as if she is going insane when no one will believe that she is really sick, we might say Giuliana is allergic to the twentieth century. To style a new collectivity out of such melancholic allergies, we will need to "hazard an improvisation" and "venture from home [together] on the thread of a tune,"[23] and this will be a blue song: rising ocean-blue and melting glacier ice-blue, blue like the stones in Virginia Woolf's overcoat, blue like Nina Simone's lilac wine that helps us to see what we want to see, blue like valium, because sometimes we need to cultivate historical forgetting, because we want to feel good, even when we feel bad. This will also be the blue-grey-green of the medieval Irish sea—*glas*, a word also associated in medieval

Irish law with the outcasts and the exiles.[24] As Ralph Ellison observes of the American blues, we will need to "finger the jagged grain" of the world's stormy weather, not to transcend it "by the consolation of a philosophy,"[25] but to get deeper into it and to "squeeze" something out of it (part tragic, part comic) that would give us the ability to "really exercise fate with extremely normal things such as our mind(s)."[26] So let's get *fated* and *outcast* together. Not as an experiment in reckless fatalism or as a collective abandonment of our hopes, but as the crafting of a more heightened sense of the co-melancholic implication of pretty much everything, of the world as a "dynamic reservoir of estrangement and enchantment"[27]—of what, quite literally, has "already been spoken" (Latin *fatum*). This is a civic project. And it is a hopeful one.[28]

On the Beach

"Somebody is living on this beach."[29] So ends the last line of David Markson's novel *Wittgenstein's Mistress*,[30] about a middle-aged woman named Kate who may be insane, or once was, and who may or may not be the last living woman on earth (what happened to everyone else is left unexplained). At one point, quite late in the novel, after having painted a rather stark narrative of herself as a "last survivor" for over ten years (or more?), Kate wonders what it might mean if she were to write a novel "about somebody who woke up one Wednesday or Thursday to discover that there was apparently not one other person left in the world," and also about how the "entire situation" of her novel's "autobiographical" heroine "might certainly often seem like an illusion on her part," so that "soon enough she would be quite mad, naturally."[31] And following these musings she realizes "she had paradoxically been practically as alone before all of this had happened as she was now."[32] Whether she is truly alone in the world or only alone in her mind is up for grabs, but what *is* certain is that Kate more than ably performs the role of the "last survivor," which may also serve as an aesthetic hedge against her always encroaching sadness—over and over again she mentions slipping into depression, especially when thinking of "Long Ago": an era that includes visiting the grave of a "little boy" she lost (her only child), the death of her parents, and failed love relationships. After traveling around the world futilely looking for other persons and visiting various cultural sites, she is spending all her time in an abandoned house on the beach banging out on a typewriter the longest "someone was here" message anyone ever left, in between bouts of feeling too sad to type.

Kate's message is a manic and associative catalog-style *dumping* of every piece of random cultural information from the Western canon she can recall (lit. call to mind), from the swirls in Vincent van Gogh's paintings to Friedrich Nietzsche crying over someone beating a horse to Maria Callas singing as Medea to Leonardo da Vinci writing from left to right in his notebooks to Spinoza's excommunication to the name of Helen of Troy's daughter, Hermione. Her narrative is not just a "someone was here" message but *the world was here*.[33] At more than one point, she confuses herself with Helen of Troy, and when she is not obsessively recounting the great cultural icons of the Western canon, she is also burning artifacts in museums and planks from the other houses on the beach to keep herself warm. In the end, there is only writing, about which we might remind ourselves the real Wittgenstein had his concerns, in terms of language's ability to describe reality. We might also reflect on the novel's title, partly a bleak joke, as the real Wittgenstein was homosexual, and given Kate's confused account of the world and of her own past and present, she is a terrible mistress to his ideas. In Wittgenstein's *Tractatus Logico-Philosophicus*, the epigrammatic structure of which Markson's novel imitates, Wittgenstein attempted to craft a theory of a mathematically precise language that would accurately "picture" the world, but according to Kate, "most of the things I write often seem to become equidistant from *themselves*, somehow. Whatever in heaven's name I might mean by that, however."[34] Kate confuses details of her own narrative and will say things like she feels too tired to type and maybe she should stop typing and in fact she stopped typing three hours ago; her dead son's name is Adam, no, it is Simon, or was it her husband who was named Simon, or Terry, or Adam? Many of her recollections of cultural "facts" are useless because they are bit-sized and lacking ample context: she knows Martin Heidegger said something important about *Dasein*, but nothing else, for example, but "what do any of us ever truly know, however?"[35] She frequently hallucinates: that she saw a cat perched on the Roman Coliseum, that another cat is scratching at her windowpane, that a piece of ash falling on the beach is a seagull, and so on. Nevertheless, Kate emphatically *writes* her way through the catastrophe, imagined or real or both. "Boneyard of names, heads never empty," as Maurice Blanchot once remarked in *The Writing of Disaster*.[36]

Regardless of whether Kate's words signify properly or even accurately describe her or the larger world's history and reality, and even though there may be absolutely no one who will ever read her manuscript or "novel," she emphatically invests herself in the project of writing her way into the wreck and detritus of the world's memory; instead of insisting on a narrative that would "make sense," she engages in what Ingold calls a "tissue of lines"—not so much inventing a *text* as a *texture* of loose ends,[37] all radiating from the multiple center(s) of her itinerant and stuttering syntax. This is not to say that, in all of Kate's narrative waywardness, that there are not some threads tying things together: there are continual returns to certain subjects: her dead son, for example, the imaginary cats, her previous (or is it her present?) "madness," and her former life as a painter, but perhaps the one subject she returns to most often is Helen of Troy, someone who shares her status as a woman left stranded on a beach after her world has ended.

When the world ends in Markson's novel, one of the first trips Kate takes is to Turkey to see the site of ancient Troy (now Hisarlik), and "it was Helen I mostly thought about, when I was at Troy."[38] And at the end of the novel, when she recounts the fires she likes to build on the beach after sunsets, she shares that,

> Now and again, too, looking at them from a distance, what I have done is to make believe for a little while that I am back at Hisarlik.
>
> By which I mean when Hisarlik was Troy, of course, and all of those years and years ago.
>
> So that what I am more truthfully making believe is that the fires are Greek watchfires, where they have been lighted along the shore.[39]

At many points throughout her narrative, Kate identifies with Helen and defends her against the charges that she caused the Trojan War, and she also recalls that she once wished to paint Helen standing at "one of the burned-out boats along the strand, when the siege was finally ended, being kept prisoner. But with that splendid dignity, even so."[40] In a sad (and perhaps

narcissistic) yet daring act of co-melancholic identification, Kate inter-
leaves herself with Helen and stands beside (and folded within) her on the
shoreline, watch- and house-fires burning beside them, thus losing the battle against the "bewitchment of our understanding by the resources of
our language" that Wittgenstein worried about so much,[41] but at the same
time demonstrating the important permeability of the self-as-atmosphere
in a gesture, not of canceling her loneliness by merging with, or binding
herself to, Helen, but actually doubling and thereby thickening that loneliness, making it ample and sensual and more livable. And the very "temperament" (in Ingold's formulation)[42] that gives rise to this atmospheric
multiplicity (Helen–Kate) is the beach itself where both women are intimate with, and registers of, the winds and storm clouds of postapocalypse.

Adrift/Drowning

There is a lot of sea and beach in Markson's novel, which are also intimate
registers of the weather. At the end of the world, it is always about the
weather, it turns out, *and* the sea and the beach, the shoreline you are stuck
on—like in Denis Johnson's *Fiskadoro,* where the end of the world by
atomic disaster leaves only the Florida Keys intact, with its "sand . . . like
shattered ivory" and its "fields of cane popping in the wind"[43]—or the
shoreline that is always receding from you as the ocean swallows you whole,
like Shakespeare's Alonso, with pearls where his eyes used to be, who in
Ariel's Song "suffer[s] a sea-change / Into something rich and strange."[44]

"The world is repeating itself. The story of the world is happening again,"
one of the characters in Johnson's novel says, foreshadowing the novel's
end, when Grandmother Wright, the oldest woman alive, is trapped in a
state of nonverbal catatonia, retreating into the memory of herself as a
young Vietnamese girl escaping from Saigon during the Vietnam War,
when the overloaded helicopter she had bribed her way onto crashes into
the sea, and she spends two days bobbing among the waves, drifting in and
out of consciousness:

> By sunset she was only a baby, thinking nothing, absolutely adrift,
> waking to cough and begin crying, drifting and weeping, sleeping
> and sinking, waking up to choke the water from her mouth and
> whimper, indistinguishable from what she saw, which was the grey

sky that held no interest, identity, or thought. This was the point
when she reached the bottom of everything, when she had no idea
either what she'd reached or who had reached it, or even that it had
been reached.[45]

She is eventually saved by a passing boat, and she lives to see another "end
of the world." And as her grandson Mr. Cheung puts it at the end of the
novel, when everyone has gathered on the shoreline expecting the arrival
of some sort of rescue operation, and Mr. Cheung is looking out over the
ocean, upon which a haze has settled, making it "seem the beach led down
to the end of all thought":

Everything we have, all we are, will meet its end, will be overcome,
taken up, washed away. But everything came to an end before. Now
it will happen again. Many times. Again and again. Something is
coming and something is going—but that isn't the issue. The issue
is that I failed to recognize myself in these seagulls.[46]

Both Grandmother Wright and Mr. Cheung touch "bottom" and sense the
end of identity and thought in the ocean, which is also always the "coming" of something else, but the larger issue in Mr. Cheung's case is that
he laments a life in which he has neglected to connect his plight, his own
end(s), with the strange strangers of his lifeworld—the seagulls—and as
Timothy Morton writes, "intimacy is never so obvious as when we're
depressed," yet the seagulls will always be beyond Mr. Cheung's ontology,
flowing underneath (or flying above) his materialism,[47] which is why the
beach also represents the end of all thought: the seagulls, and whatever
might be looming on the horizon (the future?), are beyond thought, but
they are not beyond feeling.

Consider the nameless Wanderer ("eardstapa," or "earth-stepper," and
also "anhaga," or "lone shield-bearer") of the Old English elegy who likewise fails to recognize himself in the seagulls, bathing and "spreading [their]
feathers" ("brædan feþra") and seemingly indifferent to him, rowing his
boat, alone, over the ice-cold sea after various catastrophes, especially
war ("wælsleahta" and "wig"), have laid waste to the once-noisy dwellings of men ("Yþde swa þisne eargeard ælda Scyppend / oþþæt, burgwara

breahtma lease").[48] The Wanderer is a soldier-turned-rower, temporarily bereft of his *comitatus* (band of warriors), and wending his way over the waves as a "last survivor." His song is suffused with desolate thoughts at the "daily failing and falling of this middle-earth" ("swa þes middangeard / ealra dogra gewham dreoseð ond fealleþ")[49] and his melancholic memories of having buried his lord and lost his native country, which event has set him on his current course of exile.[50] The Wanderer simultaneously mourns and dreams of his former life, when he embraced and kissed his lord and laid his head and hands on his lord's knees,[51] and when he awakens from this dream he sees before himself "the dark waves" ("fealwe wægas"), and "the fall of snow and frost mingled with hail" ("hreosan hrim ond snaw hagle gemenged"), causing the wounds of his heart to feel heavier and his sorrows to be renewed.[52] Consider also the "frost-bound" and "cold-clasped" ("forste gebunden / caldum clommum") Seafarer of Old English elegy, who likewise "dwells in winter, care-scarred, on the ice-cold sea along the exile-track, bereft of his kinsmen" ("hu ic earmcearig iscealdne sæ /winter wunade wræccan lastum / winemægum bidroren"), and who claims that the joys of the Lord are "hotter" to him than this "dead life / loaned on the land" ("deade lif, / læne on londe").[53] He endures in his boat the terrible welling of the waves ("atol yþa gewealc") and claims to hear nothing but the roaring sea ("hlimman sæ").[54]

It is a commonplace of scholarship on these two poems to liken their two lonely (and at times, terrifyingly inhuman) sea voyages to Christian pilgrimages and eremitic spiritual quests, and to also identify in the poems themes of cultural dislocation and isolation, as well as poetic registers appositionally split between a so-called Heroic Age fatalism and a Christian homiletic "wisdom" that looks more hopefully beyond and also has contempt for the always fallen world.[55] The poems, both included in the tenth-century *compilatio* of Old English works known as the Exeter Book, are seen as being bound to the belief systems of an Anglo-Saxon England that admired heroic stoicism as well as absorbed and accepted Christian consolation. The Wanderer and the Seafarer are also often assumed to be figures of extreme oblivion and alienation, wherein both the narrators and the poets who gave voice to them are ultimately, as Roy Liuzza has written in the case of the *Wanderer* poem, "beacon[s]" of "the lost oral world the Anglo-Saxons had left behind, glimpsed from the textual world to which they had journeyed; . . . [they are] *ungeþeode* [un-languaged, un-voiced, un-peopled], alienated from speech, nation, and history."[56]

The Wanderer and Seafarer are depressed, and maybe even lost, but they are also poets who sing while sinking,[57] and while they may, indeed, be alienated from a very particular human history (and human-built environments, including textual culture), they are tightly bound nevertheless to a watery world and its strange strangers within the lines of the verses that "speak" the fluid scenes of their conjoined movement and "weathering." Someone, very human someones (Anglo-Saxons), sang, spoke, and/or wrote these elegies—actual seafarers, or poets hacking into the consciousness of real and fictional seafarers, appropriating and adapting their songs. Nevertheless, for all of their teary-eyed and frost-covered remonstrations of remorse at the loss of human comradeship and an all-too-human world (while also, perhaps reluctantly, bidding that human world good riddance), the song-lines of these two poems bind together men, boats, oceans, salt waves, grains of ice, cawing sea birds, sea cliffs, eagles, hail showers, and wintery postapocalyptic affects into a meshwork where everything is literally "swept up together in the generative currents of the world."[58] The poetry itself indicates this cogeneration, which at times is even tender and affective, if also terrifying. At the outset of his lament, the Wanderer indicates he is rowing over the ice-cold sea (which is how the opening is usually translated: *rowing . . . over* the sea), but the exact words that the poet employs give us an image of the Wanderer using his own hands to stir the ocean to move his boat forward ("hreran mid hondum hrimcealde sæ"),[59] thereby offering a picture (even while likely intended as a metaphor for "rowing") of a man who is not moving in impersonal fashion *over* the waves (and thus, the world), but rather is always immersed in and part of the waves' waving, their weathering; in this sense, he is not just a boater, but a swimmer. Further, whereas the lines 23b–24, "ond ic hean þonan /wod wintercearig ofer waþema gebind," are typically translated as "and I then went, abject [or, wretched], winter-weary [or, winter-oppressed], bound *over* the waves [or, over the *bound* of the waves],"[60] indicating a man skimming *across* (or just *above*) a watery *surface* or *mass*, we might instead render the lines, "and then I went, depressed, winter-worried, *through* the *binding* of the waves." In this translation, we can glimpse a more active co-implicate (lit. enfolded) life-form (a rower?

a rower-boat-ocean assemblage?) that moves and comes into being as a binding-*with* (and not bound-*against*) the world. This world is a cold and lethal and sad one, but it is not one in which our two rowers are ever really alone or apart from the sea and its creatures that texturize the "sound" (the "hlimman") of their verses.

Indeed, in the case of the Seafarer, we have the admission that, at times, the swan's song serves him for "pleasure" ("gomene"), and the crying of a gannet reminds him of the laughter of men.[61] He also notes that he has heard the icy-feathered sea-swallows "answer" ("oncwæð") to the storms that pound the sea cliffs,[62] and therefore, his song actually calls to and materializes that event by "ringing" the strange strangers of this ocean-scape, thus making the swallows and cliffs and storms intimate with him in a vocative circuit of speech.[63] Although the Seafarer will conclude his song by urging his listeners to forget the world and hasten over it quickly, as he plans to do (at one point, he hopefully imagines his soul twisting out of his breast and soaring high above the waterways),[64] while "hanging" and weighing down everything in this ocean-world with a deadly ice and frost, he, too, is "bound by frost" ("forste gebunden") and "behung with icicles" "bihongen hrimgicelum");[65] he, too, like the Wanderer, is intimate with and bound to the weather of which he is one of many "registers."

A Minor Key

We might reflect that in the writing of these two Old English elegies, as well as in Markson's novel, we have acts of making (of poesis) that advance into the wreck and weather of supposedly "fallen" worlds in order to engage a romance of melancholic intersubjectivities that emerge *within,* and not *over,* that world, from which no flight is really possible, or even desirable. In the case of the Old English poems, no matter how much the Anglo-Saxon rowers' souls may strive to be loosened from their bodies, those bodies inhere nevertheless in the blue oceanic lines and inky materiality of the poet's "rustling tenses,"[66] which, similar to Lisa Robertson's poetry, "write through spaces that are utterly delusional,"[67] and the reader is invited to share in that delusion, which nevertheless thickens the world's very real enfolded spatiality[68] and weblike lines of relations, performing a civic erotics, because being blue together—engaging in acts of feeling weighted down, collectively, whether under the frost and hail of an oceanic winter or the sun-bleached shoreline at the end of human time—means leaving our caves and becoming more intimate with our worlding, advancing into the sense of the weather and its sea changes, which is to say, *our* sea changes, which, if felt more deeply, might make us more rich even as we grow more strange.

As Aranye Fradenburg argues, "It is difficult to understand other minds; but if it is difficult to understand the meanings of their transmissions, it is also a species of arrogance to think we could stop them from changing us."[69] As Fradenburg also argues, art and its mobile signifiers enable an intersubjective shared attention, a form of companionship across time, and even a type of therapeutic care, all of which are critical for important psychic transformations that might help us to undo the isolation and detachment that has become such a defining feature of modernity and to also become more permeable to each other. This will entail a willingness to draw close to the sadnesses of others, to seek out shipwrecks as well as gardens.[70]

Like the Wanderer, we might "awaken again" ("onwæcneð eft") from our dreams and also see before ourselves the dark waves and the frost and snow mingled with hail, but instead of seeing this only as the site of one's ultimate alienation from one's only ever human comrades, who endlessly "float away" from us ("swimmað eft onweg"),[71] we might bind ourselves to these waves as the only way down together. And like Kate in Markson's novel, we might renew our energies, even while drowning, to leave messages in the streets in "huge block letters, at intersections, where anybody coming or going would see."[72] This is how we experience the sadnesses of a blue world: as an ongoing project, as poetry, as temporary acts of co-poesis, as "brief discontinuous remarks / designed to fall apart / When read aloud."[73] I end then, via these just-quoted lines of the poet Ben Lerner's "Doppler Elegies" for a deceased friend. On the receding sound waves of a minor key.

Notes

This chapter is dedicated to Steve Mentz and to his book *At the Bottom of Shakespeare's Ocean* (London: Continuum, 2009), which deeply inspired all of my thinking here, especially his call for a "blue cultural studies" that would look "at our world through the deathly, inhuman, magical lens of the sea," so that we can begin "rebuilding narrative and interpretive practices to respond to an uncertain future" (xii–xiii). This chapter is also dedicated to Carol Braun Pasternack, whose study of the Old English *Wanderer,* which takes into account the "polyphony" of this "disjunctive, authorless text," sets an important critical framework for my readings of Old English poetry here (see Carol Braun Pasternack, "The Polyphony of The Wanderer," in *The Textuality of Old English Poetry* [Cambridge: Cambridge University Press, 1995], 33–59).

1. My thinking on a transcorporeal blue ecology is indebted to the thinking of Stacy Alaimo, who has argued that human corporeality is always a "transcorporeality, in which "the substance of the human is ultimately inseparable from 'the environment'" (*Bodily Natures: Science, Environment, and the Material Self* [Bloomington: Indiana University Press, 2010], 2).

2. Tim Ingold, "The Meshwork," in *Being Alive: Essays on Movement, Knowledge, and Description* (London: Routledge, 2011), 63.

3. Timothy Morton, *The Ecological Thought* (Cambridge, Mass.: Harvard University Press), 59, 60. In Morton's dark ecology, "strange strangers" refers to how we are both separate and interdependently enmeshed with all life forms for which we also are infinitely and melancholically responsible. See Timothy Morton, "Thinking Ecology: The Mesh, the Strange Stranger, and the Beautiful Soul," *COLLAPSE 6* (2010): 265–93.

4. Morton, *Ecological Thought,* 77, 79.

5. Following Jane Bennett, I am willing to risk some anthropomorphism in my thinking about relations between human and nonhuman agents and forces, as it might be "worth running the risks associated with anthropomorphizing (superstition, the divination of nature, romanticism) because it, oddly enough, works against anthropocentrism: a chord is struck between person and thing, and I am no longer above or outside a 'nonhuman' environment" (Jane Bennett, *Vibrant Matter: A Political Ecology of Things* [Durham, N.C.: Duke University Press, 2010], 120).

6. Spencer Reece, "Florida Ghazals," in *The Clerk's Tale: Poems* (New York: Houghton Mifflin, 2004), 40.

7. Lisa Robertson, *The Weather* (Vancouver: New Star Books, 2001), 24. Robertson, an experimental avant-garde poet and essayist, is an apt partner in my project here, as she has long been concerned with setting aside the "puppets" of pronouns and self-referentiality in favor of a more civic and communal style of writing and what she calls "rhetorical sincerity," where the "truly utopian act is to manifest current conditions and dialects" and to "practice description" (Lisa Robertson, "Soft Architecture: A Manifesto," in *Occasional Work and Seven*

Walks from the Office for Soft Architecture, 3rd ed. [Toronto: Coach House Books, 2011], 20).

8. See Tim Ingold, "Point, Line, Counterpoint: From Environment to Fluid Space," in *Being Alive*, 86; and Andy Clark, *Being There: Putting Brain, Body and the World Together Again* (Cambridge, Mass.: MIT Press, 1997), 53.

9. For important work on the idea of "furnished" environments and environmental "affordances," see James Gibson, *The Ecological Approach to Visual Perception* (Boston: Houghton Mifflin, 1979).

10. Tim Ingold, "Earth, Sky, Wind, and Weather," in *Being Alive*, 119.

11. Phreddy Wischusen, *[estuaries]* (Detroit: [sic], 2012), 16.

12. Ingold, "Earth, Sky, Wind, and Weather," 120.

13. Mentz, *At the Bottom of Shakespeare's Ocean*, 34.

14. Lisa Robertson, "The Weather: A Report on Sincerity," *DC Poetry: 2001 Anthology*, www.dcpoetry.com/anthology/242.

15. Virginia Woolf, *The Waves* (Cambridge: Cambridge University Press, 2011), 139.

16. Ingold, "Earth, Sky, Wind, and Weather," 124–25.

17. I would like to note here that we do have a long critical tradition that calls into question the supposed etiology of mental illness as inhering only in individual minds and bodies, such as the entire oeuvre of the psychiatrist Thomas Szaz (see, e.g., *The Manufacture of Madness* [New York: Dell, 1970]), the work of Michel Foucault (especially in *Madness and Civilization: A History of Insanity in the Age of Reason*, trans. Richard Howard [New York: Random House, 1965]), and other more recent studies, such as Ian Hacking, *Mad Travellers: Reflections on the Reality of Transient Mental Illnesses* (London: Free Association Books, 1999).

18. Edward Mullany, "A Suicide in the Family," in *If I Falter at the Gallows* (Baltimore, Md.: Publishing Genius, 2011), 19.

19. Lisa Robertson, "Playing House: A Brief Account of the History of the Shack," in *Occasional Work and Seven Walks*, 157.

20. See Zygmunt Bauman, *Liquid Modernity* (Cambridge: Polity, 2000), 34. It has not been uncommon to hear discussions on the political right, for example, of health care as a personal and not a national responsibility. Here I also agree with Mark Fisher that, in the face of a capitalist "realism" that seemingly swallows up all possible alternatives, we might "convert widespread mental health problems from medicalized conditions into effective antagonisms" (*Capitalist Realism: Is There No Alternative?* [Winchester, UK: Zero Books, 2009], 80).

21. *Red Desert*, directed by Michelangelo Antonioni (1964; New York: Criterion Collection, 2010), DVD.

22. Quoted in Seymour Chatman and Paul Duncan, eds., *Michelangelo Antonioni: The Investigation* (Berlin: Taschen, 2004), 95.

23. Gilles Deleuze and Félix Guattari, *A Thousand Plateaus: Capitalism and Schizophrenia,* trans. Brian Massumi (Minneapolis: University of Minnesota Press, 1987), 311.

24. See Alfred K. Siewers, "The Bluest-Greyest-Greenest Eye: Colours of Martrydom and Colors of the Wind as Iconographic Landscape," *Cambrian Medieval Celtic Studies* 50 (2005): 46.

25. Ralph Ellison, "Richard Wright's Blues," in *Living with Music: Ralph Ellison's Jazz Writings,* ed. Robert G. O'Meally (New York: Random House, 2011), 101. I want to thank Jennifer James for directing me to this essay of Ellison's.

26. Lisa Robertson, "Spatial Synthetics: A Theory," in *Occasional Work and Seven Walks,* 69.

27. Mentz, *At the Bottom of Shakespeare's Ocean,* ix.

28. I take my cue here, also, from Robertson's argument that "the most pleasing civic object would be erotic hope" ("Spatial Synthetics," 68).

29. Beaches are prominent in end-of-the-world narratives, whether medieval or modern: think of the classic of the contemporary genre, Neville Shute's 1957 novel *On the Beach,* which derived its title from these lines of T. S. Eliot's poem "The Hollow Men": "In this last of meeting places / We grope together / And avoid speech / Gathered on this beach of the tumid river" ("The Hollow Men," in *Collected Poems, 1909–1962* [New York: Harcourt Brace, 1963], 81).

30. David Markson, *Wittgenstein's Mistress,* 3rd ed. (Champaign, Ill.: Dalkey Archive, 2012), 240.

31. Ibid., 230.

32. Ibid., 230, 231.

33. As David Foster Wallace has written about Kate, "She, no less than Wittgenstein, or Kant, or Descartes, or Herodotus, is writing a world" ("The Empty Plenum: David Markson's *Wittgenstein's Mistress,*" in Markson, *Wittgenstein's Mistress,* 273).

34. Markson, *Wittgenstein's Mistress,* 232. In his *Tractatus,* Wittgenstein argues, "What can be said at all can be said clearly; and whereof one cannot speak thereof one must be silent" (*Tractatus Logico-Philosophicus,* trans. C. K. Ogden [New York: Harcourt Brace, 1922], 27).

35. Markson, *Wittgenstein's Mistress,* 227.

36. Maurice Blanchot, *The Writing of Disaster,* trans. Ann Smock, new ed. (Lincoln: University of Nebraska Press, 1995), 7.

37. Tim Ingold, "Bringing Things to Life: Creative Entanglements in a World of Materials," unpublished paper (2008), 19. See also Henri Lefebvre, *The Production of Space,* trans. Donald Nicholson-Smith (Oxford: Blackwell, 1991).

38. Markson, *Wittgenstein's Mistress*, 1.

39. Ibid., 239.

40. Ibid., 25.

41. Ludwig Wittgenstein, *Philosophical Investigations,* ed. P. M. S. Hacker and Joachim Schulte, trans. G. E. M. Anscombe, P. M. S. Hacker, and Joachim Schulte, rev. 4th ed. (Oxford: Blackwell, 2009), 52e.

42. See Tim Ingold, "Footprints through the Weather-World: Walking, Breathing, Knowing," special issue, *Journal of the Royal Anthropological Institute,* n.s., 16 (2010): S121–S139.

43. Denis Johnson, *Fiskadoro: A Novel,* 4th ed. (New York: HarperPerennial, 1995), 1.

44. William Shakespeare, "Ariel's Song," *The Tempest,* in *The Riverside Shakespeare,* ed. G. Blakemore Evans, 2nd ed. (Boston: Houghton Mifflin, 1997), 1.2.564–65.

45. Johnson, *Fiskadoro,* 216.

46. Ibid., 219.

47. Morton, *Ecological Thought,* 94, 96.

48. T. P. Dunning and A. J. Bliss, eds., *The Wanderer* (London: Methuen, 1969), 1, 6a; l. 47b; ll. 7a, 80b; ll. 85–86. All translations are mine.

49. Ibid., ll. 62b–63.

50. Ibid., ll. 19–29a.

51. Ibid., ll. 39–43a.

52. Ibid., l. 46b, l. 48, ll. 49–50.

53. *Seafarer,* in George Philip Krapp and Elliott V. K. Dobbie, eds., *The Exeter Book,* Anglo-Saxon Poetic Records 3 (New York: Columbia University Press, 1936), ll. 9b–10a; ll. 14–16; ll. 65b–66a. Translations are mine, although I note here that "lone shield-bearer" for "anhaga" (typically translated as "lonely one," "recluse," "exile," "solitary man," and "wanderer") was first brought to my attention by Karma DeGruy and Jeff Massey, "*Ic eom anhaga, saga hwæt ic hata*: Riddling Meaning from Old English -haga Compounds" (unpublished paper).

54. *Seafarer,* l. 6a; l. 18b.

55. See, to cite just some examples of these approaches, R. C. Boer, "*Wanderer* and *Seafarer,*" *Zeitschrift für deutsche Philologie* 35 (1903): 1–28; Thomas D. Hill, "The Unchanging Hero: A Stoic Maxim in *The Wanderer* and Its Contexts," *Studies in Philology* 101, no. 3 (2004): 233–49; Bernard F. Huppé, "*The Wanderer*: Theme and Structure," *Journal of Germanic and English Philology* 42 (1943): 516–38; Clair McPherson, "The Sea a Desert: Early English Spirituality and *The Seafarer,*" *American Benedictine Review* 38, no. 2 (1987): 115–26; and John C. Pope, "Second

Thoughts on the Interpretation of *The Seafarer*," in *Old English Shorter Poems: Basic Readings*, ed. Katherine O'Brien O'Keeffe (New York: Garland, 1994), 213–29.

56. R. M. Liuzza, "The Tower of Babel: *The Wanderer* and the Ruins of History," *Studies in the Literary Imagination* 36, no. 1 (2003): 23.

57. The Seafarer begins by invoking his ability to "work truth-songs" ("soðgied wrecan," l. 1b).

58. Tim Ingold, "The Textuality of Making," in *Being Alive*, 214.

59. *Wanderer*, l. 4.

60. To cite just a few examples, Robert E. Diamond translates the lines "I, abject, winter-grieving (i.e. in a mood as dreary as winter? oppressed by advancing years?) went from there over the surface (lit. binding) of the waves" (*Old English Grammar and Reader* [Detroit: Wayne State University Press, 1970], 153). Burton Raffel's more modern poetic translation gives us, "Weary with winter I wandered out / On the frozen waves" (in *Poems and Prose from the Old English*, ed. Burton Raffel and Alexandra H. Olsen [New Haven, Conn.: Yale University Press, 1998], 8). In one of the first translations, Benjamin Thorpe offers, "I abject thence / went, stricken with years, / over the billowy mass" (*Codex Exoniensis: A Collection of Anglo-Saxon Poetry* [London: William Pickering, 1842], 287–88). In most cases, the sea is a mass, or a "bound" (a well-demarcated extension in space) to be prepositionally traveled *over*, although Diamond's parenthetical note hints at the more active co-implication I argue for here.

61. *Seafarer*, l. 20, ll. 20–21.

62. Ibid., ll. 23–24a.

63. On the subject of the poet's close attention to the rich variety of birds that populate the winter seaside in early medieval northern landscapes, see Margaret E. Goldsmith, "*The Seafarer* and the Birds," *Review of English Studies*, n.s., 5 (1954): 225–35.

64. *Seafarer*, ll. 58–61.

65. Ibid., l. 9, l. 17.

66. I borrow the phrase "rustling tenses" from Ben Lerner, "Doppler Elegies," *Jacket* 38 (2009): http://jacketmagazine.com/38/lerner-doppler.shtml.

67. Robertson, "Weather."

68. On the idea, propounded by some physicists, that the entire universe is enfolded, see David Bohm, *Wholeness and the Implicate Order* (London: Routledge, 1980) and "The Enfolding-Unfolding Universe and Consciousness," in *The Essential David Bohm*, ed. Lee Nichol (London: Routledge, 2003), 78–138.

69. L. O. Aranye Fradenburg, "Living Chaucer," *Studies in the Age of Chaucer* 33 (2011): 45.

70. In *At the Bottom of Shakespeare's Ocean,* Steve Mentz urges us to let go of "certain happy fictions" and replace them with "less comforting narratives. Fewer gardens, and more shipwrecks" (98).

71. *Wanderer,* l. 45, l. 53.

72. Markson, *Wittgenstein's Mistress,* 10.

73. Lerner, "Doppler Elegies."

Violet-Black

STACY ALAIMO

We are unfaithful to our trust if we allow biology to become a
colorless, aridly scientific discipline, devoid of living contact with
the humanities.

—WILLIAM BEEBE, *Half Mile Down*

The edge of being, and therefore of the being that I am, in the first
place because what is here called the "animal abyss" is not a hole, a
gulf, but too much being and the fact that there is being rather
than nothing.

—JACQUES DERRIDA, *The Animal That Therefore I Am*

Aviolet-black ecology hovers in the bathypelagic, abyssopelagic, and
hadal zones, the three regions of the deep seas, one thousand meters
down and much deeper, where sunlight cannot descend. The violet-
black depths—cold, dark regions under the crushing weight of the water
column—were long thought to be "azoic," or devoid of life. It is not surprising that Edward Forbes's azoic theory of the 1840s (preceded by that
of Henry de la Beche a decade earlier) stood as the accepted doctrine for
a quarter century, since it is difficult for terrestrial creatures to imagine
what could possibly survive in the unfathomable seas. William J. Broad
argues that generations of scientists "dismissed the abyss (a dismissive
word in some respects) as inert and irrelevant, as geologically dead and
having only a thin population of bizarre fish." Even as deep-sea creatures
have been brought to the surface, it remains convenient to assume that the
bathyl, abyssl, and hadal zones are empty, void, null—an abyss of concern.[1] The deep seas epitomize how most ocean waters exist beyond state
borders, legal protection, and cultural imaginaries. Even as some marine
areas such as coastal zones are considered inexhaustibly abundant, the

open seas have long been considered empty space. As Philip Steinberg argues, the social construction of the ocean in industrial capitalism has been that of a "vast void," an "empty transportation surface, beyond the space of social relations."[2] The emphasis on the transportation surface here neglects vertical zones in favor of horizontal trajectories, making the deep seas the void of the void. Such a colossal, global, oceanic void is of an entirely different scale than Jacques Derrida's domestic encounter with the gaze of his cat, certainly. Yet Derrida's ruminations are already drenched in the language of the depths, as he describes the question of human and nonhuman subjectivity as "immense and abyssal," requiring that he wrestle with the "several tentacles" of philosophies that become, together, "a single living body at bottom."[3] If we shift Derrida's ruminations on the "animal abyss" from an encounter with the gaze of a specific animal to the collective "composition" (in Bruno Latour's terms) of the vast abyssal zone and its surrounding territories,[4] we discover the same sort of vertiginous recognition that there is, indeed, "being rather than nothing." But what does it mean for the abyssal being to be or become "too much"?

When historic expeditions have dredged up creatures from the depths, the profusion of animals has been met with astonishment. The British *H.M.S. Challenger,* sailing from 1872 to 1876, hauled up "tens of thousands of animals, some writhing and squirming on deck," and identified "4,717 new species, giant worms and slugs, spindly crabs and prawns, delicate sponges and sea lilies."[5] The Danish *Galathea,* from 1950 to 1952, also dredged up thousands of creatures estimated to be part of a "global mass of deep diversity whose ranks held as many as ten million species—far more than the million or so varieties of life identified on land."[6] The profusion of creaturely life should not be surprising given the sheer magnitude of the violet-black zones of the ocean. The deep sea comprises, by volume, 78.5 percent of the planet's habitat, a stunning mass compared with only 21 percent of the rest of the sea and the paltry 0.5 percent of land habitats.[7] Rather than scrutinize deep sea creatures as they writhe and squirm in suffocating air and glaring light, a violet-black ecology would descend, in highly mediated ways, to zones of darkness to witness diverse animals in their own watery worlds, but it would also grapple with the watery "environment" itself. As the contemplation of the deep seas is always already a politically charged, scientifically mediated process—partly because of the staggering costs of even the most basic investigations conducted at these depths—it exemplifies Latour's call to "compose the common world from disjointed pieces."⁸ As a new materialist endeavor, a violet-black ecology would attempt to understand the water of the abyssal zone as something rather than nothing, as substance rather than background, as a significant part of the composition.

At the turn of the twenty-first-century, scientists and environmentalists warn of the devastating ecological effects of ocean acidification, massive overfishing, bottom trawling, deep-sea mining, shark finning, and decades of dumping toxic and radioactive waste into the oceans. Marine science, which is still in its infancy, struggles to keep up with the devastating effects of capitalist waste and plunder as countless species may be rendered extinct before they are even discovered. William Beebe's worry, however, that biology would become "colorless" and "aridly scientific," would be assuaged by the early twenty-first-century representations of sea creatures in which science, aesthetics, and politics swirl together. The massive, international, decades-long Census of Marine Life, for example, produced not only a treasure trove of scientific disclosures but a vibrant profusion of still and moving images for wide audiences. While the Census of Marine Life's gallery of photos on its website and Claire Nouvian's stunning photographic collection *The Deep: Extraordinary Creatures from the Abyss* attempt to gain support for deep-sea conservation by featuring newly discovered life forms, it may be worthwhile to scrutinize what is intentionally out of focus in their photographic compositions—the violet-black background of the photos. What possibilities does this eerie and entrancing hue pose for new materialist and posthumanist ecologies of the depths? And how do the prismatic bioluminescent displays of creatures in the abyss provoke recognitions of the multitude of aquatic modes of being, communicating, and knowing? Violet-black ecologies of the abyssal zones entice us to descend, rather than transcend, to unmoor ourselves from terrestrial and humanist presumptions, as sunlight, air, and horizons disappear, replaced by dark liquid expanses and the flashing spectrum of light produced by abyssal creatures.

William Beebe, *A Half Mile Down*

Ocean ecologies are particularly suited for prismatic consideration, in that seawater absorbs and scatters light. The ocean acts like a vast liquid prism that subtracts rather than diffracts different frequencies of light at different depths. Red, the longest wavelength of light visible to humans, disappears at shallow depths, followed by orange, yellow, and green. As the sea absorbs nearly the entire spectrum of light that is humanly discernible, it marginalizes human modes of perception and, moreover, rebuffs the terrestrial dominion of the sun. William Beebe, an explorer and scientist, who penned an account of his famous, record-breaking, bathysphere descents in the 1930s, was fascinated by the prismatic seas. In his typed notes titled "Dive Number X: Spectrum," he details how colors disappear as he and Otis Barton descend to eight hundred feet. At fifty feet red is "invisible," at two hundred feet orange is gone, at three hundred feet, "yellow green" is "almost gone," at four hundred feet violet "has completely eclipsed blue," at five hundred feet, "Every color gone but violet, and by eight hundred there is "no color": "Not a particle of the faintest color distinguishable by either Barton or myself."[9] Beebe was mesmerized by the indescribable color of the water, which underscored the fact that the fish inhabited a world so utterly different from his own. As he and Barton descend in their first bathysphere expedition to seven hundred feet, Beebe attempts to register the liquid hue: "I brought all my logic to bear, I put out of mind the excitement of our position in watery space and tried to think sanely of comparative color, and I failed utterly."[10] He switches on the searchlight, using it as a miniature sun to normalize his color perceptions but to no avail: "The blueness of the blue, both outside and inside our sphere, seemed to pass materially through the eye into our very beings. This is all very unscientific; quite worthy of being jeered at by optician or physicist, but there it was."[11] Logic, sanity, and imperviousness, the bedrocks of scientific objectivity, fail him as the color of the water "materially" enters their "very beings." Unable to directly experience the deep waters without the protection of the bathysphere, they nonetheless experience a direct encounter with the color—the light—that penetrates them.

Beebe, who was rightly concerned that his bathysphere dives would be seen as a stunt rather than as science, partly because they were unable to capture specimens, worries he will be mocked for remarking how deeply the color affected him. In his many ruminations on the color of the water in *A Half Mile Down*, he mixes scientific, philosophical, and aesthetic perspectives. At one point he suggests that the color exceeds standard classifications. Beebe notes, "I think we both experienced a wholly new kind of mental reception of color impression. I felt I was dealing with something too different to be classified in usual terms."[12] While Beebe's vague observations on the colors of the deep-sea waters hardly seem noteworthy, Henry Fairfield Osborn claims that the "two most surprising phenomena [of the bathysphere dives] were, first, the abundance of life observed, and the clarity and certainty with which it could be seen and identified, and second, the blue brilliance of the watery light to the naked eye, long after every particle of color had been drained from the spectrum."[13] On their seventh dive, Beebe continues to study "the changing colors, both by direct observation and by means of the spectroscope," recording each color as it disappears at a particular depth. At eight hundred feet, for example, he sees "only the deepest, blackest-blue imaginable," adding that "this unearthly color brought excitement to our eyes and minds" on every dive.[14] He waxes poetic about the color of the water throughout *A Half Mile Down*, marveling at "a solid, blue-black world, one which seemed born of a single vibration—blue, blue, forever and forever blue."[15]

Ravished and overcome by the blue-black of the waters, Beebe revels in the powerful strangeness, the indescribable difference of this watery world. In a chapter titled "At the End of the Spectrum," Beebe describes how, at seventeen hundred feet down, he "attained one of the chief objects of the whole dive, namely to get below the level of humanly visual light." He "was beyond sunlight as far as the human eye could tell, and from here down, for two billion years there had been no day or night, no summer or winter, no passing of time until we came to record it."[16] Beebe imagines the depths as timeless, since the rising and setting of the sun have no significance. The "human eye" is capable of only a limited perspective, but the timeless seas are saturated with that mesmerizing, eternal blue. While Beebe was not himself engaged with conservation projects, and, in his defense, during the early twentieth century it hardly seemed that the oceans would need to be conserved, his writings about the seas often insisted that human perspectives, perceptions, and understandings are partial. In some ways his writings resonate with an animal studies, rather than an ecological, perspective. His story "Argyropelecus," which he intended to include in his unpublished book, "Mid-Ocean," traces the life of a fish, "young Argy," from the time when he swims with his mother to the time when he is caught by a "famous ichthyologist" and put in a glass jar. Beebe begins by asking "who can prove that the story of a tiny fish is less important than our own?" and concludes by asking "who can say that their little silver souls were not conscious of the peering eyes that gazed down on them in wonder and admiration?[17] I would not use the term *biocentric* to describe Beebe's philosophy, as Gary Kroll does, since Beebe emphasizes individual creatures, their perceptions, and their lifeworlds, rather than ecological systems, but I do agree with Kroll that Beebe "invested in nature an inherent value that was in no way contingent on humans."[18] The enthralling blue-black light, as well as the colors emanating from bioluminescent creatures, destabilize terrestrial assumptions, values, and modes of life. The first paragraph of "Argyropelecus" reads almost like science fiction, with its Haraway-esque emphasis on animals as "other worlds."

> It was the same beautiful black day that it had been for aeons and aeons and would be for aeons and aeons to come. The blackness was lit by a firmament of moving worlds, [whose] glowing spots of myriad-hued lights glided and flashed through the hydrosphere. Uncharted and trackless were the courses of these worlds.

When Beebe does attempt to chart and track the unknown animals that are themselves imagined as moving, glowing, worlds, his observations wash out into repetitive, not at all illuminating, observations. His scientific method fails to graph or illuminate this dark, timeless place. Organized by depth, from shallower to deeper, the typed notes titled "Unknown Animals" were probably intended to find correlations between depths and types of bioluminescence observed. The notes, however, do not reveal any success, as the observations seem random and not exactly systematic: "very brilliant animal lights," "faint lights in distance," "sparks," "first little flash," "three tiny sparks in distance," "first brilliant spark near window," "tens of thousands of tiny dots," "school of sparks," "water a dark blue with few sparks," "animal lights dim," "brilliant light, pale greenish in color," "pale rose red flash," "lots of lights that come and go," "very brilliant animal lights," "something like a rocket bursting."[19] One observation, "lovely bright solid pale blue light close to glass. Probably------," leaves a string of hyphens where the name of the creature could be, but was not, filled in later. Tony Koslow notes that Beebe's bathysphere dives "had more influence on the popular imagination than on oceanographic science,"[20] and Kroll contends that "Beebe made the ocean something worth protecting."[21] I would add that Beebe's observations—so often dominated by the captivating colors of the seas and its creatures—embody a nascent posthumanist philosophy in which human knowledge systems and terrestrial horizons are overwhelmed, overtaken, undone. Dry scientific epistemologies of rational "objectivity" become drenched with embodied aesthetic, emotional responses. And the "data" that are gathered drifts—eluding systems or grids. The glimmers of a violet-black posthumanist onto-epistemology here may be more ethically significant than determining exactly what creature made that "lovely bright solid pale blue light."

Portraits from the Abyss

Beebe's rapturous outpourings attempt to convey the stunning blue-blackness of the deep seas, but the grainy black-and-white photographs included in *Half Mile Down,* published in 1934, disappoint. At the turn of the twenty-first century, however, vivid, even radiant images of deep sea creatures proliferate in coffee-table books, scientific journals, popular magazines, and websites. The Census of Marine Life, as it explains on its website, is a "10-year international effort undertaken to assess the diversity (how many different kinds), distribution (where they live), and abundance (how many) of marine life—a task never before attempted on this scale. The Census stimulated the discipline of marine science by tackling these issues globally, and engaging some 2,700 scientists from around the globe, who participated in 540 expeditions and countless hours of land-based research. The scientific results were reported on October 4, 2010."[22] In an age of genetically oriented research in which the gene and not the organism reigns supreme, and in which science, engineering, and even bioart remake rather than discover life forms, the Census seems to inhabit an earlier time. Indeed the impossible aims of the Census assume Enlightenment models of knowledge where creatures from the depths are brought into the light of scientific reason. The popular media of the Census of Marine Life—books, web pages, photographs, videos—intertwine science, aesthetics, and environmentalism, attempting to entangle us in networks of aesthetic pleasure, responsibility, and concern. Despite the website's subtitle, "Making Ocean Life *Count,*" a pun suggesting that the exhibition of numerical magnitude will make the ocean matter to humans, it seems that the primary way the Census appeals to the wider public is through highly aestheticized images—framing, not counting. The predominant mode of representing deep-sea environments—for example, on the official Census of Marine Life website and in Nouvian's *The Deep: Extraordinary Creatures of the Abyss*—is a portraitlike photo of one single specimen of one species, usually rendered in a hyperreal, highly aestheticized manner, against a solid black background.[23] These photos feature saturated, bright, distinctive colors and a sharp contrast between the animal and the black background. The beautiful but blatant images would seem to exemplify Enlightenment epistemologies where objective truth is available to all, free of perspectives, systems of power, or other entanglements. In some sense the taxonomical and enumerating aims of the Census assume this epistemological stance, as scientists discover and photographically capture each species. Unabashed realism, indeed, a kind of luminous hyperrealism reigns.

A French film director and journalist, Nouvian "worked alongside Census scientists studying the continental margins to capture some amazing photographs."[24] Nouvian's preface to the massive book tells how in 2001, after watching "a stunningly beautiful film" at the Monterey Bay Aquarium, her life "changed direction," as she became fascinated by creatures that she thought could not possibly be real.

> I was dazzled . . . speechless . . . astounded . . .
>   As crazy as it might seem, I had fallen in love at first sight. . . .
> It was as though a veil had been lifted, revealing unexpected points
> of view, vaster and more promising. . . . I imagined this colossal
> volume of water, cloaked in permanent darkness, and I pictured the
> fantastic creatures that swam there, far from our gazes, the surrealist
> results of an ever inventive Nature.[25]

Nouvian's crazy love produced a stunning volume, combining essays by scientists with unrivaled photographs of the creatures (many of them taken by scientists). The essays are often passionate about the creatures they describe, but it is the large, astoundingly beautiful photographs that transport their viewers to the place where Nouvian found herself "dazzled . . .

speechless . . . astounded." The critic Andrew Robinson, asserting that *The Deep* will have an impact similar to that of Robert Hooke's *Micrographia* (which Samuel Pepys "sat up until 2am reading") called Nouvian's book "eye-poppingly magnificent": "So much so that it provokes gasps of amazement and awe at the complexity, beauty and uniqueness of life in the abyss."[26] Notwithstanding the book's oversized format that makes the pictures even more powerful, it is the exquisite composition of each photograph that is so effective. The strange, incredibly vibrant animals are skillfully positioned within black pages, as the "nothing" of the darkness spotlights an individual creature. Each animal hovers in a great expanse of black space. The aesthetically arresting expanse signifies the vastness of the oceans. Nouvian, when asked about how she edited the photos for the collection, replied that the "biggest amount of work was put into color editing the black backdrops because it took my writing this book in order to understand that there are as many different blacks as there are pinks or blues. We didn't do anything else but clean up the files and make sure the blacks were even all throughout the book."[27] Despite her own metaphors of lifting the veil of nature, the water itself, impervious to the slightest solar rays, remains exactly the same impenetrable hue. The solid blackness is vertiginous—viewers are denied any sense of scale, perspective, or depth. The flat wall of blackness denies us any foundation, direction, or orientation toward a horizon. We hover, like the pelagic creatures, unmoored.

From a new materialist perspective the predominant aesthetic mode of both the Census website and Nouvian's volume may be problematic, as the substance, agencies, and significance of the seas disappear. The dynamic liquid materiality is rendered a flat, static background, evident yet disclosing nothing. The backdrop belies not only the vast expanse of the oceans but the intra-acting material agencies of oceanic ecologies and human entanglements. The genre mirrors the myth that the deep sea is an abyss, a nothingness, an immaterial zone separate from human incursions and transformations and, thus, a sort of anachronistic space for the innocent pleasure of "discovery," free from environmentalist hand-wringing. The clean aesthetic, in other words, may mask the contaminated waters. It is one thing for William Beebe, in 1932, to encounter a fish while in his bathysphere and propose that it be called "Bathysphaera Intacta: The Untouchable Bathysphere Fish,"[28] but at this point everything in the ocean has already been touched by human practices, if not human hands. As Tony Koslow puts it, "We may think of the deep sea as pristine, but in fact no portion of the deep sea is today unaffected by human activities."[29] The substance of the deep waters is by no means immune to the dumping of toxic and radioactive waste, the acidification of the ocean, the microplastics, and other factors.

Even as the flat, black aesthetic of the abyss mirrors the darkness of bathypelagic, abyssal, and hadal zones; it results from particular photographic techniques that eliminate "backscatter," the soupy mix of particles and tiny creatures in the water, from view. Simon Foale and Martha Mcintyre argue that photos of coral reefs maintain the fantasy of pristine nature by eliminating backscatter, which is, ironically, essential for marine life: "Many of these aesthetically annoying specs are vitally important food sources for the pretty reef fish that are so often photographed."[30] As the particles and tiny creatures of deep-sea waters are concealed, the ocean as a habitat, an ecosystem, is obscured. By contrast, Koslow's book, *The Silent Deep,* contains an inset of sixteen color plates, which do not feature backscatter but which do highlight lively interminglings of creatures: the scavengers of a whale carcass, a black coral with an orange starfish, a benthic octopus and clam on a rock, an eel and some crabs hiding in a coldwater coral, a bubblegum coral with a basket star and shrimps on its branches, a rich profusion of creatures on a "soft coral and sponge garden."[31] His photographs represent ecosystems, habitats, lively interrelations between creatures, rather than isolated, taxonomical captures. The photographs are consistent with the conclusion of the book that, after discussing the many threats to deep-sea environments—climate change, mining, overfishing, bottom trawling, pollution, the lack of international laws or law enforcement—advocates "a new approach to ocean management: an ecosystem-based approach that is comprehensive, integrated and effective, and that addresses all activities and threats in a precautionary fashion."[32]

Although the black background of the photos on the Census of Marine Life website does not intimate ecosystems, the fact that the photos are highly stylized, rather than a window onto the aquatic world, suggests their networks of production. The "Gallery" of images delivers heretofore undiscovered species to computer screens, where they glow against their black backgrounds. The Gallery is an orderly, symmetrical presentation of each creature as it is distinguished from the depths, which is visually striking, but may, problematically, render each creature an object of art. The site, however, encourages its viewers not to view each image in isolation but as a series, tempting us with over one hundred stunning photos. Thus these scientific images could be read as a "set of instructions to reach another one down the line."[33] On the left of each page is an orderly array of square images, three columns wide, five images tall, mimicking a photographic exhibition in an art gallery. Clicking on the arrows below leads to more orderly columns of creatures. Clicking on these squares makes a larger image of that life form appear, with explanatory text below it, which, together, take up the bulk of the page. The black background of the web pages themselves signifies how much is as yet unknown about ocean life, but it could also dramatize the photos of each creature as "artifacts," in Latour's sense. The fact that the photos are highly mediated and humanly made increases, rather than decreases, their status as truth, as they embed the creatures within the networks that have made them visible.[34] The distinctive web pages exhibit the human labor, the technologies, the fabrications, and the huge cost of the Census itself. Moreover, the first image on the "New Species" page informs us that "twelve hundred new species were formally described during 2000–2010 by Census scientists, with another five thousand or so in glass jars awaiting formal description,"[35] asking us to imagine these photos as a much larger network of scientific and aesthetic capture, as yet unavailable to the public. Could the black background, which fails to register ecosystems, signify instead the densely populated space where mediations—the swirl of science, economics, politics, technology, and aesthetics—deliver sea creatures from the oceanic depths to labs, scientific journals, computer screens, and coffee-table books? If truth is to be found "in taking up the task of continuing the flow, of elongating the cascade of mediations one step further,"[36] the images pull not only scientists, environmentalists, and policy maker into their currents but ordinary citizens and activists who find themselves descending into as yet unfathomable violet-black ecologies.

Does it make sense to imagine these carefully fashioned photos functioning politically? While it would be simple to critique the overt commodification of sea creatures as coffee-table books or computer images—just more fodder for aesthetic consumption—there is something about these photos that is arresting, moving, compelling. As the black screens and pages dramatically stage each creature, perhaps these photos act in an aesthetic-political manner, "reconfiguring the sensible" in Jacques Rancière's terms, by posing heretofore invisible marine creatures for consideration. It is tempting, despite Rancière's own humanism, which defines the "human" animal as that which "possesses the ability to articulate language and its power of demonstration," to nonetheless consider the "political" potential for portraits of deep-sea creatures to intervene "into the visible and the sayable."[37] If, as he argues, politics consists in "refiguring space," could representations of diverse and multitudinous sea creatures reshape oceanic geopolitical territories as places of concern for sea cucumbers, squid, and other creatures? If the "essential work of politics . . . is to make the world of its subjects and its operations seen" and to demonstrate "the presence of two worlds in one,"[38] such a manifestation of dual worlds would be perhaps most profoundly embodied by a violet-black ecology that demands recognition of the abyssal zone, a realm that scrambles terrestrial orientations with aquatic immensities. I am not alone in my desire to recast Rancière for posthumanist purposes. Jane Bennett argues that "even against his will," Rancière's "model contains inklings and opportunities for a more (vital) materialist theory of democracy."[39] She explains that since Rancière "chooses to define what counts as political by what effect is generated," we "see how an animal, plant, mineral, or artifact can sometimes catalyze a public."[40] Strangely, one of the official Census of Marine Life books written for a popular audience is the National Geographic collaboration titled *Citizens of the Sea: Wondrous Creatures from the Census of Marine Life.*[41] Nancy Knowlton introduces the book by noting that the ocean is "out of sight, out of mind, for most people." Yet the sea "is in trouble": "Its citizens have no vote in any national or international body, but they are suffering and need to be heard."[42] The Census does not convey the voices of sea creatures, as they tend to "speak" in visual modes, but it does stage them as living beings that demand consideration. The dramatic black background throughout *Citizens of the Sea* announces that these "citizens" occupy another world. The very provocation to consider these creatures as "citizens" engulfs viewers with posthumanist, not necessarily terrestrial, modes of (political) life, challenging us to reconfigure geopolitical parameters so as not to exclude abyssal ecologies.

Prismatic Constellations of Animal Worlds

The unnervingly violet-black seas entice us to envision posthumanist perspectives that renounce mastery, transcendence, and stable, terrestrial frames of reference that center the human subject within visible horizons. That flat wall of black, used so effectively in Nouvian's compositions, may, however, lead us to believe that the deep seas are devoid of light. Edith Widder, a marine biologist specializing in bioluminescence, or, as she calls herself, "a bioluminescence junky,"[43] says this is not the case: "The deep sea is often described as 'a world of eternal darkness.' That is a lie. While it is true that sunlight does not penetrate below 1000m, that does not mean that it is a lightless world down there. In fact, there are lots of lights—billions and billions of them. These are animal lights and they serve many life sustaining functions."[44] Widder's TED talk, "Glowing Life in an Underwater World," describes how her "addiction" to bioluminescence began in the Santa Barbara Channel:

> I knew I would see this phenomenon of animals making light called bioluminescence. But I was totally unprepared for how much there was and how spectacular it was. I saw chains of jellyfish called siphonophores that were longer than this room, pumping out so much light that I could read the dials and gauges inside the suit without a flashlight; and puffs and billows of what looked like luminous blue smoke; and explosions of sparks that would swirl up out of the thrusters. . . . It was breathtaking.[45]

Thus a violet-black abyssal ecology is not a single hue but is instead populated with a spectrum of colors extending across the range of what is humanly visible and beyond. A veritable constellation of creatures who create their own light supplants a terrestrial, heliocentric model of sovereign, unitary, human (or divine) knowledge. Prismatic, fluid constellations of bioluminescent animals in the violet-black abyss experience a world where the Copernican revolution is irrelevant. (Even the "fact" that all life depends on the sun, which most of us learned in elementary school, is no longer quite true, as chemosynthesis in marine vent ecologies does not depend on photosynthesis.)

In the depths, millions of light-creating creatures dramatize a multitude of species-specific ways of being, communicating, surviving, and seducing. Widder explains that bioluminescence "can aide animal survival in at least three critical ways: (i) It can serve as an aid in locating food, either by means of built-in headlights or by the use of glowing lures. (ii) It can be used to attract a mate by means of species-specific spatial or temporal patterns of light emission. (iii) It can function as a defense against predators."[46] As 80 to 90 percent of deep-sea life forms use some type of bioluminescence—a much larger percentage than those found on land—it is not the broad categories of use that are intriguing but the incredible diversity, ingenuity, and artistry involved in the deployment of light. For example, "The male sea firefly, a crustacean the size of a sesame seed, squirts out light that hangs as a bright dot in the water, then zips upward and squirts out another and another, leaving a string of hanging dots spaced out like smoke signals. The spacing is species specific; mate-ready females can go to the head of the dot string and find an appropriate male."[47] The sea firefly uses light as his artistic medium of seduction; another fish, the shining tubeshoulder, uses light as a weapon, as he or she "literally squirts light out of a tube on its shoulder into the face of an enemy, much as a squid shoots ink."[48] Deep-sea anglerfish are so named because the female possesses a fishing pole–like lure, positioned in front of its mouth, glowing with bioluminescent bacteria. In the violet-black waters, animals use light as lures, alarms, distractions, weapons, and semiotic systems. Widder states, "So there's a language of light in the deep ocean, and we're just beginning to understand it."[49] To attempt to decipher the language of light, Widder has sent the camera she designed, called "Eye-in-the-Sea," which uses a frequency of light that most creatures cannot see, to make the camera less disruptive. The Eye-in-the-Sea includes an electronic jellyfish that lights up to provoke bioluminescent displays. At two thousand feet in the Bahamas, the flashing jellyfish provokes a lively discussion: "We basically have a chat room going on here, because once it gets started, everybody's talking. And I think this is actually a shrimp that's releasing its bioluminescent chemicals into the water. But the cool thing is, we're talking to it. We don't know what we're saying. Personally, I think it's something sexy."[50] Not unlike David Rothenberg who makes music with birds and whales, attempting to interact with them in their own languages, cobbling together a common tune, rather than studying them from a distance, Widder hints at her desire for intimacy with these creatures that are too often termed "alien."[51] She hopes that the messages of light will be interpreted as "something sexy." There is a joyful abandon here, as the technologically proficient, physically intrepid, renowned scientist is exhilarated by the prospect of speaking in a language she does not understand, daring to talk without knowing what she is saying. If, as Cary Wolfe contends, "the nature of thought itself must change if it is to be posthumanist,"[52] then Widder's attempt to speak a language of light, to seduce abyssal creatures with her electronic jellyfish, certainly exceeds a mere "thematics of the decentering of the human."[53] Thinking with and through the electronic jellyfish, seeing through the prosthetic eye, playing open-ended, improvisational language games with deep-sea creatures, being transformed by astonishment and desire enact a posthumanist practice. Yet Widder, safe from the consequences of her speech, may unwittingly be sending harmful messages, akin to shouting "Fire!" in a crowded theater. The creatures with whom she speaks are certainly more vulnerable to the potential effects of these conversations than are the terrestrial scientists.

Posthumanists, nonetheless, may rejoice in how the multitude of light-emitting abyssal creatures dethrones the monotheistic idea that one sovereign, transcendent, celestial deity is the source of true, holy, knowledge—knowledge that he imparts solely to the one creature cast in his image. Bioluminescence epitomizes animals as other worlds, as creatures profoundly different from, not inferior to, ourselves. As Mick Smith advocates, "Instead of looking for the divine in Man (the metaphysics of the anthropological machine), we might instead try to divine, to sense something of, (as a water diviner does), the flows and depths of diverse worldly existences happening beneath their surface appearances."[54] In *Against Ecological Sovereignty*, Smith develops a potent ecological ethics and politics, but his theory does not account for the extent to which environmental politics requires scientific data. "Divining" the deep seas, for example, requires costly scientific expeditions, expensive technology, artistically rendered images, and savvy modes of dissemination. So little is currently known about the majority of sea animals and ecosystems, so rarely do they figure into ethical or political consideration, that without a "reconfiguration of the sensible," which could occur only via the intermingling channels of science, aesthetics, and advocacy, there is little chance these creatures would be divined. Notwithstanding the lack of attention to science in Smith's theory, his sense of the "infinite" dimension of ecological ethics and politics is essential for coming to terms with the rather sudden disclosure of thousands of "new" species in the seas as well as the many threats to their existence. Smith writes, "Ecological politics as such emerges through facing up to and recognizing our potentially infinite ethical responsibilities for Other (other than human) beings."[55]

In the same essay in which Derrida contends that the "animal abyss" is "not a hole, a gulf but too much being" he describes his own philosophical exertions as something akin to the efforts of an amateur marine biologist.[56]

> At the moment of bringing and including together, in a single embrace, Descartes, Kant, Heidegger, Levinas, and Lacan, as a single living body at bottom, indeed as a single corpus delicti, the mobile system of a single discursive organization with several tentacles, I have the impression that I am myself trying to gain— as though wrestling, fishing, or hunting—a sufficiently expert or knowledgeable purchase [prise] on what might touch the nervous system of a single animal body. A little like someone who would claim to know which way to take hold of a cuttlefish or octopus, without hurting it too much, and especially without killing it, keeping it at a distance long enough to let it expel its ink. In order to displace its powers without doing anybody too much harm. Its ink or power would here be the "I," not necessarily the *power to say* "I" but the ipseity of being *able to be or able to do* "I," even before any autoreferential utterance in language.[57]

For the philosopher, the tentacles are merely metaphorical and the grasping of the cuttlefish, despite the palpable prose, is just a simile. Yet he seeks to gain "a sufficiently expert or knowledgeable purchase [prise] on what might touch the nervous system of a single animal body." Oddly, despite the wrestling, the scene is not described as a two-way encounter in which the philosopher is touched or altered; the cephalopod is kept at a distance. The passage is still relevant, however, because the multitude of lights in the abyssal zone, like the ink, are "*able to be or able to do* 'I.'" As constellations of luminous creatures populate the seas being and doing diverse things with the light they generate, the irreducibility of their ipseity lures terrestrial humans to imagine posthuman worlds. Smith, speaking of commonplace "birds, stones, trees," insists that even they are "alien," as they "exhibit radically different and sometimes extraordinarily strange ways of being-in-the-world."[58] Drawing on Emmanuel Levinas and Iris Murdoch, Smith advocates an ethics that emerges from a "non-self-centered response to the recognition of such alienation from the world and from others."[59] The violet-black seas themselves, which entranced William Beebe, and the addictive bioluminescent creatures, underscore the significant differences between the lifeworlds of human beings and abyssal beings, as well as the potential for prismatic ecologies to lure us into less anthropocentric, less "grounded" modes of knowledge, politics, and ethics. We can only hope that violet-black compositions will, somehow, catalyze concern for creatures and habits we can barely begin to imagine.

Notes

1. William J. Broad, *The Universe Below: Discovering the Secrets of the Deep Sea* (New York: Touchstone, 1997), 331.

2. Philip E. Steinberg, *The Social Construction of the Ocean* (Cambridge: Cambridge University Press, 2001), 113.

3. Jacques Derrida, *The Animal That Therefore I Am* (New York: Fordham University Press, 2008) 95, 91.

4. For convenience, I use the term *abyssal* throughout to signify the bathyl, abyssal, and hadal zones, which together make up the deep seas. Technically, the abyssal zone is between three thousand and six thousand meters deep; the bathypelagic zone is between one thousand and three thousand meters; and the hadal zone is below six thousand meters. The benthic zones, which lie at the bottom of the oceans, vary in depth according to the depth of the ocean floor. The epipelagic zone comprises the top two hundred meters of water, and the mesopelagic ranges from two hundred to one thousand meters. For this particular essay, it makes sense to focus on the bathypelagic zones and the zones below it, since sunlight cannot descend below one thousand or twelve hundred meters.

5. Broad, *Universe Below,* 37.

6. Ibid., 45.

7. Ibid., 44.

8. Bruno Latour, "An Attempt at a Compositionist Manifesto," *New Literary History* 41 (2010): 485.

9. William Beebe Papers, Department of Rare Books and Special Collections, Princeton University Library, Collection C0661 (hereafter cited as PUL), box 12, folder 8.

10. William Beebe, *Half Mile Down* (Chicago: Cadmus Books, 1934), 109.

11. Ibid.

12. Ibid., 111.

13. Henry Fairfield Osborn, "A New Method of Deep Sea Observation at First Hand," *Science,* July 11, 1930, 28.

14. Beebe, *Half Mile Down,* 119.

15. Ibid., 132.

16. Ibid., 165.

17. William Beebe, unpublished papers, PUL, box 12, folder 10.

18. Gary Kroll, *America's Ocean Wilderness: A Cultural History of Twentieth-Century Exploration* (Lawrence: University Press of Kansas, 2008), 94.

19. Beebe papers, PUL, box 12, folder 7.

20. Tony Koslow, *The Silent Deep: The Discovery, Ecology, and Conservation of the Deep Sea* (Chicago: University of Chicago Press, 2007), 54.

21. Kroll, *America's Ocean Wilderness,* 94.

22. Census of Marine Life, "About the Census," http://www.coml.org/about-census (accessed May 14, 2012).

23. Claire Nouvian, *The Deep: The Extraordinary Creatures of the Abyss* (Chicago: University of Chicago Press, 2007).

24. Census of Marine Life, "Census in the Arts: The Deep," http://www.coml.org/census-arts/the-deep (accessed May 14, 2012).

25. Nouvian, *Deep,* 12.

26. Andrew Robinson, "Yeti Crabs and Vampire Squids," *Literary Review,* http://www.literaryreview.co.uk/robinson_05_07.html (accessed May 14, 2012).

27. Nouvian, e-mail to author, April 23, 2011.

28. Beebe, *Half Mile Down,* 173.

29. Koslow, *Silent Deep,* 3.

30. Simon Foale and Martha Macintyre, "Green Fantasies: Photographic Representations of Biodiversity and Ecotourism in the Western Pacific," *Journal of Political Ecology* 12 (2005): 14.

31. Koslow, *Silent Deep,* plate 13.

32. Ibid., 236.

33. Bruno Latour, *On the Modern Cult of the Factish Gods* (Durham, N.C.: Duke University Press, 2010), 93.

34. Ibid., 71.

35. Census of Marine Life, "Image Gallery," http://www.coml.org/image-gallery (accessed May 14, 2012).

36. Latour, *On the Modern Cult,* 123.

37. Jacques Rancière, *Dissensus: On Politics and Aesthetics,* ed. and trans. Steven Corcoran (New York: Continuum, 2010), 37.

38. Ibid.

39. Jane Bennett, *Vibrant Matter: A Political Ecology of Things* (Durham, N.C.: Duke University Press, 2010), 106.

40. Ibid., 106, 107.

41. Nancy Knowlton, *Citizens of the Sea: Wondrous Creatures from the Census of Marine Life* (Washington, D.C.: National Geographic, 2010).

42. Ibid., 9.

43. Edith Widder, "The Weird, Wonderful World of Bioluminescence," TED talk, March 2011, http://www.ted.com/talks/edith_widder_the_weird_and_wonderful_world_of_bioluminescence.html.

44. Edith Widder, "Living Lights in the Sea," in Nouvian, *Deep,* 85.

45. Edith Widder, "Glowing Life in an Underwater World," TED talk, April 2010, http://www.ted.com/talks/edith_widder_glowing_life_in_an_underwater_world.html.

46. Edith Widder, "Bioluminescence in the Ocean: Origins of Biological, Ecological, and Chemical Diversity," *Science* 328 (2010): 704.

47. Jack McClintock, "Splendor in the Dark," *Discover* 25, no. 5 (2004), 3.

48. Ibid.

49. Widder, "Weird."

50. Ibid.

51. For a critique of the how the oceans are often cast as alien, by James Cameron, Tony Hayward of British Petroleum infamy, and others, see Stacy Alaimo, "Dispersing Disaster: The Deepwater Horizon, Ocean Conservation, and the Immateriality of Aliens," in Christof Mauch and Sylvia Mayer, eds., *American Environments: Climate-Cultures-Catastrophe* (Heidelberg: Universitätsverlag, 2012).

52. Cary Wolfe, *What Is Posthumanism?* (Minneapolis: University of Minnesota Press, 2010), xvi.

53. Ibid.

54. Mick Smith, *Against Ecological Sovereignty: Ethics, Biopolitics, and Saving the Natural World* (Minneapolis: University of Minnesota Press, 2011), 63–64.

55. Ibid., 177.

56. Derrida, *Animal,* 66.

57. Ibid., 92.

58. Smith, *Against Ecological Sovereignty,* 44.

59. Ibid., 45.

Ultraviolet

BEN WOODARD

Nature is often taken to be a visible entity or set of easily identifiable entities: a forest populated with squirrels, deer, birds, worms, small plants. The very title of this collection testifies to the purported visibility of nature and the connection of that visibility to ecology and subsequently to ecological politics. This is not an original or spectacular thought: we think of nature and of the nature we wish to (or are told to) protect as this or that plant, this or that animal, this or that landscape. This thinking of the visible runs into trouble as soon as we begin to think of ecosystems, to think the relations between things. The unveiling of systems brings in relations between things as well as the powers or abilities those things have to not only affect one another but change the contours of the environment around them. Given that these entities of nature feed off of and utilize not only each other but also nonanimal actors (plants, microorganisms) as well as inorganic entities (the ground as burrow, rocks and caves as habitats, rivers and lakes as spawning grounds), the system of living things is dependent on systems that, as we follow it a few steps down, brings us to basic physical reality (the formation of the earth, the movement of tides, the chemical necessity of the sun's rays). Thus each natural thing appears nested in a system, and each system, in turn, is nested in larger and older systems the closer one looks. Furthermore, this also troubles the very division of us (as human entities) and nature (out there) both materially and nonmaterially; we share substances but we also exist in the same field of forces. From a philosophical viewpoint the issue to be explored in terms of ecological theory is the degree of connection and disconnection between thoughts, between things, and between thoughts and things.

The nineteenth-century German philosopher F. W. J. von Schelling is an adept examiner of this doubled tension of the visible and the invisible, and the *us* (subject) and the *it* (object). Instead of shoring up these divisions, Schelling's thought spirals ever downward, and explains the coemergence of a nature composed of forces and the resultant stages of actual things, alongside the seemingly unlimited freedom of the mind and the constraint of actually existing things. This is why Iain Grant defines Schelling's *Naturphilosophie* as the dynamics of nature coupled with the dynamics of the idea.[1]

More generally, *Naturphilosophie* is an attempt to theoretically determine all of nature. Beyond stating that there are systems upon systems upon systems resulting in an incredibly large collection of things, Schelling's nature is not a finite collection of things but a process of thing-ing that in turn means that the dynamism of our own freedom is no different from the dynamism at the core of nature itself. This distances Schelling from Immanuel Kant and others who adhere to a human exceptionalism based in our apparent capacity to perform free acts. Kant is able to valorize human freedom by devaluing the productivity of nature, reducing nature to its products. Only by ignoring the invisible forces of nature is Kant able to assert the artificial power of human freedom over nature. If, as Schelling does, we equate nature's dynamism with our own freedom, then ecology becomes a task of sorting out the limits and damages of choosing one material entanglement over another (such as coal power versus nuclear versus solar).

To draw a line from these seemingly abstract assertions to an ecological politics (or at least to a more ecologically sound way of thinking nature), we can pursue an example that is simultaneously concrete as it is purportedly ephemeral: that of Johann Wilhelm Ritter's body and the phenomenon of ultraviolet radiation. Following from these interconnections, we can posit an ultraviolet ecology that would reveal the deeper dimensions of the seen by the unseen as well as expose unthought unseens and the possible connections between actualities already known. It shows historically and aesthetically how the connections and disconnections between thoughts, things, and thoughts and things is complicated in terms of an unseen connectivity of nature (Schelling's speculative *Naturphilosophie*) and the apparent or visible discontinuity (Ritter's body) of ecological practice (Ritter's experiments).

The corpse of Ritter discovered as it was in his cluttered Munich apartment in 1810 would have produced puzzlement. Thanks to television crime shows, ultraviolet radiation is already familiar lighting for a corpse, as the black light causes bodily fluids to luminesce, making traces of lost vital liquids apparent to the eye. That Ritter's lack of academic credentials led to rather extreme poverty and in turn to drug and alcohol abuse, all bound by a deep depression, would be fairly straightforward. Yet his body would show peculiar signs. Ritter's dysenteric body, bearing rotten teeth in a mouth itself a cluster of sores, was not the result of a self-destruction caused by depression but caused by the use of his body as an experimental medium.[2] The anachronistic impossibility of examining Ritter's body with a black light is brought up to illustrate the origin of that very device, as Ritter was (arguably) the discoverer of ultraviolet radiation, a discovery that was part of Ritter's belief in a fundamentally polarized nature, a polarity pursued through research in galvanism (hence his shock-torn and scorched body) as well as in investigations into the nature of light, a light more real than thought (its invisible continuity) and more ideal (illuminating our very concept of thinking).

Ritter's contested discovery of ultraviolet was not predominantly challenged on the grounds of his experimental procedures (as extreme and self-destructive as they were) but because of it being part of Schelling's *Naturphilosophie,* derided then and now as the worst kind of armchair theorizing.[3] This not only underestimates or misreads Schelling's *Naturphilosophie* on a specific level, it also misunderstands the larger relation between speculation and the sciences, between postulates of creative thinking and experimental practice. Numerous authors have questioned whether Ritter deserves the moniker of discoverer of ultraviolet radiation either because of the fact that he was a sloppy experimenter and/or because the influence of *Naturphilosophie* corrupted his scientific worldview.[4]

Ritter's interest in a polarized and processual nature started with his study of the experiments of Luigi Galvani on so-called animal electricity that Ritter furthered by examining galvanism in relation to both physics and chemistry.[5] Galvani, who discovered animal electricity accidentally during a dissection (by touching a scalpel to an iron hook to a dead frog leg, stimulated the muscles with static electricity causing the leg to flex) argued that this electricity was its own kind of special force located in the biological world.

Ritter, doubting this narrow view, improved and expanded these experiments using more extensive chains of frog legs and eventually batteries to demonstrate the relation between the electrical and the chemical. These experiments impressed numerous intellectuals in Germany including the poets Novalis and Goethe.[6] Some combination of Ritter's exposure to this intellectual milieu (which included Schelling's *Naturphilosophie*) and the discovery of infrared in 1800, as well as Karl Scheele's experiments on silver chloride, led Ritter to search for these rays' polar opposite in 1801.[7] How do these three material and real forces come together for Ritter? Since Ritter accepted Schelling's idea of nature as a deeply unified field of polarized forces, Ritter assumed that Herschel's hot rays must be accompanied by cool dark rays at the other end of the spectrum. In addition, Scheele had demonstrated that heat and light had chemical effects on substances because of oxygen's reactivity to solar radiation.

Given this nascent form of ecological interconnectedness (the polarized connectivity between forms of light and the actions of gases), following Schelling, Ritter's self-experimentation becomes less surprising. The resistance, to connect back to Kant, resides in a critical view of the experimenter in which the operator making the experiment (the human, or the human capacity for reason) must be ontologically separate from what is being experimented on (nature). An ultraviolet ecology with a Schellingian scaffolding would, on the other hand, attempt to demonstrate the connectivity of the seen and unseen (as well as the created and its creation). While Kantian critics would point out that this too easily leads to leaning on occult qualities (and the end of Ritter's life illustrates this all too well), the very division of the thinker and the thought is just as occult and ungrounded as hyperconnectivity. Ritter's autogalvanism has also been critiqued as evidence of Ritter's rampant individualism.[8] But given Ritter's adoption of Schelling's processural and unified nature, his romanticism, however dark or brooding, seems less about a selfish individuality than about the utter *testability* of the subject, of the subject as a body *for* the expansive forces of nature. Such critique also neglects the fact that it

was not an entirely uncommon practice among romantic scientists to use
their own bodies as laboratory instruments.[9] As Iain Hamilton Grant puts
it in *Philosophies of Nature after Schelling*: "Naturephilosophy therefore
favours the extremes to which Ritter subjected his body, in his 'galvanic
self experiments,' in order to generate new forms of possible experience
over any rearguard humanist conservativism regarding the constitution of
that experience *for us*."[10] For Grant, Ritter's self-experiments speak to the
radical form of Schelling's empiricism extended to the unconditioned, to
what is as of yet, and may remain always, unexperienceable,[11] what we have
been calling invisible and processural nature. Yet Schelling still attempts
to outline *an empiricism* because the course of nature (and in particular
physics and physiology) determines the production of experience in nature
outside us and the production of our means to experience *in us*. Experience
for Schelling is about the various degrees to which nature can be detected
in the sensible while determining the various biological senses. Later on,
Grant argues via Schelling that if nature preexists thought, then experience must be the result of the capacity of things, a capacity that Ritter
attempted to prove through his autogalvanic experiments.[12] The strangeness of ultraviolet light becomes even stranger here, since, to sum up, there
is a nature that produces and a nature of products (with the Kantian tradition overdetermining the former at the expense of the latter). In addition,
there is the experimenter who is in a body, a body produced by that nature
which it studies, a nature that produces the body's senses and abilities that
are a part of that nature. For instance, we can produce (through technological means) objects that produce ultraviolet light that let us see objects
we could not otherwise see; we are, for Schelling, seeing nature through
nature.

If we could pick through the neuronal corridors of Ritter's overcooked
brain, we would see that it was his zealotry on this last point that separated
him from Schelling in the end. While Ritter was obviously enthralled by
Schelling's *Naturphilosophie* (referring to Schelling as the great electrical
philosopher as late as 1810), the latter seems to have eventually tired of
the former.[13] This is connected to Schelling's critique of experiment that
disavows its speculative grounding while celebrating experiment as the
necessary way to change our thinking about the real world outside ourselves.[14] In this sense, we could say that Schelling is more concerned with

ecological connectivity (of the invisible revealed), whereas Ritter is more interested in the body as a medium exposing the limits of the visible. That is, the danger of Schelling is falling into an endless search for the broadest ecological model, whereas for Ritter the danger is falling back into an ecology of visible (and often aesthetically attractive) things.

While Grant shows Ritter's experiments partly enacting Schelling's theoretical apparatus, Grant distances Schelling's broader articulation of nature from Ritter's.[15] For Ritter, the human mind (in conjunction with the medium of the body) has power over nature because of its privilege *as a human being.* For Schelling, this privilege ignores the genetic history of nature as well as the history of ideas. What this means is that for Schelling, the animal body is not the best model for nature but that light, as an extensive manifold embodying and representing the widespreadness of polarized nature and the efficacy of ideas, is. This is not to say that Ritter is a materialist, whereas Schelling is too focused on becoming, but to suggest that, for Ritter, the medium of experimentation is the body of the experimenter, whereas for Schelling, experiment is more bound to self-reflective thought and intuition. Schelling's concept of nature is not divorced from reality, but given that his *Naturphilosophie* is supplemented with a transcendental philosophy, the methodological division of the one from the other (thinking nature versus thinking thought) would be somewhat problematic for Ritter's empirical self-induced torture, as for Ritter thinking is empirical.[16] Here we continue to drag Ritter's corpse into another room bathed in purplish light, in that the dead medium of Ritter's body (as speculative and real) illustrates the strangeness of light itself; the body casts its own light (as experimental medium) on the very nature of light. Schelling moves closer to Ritter and embodied nature when Schelling discusses light's chemical affinities relating sunlight to chemical processes on the earth going back to Ritter's use of Scheele's experiments.[17] Light is analogous to the chemical process, and light, for us, is a phenomenon of a deeper unity in nature. As Schelling writes:

> For if everything that "is" is only as it were, the color of the unconditioned, then the unconditioned itself must everywhere become manifest through itself—like light that requires no higher light in order to be visible.[18]

Simply put, we do not need light to see light; light is a phenomenon index-ing a deeper albeit invisible continuity. Beyond this, the light phenomenon (what we know and perceive as light) functions as a chemical bridge be-tween the sun of our solar system and the earth. *Naturphilosophie,* which is shorthand for an empiricism extended to the unconditioned, an empiricism that begins to undo itself does not seek an unconditioned as a definite strata of nature but works always to uncondition any given product of nature (including thought) to its grounds.[19] The unconditioned then is not an ultimate state but the most recent strata of unconditioning.[20] This begins to explain the strange energetic instability caused by the sun as well as the strange usefulness of a light (and a nature, and an ecology) fragmented into spectra. To plug this back into the odd machine of ultraviolet ecol-ogy, thought appears as a light that needs no light, yet it is contoured by objects—the unseen of our thoughts is guided by the seen that, in terms of ultraviolet, means that there are particular divisions in ecology always pointing to a more diffuse, more deep connectivity of light. But it is also variations of that light, at more visible modes, that allow us to see that con-nectivity, however indirectly.

Schelling's light as self-evident (the light that needs no other light) can easily supplant the deep, dark continuity of nature for a shallow sense of "everything is connected" for a purely visible continuity or economic or aesthetic continuity; everything is connected to the degree it is affordable to appear connected. But Ritter's corpse litters the floor. The eyes are clouding. Because, as Ritter showed, what appears simply self-evident and visible contains variations that speak not only to the complexity of any particular object, force, or process but to the continuity in nature that lies steps deeper than what we can easily perceive. Yet, at the same time, ultra-violet (at least in its effects) is easier to perceive.

That Ritter used his body as medium to discover ultraviolet radiation appears as an odd retroactive warning of the eventual damage of ultra-violet radiation, a form of energy that we experience through blacklights but also most notably through sunburn in which UV light excites DNA and the body in turn reacts to produce melanin, to darken to prevent fur-ther damage. It has even been suggested that UV light tested the earliest organisms that broke the surface of earth's early oceans, eradicating those that could not adequately repair their DNA,[21] giving a twist to Schelling's claim that the sun grants us the combustible life/light of existence.[22] Ritter's discovery of a new form of light then, an essentially invisible form of light, fits into Schelling's system insofar as it is just another example of the spread of light in the universe as becoming. In this sense we can see the difference of Ritter and Schelling, not in terms of experiment (Ritter) versus speculation (Schelling) but in terms of the pervasiveness of connectivity and the various depths of visible objects.

While Novalis stated that Ritter was searching everywhere for the World Soul, he may have been in fact seeking the world animal (the experimental body) in a very Schellingian sense by attempting to uncondition his own sensory powers,[23] but relied too much on the speculative ground of a cosmic electricity. Ritter's World Soul was too electrical. Looking at Ritter's own experiments with light and vision, light is subject to the electrical as Ritter performed experiments that altered his perception of color through lengthy exposure to solar radiation and because of electrical current being fed directly into his eyes.[24]

In the *System of Transcendental Idealism* Schelling states that "self-consciousness is the lamp of the whole system of knowledge, but it casts its light ahead only, not behind."[25] For Ritter, this lamp is indissociable from the human organism. For Schelling, on the other hand, it must be at least methodologically separate, as it is not the organism that holds the lamp but a subject. Though Schelling suggests the organism as a possible medium, it is not the *universal* medium.[26] But this is not to disabuse the weight of sense, and sense experiment, however weird.[27] For Ritter, ultraviolet light is the negative aspect of a spectrum visible through the body; it is one side of connectivity that itself is visible only through its effects on a body. For Schelling, ultraviolet light is a mode of a phenomena of light (light as we see it) that speaks to a connectivity deeper than what could ever be visible or expressible in the body. For Ritter, material experiment speaks to the human as a privileged instrument (what is the ecologist of all ecologies), whereas for Schelling, the experiment demonstrates the limit of the human in the face of nature. For Ritter, the crime scene investigator with the ultraviolet lamp is delving into the darkest tombs of nature; for Schelling, that investigator is nature investigating itself *through us*.

Flinging Ritter's putrescent corpse into the twentieth century, the weird-fiction author H. P. Lovecraft is another source of illumination, as he shares with Schelling a concern for a nature composed of forces that are at times horrifying and at times cosmologically bewildering, and shares with Ritter a predilection for weird experiments testing the very limits of the sense organs. Lovecraft's tales make frequent reference to the laws of nature and the tension between nature as we know it (what I designate with nature) and Nature as it appears in itself (Nature thusly capitalized). Two stories of Lovecraft's that relate to color—one specifically to ultraviolet radiation—are "From Beyond" and "The Colour out of Space." Both center on visibility and on the limits of science specifically in relation to color and sense.

In "From Beyond" an unnamed narrator goes to visit the scientist Crawford Tillinghast, who studies both the physical and the metaphysical and who has invented a machine that stimulates one's pineal gland to allow one to perceive beyond the normal senses, indirectly indexing Schelling's *Naturphilosophie* as empiricism extending to the unconditioned as well as Ritter's self-experimentation.

To quote at length from the tale:

He now seated me near the machine, so that it was on my right, and turned a switch somewhere below the crowning cluster of glass bulbs. The usual sputtering began, turned to a whine, and terminated in a drone so soft as to suggest a return to silence. Meanwhile the luminosity increased, waned again, then assumed a pale, outré colour or blend of colours which I could neither place nor describe. Tillinghast had been watching me, and noted my puzzled expression.

"Do you know what that is?" he whispered. "That is ultra-violet." He chuckled oddly at my surprise. "You thought ultra-violet was invisible, and so it is—but you can see that and many other invisible things now.

"Listen to me! The waves from that thing are waking a thousand sleeping senses in us; senses which we inherit from aeons of evolution from the state of detached electrons to the state of organic humanity. . . . You have heard of the pineal gland? I laugh at the shallow endocrinologist, fellow-dupe and fellow-parvenu of the Freudian. That gland is the great sense-organ of organs—I have found out. It is like sight in the end, and transmits visual pictures to the brain. If you are normal, that is the way you ought to get most of it . . . I mean get most of the evidence from beyond."[28]

Lovecraft (through Tillinghast) suggests that we have the capacity for expanding the senses (and our understanding of nature) technologically but possibly at our own expense. The characters of Lovecraft's tales more often than not suffer death or madness at the end of their paranormal adventures, reflecting the real risks and gains of Ritter's work, albeit hyperbolically. As the well-known Lovecraft commentator S. T. Joshi has noted, the reference to the pineal gland is no doubt a parody of Cartesianism, as the pineal gland was identified by René Descartes as the seat of the soul.

If "From Beyond" is Ritterian in its corporealization of seeing the unseen, then Lovecraft's "Colour out of Space" is far more Schellingian. In this tale a small meteorite lands in a farming community, causing peculiar changes and eventually death in a nearby farm's inhabitants. The meteorite is studied by local scientists and is a substance that possesses an unearthly color and seems to break every known law, giving no results to any and all tests.

"The Colour out of Space" speaks to the intrusion of an outside unthinkable entity that while appearing completely alien is simply another part of Nature able to affect and destroy human thought and existence because it is continuous with us, that is, because we are both a part of the same Nature while having very different observable natures. The story opens with a pastoral description of the region before stating that everyone has left because of an imagined horror. The story proceeds to unveil the extraterrestrially caused events that slowly transform the landscape.

Toward the story's conclusion:

This was no fruit of such worlds and suns as shine on the telescopes and photographic plates of our observatories. This was no breath from the skies whose motions and dimensions our astronomers measure or deem too vast to measure. It was just a colour out of space—a frightful messenger from unformed realms of infinity beyond all Nature as we know it; from realms whose mere existence stuns the brain and numbs us with the black extra-cosmic gulfs it throws open before our frenzied eyes.[29]

Compare with Schelling: "Light, this element of the heavens, is too generally distributed, too universally active, for the eye of the ordinary man, fettered to the soil, to seek it, in order to enjoy the blessing of sight with consciousness."[30] Ultraviolet ecology probes the historical and aesthetic connections and disconnections between thoughts and things through the matrix of an unseen connectivity of nature and a visible discontinuity of things. For Schelling this ecology unfolds at a limit of color, whereas for Ritter ultraviolet is one shade of the key to the electrical cosmos.

In this way "From Beyond" is more about an overproximity of nature, whereas "The Colour out of Space" is more about the impressive continuity of nature/Nature. The relation between these issues is a philosophical problem but equally an ecological one: nature continually produces more and different kinds of thoughts in us about us and about nature, and Nature is always beyond our capacity to know it. This is not to say that continuity implies a comfortable stasis or a teleology. While there may be stasis or apparent stasis at apparent scales, this is possible only through visible nature and, furthermore, a visible nature that itself is a selection, a view, or a landscape. In this sense, direct knowledge about the depths of nature is always colored by the selection of it we are viewing. This is why Ritter's and Kant's faith in the instrument of human reason is problematic and why Schelling's genetic nature and genetic ideas are right for ecological investigation.

In a letter to Schelling, Caroline Michaelis-Bohmer-Schlegel writes:

> It occurs to me that for all his [Johann Gottlieb Fichte's]
> incomparable power of thought, his powerful mode of drawing
> conclusions, his clarity, exactness, his direct intuition of the I and
> the inspiration of the discoverer, that he is yet limited. . . . When
> you have broken through a barrier that he has not yet overcome,
> then I have to believe that you have accomplished this, not so much
> as a philosopher—if I'm using this term incorrectly, do not scold
> me—but rather because you have poetry and he has none. It leads
> you directly to production, while the sharpness of his perception
> leads him back to consciousness. He has light in its most bright
> brightness, but you also have warmth; the former can only
> enlighten while the latter is productive.[31]

Here what is seen as absolutely outside (light) is taken in as warmth, at least to the extent that the eye can perceive it and the body, as the medium of measurement, can register that warmth. While the road of experimentation and light always leads back to the mind for Ritter, for Schelling this warmth, the felt effects of nature, pull the jaws of nature even wider beyond the mind's reach. Caroline's kind words reference Schelling's infamous break with his former mentor Fichte (who was a hyper-Kantian particularly in regard to the separation of our freedom from nature's dynamism previously discussed), a break that, while strictly philosophical, now appears equally ecological.

In a letter to Fichte, Schelling writes: "I am thoroughly aware of how small an area of consciousness nature must fall into, according to your conception of it, . . . But are you really of the opinion, for example, that light is only there so that rational beings can also see each other when they talk to each other?"[32] As Bruce Matthews points out, the ecological push of Schelling can be traced back to a resistance to the Cartesian method, what is lampooned in the figure of Tillinghast in Lovecraft's "From Beyond." At the same time, Andrew Bowie and Matthews make clear that Schelling was attentive to the force of thought against nature, and that nature as it is visible will have more weight than nature as an engine of production. Schelling's interesting (ecological and philosophical tactic) is to oppose connectivity to mentality through strategic uses of mentality against itself.

As I have shown, ecology is mired in aesthetics, particularly in the visual as nature—or that idea of nature that is supposed to be preserved, saved, otherwise benignly targeted, is made visible. Yet, as even the most shallow dive into physics shows, much of nature and many pivotal aspects of nature are unseen forces, powers, fields, particles, and the like. If one heard the phrase *invisible nature,* what would be imagined? I would argue that we would most likely respond along the lines of "a field of invisible grass" or "a grove of invisible trees." The phrase evokes a somewhat absurd projection of the imagination. Yet I believe this speaks to the aesthetic problem of ecology—that nature, as a thing to be saved, is colored (is green, and nonnatural things are greenwashed to make them friendlier to the environment) and that nature is equated with a pleasant view. The nature that ecology is supposed to save is pristine and visible. We must accept that nature is not merely a verdant forest filled with trees, birds, worms, small mammals, and the like, but that nature is shorthand for the generative and the generated capacities of existence (thought itself being one such capacity, a capacity that has the troubling ability to create its own series of things that we generally refer to as technology, culture, or more broadly civilization). While a nature thus capable and broadly conceptualized is frustrating, it is the logical materialist alternative to both a rampantly Promethean humanism and a Gaia-like theology of a nature separate from us. As Keith R. Peterson puts it in his introduction to the *First Outline,* *Naturphilosophie* was, for Schelling, not merely another means of representing a distant nature that humans were separate from but an attempt to redefine the necessary synthesis of self and world.[33]

This is the more obvious reading of the light from the lamp of knowledge: the past conditions of productivity are generally lost to us but with a Schellingian twist. It is not merely that knowledge as light makes all that is dark clear, but that knowledge brings the real conditions of the world outside the mind into the mind. This again relies on Schelling's valorization of, and not simple dismissal of, the experimental. Again following Peterson: "Construction is the deduction of the unconditioned conditions of natural production and also the reproduction of these conditions in thought. Therefore, construction by means of experiment is, after all, an absolute self-production of phenomena."[34] One clue to this somewhat enigmatic statement can be taken from Schelling's musings on thinking a cube in *The System of Transcendental Idealism.* When one thinks an object, according to Schelling, one thinks in the form of that object trying to think that object.[35] We can plop down Ritter's corpse once more: in following Schelling's ideas, the unseen is seemingly absorbed by the mind but not merely equated with it. Ritter's corpse is ingested (always imperfectly) in our thoughts.

This is particularly strange when we take light as an object (as a natural product). Since light is the phenomenon that allows us to see, thinking light means attempting to think the conditions of visibility. When we think light then, we not only think the phenomenon light (i.e., light as it appears for us or at least to us) but think the conditions (not visible) that allow light to be for us and allow light to be in itself. Light as phenomenon becomes released into the gene pool of our thinking. That is, as we attempt to contract light for ourselves and, having definite conditions light (as concept), expands in our thought as the light of reason; thinking churns anew because of a concept of illumination. Put most directly, thinking illumination illuminates our thinking both consciously and in other forms.

Yet, at the end of his introduction, Petersen seems to suggest that this is only ever a logical progression and not a naturalistic one—a statement that seems to undo the methodological split of *Naturphilosophie* and the transcendental project that is possible because of an underlying unity in nature. To think ultraviolet light in a *Naturphilosophical* sense is to think it as a form of becoming (nature thinging, and processing) and a form in itself (as a natural thing) that nature allows us to think as ultraviolet, which in turn illuminates not only a form of radiation outside us but enlightens (albeit in a possibly dark sickly glow) the idea of light and the real of light in us.

But this issue seems a bit more complex in Schelling: "The succession of our ideas arises in us, and indeed a necessary succession; and this self-made succession, first brought forth in consciousness, is called the course of Nature."[36] For Schelling, philosophy becomes a natural history of the mind that we must also take as an ecology of the mind. What, then, is the ecological lesson of Ritter? That of Schelling seems more obvious: simply that nature is not just the seen but also the unseen, the capacity of production. We do not know the limits to which we can alter the course of nature, but it has become quite apparent that we can destroy the products of nature and enough of them as to alter those nested systems mentioned at the outset of this chapter. Even if we could not undo the fundamental processural being of nature, it seems clear that we can rearrange it to the extent to destroy vast swaths of life (including our own).

Given the spread and breadth of technology, we have begun to test ourselves unknowingly and consistently, thereby experimenting on our own bodies. Widespread use of pesticides (such as glyphosate) has started to slowly alter our own composition as animals. As Jane Bennett notes, as we learn we as human beings are made of assemblages of other organisms, chemicals, and so forth, we are presented with the choice of determining what alliances we wish to pursue and what connections we wish to sever.[37] And, as Timothy Morton repeatedly argues, ecological interconnectedness is not a happy-go-lucky fact but one that can easily be seen as a terrifying overproximity. The statement "everything is connected" seriously questions what makes up any one of those things, nested as they are in other things and systems.

In a Schellingian sense, the light from the lamp of knowledge is double-edged: since our senses can reach back only so far, we have to speculate with the light of reason (without intuition), but at the same time that light is productive of actual changes in the world: light gives us the opportunity of creating new things, new systems, of altering nature at least at the surface. This is why for Schelling nature is *visible* mind[38] and why *Naturphilosophie* is both the dynamics of nature and the simultaneous dynamics of the idea.[39] This means that to experiment is not to simply entertain our speculative minds but to submit our bodies to the consequences of those ideas in order for them to be real ideas at all.

Put another way: if there is a cocreative and not strictly correlative relation between the dynamic of thinking and the dynamic of being, then ecology and ecological practices are not those practices that uncondition or simply reduce the natural to its more base constituents (in the form of a strict, i.e., nonreflective reductionism or eliminativism), thereby reducing the actual pluralism of the world in the name of preserving it or in order to use it. Rather, they are those practices that capture a specimen of nature that in turn allow the capturer to be captured by the bounds of the specimen.

To make one last use of Ritter's now-bloated corpse, we launch it into space aboard the starship Enterprise. In the original series episode titled "Operation Annihilate!" Captain James T. Kirk and company investigate an epidemic of mass insanity sweeping across a sector of the galaxy (a Lovecraftian tone to *Star Trek* if there ever was one). When yet another colony falls silent, the crew investigates and finds strange flying bloblike creatures that attach themselves to humanoids and direct them to spread their influence by causing incredible pain. When one infects Mr. Spock nothing seems to stop it. Kirk, having previously witnessed an infected colonist become lucid while flying suicidally into the sun, guesses that perhaps light is the answer. Dr. Leonard "Bones" McCoy submits Spock to a light so bright it blinds him, and only afterward McCoy realizes that it was not necessary to do so, as the creatures (being so alien to our universe) are vulnerable to ultraviolet radiation. The illustration is silly but useful: in trying to find (see) a way to kill the creatures McCoy overlooks an unseen part (ultraviolet) of light (seeing) and in turn blinds Spock (logic, reason) to the visible world but makes visible the invisible. Ecology is the choice, through this murkiness, of picking what lives and what dies, what is to be constructed and what should be demolished.

This is difficult, as the preservation of an object of nature simultaneously preserves a thought-lineage and an actual lineage, the former being ontologically dependent on the latter but with the former's creativity accelerated by the latter. Even if we limit our view of nature to inspiration for our own thinking, a transcendental idealist twist on the ecological crisis emerges: can an imagined creature ever cause the impetus for thought and for creation as a newly discovered one? Schelling's and Ritter's answer in the negative is what defines *Naturphilosophie* and is what separates them from those thinkers who believe the mind enlightens the mind and the world without source and without regard for the innumerable grounds beneath it. For Ritter and Schelling, it is not that everything is connected but that things are always more separated in our thoughts than they are in nature and, even more strangely, our very thoughts are a product of that nature as well.

Notes

I wish to thank Karen Dewart McEwen for her insightful comments on an earlier draft of this chapter as well as for her kind support throughout.

1. Iain Hamilton Grant, "Philosophy Become Genetic," in *The New Schelling*, ed. Judith Norman and Alistair Welchman (London: Continuum, 2002), 166.

2. Siegfried Zielinski, *Deep Time of the Media: Toward an Archeology of Seeing and Hearing by Technical Means* (Cambridge, Mass.: MIT Press, 2006), 177.

3. R. A. R. Tricker notes that *Naturphilosophie* wholeheartedly depreciates empirical knowledge (*Early Electrodynamics: The First Law of Circulation* [Oxford: Pergamon, 1965], 11), while Brian Dibner refers to Ritter's "fertile but disorganized mind" (Bern Dibner, *Oersted and the Discovery of Electromagnetism* [New York: Blaistell, 1962], 20). Henrik Steffens in his autobiography notes that Ritter became lost in the darkness of his own mind (quoted in Jocelyn Holland, *German Romanticism and Science: The Procreative Poetics of Goethe, Novalis, and Ritter* [New York: Routledge, 2009], 114). Other commentators such as Dale Snow and R. C. Stauffer have argued that *Naturphilosophie* was the driving force behind Ritter's discovery of ultraviolet light (see Dale E. Snow, *Schelling and the End of Idealism* [Albany: State University of New York Press, 1996], 113; and Robert Stauffer,

"Speculation and Experiment in the Background of Oersted's Discovery of Electromagnetism," *Isis* 48 [March 1957]). While Jan Frercks, Heiko Weber, and Gerhard Wiesenfeldt argue for Ritter as the discoverer of ultraviolet light, they do not address *Naturphilosophie* or Ritter's relation to Schelling in any direct way (see Jan Frercks, Heiko Weber, and Gerhard Wiesenfeldt, "Reception and Discovery: The Nature of Johann Wilhelm Ritter's Invisible Rays," in *Studies in History and Philosophy of Science* 40 [2009]: 144). As a point of comparison one can look at Hans Christian Oersted (a thinker and scientist similarly inspired by *Naturphilosophie* and in the same field as Ritter), who ascended the ladder of scientific success; Ritter toiled in obscurity and eventually wrote a massive and confused tome entitled *Posthumous Fragments of a Young Physicist* that purported to be about a fictionalized and already deceased version of Ritter (written disturbingly close to his actual death) (see Zielinski, *Deep Time*, 175). Oersted arranged lectures for the impoverished Ritter that displayed the latter's disorganized state in 1806. See Joan Steigerwald, "The Subject as Instrument: Galvanic Experiments, Organic Apparatus, and Problems of Calibration," forthcoming in *Human Experimentation*, ed. L. Stewart and E. Dyck, 24–25.

4. Holland, *German Romanticism and Science,* 113.

5. Zielinski, *Deep Time,* 167.

6. Ibid., 174.

7. Ibid., 175.

8. Holland, *German Romanticism and Science,* 114.

9. Zielinski, *Deep Time,* 175, 177. See also Richard Holmes, *The Age of Wonder: The Romantic Generation and the Discovery of the Beauty and Terror of Science* (New York: Vintage, 2010), 328.

10. Iain Hamilton Grant, *Philosophies of Nature after Schelling* (London: Continuum International, 2006), 149–50.

11. Grant, *Philosophies,* 150.

12. Grant, *Philosophies,* 160–61; and Steigerwald, "Subject as Instrument," 2, 5.

13. Grant, "Philosophy Become Genetic," 146.

14. Grant as well as Frederick Beiser have made this argument. See Beiser's "German Idealism: The Struggle against Subjectivism," 508, and Grant's "Philosophy Become Genetic," in *The New Schelling,* 148.

15. Grant, *Philosophies,* 93.

16. Another piece of evidence in possibly explaining Schelling's break with Ritter is Schelling's experiments conducted with Christoph Heinrich Pfaff (a harsh critic of Ritter) in 1798 for several days. See Steigerwald, "Subject as Instrument," 10.

17. Joseph von Schelling, *First Outline of a System of the Philosophy of Nature,* trans. Keith R. Peterson (New York: State University of New York Press, 2004), 9.

18. Ibid., 13.

19. Grant, "Philosophy Become Genetic," 132–33.

20. Ibid., 138.

21. See Loren Cordain and Matthew Hickey, "Ultraviolet Radiation Represents an Evolutionary Selective Pressure for the South-to-North Gradient of the MTHFR 677TT Genotype," *American Journal of Clinical Nutrition* 84, no. 5, http://www.ajcn.org/content/84/5/1243.full.

22. Schelling, *First Outline*, 226–27.

23. Grant, "Philosophy Become Genetic," 144.

24. Zielinski, *Deep Time*, 193.

25. F. W. J. Schelling, *System of Transcendental Idealism (1800)*, trans. Peter Heath (Charlottesville: University Press of Virginia, 1978), 18.

26. Andrew Bowie, *Schelling and Modern European Philosophy: An Introduction* [New York: Routledge, 1994), 39.

27. For a longer engagement between Lovecraft and Schelling, see my essay "Thinking against Nature: Nature, Ideation, and Realism between Lovecraft and Schelling," *Speculations: The Journal of Speculative Realism* 1 (2010): 47–65, spec ulations.squarespace.com/speculations-1.

28. H. P. Lovecraft, "From Beyond," in *H. P. Lovecraft: Complete and Unabridged* (New York: Barnes and Noble, 2008), 117.

29. H. P. Lovecraft, "The Colour Out of Space," in *H. P. Lovecraft*, 616.

30. F. W. J. Schelling, *Ideas for a Philosophy of Nature*, trans. E. Harris and P. Heath (Cambridge: Cambridge University Press, 1988), 130.

31. Robert Richards, *The Romantic Conception of Life: Science and Philosophy in the Age of Goethe* (Chicago: University of Chicago Press, 2002), 130.

32. Bowie, *Schelling*, 58.

33. Peterson, introduction to *First Outline*, xv.

34. Ibid., xxiv.

35. Grant, *Philosophies*, 182.

36. Schelling, *Ideas*, 26.

37. This was in the question and answer period of Bennett's talk at the "Nonhuman Turn" conference at the Center for Twenty-First Century Studies, Milwaukee, Wisconsin, May 4, 2012.

38. Bowie, *Schelling*, 39.

39. Grant, "Philosophy Become Genetic," 133.

Grey

JEFFREY JEROME COHEN

For Michael O'Rourke

Grey is the fate of color at twilight. As the sun's radiance dwindles, objects receive less light to scatter and absorb. They yield to the world a diminishing energy, so that the vibrancy of orange, indigo, and red dull to dusky hues. A grey ecology might therefore seem a moribund realm, an expanse of slow loss, wanness, and withdrawal, a graveyard space of mourning. Perhaps with such muted steps the apocalypse arrives, not with a bang but a dimming. Or maybe ashen grey is all that remains after the fires of the world's end have extinguished themselves, when nothing remains unburned.

Yet this affective disposition in which greying signals depletion and life-lessness reveals only the stubborn embedding of our anthropocentricity: as if the earth greys to mourn with us, to lament the absence of our tread. *Entre chien et loup,* twilit grey is materialized uncertainty. The shade marks a moment of mesopic vision, when the colors constituting the small portion of the spectrum humanly apprehensible recede, but they do not take the world's vitality with them. The grey hour is liminal, a turning point at which owls, mosquitoes, monsters, and the wind thrive, when stone cools for a while and persists in its epochal process of becoming dust, when animals and elements continue indifferent to our proclivity to think that an evening's color drain is a metaphor for human impermanence, a cosmic acknowledgment of our little fits of melancholy. Grey includes exhaustion, even obliteration, but also reminds that death is a burgeoning of life by other means. Grey is unimpressed by fantasies of disaster and finality. We are too enamored of the red and blue of catastrophe—of a world destroyed in flame and flood—and of the etiolation that follows. We like to imagine our own end and assume at our demise the world likewise terminates (fade to black) or that planet Gaia returns to the balance it possessed before apes became profligate humans (fade to deepest green). The apocalyptic imagination has difficulty discerning the vibrancy of grey. The gloaming is a place of life, but not necessarily in those sublime forms we expect life to assume. Despite our indolent habit of aligning dusk and evening with the declining and the still, neither are terminal. Grey mornings inevitably arrive, with roiling fogs and air restlessly astir.

A sensual grey ecology is inhuman, but that does not render it misanthropic, disembodied, or wholly foreign. *Inhuman* signifies "not human," of course, and therefore includes a world of forces, objects, and nonhuman beings. But *in-human* also indicates the alien within (any human body is an ecosystem filled with strange organisms; any human collective is an ecosystem filled with strange objects), and requires as well a consideration of the violently inhumane.[1] Grey, polychrome hue of the in-between and the uncertain, a miscellaneous zone, is not easily circumscribed. Like a cloudbank, a grey ecology teems with varying densities of matter and shifting velocities: stormy thicknesses as well as serenely heterogeneous clumps (*cloud,* after all, comes from the same word as *clot* and *clod*), composites and microclimates. Grey rolls, thins, inspissates, comes on little cat feet. It is an open aesthetic.

If an ecology is an *oikos,* a dwelling or a home, it must also include the one who writes about grey materiality while sitting at a laptop on a particularly fine morning just at the border of Washington, D.C., listening to traffic and birdsong through an open door. I know that nature is not outside with the melodies of trucks and finches, but resides also within this house (a structure built of trees, after all: birds are not the only architects of arboreal habitations), a home shared with a spiny-tailed lizard named Spike and a basil plant and dust mites and a ridiculous number of small rocks I have brought indoors. This porous and fragile dwelling is built on both life and death, and not just because its foundational soil is a seething expanse of decay and renewal, a necropolis of vitality. This field become a little yard was probably at some point worked by enslaved people. Not far from here is the church attended by those transported into hard lives they did not choose, the ruins of the segregated school built for their descendants, the remains of a burial ground. When this small brick house was erected quickly in 1940, one of many hundreds for an influx of wartime workers, the neighborhood's covenant declared what skin color and what religion would bar potential owners from possession. As I was reminded by a neighbor when we moved here, Jews like us were not allowed.

A grey ecology will not forget this difficult past, limned by exclusions and brutality. A community comes into being through boundary. Forces, beings, and things left outside dwell in an unsettled, "inexcluded" space. This liminal expanse marks the habitation of unfinished business. The story it conveys includes histories of injustice, trauma, violence. Grey is the realm of the monster, what appears at the perilous limit between what we know and what we do not wish to apprehend, what we are and what we must not be, what we fear and what we desire.[2] Like the monster, a grey ecology will often take anthropomorphic form. Our perceptions of the world are irremediably shaped by our humanity, and although we can attempt to discern what it is like to be a thing, "one can never entirely escape the recession into one's own centrism."[3] Grey is an expanse for what might be called disanthropocentrism: a sweep in which an environmental justice may flourish, with its attention to lived human existence, as well as the vibrant matter, dark ecologies, and object orientations that are so much a part of the new materialism. In grey—a process more than a color—can be discerned the inhumanity through which dominating notions of the human come into being, hegemonies that emerge through the sorting of who and what gets to dwell in the house and own a proper life, who and what will be excluded. Grey reveals the inhuman as a thriving of life in other forms, a vitality even in decay that demonstrates how the nonhuman is already inside, cohabitating and continuing. Grey is the human in the microbe and the stone as well as the virus and the rock in the human. It propels us beyond our own finitude, opens us to alien scales of both being (the micro and the macro) and time (the effervescent, barely glimpsed; the geologic, in which life proceeds at a billion-year pace).[4] A grey ecology is an expanse of monsters, but that is not in the end such a dark place to dwell.

Grey is the tint our flesh acquires as cells deprived of nutrients become energy for other creatures, for whom our demise is a flourishing. At this mortal boundary grey is *undead*—that strangely evocative word, the negative of a noun that is already a kind of ultimate negative. *Undead* names the zone of restless and perplexing activity from which monsters arrive, a sensual as well as epistemic threshold at which the familiar loses certainty. *Un-dead* marks a kind of contact zone between the human and the nonhuman, in which the human reveals the monster always already enfolded in whatever dispersed amalgamation we are.

A green ecology judges a culture by its regard for nature, where "nature" is typically regarded as an external entity, culture's other. A grey ecology refuses such separations, and believes that the haunting of monsters reveals communal values, shared aspirations and lived ethics (the anthropomorphic) as well as the coinhabitance and alien thriving of the nonhuman (the disanthropocentric). Changes in a people's dominant monster manifest restless processes of transformation. The undead with the most enduring history of haunting are no doubt ghosts: sublime, frighteningly aesthetic creatures with cerebral narratives and noble pedigrees, tracing their descent from Virgil, Shakespeare, Henry James, Karl Marx, Jacques Lacan, and Jacques Derrida. The specters haunting Europe and its former colonies have a deep history and long postcolonial reach. Yet these intangible spirits have yielded over the last decade to a relentlessly corporeal zombie onslaught. The discarnate enigma of *The Turn of the Screw* seems anemic compared with the harrowing eyewitness accounts of apocalypse in Max Brook's *World War Z* (2006), modeled on an oral history of World War II.[5] Our monsters are no longer ethereal and philosophical specters, but shambling, putrefying corpses. Existential riddles, ghosts and the vampires that followed them sought to challenge our minds. Now the undead just want to eat our brains. What is at stake in this material turn, this movement from cognition to consumption, from subjectivity to grey matter, from ectoplasm to ashen flesh, the human as yet another object in an object-filled world?

Whereas a ghost is a "soul without a body," the zombie (according to Zora Neale Hurston in her seminal account of folklore in Haiti) is a body deprived of soul.[6] A corpse unearthed from the cemetery, the zombie is reanimated without possession of its personhood and forced into interminable labor on a Caribbean plantation. Zombies are therefore intimates of colonial history and the burgeoning of capitalism. Hurston published her research in 1938, and although zombies enjoyed a brief vogue in contemporary film, they did not so thoroughly saturate pop culture until the last decade or so. Their Haitian origin has mainly been forgotten, as the animated dead have migrated from film into novels, video games, and advertisements. With tiresome repetition the future now promises a zombie apocalypse, an end to all hope of righting an unjust world. Our inevitable fate is to become zombies ourselves or to perish within their insatiable stomachs.

Because they possess a subjectivity that makes them seem like us, a ghost or a vampire is a monster to which a connection is easily felt. Not so the zombie. Despite its human form, these undead are far less anthropocentric. Their barrier to desire is evident in the love poems in the recent collection *Aim for the Head: An Anthology of Zombie Poetry,* replete with ironic lines like "gazing deep into your glazed eyes / you make me feel so vaguely alive."[7] In variations like "I love you for your brains," tongue-in-cheek effusions that replace soul with mere body are the best intimacies that zombie verses muster. Grey ecology, it seems, is a space of foundering attachment, of withdrawal rather than collaborative composition. Yet to write poetry about zombies, to dress as them during "Zombie Runs" and to imagine at such great literary lengths their depredations enacts a kind of desire, indicating their monstrous pull. Ugly, gauche, and anything but ethereal, zombies possess a shadowy but undeniable magnetism. Like vampires, they are embodied monsters; unlike their debonair cousins, zombies are nothing but their bodies. Whereas many familiar monsters are singular and alluring characters, zombies are a collective, a herd, a swarm. They do not own individualizing stories. They do not have personalities. They eat. They kill. They shamble. They suffer and they cause suffering. They are dirty, stinking, and poorly dressed. They are indifferent to their own decay. They bring about the end times. They are the perfect monster for a human world more enamored of objects than subjects, in which corporations are people and people are things.

The notion of an impending zombie apocalypse is so widespread that a best-selling handbook instructs readers on the supplies, shelter, and proper selfish behaviors necessary to survive the event. Over a million copies have been sold of Max Brooks's *Zombie Survival Guide: Complete Protection from the Living Dead.*[8] Its ardor for a doomsday when the earth is so catastrophically unbalanced that humans forfeit their dominion is a translation into a monstrous register of the vibrant genre of ecocatastrophe, what James Lovelock calls *The Revenge of Gaia*.[9] Inspired perhaps by the success of Brooks's book as well as the triumph in the United States of a secular apocalyptic imagination (the intoxication of imagining all things coming to their catastrophic end), the Centers for Disease Control (CDC) in Atlanta recently published the graphic novel *Preparedness 101: Zombie Pandemic*. The book is described as "a fun new way of teaching about emergency preparedness."[10] The CDC also offer a tongue-in-cheek web page devoted to the management of virally induced zombie plagues, where the following announcement appears:

> If zombies did start roaming the streets, CDC would conduct an investigation much like any other disease outbreak. CDC would provide technical assistance to cities, states, or international partners dealing with a zombie infestation. . . . CDC and other federal agencies would send medical teams and first responders to help those in affected areas.[11]

Viewers of the AMC series *The Walking Dead* as well as readers of the graphic novels on which the show is loosely based know that the CDC will not live up to any of these promises. In season 1, episode 6, the Atlanta headquarters of the CDC is self-incinerated after its last remaining scientist fails to identify any means of combating the agent reanimating the brain stems of the dead. To the survivors seeking its refuge, the Centers for Disease Control promise knowledge and safe harbor. The institution delivers neither. Stealing a topos from Richard Matheson's vampiric zombie novel *I Am Legend* (1954), the lone scientist who mans the abandoned headquarters has been traumatized by the death and subsequent reanimation of his wife. His experiments have demonstrated that whatever agent causes corpses to become ravenous zombies has already infected the living. To be human means to inhabit the zombie's juvenile form. The scientist can see no escape from the future's bleakness, despite his frantic efforts to restore the past. He blasts the CDC to fiery pieces, perishing in the explosion. The scene is typical of the zombie's doom-laden domain, an out of kilter ecology that systematically robs family, neighborhood, city, and nation of protective power. Grey, the ashen shade that colors Atlanta after the blast vaporizing the CDC, is the color that moves the earth toward its ecological destiny as *The World without Us*.[12]

Like the meteors, plagues, floods, alien invaders, and personified earth that also populate the apocalyptic imagination, the advent of the zombie heralds the termination of human hegemony. The sleepers of *The Walking Dead* and *28 Days Later* awaken to a reconfigured world, a history that is literally posthuman. They are tasked with navigating a landscape of catastrophe, but do so without much hope. They suffer so that their audience will not have to. Such narratives are not alarmist, but instead are excellent at inculcating passivity. The world we know may well be coming to its horrible and human-caused close. It is perversely reassuring to be told that there is not much we can do about this ruinous advent besides spectate and carry on.

Because the word *zombie* migrated from Africa to Haiti to the United States and thence to Europe, zombies are transnational and epochal, but that does not mean they are not historicizable. George Romero's ghouls in *Night of the Living Dead,* for example, offered "an allegorical condemnation of the atrocities of Vietnam, violent racism, and the opposition to the civil rights movement."[13] Like all monsters, zombies are metaphors for what disquiets their generative times. But while it is clear that images of the violence in Vietnam resonated with the early viewers of Romero's film, few who watch today will associate that war with the movie's profaned bodies. Yet *Night of the Living Dead* remains powerful forty-four years later. No single interpretation can capture a monstrous totality, no matter how persuasive that analysis might be. Monsters are more than the contexts that attended their births. They move through spaces even more potent than their own bodies. A monster is best understood as an extension of and collaboration with the unsettled ecology in which it dwells.

Zombies seem wholly natural. They are "just" dead human bodies, after all. Yet their haunting is the product of prosthetics, special effects, and digital enhancement, rendering them among the most industrially mediated of monsters. Multiple technologies have aided the exponential growth of the zombie population. Anyone with a smartphone, friends, and inexpensive makeup can create a zombie video for YouTube. Zombies are the perfect fodder for munitions-centric action films and video games (and sometimes, as with the *Resident Evil* series, it is impossible to tell the two apart). While social media can enable us to be more connected, more affiliated, more humane, the callous culture of the Internet can also trigger a profound affective disconnect. Zombies are its perfect monster. They are human beings against whom the most horrendous violence may be ethically perpetrated. They are to be shot through the head, and such execution is never a war crime. Offering the possibility of a murder that does not count, the zombie is the perfect monster for guilt-free slaughter. They are also relentless. Video games require enemies that turn us into zombies, pounding away at the FIRE button without cessation and without remorse. Maybe that is why games used to be marketed as enjoyable, but now they simply announce themselves as addictive.[14]

Our dreams used to be bucolic, pastoral, green. Now we fantasize the past in violent shades of crimson. The Gaia hypothesis in its many guises offers either an agrarian or georgic reverie of primeval subsistence. We do not imagine the past in such pacific frames anymore. Now prehistory is a space for eating meat, running, and having our genes inalterably set to propel us toward destructive choices (evolutionary biology in its pop forms is the best thing to ever happen for white male privilege, because what used to be horrendous can now be naturalized as a response hardwired through environmental conditioning). Zombies are proliferating at the same time as our reigning fad diet is the Paleolithic, extolling the consumption of raw foods.[15] Meat loving and contemptuous of grains, the Paleo Diet renounces agricultural humanity for a fantasy of primitive hunter-gatherers who devoured what they killed or snatched with their own hands, a primal masculine ecology. Everyone was supposedly healthier when they resembled Bear Grylls, despite the fact that most hunter-gatherers probably lived very short lives that terminated in the stomachs of predators. Like the "Born to Run" movement, which insists that human bodies were designed on the savanna to run long distances without shoes, this diet is propelled by a fantasy that the past was a better space, and that the current imperfections of our bodies were in distant history its flawless adaptations. The Paleo Diet, like the Zombie Diet, imagines that it is best to consume without adding culture to your food (do not process what you devour), and that what we eat should arrive through no intermediary (nature offers bounty enough). We might even be tempted to label both diets *green:* what could be more natural, more ecofriendly, than a locavore culinary regime that leaves so small an environmental footprint? In the end, however, zombie diets are actually the more sustainable, since humans are the most-neglected meat in a flesh-loving culture. Zombies know that deer, horses, and humans all make good eating, and they were early practitioners of snout-to-tail dining. A grey ecology has very little waste—or, rather, what would be waste is revealed as intimate to life in other forms.

Environmental justice is a mode of analysis that urges close attention to the populations paying the highest price for the comfortable modes of living enjoyed by elites. In Stacy Alaimo's words, "Environmental justice insists upon the material interconnections between specific bodies and specific places, especially the peoples and areas that have been literally dumped upon."[16] These are the poor and the underserved: those who live downstream from toxic chemical spills, those whose drinking water has been poisoned, those whom economic necessity compels to mine toxic substances without proper protective gear. Racism is as environmental as it is social.[17] The undead as another category of "unthought" share much with such victims, most of whom suffer in their bodies for ecological devastation. The state of undeath is frequently triggered by environmental hazards: radiation, toxic chemical spills, viruses. Racism is intimately entwined within monsterization, and so it is perhaps not surprising to discover that the zombie offers a racialized body. Never individualized, zombies present the single human collective about whom we can without hesitation speak in terms of determinative mental traits, communal bodily designators, and stereotyped characteristics. Zombies offer a permissible groupthinking of the other, the slough where we find ourselves besmirched by modes of thinking we claim to have surpassed. We feel no shame in declaring the discolored bodies of the undead repulsive. Zombies eat disgusting food. They possess no coherent language; it all sounds like grunts and moans. They desire everything we possess. They are a danger from without that is already within. We need to erect walls, secure borders, build fortresses, and amass guns against their surging tide. Applied to any other group, such homogenizing reduction and obsession with physicality, communal menace, and fantastic consumption should be intolerable. But the zombie is a body from which the person has departed, so we can talk about them without worry over bigotry.

The word *zombie* came into English by way of Haiti, where it arrived from Africa along with that island's population of enslaved peoples.[18] The folkloric zombie is a reduction of person to body: an utterly dehumanized laborer, compelled relentlessly to toil, brutally subjugated even in death. Old tropes gain new life in the contemporary zombie's body. Regardless of its skin color, we speak of the undead in terms inherited from racialist discourse. This undeath of some fairly ugly rhetoric suggests that, despite the fervent assertions of some political commentators, the United States is nowhere near postracial. As *The Walking Dead* TV series made clear in an episode titled "Vatos" (season 1, episode 4), featuring a Latino gang whose bluster hides the fact that they are caring for the elderly in an abandoned nursing home, life after the zombie apocalypse does not mark a radical break for everyone. Guillermo, the leader of the group and the nursing home's former custodian, declares that things did not really change all that much once the zombies appeared. Survival has always been difficult.

Derrida obliquely predicted the zombie advent (where zombies convey real human suffering) when he composed a ghostly book, *Specters of Marx,* critiquing the triumphalism that attended the fall of the Berlin Wall. Before we start celebrating the end of history or ideology, Derrida wrote, we should recall

> Never have violence, inequality, exclusion, famine, and thus economic oppression affected as many human beings in the history of the earth and of humanity . . . instead of celebrating the "end of ideologies" and the end of the great emancipatory discourses, let us never neglect this obvious macroscopic fact, made up of innumerable singular sites of suffering: no degree of progress allows one to ignore that never before, in absolute figures, have so many men, women and children been subjugated, starved or exterminated on the earth.[19]

These words have become only more true since Derrida penned them in 1993. Our exultant self-satisfaction at communism's end—our very love of things coming to ends—blinds us to abiding, proliferating human suffering. From specter to zombie: is it any wonder that an ardor for the end of history has been swept along by an apocalypse that involves "violence, inequality, exclusion, famine . . . innumerable singular sites of suffering"? The zombie figures the return of the injustices we quietly practice against people we prefer to keep dim in a twilight that marks a willed blindness.

In its limbo of body enduring beyond death, the zombie offers a vision of an afterlife that we have decided is otherwise impossible. Imagine there's no heaven, no hell below us, and we get the endless nightfall of the zombie apocalypse, a place indifferent to good and evil, a hereafter without gods. Yet the walking dead are also very much of this world. We are haunted by zombies because we experience embodiment as a drag against the Internet-induced fantasy of incorporeality. Perhaps we no longer dream of ghosts because we have become them. We disidentify with zombies by slaughtering them en masse, allowing us to sustain our desire for an electronic realm where we are freed from fleshly restraint. Battling zombies is a wild liberation—or at least a powerful vehicle for our fantasy that we can escape our own embodiedness and become high-speed avatars, quick souls divorced from slow flesh, from our own worldedness.[20] Paradoxically, however, a bond of desire continues to entwine us with the zombie we murder. During a television interview to promote *Land of the Dead* (2005), George Romero asserted that should zombies actually appear, he would offer himself to be bitten so that he could live forever. As Sarah Juliet Lauro and Karen Embry observe in "A Zombie Manifesto": "The irony is that while the statement prompts us to ask what kind of life that would be, it reveals that our fascination with the zombie is, in part, a celebration of its immortality and a recognition of ourselves as enslaved to our bodies."[21] And lovers of the world we inhabit as well. We will stay here forever even if the price is undeath.

Zombies are a kind of ultimate enemy, because they are so utterly inhuman . . . yet we the living always turn out to be worse than the zombies they fight. We form our collectives to do battle with these monsters, and then we turn on each other and display a zombielike aggression against what should be community. In *Night of the Living Dead,* the "hero" Ben participates in but survives the violence practiced within the besieged farmhouse. Emerging from the place the next day he is shot by the police. *The Walking Dead* series seethes with brutality perpetrated by the living against each other, offering a sustained meditation on racism and class enmity. Its cast of traumatized men also expose as a lie the idea that zombies have no feelings. Men in the narrative have trouble articulating needs, desires, and emotions; when they do, disaster ensues. The zombies meanwhile are not emotionally dead; they are unremittingly expressive—of anger, of insatiable hunger, of trauma. They are raw. The zombies embody what the men feel.

To return to the "Vatos" episode of *The Walking Dead* and its ecology askew: though sometimes too saccharine, the narrative of the Latino gang brilliantly juxtaposed a fortresslike industrial building where the elderly had been placed to spend their last days with the transformed streets of Atlanta, an urban space made strange because traversed by nonnormative bodies. The zombies crowding the city blocks offer the corporeal forms communities typically render invisible, now released from their warehousing in assisted living centers, group homes, mental hospitals, and hospices to fill spaces once purged of all signs of nonablebodiedness. We live in a disability-fearing, youth-loving, deathphobic culture. When the elderly and the disabled are institutionalized to dwell secluded from public view, when cognitive and physical disability are conflated first with mere corporeality and then with the moribund, when we associate the end of life with the smell of disinfectant and the scrubbed walls of a hospital, when bodies simply vanish after the person inside perishes, quietly carted away by people paid a trifling wage to ensure that we do not have to stand in the presence of a corpse, to stand in the presence of our own mortality, then the zombie offers a chance to behold our bodily future. What lies ahead for most of us is disability, and for all of us, death. The zombie is the perishable carnality that we hide from ourselves, the declaration of our own thingly existence.

Yet the zombie's decay is not an indication of its deadness. The zombie is our window to the visceral world to which we have always belonged and into which we are absorbed as food for growth. It is a world we close off from ourselves yet yearn to see. We know that we are something more and something less than human, yet we hide that knowledge from ourselves. Surrounded by injunctions to conceal, costume, and enjoy, we outsource the corpse to morticians, health care personnel, hospice workers, and custodians. The zombie vividly exhibits the indifference of our materiality to the supposed superiority or control or beauty of the subjectivity that is supposed to reside within, grey life in death. Decomposition is the flourishing of bacteria, the autonomy of the world, an unyielding demonstration of the inhuman agency that resides in the pieces and substances that we totalize for a while into a body we call ours. Decay is a process of transformation. It seems final, fatal, and terminal, but this activity is future directed, creative, and uninterested in our mourning.

Such inhuman indifference finds a parallel in our propensity to regard others in ways patently inhumane, a withdrawal of ethical relation. As I compose this chapter, the news has been full of stories of cannibalism labeled, tongue in cheek, as signs of the advent of the zombie apocalypse. High on drugs, a man in Miami was shot by the police while chewing the face from a homeless victim. The event illustrates some profound human failures: of a social safety net that should ensure a world where indigent people do not have to sleep under bridges, of a health care system in crisis. To say that a mentally ill substance abuser and a person without a home should be omens of a zombie apocalypse is to guard ourselves from knowledge we possess but prefer to dismiss: that we are a class-riven society, that ablebodiedness is impossible to maintain, that we are in the end too selfish to care adequately for the elderly, the impoverished, the disabled. There are no monsters visible at such horrific encounters, at such foundering of our sympathy, only us.

Humans ought never to be reduced to the bare life of an object. Yet our inclination to imagine that things have no agency, vitality, or autonomy also deserves interrogation. Thingly existence is very different from existence reduced to inert thingness. What if the world is not passive? What if objects are livelier than we suppose? In the zombie's ongoing putrefaction, in its inability to remain still long, in its status as animated body indifferent to human subjectivity is evident what has been called an object-oriented ontology (OOO). Graham Harman defines this thing-centric mode of philosophical analysis as one in which "individual entities of various different scales . . . are the ultimate stuff of the cosmos," and "these entities are never exhausted by any of their relations or even by their sum of all possible relations."[22] OOO is a nonanthropocentric philosophy in which things possess agency, autonomy, and ultimate mystery. The walking dead offer what might be called a ZOO, a zombie-oriented ontology—or , even better, a ZOE (zombie-oriented ecology), which makes evident the objectal status of the body as a heterogeneous concatenation of parts, working in harmonious relation, or exerting their own will, or entropically vanishing, or willfully relating to other forces, other things. The zombie becomes organs without a body, an assemblage of autonomous zones without a necessary totality. The zombie is the inhuman reality of the body, our composition by volitional objects that sometimes work together and sometimes do not, as well as the dependence of this composing process on an agentic, active nonhuman world. We do not like to behold our own viscerality, our own material composition, and the zombie is therefore repugnant. Obscure, worldly, challenging, and embodied, the zombie's grey is also strangely beautiful.

Like dragons and giants, the walking dead are transcultural monsters, haunting nearly every geography and history. Our hope and our fear that death is not the end of life amount to same thing, yielding gods who rise from the dead to redeem us as well as humans who rise from the dead to feed on us. Yet the world is seldom so small as this anthropocentric feeding and believing cycle would posit. A vigorous tradition of animated corpses unfolds (for example) in medieval Icelandic texts, where the sagas speak of a revenant called the *draugr* or *aptrgangr* who once interred will not remain still. In *Grettir's saga,* a work of the fourteenth century, we learn of Glam, a pagan from Sweden hired by a farmer to tend sheep on a haunted mountainside.[23] Glam refuses participation within the farmhouse community and will not attend Christmas services or even fast before the holy day.[24] He is murdered by an unseen monster during a snowstorm, and his employer finds it impossible to bring the corpse to Christian burial. Once interred in a cairn—beneath a heft of stones that cannot hold him down— Glam begins haunting the farm, riding atop its roof at night and descending to smash to pieces the bones of any animal or human foolish enough to slumber nearby. The young warrior Grettir offers to rid the farm of this *aptrgangr,* this "again walker." In life Glam had been "extremely large . . . a strange appearance, with wide-open blue eyes and wolf-grey hair," and in death "large and horribly deformed, with strange oversized features": an intimacy of the pre- and postmortem.[25] Grettir wrestles with this monster furiously, destroying parts of the house and then tumbling through the door:

> Glam, now off balance, came crashing out of the house with Grettir
> on top of him. Outside it was bright in the moonlight, with gaps

here and there in the cloud cover. On and off, the moon shone
through. Just as Glam fell the clouds moved, revealing the moon.
Glam stared up at the light, and Grettir later said that this sight was
the only one that ever scared him.[26]

At this moment when Grettir himself seems undead ("he lay between life
and death"), Glam curses his foe, declaring that he will never reach more
than half his strength, that he will forever fear the dark. Grettir recovers,
decapitates Glam, and places the head against the buttocks, ensuring the
monster will not return. Glam's prediction will, however, hold true. Grettir
forever fears darkness and isolation. His death will unfold as a result.

Glam is clearly the walking dead, but not exactly a zombie in the contemporary sense. He murders, but not for food. After death his personhood endures within his body. Yet the episode well illustrates something
lurking within but often hidden by modern zombie narratives: the twilight
environmental aesthetic of the undead. Zombies are creatures who have
no need of shelter. They do not build. They exist in an uncultured state.
Perhaps they incarnate our fantasies of nature as an exterior and inimical
force, our ecophobia.[27] They are also in the end too separate from their
worlds, too solitarily human. Zombies never break anthropomorphism.
Humans living and undead continue to inhabit a shared and limited ambit.
Even if they sometimes devour animals, zombies generally eat only live
human beings, not each other, never plants. Their limited diet is evidence
enough of how circumscribed their monstrosity remains. Creatures of relation, found only in herds, their insistent human connection also constitutes a silent sociality, one that disallows the invention of wider modes of
worldly inhabitance. Unlike some of the lonely bodies described by object-
oriented philosophy—dim, rogue, and dark objects, things that recede infinitely from relation, objects that cannot ever directly touch—zombies
are unremittingly gregarious.[28] They do not thrive in solitude but seek
others with whom to compose their vagrant herd. A zombie is a body in
insistent relation, but only with other human bodies.

Zombies could learn much from their forebears. Frankenstein's Creature, who apprehends the language of the earth through the groaning of
glaciers in the Alps, who is spotted most often in resplendent, icy spaces,
knows as undead Glam does that a continuity binds body and world. Glam

could have taught our modern monsters the potency of lunar radiance, of dwelling at margins, of trackless snow. The love of icescapes shared by Frankenstein's Creature and Glam, expanses where the movement of the earth is constant, suggests that their undeath is perhaps the same as the animation of what was never supposed to have held life. They are undead as the world is undead—which is to say, that the world is differently alive. Monster, human, and world are *transcorporeal*. I take that term from Alaimo, who coins it to designate the "entangled territories of material and discursive, natural and cultural, biological and textual,"[29] where "concern and wonder converge" in a material ethics that involves "the emergent, ultimately unmappable landscapes of interacting biological, climatic, economic, and political forces," where "human corporeality" intermeshes with the "more-than-human."[30]

And so Glam's power is not fully exerted until he is outdoors, in those wild spaces where during his life as a shepherd he dwelled. His curse is delivered only when clouds cease to obscure the moon, when the cold night is bathed in a radiance that makes Glam's eyes glisten. A being of lunar luminescence, broken stones, and blizzards, Glam in his undeath is that against which we build our houses, the excluded as well as the inhuman. The *aptrgangr,* the again-walker is a monster whose life in death makes us realize the precariousness of our own dwellings, of our lives: the weakness of our doors and roofs, the penetrative power of the moon, storms and night. This inhuman ecology is a part of our zombie-oriented ontology, one in which we realize it is not simply the human body that is an assemblage of discordant, agential, and envitalized objects, but the earth itself. "Undead" means "differently alive." The very ground we walk on, our future tomb, is alive in its supposed inertness, forever on the move, a foundation as well as our ruin, the undead material from which we construct our worlds. No wonder our zombies revive through the agency of inhuman but fully mundane agents like radiation and viruses.

A *kakosmos* of flowing crimson and grey body parts autonomously alive, the zombie aesthetic is disturbing, and thereby fruitful to think with.[31] Yet in the end I wish we could have our zombies without desiring so ardently an apocalypse to accompany them. Apocalypse is a failure of the imagination, a giving up on the future instead of a commitment to the difficult work of composing a better present. Those who dream of the purgation of our problems rather than deliver themselves to the labor of repair choose an easier path. No wonder the zombies devour them. To be undead might mean something more than to inhabit a terminal world, a vastness reduced to the grey of an earthbound despair. Zombies without apocalypse might offer a future in which we recognize the suffering, the possibilities, the potency, and the dignity of humans and nonhumans alike: grey as the color of unexpected life.

Notes

A substantially different version of this chapter appears in the *Journal for the Fantastic in the Arts*. I thank the journal for permission to reprint some of that material here. I would like to thank the audiences in Orlando and Edinburgh who gave me valuable feedback on this chapter; China Miéville and Kamillea Aghtan for their critical responses; and Karl Steel, Lara Farina, Alan Montroso, Richard Morrison and Michael O'Rourke for their suggestions for revision.

   1. I quietly argue throughout this chapter that a grey ecology is consonant with scholarly work being conducted under the rubrics "object-oriented ontology" and "the new materialism," and cannot exclude a consideration of ethics, especially in the form of environmental justice. Profoundly helpful in framing this investigation have been Stacy Alaimo, *Bodily Natures: Science, Environment, and the Material Self* (Bloomington: Indiana University Press, 2010) and Jane Bennett, *Vibrant Matter: A Political Ecology of Things* (Durham, N.C.: Duke University Press, 2010).

   2. For some of my early work on monsters, see "Monster Culture (Seven Theses)," in *Monster Theory: Reading Culture,* ed. Jeffrey Jerome Cohen (Minneapolis: University of Minnesota Press, 1996), 3–25. For a vivid exploration of the confluence of monster theory and ecocriticism, see Simon C. Estok, *Ecocriticism and Shakespeare: Reading Ecophobia* (New York: Palgrave Macmillan, 2011), 67–83.

   3. Ian Bogost, *Alien Phenomenology, or What It's Like to Be a Thing* (Minneapolis: University of Minnesota Press, 2012), 80. On the unavoidability of anthropocentrism, see also page 64. Bogost's work, like that of Graham Harman, Timothy Morton, Levi Bryant, and the other writers associated with object-oriented philosophy, is often carelessly accused of possessing no evident ethics or politics. Yet thickening human understanding of the inhuman world and interrogating relations to it is an ethical practice (and in the case of Morton and Bryant, one conducted within an explicitly ethical mode). See especially Timothy Morton, *The Ecological Thought* (Cambridge, Mass.: Harvard University Press, 2010); and Levi Bryant, *The Democracy of Objects* (Ann Arbor, Mich.: Open Humanities Press, 2011). I am attempting in this essay a humane account of a subject ethically,

ontologically, and phenomenologically messy, as Jane Bennett accomplishes through her refusal to pathologize hoarding in her essay "Powers of the Hoard: Further Notes on Material Agency," in *Animal, Vegetable, Mineral: Ethics and Objects,* ed. Jeffrey Jerome Cohen (Washington, D.C.: Oliphaunt Books, 2012), 237–69.

4. In writing these lines I am thinking both of Quentin Meillassoux, *After Finitude: An Essay on the Necessity of Contingency* (London: Continuum, 2008), especially his disruptive notion of the arche-fossil; and, conversely, Paul Virilio, *Grey Ecology,* trans. Drew Burk (New York: Atropos, 2009) about the scale and the power of finitude, as well as the necessity of rethinking progress narratives.

5. Max Brook, *World War Z: An Oral History of the Zombie War* (New York: Random House, 2006).

6. "The stereotypical zombie is essentially the opposite of such a 'ghost': it is a soulless body, rather than a disembodied soul" (quoted in Peter Dendle, "Zombie Movies and the 'Millennial Generation,'" in *Better Off Dead: The Evolution of the Zombie as Post-Human,* ed. Deborah Christie and Sarah Juliet Lauro [New York: Fordham University Press, 2011], 177). For the zombie as body without soul, see Zora Neale Hurston, *Tell My Horse: Voodoo and Life in Haiti and Jamaica* (New York: Harper and Row, 1938), 179.

7. Sean O'Neil, "Visceral Love," in *Aim for the Head: An Anthology of Zombie Poetry,* ed. Rob "Ratpack Slim" Sturma (Long Beach, Calif.: Write Bloody Publishing, 2011), 46.

8. Max Brooks, *The Zombie Survival Guide: Complete Protection from the Living Dead* (New York: Three Rivers, 2003).

9. James Lovelock, *The Revenge of Gaia: Why the Earth Is Fighting Back—and How We Can Still Save Humanity* (New York: Basic Books, 2006).

10. http://www.cdc.gov/phpr/zombies_novella.htm.

11. http://www.bt.cdc.gov/socialmedia/zombies_blog.asp.

12. *The World without Us* is the title of a best-selling book by Alan Weisman (New York: St. Martin's Press, 2007) that imagines life on the planet should its human population vanish: a delirium of buildings falling apart, forests eagerly expanding, subways aflood with cleansing water, farms that had been sustained by chemical interventions reverting to wilds, human traces reduced to thin lines in the geological strata and some lingering synthetic molecules. For a rich exploration of what the "spectral and speculative" *world without us* might offer as a negative concept for thinking about the world itself, on the other hand, see Eugene Thacker's *In the Dust of This Planet* (Winchester, U.K.: Zero Books, 2011), especially pp. 4–5.

13. Kyle William Bishop, *American Zombie Gothic: The Rise and Fall (and Rise) of the Walking Dead in Popular Culture* (Jefferson, N.C.: McFarland, 2010), 14.

14. Karl Steel made that point to me via Twitter, and it seems exactly right.

15. See the multimedia spectacle of a website at http://thepaleodiet.com/.

16. Alaimo, *Bodily Natures,* 28.

17. Ibid.

18. For the Haitian context of the zombie, see Franck Degoul, "'We Are the Mirror of Your Fears': Haitian Identity and Zombification," trans. Elisabeth M. Lore, in *Better off Dead: The Evolution of the Zombie as Post-Human* (New York: Fordham University Press, 2011), 24–38.

19. Jacques Derrida, *Specters of Marx: The State of the Debt, the Work of Mourning, and the New International,* trans. Peggy Kamuf (New York: Routledge, 2004), 85.

20. Peter Dendle maps the "relationship between history's least energetic monster and history's most energetic generation" in "Zombie Movies and the 'Millennial Generation,'" 181.

21. Sarah Juliet Lauro and Karen Embry, "A Zombie Manifesto: The Non-human Condition in the Era of Advanced Capitalism," *boundary* 2 35, no. 1 (2008): 88.

22. http://doctorzamalek2.wordpress.com/2010/07/23/brief-sr000-tutor ial/. A fuller discussion of OOO may be found in the second half of Harman's recent book *Prince of Networks: Bruno Latour and Metaphysics* (Melbourne: re.press, 2009) and *Towards Speculative Realism: Essays and Lectures* (Winchester, U.K.: Zero Books, 2010), as well as the collection *The Speculative Turn: Continental Materialism and Realism,* ed. Levi Bryant, Nick Srnicek, and Graham Harman (Melbourne: re.press, 2011).

23. *Grettis saga Ásmundarsonar,* ed. Guðni Jónsson (Reykjavík: Íslenzk fornrit 7, 1936); trans. Jesse Byock (Oxford: Oxford University Press, 2009). References by chapter number. For a good introduction to undead figures in Norse sagas, see William Sayers, "The Alien and Alienated as Unquiet Dead in the Sagas of the Icelanders," in *Monster Theory: Reading Culture,* ed. Jeffrey Jerome Cohen (Minneapolis: University of Minnesota Press, 1996), 242–63.

24. "I liked the customs better when men were called heathens," Glam declares, "and I want my food without tricks" (*Grettis saga Ásmundarsonar,* 32).

25. Ibid., 32, 35.

26. Ibid., 35.

27. "Ecophobia" is David Sobel's coinage in *Beyond Ecophobia: Reclaiming the Heart in Nature Education* (Great Barrington, Mass.: Orion Society, 1996).

28. This taxonomy of bodies according to their luminescence and relation making (a list also includes "bright") is taken from Levi Bryant, who uses it throughout his work. For an especially lucid explication, see his blog post, http:

//larvalsubjects.wordpress.com/2012/04/22/a-brief-observation-on-relation-language-and-logic/.

29. Alaimo, *Bodily Natures,* 3.

30. Ibid., 2.

31. "Kakosmos" is Bruno Latour's wonderfully messy term in *Politics of Nature: How to Bring the Sciences into Democracy* (Cambridge, Mass.: Harvard University Press, 2004).

Black

LEVI R. BRYANT

The Twilight of the Idols

Like the story of Adam and Eve where hominids once lived in paradise and were then exiled for disobeying God's commandment not to eat from the tree of knowledge, the story of contemporary green ecology either seems to be that once there was an idyllic and harmonious nature that was then destroyed through the advent of humans, or that once nature and hominids lived in harmony only to have this harmony destroyed by the advent of modern science, technology, and capitalist economy. The story runs that something has upset the balance of nature and that we must return to equilibrium. Such a return would also be a return to Eden.

Accompanying this narrative is a spiritual conception of nature as something that possesses a wisdom that, while not cognitive, nonetheless "knows" the best way to harmonize things. In nature, the story goes, *everything* is interconnected, everything is interrelated, and governed by *negative* feedback relations. Where positive feedback refers to relations between entities where interactions increasingly intensify and run out of control, negative feedback relations refer to interactions that maintain sustainable equilibrium. Popular "green" ecological discourses tend to speak as if negative feedback loops are the *truly* natural, such that positive feedback relations that push things out of homeostasis are deviant aberrations that are *unnatural.* This suggests a *teleological* conception of nature where nature perpetually strives for equilibrium, akin to a god providentially organizing the world for certain ends. If everything is interrelated, then all is somehow a part of a comforting, unifying One. This Nature is disturbingly similar to neoliberal economic theories holding that unregulated markets always wisely correct themselves and are best at providing for all.

These ideas can be seen in James Cameron's blockbuster hit *Avatar,* where the sacred tree perpetually seeks equilibrium among all the entities of the planet and intervenes to right the unbalance produced by capitalist exploitation by unleashing the animals of the planet against the invading corporations. Again, we get a variation of the legend of fall—the planet was harmonious until humans, technology, and capitalists invaded—and a thesis that nature, as a sort of divine being, will right itself, returning to paradise, through negative feedback mechanisms. Like neoliberalism, green ecology sees homeostasis as the truly natural force regulating the universe, failing to recognize positive feedback being every bit as natural. It is thus a mystified conception of nature that confuses its own normative preferences with the being of nature as such.

Black ecology rejects these claims as both ontologically false and potentially dangerous for ecological thought and practice. The color black nicely provides a unifying thread for thinking the ecological in contrast to spiritualist visions prominent in green, deep, and other popular ecological discourses. On the one hand, the color black has connotations of despair and abandonment, fitting for both the ecological circumstances we find ourselves in today, as well as an ecological vision that abandons comforting spiritualized conceptions of nature as a warm and inviting place outside culture to which hominids can go. Black also draws attention to issues of race, minoritization, and second- and third-world countries, underlining how these groups are often disproportionately affected by climate change. Here it is worthwhile to recall Friedrich Nietzsche's declaration of the death of God in *The Gay Science.*[1] Nietzsche's narrative of the death of God is not a disproof of the existence of God, but rather shows how the will to truth embodied in philosophy and science led to the collapse of teleological conceptions of existence, designed and organized by God, where there is meaning and purpose to existence. With this collapse of meaning, purpose, and design, existence becomes, as Nietzsche emphasizes, increasingly dark. The "stars" that once guided our way disappear, and we find ourselves adrift in a black universe without any ultimate or transcendent guides. Black ecology argues that we need to undergo a similar "twilight of the idols" with respect to our thinking about nature, and that we must abandon comforting ideas such as the homeostatic conception of nature and the idea that everything is interconnected. Indeed, we could call black ecology an "existential ecology," insofar as it presents an image of the universe that is indifferent to our existence, without design, teleology, or built-in equilibriating mechanisms that will ineluctably save us from catastrophe. Such a refusal of comforting supplements is intended to spur us to action.

Yet apart from these melancholy existential connotations of the color black, black also has connotations that draw our attention to important ecological features of things or entities. Black entities absorb all frequencies of light, while not reflecting or emitting light in that spectrum of color visible to us. In its absorptive dimension, the color black provides us with a nice metaphor for how entities are modified and transformed as a result of their interactions with other entities. As the great first-century Roman philosopher Lucretius argued, objects are *porous,* such that they can absorb the matters and causal influences of other entities.[2] Far from having stable and impenetrable boundaries, things are modified as a result of their encounters with other things. This porosity is a central dimension of the blackness of objects and is of crucial concern to ecological thought, for often what ecological thinkers are most concerned with is how encounters with other substances change the nature of things, as in the case of the impact of oil on wetlands and ocean life as well as economies and livelihoods from the 2010 British Petroleum oil spill. Stacey Alaimo captures this porosity of things nicely with her concept of "trans-corporeality," where she shows how bodies interpenetrate and modify one another.[3] For example, mercury in fish enters our diet, modifying our nature and perhaps contributing to autism and other health problems.

However, the nonreflective nature of black for things visible in the *human* color spectrum also draws attention to the power of entities to *surprise* when circumstances change. Our tendency is to think that the nature of entities is given in a glance, that their being is exhausted by how they are given here and now. We treat them as having a fixed essence or nature that can be read off from their appearances or qualities. However, if objects are black objects, if there is a sense in which they are nonreflective, then this suggests that things are characterized by a sort of mysteriousness harboring hidden powers that hold themselves in reserve, waiting to erupt under the right circumstances when they enter into the appropriate inter-actions with other things. The nonreflective nature of objects—that they are not given all at once and in the same way in all circumstances—culti-vates an awareness that we do not know "what [a] body can and cannot do."[4] This awareness, in turn, encourages attitudes of humility and caution with respect to practices like genetic engineering, the use of pesticides, the destruction of ecosystems, and so on. What will this body *do* when it enters into interactions with these entities with which it has not yet been in contact? How will the behavior of this entity be modified when it enters into these new relations?

That black is nonreflective in *human* spectrums of color also helps us to move beyond anthropocentrism, as is crucial for any ecological dis-course. For while black bodies might not reflect or emit light in *our* visible spectrum, there are other spectrums in which the bubbling power of the black object can be seen. Many snakes, fish, and insects such as mosqui-toes encounter the world through infrared. A black ecology is one that invites us to explore the perspectives of *other* entities, investigating how the world is encountered *for them,* thereby overcoming that anthropo-centric perspective that focuses on what things are *for us* and that places humans at the center of being.[5] It invites us to engage in what Ian Bogost has called "alien phenomenology," exploring how the world is for other entities.[6] Such a form of thought is crucial to understanding ecosystems, for we cannot understand why things are assembled as they are and behave as they do without understanding the unique ways in which entities other than ourselves encounter the world about them.

Finally, the color black raises associations to things like black holes and the mysterious dark matter and energy that is purported to explain why the universe is expanding at the rate it is expanding, why the outer reaches of galaxies spin at a faster rate, and why galaxies take on the shape they do. Concepts like dark matter and energy, as well as black holes, provide nice metaphors for all those things that powerfully contribute to orga-nizing the world in the way we find it while often going unnoticed as if they were invisible. In many respects, ecological thought has consisted in drawing our attention to "black bodies," objects akin to dark matter, that are extremely humble and innocuous—like the chemicals released by aerosol cans—while nonetheless producing big effects. "Black bodies" also draw attention to oppressed human populations and how their oppression is bound up with both social and natural ecological relations.

Where the Wild Things Are: Nature without Culture

Perhaps the central idol a black ecology must shatter is that ecology is solely about *nature,* and that ecotheory is a form of theory distinct from theory about society and culture. Both inside and outside ecotheory, there has been a tendency to see ecology as restricted to an investigation of *nature,* such as the study of coral reefs and rain forests, and the impact of pollutants on these systems. Within this framework, there is, on the one hand, the study of natural ecosystems and, on the other, the study of culture. This is a destructive thesis insofar as it suggests that culture is outside nature, such that it neither affects nor is affected by natural systems. The cultural critic can then focus solely on cultural phenomena, ignoring how cultures are intertwined with a broader natural world. Black ecology rejects this thesis, instead proposing that ecology is the study of relations and interactions between entities, full stop: an ecology of classrooms, economic relations, institutions, and families, no less than of coral reefs and rain forests. Social systems are always intertwined with a broader natural world that affects the nature of social relations, what form they take, and where social ecologies affect the broader natural world. The two can never be separated, and we will never understand why social relations take the form they take without also understanding how features of, for example, natural geography contribute to social relations.

Societies are themselves ecologies that are embedded in the broader ecologies of the natural world. Indeed, in this connection, it might be advisable to abandon the word *society* altogether, as it suggests something outside nature, instead adopting the term *hominid ecologies.* The advantage of such a move would be threefold. First, it would emphasize how social relations are a type of ecological relation. Second, it would emphasize that societies are embedded in natural ecologies, thereby curbing the tendency among social scientists and cultural theorists to bracket or ignore the natural world. And finally, use of the term *hominid* would help curb human exceptionalism and anthropocentrism by reminding us that humans are animals among animals, unique in their own ways and possessed of powers that other organisms do not have, but certainly not sovereigns of the world and different in kind from other organisms.

This pan-ecologism also helps distinguish existential ecology from traditional existentialism. From Sartre, existential ecology retains the notion of a dark and indifferent universe with no ultimate teleology, purpose, or providential design. Nonetheless, Sartrean existentialism practices a sort of human exceptionalism, emphasizing the transcendence of humans to the natural world and the manner in which we freely structure the world. Existential ecology, by contrast, emphasizes how societies are ecosystems embedded in broader natural ecosystems. It readily recognizes that we are free, but also points to how our freedom is embedded within constraints of the natural world and the institutions that surround us. As Jane Bennett has argued, our freedom is distributed, such that it must be negotiated in highly complex and aleatory networks of human and nonhuman networks.[7] Humans—and other entities—make history, but not in conditions of their own making, for their action always occurs in alliances with other entities such as the tools we use or features of the natural world.

As Timothy Morton argues, the association of ecology with discourse on nature and the idea that culture is outside nature contribute to the idea that ecology is of concern only to those who are interested in preserving rain forests and saving spotted owls.[8] Here ecology is only of interest to "granola eating and patchouli wearing hippies." Elsewhere Morton tries to show that ecological concerns are not about matters *elsewhere* that are only of concern to hominids in those instances where we *value* things like spotted owls, but rather that we are right there in the thick of ecological relations when we are eating a Big Mac.[9] The Big Mac is related to the clearing of forests to support bovine grazing, the burning of fossil fuels in transporting and producing various food products, the results of waste both in the form of methane gas produced by cows as they graze and through waste products thrown into landfills, and many things besides. Morton's point is that we cannot neatly separate society from the natural world, but that we are imbricated in it from start to finish.

Morton advocates abandoning the notion of "nature" as it gives rise to connotations of an *elsewhere,* an "over there," that is outside society; but it seems that this risks reducing the natural world to *cultural constructions.* The winning move, it seems, would lie not in abandoning the concept of nature but in abandoning the idea that *culture* is something *outside* nature. The advantage of this move is twofold: it undermines the human exceptionalism implicit in the distinction between nature and culture, and highlights the manner in which social and cultural formations are imbricated with broader material domains. Thus Bennett sees social and political issues as subsets of the ecological in general, and Hasana Sharp sees all things as things of nature.[10]

"Ecology" can no longer denote a discourse about *nature* because now *everything* is nature. As the band Love and Rockets put it in their 1987 song "No New Tale to Tell," "you cannot go against nature, because when you do, it's nature too." The first point, then, is that there is no longer a distinction between the natural and artificial. Yet, since ecology can no longer be a discourse on nature distinct from culture, it follows that ecology must be a discourse on *relations and interactions.* To think ecologically is not to think nature per se but to think relations between things, what happens when things relate, what happens when relations are severed, and positive and negative feedback loops that emerge in interactions between things. This relational, rather than nature-based, object of thought is truly unique to what ecological thought has to offer. One is thinking ecologically not simply when thinking the interrelations between species on a coral reef but also when investigating the impact of certain physical media like smartphones on social relations, when thinking the manner in which discourses, language, and institutions contribute to the formation of gender identities, or when thinking the impact of certain architectural designs such as the panopticon on the formation of subjectivity. Depending on the hominid ecosystem we are dealing with, that system will include semiotic, technological, and nonhuman material components.

Charles Darwin's theory of evolution, coupled with animal ethology, completely explodes the modernist and scholastic conception of nature, yet strangely this conception of nature still haunts ecological thinking. Under the pre-Darwinian concepts of nature, the distinction between the natural and the cultural is a distinction between the natural and the artificial. The "natural" refers to that which emerges from within and out of the thing itself according to its eternal *essence,* what is "authentically itself." We say "birds *naturally* build nests," and by this we mean that they do not *learn* to build nests but that as a result of their own predetermined essence they build nests of their own accord. By contrast, the cultural was conceived as the *artificial* insofar as a craftsman or designer brings something to entities that were not already there in entities of their *own accord*. There is nothing about a tree that *of itself* "blooms" into a table, but rather it is the artisan that brings this form to bear on the wood of the tree. The natural is thus conceived as what arises out of itself, while the cultural is conceived as the artificial, as the technological, that brings something into the world that was not immanently there in the essence of the thing.[11] The natural is seen as the domain of the ahistorical in that the essences of natural things are eternal and unchanging, while the cultural is seen as the domain of the historical as it is characterized by unpredictable revolution and invention that unfolds in different, surprising directions. What is more, those entities that deviate from their "naturally" predelineated essence through, for example, mutations are seen as "monstrous" by violating the order of nature. Finally, the capacity to create the artificial or technological is seen as the exclusive domain of humans.

Yet within the Darwinian framework, nature is not static, eternal, and unchanging, but rather creative, constructive, and inventive. Species are no longer eternal essences but statistical effects of random mutations in individuals passed on in a population as a result of natural selection and geographic isolation. In this regard, deviation—mutation—is no longer seen as *monstrous* but as *inventive*. Here "nature" begins to look more and more *historical*, and it becomes increasingly difficult to contrast the natural with the artificial. To be sure, some habits of organisms are more intractable than others, but this is a difference in scales of time. In the Darwinian universe, *everything* is constructed, everything is a habit, all of which can become otherwise. Moreover, as developmental systems theorists have shown, we can no longer speak of genes as a master blueprint *predelineating* form, but must instead understand development as a play of factors involving genes, protein replication, cellular metabolism and neighborhoods, niches, and social factors without one of these factors presiding over the rest.[12]

Likewise, animal ethnography has significantly undermined the uniqueness of hominid technology and culture. Dolphins, octopuses, and squid show signs of having significant linguistic capabilities. The mimic octopus shows signs of being capable of *lying* in that it appears not to have an *innate* repertoire of other animals that it mimics, but rather learns about the

predators in its specific environment and imitates animals that would be
a threat to that predator such as poisonous sea snakes. It is sometimes suggested that what is unique to *human* language is reflexivity or the capacity
for language to both talk about itself and to adopt the perspective of a
listener and theorize how he or she is likely to receive the message. As
Umberto Eco famously put it, "Semiotics is the study of the conditions
under which it is possible to tell a lie."[13] Here it is argued that the language
of humans must certainly be distinct from that of animals, for while animals might be able to camouflage themselves, they certainly cannot tell
lies, for lying involves a level of reflexivity that requires the liar to be cog-
nizant of a sign *as* a sign and how the receiver is likely to interpret that sign.
Yet here, in the behavior of mimic octopuses, we find what appear to be all
the components of telling a lie.

Koshimi monkeys in Japan taught *themselves* to wash potatoes in the
ocean. Certain apes use thin sticks to capture ants. Beavers build dams.
Certain leaf-cutter ants harvest leaves not for *food* but for their nest to use
as fertilizer to grow the fungus on which they live. They are true farmers.
The point here is not that animal technology and language rises to the
level of human complexity, but that the distinction between the artificial
and the "natural" does not neatly map onto a distinction between "animal"
and human. We find artifice—technology, where τέχνη (techne), in Greek,
signifies "art" or "craft"—throughout "nature." From the standpoint of existential ecology, this entails (1) that human exceptionalism must be abandoned, (2) that the nature–technology distinction cannot be sustained,
and (3) that our social world is not simply a product of our own agency
but also requires the agency of nonhuman organisms to exist as it does.
For example, Bennett draws on Darwin's investigations of how worms
form soil, showing how farmable land is dependent on the agency of
worms preparing soil on which our food is dependent.[14] Here she shows
how worms make a central contribution to society, without which society
could not exist as it does. Given this, should not we see worms as among
the actants populating "human made" society?

Wilderness Ontology

Elsewhere I have referred to that ontology that sees culture as a formation
of nature as "wilderness ontology."[15] Here *all* of being or existence, including

formations of culture, are elements existing in the great and savage wilderness. Wilderness is thus not a *place* to which one can *go*; rather, we are always already in the wilderness. Even when I am in the center of Paris I am in the wilderness. The wilderness is not *elsewhere,* but pervades everything. If "wilderness" is an apt name for being, especially when thinking the social, then this is because it reminds us that our cultural world is not separate from nature. Cultures are never isolated islands floating in the clouds, unconnected to everything else, but always take the form they take, in part, because of the geography of the land, and draw on material resources from the world about them.

This dimension of material flow through social systems is too often ignored by cultural studies. In our social constructivist moods we often speak as if humans create the world wholesale through language, concepts, and signs. Under this model, to analyze the world is to analyze how it is produced and structured in and through language. Adopting the stance of human exceptionalism, we proceed as if we were sovereign creatures able to weave the world entirely from our signifying activity. We end up ignoring the features of geography that contribute to the form societies take,[16] the material resources that pull people together and separate them, as well as the impact that various social formations have on the world around them. In other words, we entirely ignore the *ecology* of human societies. The concept of the wilderness helps draw our attention to these networks by underlining how culture is deeply and inextricably intertwined with the broader world and the role that nonhuman entities contribute to social formations. Black ecology calls for us to think the manner in which signs, signifiers, ideologies, technologies, foods, energies, natural organic and inorganic beings, institutions, and economies are intertwined.[17]

In claiming that society and culture are formations of nature, one immediately worries that such a move will imply a *reduction* of social formations to biology and neurology. However, following in the steps of the groundbreaking work of Hasana Sharp, this entirely misses the point.[18] This worry is premised on the idea that the biological and neurological are the "really real" beings and that signifiers, texts, signs, and so on are just epiphenoma of this real substrate. While biology and neurology should certainly be included in any account of social formations,[19] signifiers, concepts, norms, technologies, and so on are also real, *natural* features of the world that belong to the ecology in which humans are embedded as well as the ecology in which all sorts of other entities are embedded. The call to abandon the nature–culture divide is not a call to *eliminate* entities such as texts and signifiers but to think the imbrications of human and nonhuman beings together. Texts, beliefs, technologies, and signifiers are every bit a part of certain ecosystems as salamanders, aardvarks, coral reefs, rain forests, tardigrades, and mantis shrimps.

Ecologically the value of this move is threefold. First, over against social constructivism so common in cultural studies, it refuses the transformation of all beings into cultural constructions, leading us to recognize the real impact of nonhuman beings in our collectives and how they contribute to organizing relations of power or the forms that societies take. To think societies is not to think something *distinct* from ecology but to think particular ecological formations. Rather than seeing social and political thought as an endeavor distinct from ecological thought, we should instead see it as a variation of ecological thought. If I insist that societies are ecologies, this is to draw attention to those nonhuman entities such as technologies, animals, microorganisms, features of geography, and so on that play a role in the forms that societies take. Second, over against the eliminativists such as the evolutionary psychologists and sociologists, treating signs, signifiers, texts, and narratives as real, natural entities in the world forestall that move that would *reduce* everything to biology, leading us to explore the real difference that things such as texts, narratives, and discourses contribute to the world. The destiny and lives of inhumans are every bit as entangled in scientific and cultural discourses, narratives, and webs of significations as people.

Finally, refusing the nature–culture divide entails that we must think ecologically about our *own* ecological discourses and practices, introducing *reflexivity* into our ecological theorization. Insofar as culture and thought are no longer treated as *outside* nature, we must now treat our theorizing as a natural formation and our theories as real entities in the world. Ecology has, above all, taught us that all entities exist in networks of relations to other entities that respond to their actions affording and inhibiting possibilities of action. The possibilities of action for cane toads living in Central and South America are different than those living in northern Australia because the ecosystems differ. In the first instance, there are natural predators that restrict the population of cane toads, while in the latter there are none.

Thinking ecologically about ecological theorizing means that the ecotheorist does not simply *represent* ecosystems but also investigates how their theorizations will function ecologically in social ecosystems: are these forms of theorizing adequate for generating action and new ways of living? Will they be capable of assembling other people, organic and inorganic entities, and technologies to bring change? Theories too are agents, entities in the world.

Yet the concept of the wilderness has darker connotations. In ordinary language, "wilderness" evokes connotations of an environment hostile to us, where we are not masters, and where we are abandoned. Here is one place where a black or existential ecology differs markedly from green ecology, recognizing that the wilderness is just as prone to disequilibrium as it is to balance. Given the size of the universe, it is likely that countless planets with rich, living ecosystems have been destroyed by dying stars, supernovas, black holes, planetary collisions, and asteroids. It is likely that Mars was once on its way to evolving life, yet because its core ceased to be active, thereby destroying the electromagnetic field that protected it from highly charged cosmic particles, its atmosphere seeped away. Venus is in that area of the solar system that should render it capable of supporting life, yet its volcanic activity transformed the planet into an inhospitable place through greenhouse gases released into the atmosphere, making it into an environment that can melt lead in minutes. Volcanic activity on the planet earth in the Siberian Traps may be responsible for the climate change that caused the Permian–Triassic extinction. In each of these cases we see *positive* feedback loops arising from within the wilderness, destroying complex ecosystems.

One might object that all these examples of the indifference of the wilderness to life arise from *geological* and *astronomical* events destroying life, and that living ecosystems are characterized by homeostasis so long as geology, the astronomical, and human technologies do not intervene. While this should not matter given that the geological and astronomical are of "nature" as well, it is not true that such disequilibriums or positive feedback relations are restricted to the inorganic. It is suspected that during the Precambrian era about 2 billion years ago, for example, cyanobacteria so saturated the atmosphere with oxygen produced from the new trick of photosynthesis they had learned they created an environment inhospitable to other prokaryotes, causing mass extinctions. This event is sometimes referred to as the "Great Oxygenation Catastrophe." Here we have an example of a disequilibrium or catastrophic positive feedback loop arising from nonhuman living organisms.

The point here is *not* that we should celebrate positive feedback loops, or ignore *anthropogenic* disequilibriums, but that the wilderness is not "naturally" a balanced and harmonious place, but is rather every bit as prone to positive feedback relations as negative feedback relations. Negative feedback relations or homeostases are a preference of *our* own—a wise preference—and are not a feature of the wilderness *as such*. We cannot draw normative criteria from the wilderness, but must recognize that these normative preferences are *our* "artificial" creations.

And here we encounter yet another dark and melancholy dimension of black ecology. As Justine remarks in Lars von Trier's *Melancholia,* we are adrift in a wilderness, in a universe, that is indifferent to us and life. There are those conditions that are capable of supporting life and intelligence and those that are not. As a consequence of either self-destruction, destruction through other agencies such as diseases or asteroids, or simple evolution, humans will blink out of existence at some point in time, only to be replaced by something else or nothing at all. There is no necessity to our existence or the existence of other living beings. Far from teaching us that we ought to be indifferent to life, black ecology reveals just how precious, rare, and precarious life is, reminding us that we have to fight hard to preserve it.

Precarious Relations

Popular green ecological discourses often articulate the thesis that everything is *interconnected.* This thesis seems to provide spiritual comfort through the idea that we are all a part of a being that is a sort of pantheistic god (Gaia), and is designed to draw our attention to the importance of relations. Here black ecology differs fundamentally from traditional green ecologies; for black ecology, following Gilles Deleuze, rejects the thesis that everything is interrelated and that entities *are* their relations. As Deleuze puts it,

> *Relations are external to their terms.* "Peter is smaller than Paul,"
> "The glass is on the table": relation is neither internal to one of the
> terms which would consequently be subject, nor to two together.

> Moreover, a relation may change without the terms changing. One may object that the glass is perhaps altered when it is moved off the table, but that is not true. The . . . glass and the table, which are the true terms of the relations, are not altered. Relations are in the middle, and exist as such.[20]

While black ecology both commends and shares green ecology's efforts to draw attention to relations, it believes that the view that entities *are* their relations and that *everything* is interconnected renders the project of ecology incoherent. The point is *not* that things do not *enter* into relations and that they are not often significantly changed as a result of breaking relations, or that they are not related, but that relations can always be broken, often with dire consequences.

The greatest contribution and insight of ecological thought has been to draw attention to relations. Yet the addition and subtraction of relations is possible only where relations are *external* to their terms, for only where terms exist independent of their relations can they break with relations or enter into new relations. Relations are not guaranteed as the thesis of holism or interconnectivity would have it, but are fragile and always in danger of breaking. What ecology should teach us, and what a melancholy black ecology foregrounds, is that relations are *precarious*. At the level of green ecological *theory* we are told that everything is interconnected and that relations are *internal* to their terms. Yet at the level of ecological *practice* we everywhere see ecologists unconsciously presupposing that relations are external to terms or entities. Everywhere ecologists draw attention to what happens when entities are separated from relations they previously enjoyed and what happens when new entities are introduced into networks of existing relations. Ecologists investigate what happens when cane toads are introduced into northern Australian ecosystems, which is a new relation for both the cane toads and the other plants and animals of northern Australia. They investigate the effects of chemicals used in fracking or the mining of natural gas on water resources. Media ecologists investigate the effect of smartphones on human relationships. Other ecologists investigate what happens to various animal species as a result of suburbanization that destroys natural habitats, which is a destruction, a subtraction, of relations.

Ecological theory ought to be rendered consistent with ecological practice. The problem with the thesis that entities possess no separability from
one another is that it paradoxically risks rendering us blind to relations.
Because we begin with the premise that everything is interrelated, we risk
not doing the hard work to determine how things are linked and related,
with disturbing political and practical consequences. We forget that many
of our central political problems arise from the fact that people and other
living beings are *not* related. People suffer because they are unrelated to
jobs, food, water, opportunity, and political representation. Many nonhumans, on which we rely, suffer because they are unrelated. Increasingly
ocean life and other oceangoing microorganisms find themselves separated from oxygen as a result of algae blooms produced by our fertilizers.
Efforts to fight apocalyptic climate change suffer because they are unrelated to the forces of government and big business. Much of our work as
ecological activists consists not simply in getting people, governments,
and businesses to recognize how things are related but in *forging* relations
that do not currently exist and in *preserving* relations that are in danger of
being broken. This form of theoretical and practical engagement makes
sense only where relations are external to their terms.

Black Bodies and the Gravity of Things

The color black absorbs all frequencies of light visible to human beings, and
therefore provides a nice metaphor for thinking what *happens* to objects
when they enter into relations. In other words, what is ecologically important is not simply investigating networks of relations, but how entities are
changed as a result of their *interactions* with other entities. There is a sense
in which all entities are "black bodies" insofar as they absorb the effects
of other objects to which they relate, such that their nature is modified or
changed. This can readily be seen in our bodies. Any trip to a Civil or Revolutionary War museum engenders the striking impression that humans
have grown much taller than they were in the last century. Initially we
might conclude that humans have changed *genetically,* leading us to grow
taller. However, studies indicate that we have not significantly changed at
the level of our genes. Rather, it appears that because of changes in diet
arising from the greater availability of proteins and milk, we now grow
taller than we did in the past. We ourselves are black bodies, absorbing the

effects of other entities with which we have entered into relations and thereby manifesting striking differences in our phenotype.

A more disturbing example of entities as black bodies is that of the relationship between birds and the chemical DDT used in pesticides. As a result of DDT entering the food chain, the shells of bird eggs such as the bald eagle became thinner, nearly leading to these birds' extinction. Once again, it was not that these birds underwent a genetic change—though clearly chemicals in the environment can also affect and change genetics—but rather that as a result of a new relation between birds and DDT that was entering their system through their diet, a profound change took place at the level of the phenotype of their eggs. Birds here are black bodies that are transformed as a result of the other entities they interact with.

The concept of objects as black bodies entails that entities are dynamic activities where qualities are *actions* on the part of objects arising from their interactions with other entities in the world.[21] We do not know what a body can do because every object harbors mysterious depths that can be actualized in different ways as a result of their environmental interactions or encounters with other entities. Objects are *split* between these mysterious depths composed of powers or capacities and whatever qualities they happen to actualize at a particular point in time. In conceiving objects as black bodies that, as porous or transcorporeal, both absorb their environments and harbor mysterious possibilities of behavior in changing contexts, our attentiveness to the surprising nature of the world is enhanced, leading us to be more cautious about what we introduce into the environment. Things are dynamic machines in a sense related to that proposed by Deleuze and Félix Guattari, where these machines perpetually code flows from other machines and are modified by the encounters or interactions they have with other entities. Black ecology is a machine-oriented ontology that sees all beings as machines interacting with and modifying one another in their encounters.[22]

Black bodies also bring to mind issues of race and minoritization. There is an entire ecology of minority groups and the various mechanisms, social and natural, by which oppression is sustained that involves scientific and political discourses, narratives, economics, institutions, geography, resources, and many things besides. Jennifer James has shown how African American attitudes toward wilderness sites have been influenced by a long history of violence that took place in these secluded regions, but also how it might be possible to develop a different attitude toward nature drawing on African American history and experience.[23] Alaimo has shown that minorities are particularly affected by ecological catastrophes, with damage to their bodies often going unredeemed and ignored by the industries and governments that have perpetrated them. Black bodies are not simply entities harboring hidden powers but also entities caught in ecological networks that perpetuate their disadvantage and lack of representation and that are particularly vulnerable to economic, natural, and institutional inequalities and forms of destruction. Black ecology, in part, seeks a framework powerful enough to think the interrelation between discourses, narratives, institutions, before the natural world that perpetuate these forms of inequality and invisibility.

Yet the concept of objects as black bodies also draws our attention to the *gravity* of things. In 1916 Albert Einstein introduced his general theory of relativity showing how the mass of objects bend time and space, thereby affecting the movement of other objects in their vicinity. Einstein's theory of relativity also predicted the possibility of objects so massive that light cannot escape from them. Today we know these objects by the name "black holes." More recently, cosmologists have postulated the existence of dark matter and energy to account for the expansion of the universe and why galaxies take the form they take.

The concept of black bodies and the gravity of things provides a nice metaphor for how objects modify relations, as well as the seriousness of the circumstances we now find ourselves in with respect to climate. One of the greatest achievements of ecological thought has been to draw our attention to humble things, little things, invisible things and the big differences they make. These humble things are things such as aerosol cans and how they deplete ozone, disappearing bees and how our entire civilization is based on their pollination of the plants on which we depend, fertilizers that enter the oceans, and many things besides. Ecological thought teaches us to attend to the "gravity" of things—to these things that are akin to black holes in being invisible—and the role that all sorts of nonhuman things play in organizing relations between things as well as organizing human relations. To investigate the wilderness ecologically is to investigate the gravity of things or how things, human and nonhuman, organize networks of relations both affording and inhibiting possibilities of movement and action. Elsewhere I have proposed that we call this sort of practice and analysis "terraism," meaning "a practice of the earth."[24] Terraism consists in mapping relations and flows between machines or objects in their ecology to see how power is structured (cartography), devising strategies to respond to destructive and oppressive ecological relations (deconstruction), and building new ecological relations that would be more just and sustainable (construction).

A New Enlightenment

It is often suggested that the Enlightenment is responsible for oppression and the climate catastrophe now approaching us, because it generated an attitude of mastery and control that saw everything as something to be dominated and used by human beings.[25] Yet this thesis seems to cut too deep, for here we already see nature depicted as something over which humans are sovereign, as in the *Genesis* account of creation. Additionally, there are well-documented cases of environmental devastation by non-Enlightenment cultures,[26] and the idea of a reason that fails to take into account how we are embedded in the broader material world and where we do not have mastery over the effects of all our actions does not seem very rational. Nonetheless, there is something to the thesis that Enlightenment ideals of mastery and autonomy have led to a blindness of how we are embedded in a broader world that we do not entirely control.

Black ecology calls for a new type of enlightenment that would respond to these problems. With the Enlightenment as traditionally conceived, it calls for an overcoming of superstitious and spiritualized conceptions of nature that see it as a homeostatic and self-organizing organism that always strives for balance and harmony. It is argued that this view of nature is both untrue and contributes to ecological apathy in that it leads people to believe that nature will always right imbalances. In contrast to this view, black ecology proposes the melancholy concept of being as a wilderness, where nature, while generating life, is indifferent to life and every bit as prone to disequilibrium as equilibrium. It is hoped that recognition of the harsh wilderness in which we exist will lead us to both value the preciousness and rarity of homeostatic relations, while also understanding that a preference for homeostasis and sustainability is a normative value-judgment that arises from us, not something that can be read off the wilderness as such. Black ecology rejects comforting notions such as the idea that everything is interconnected, instead drawing attention to the fragility of relations, disconnections, and the necessity of preserving relations.

With green ecology, however, black ecology draws attention to relations and networks, the surprising behavior of entities when they enter into new relations, and carries out a critique of that *traditional* Enlightenment belief that we are sovereigns of the wilderness capable of mastering all about us. Insofar as all action takes place in networks of externally related entities, we can never completely master the effects of our action. Moreover, human action and society is enabled by all sorts of nonhuman entities such as resources, food sources, rivers, mountains, climate patterns, and so on, without which life as we know it would not be possible. Within this framework, to be rational and enlightened is to be attentive to how we are embedded in the wilderness, how our form of life is dependent on all sorts of nonhumans that populate the wilderness, how we are not sovereigns but beings among an array of other beings, and to be cautious about the potential effects of our actions and technologies. The failure to embody this ideal of enlightenment might very well spell our destruction or a future far blacker than the melancholy affront to our narcissism proposed here.

Notes

1. Friedrich Nietzsche, *The Gay Science: With a Prelude in Rhymes and an Appendix of Songs,* trans. Walter Kaufmann (New York: Vintage, 1974), para. 125.

2. Lucretius, *The Way Things Are: The De Rerum Natura of Titus Lucretius Carus,* trans. Rolfe Humphries (Bloomington: Indiana University Press, 1969), 30.

3. Stacy Alaimo, *Bodily Natures: Science, Environment, and the Material Self* (Bloomington: Indiana University Press, 2010).

4. Benedict de Spinoza, *Ethics,* in *Spinoza: Complete Works,* ed. Michael L. Morgan (Indianapolis: Hackett, 2002), 280.

5. Here the pathbreaking animal ethology proposed by Jakob von Uexküll is of crucial importance. See Jakob von Uexküll, *A Foray into the Worlds of Animals and Humans: With a Theory of Meaning,* trans. Joseph D. O'Neil (Minneapolis: University of Minnesota Press, 2010).

6. Ian Bogost, *Alien Phenomenology, or What It's Like to Be a Thing* (Minneapolis: University of Minnesota Press, 2012).

7. See Jane Bennett, *Vibrant Matter: A Political Ecology of Things* (Durham, N.C.: Duke University Press, 2010).

8. Timothy Morton, *Ecology without Nature: Rethinking Environmental Aesthetics* (Cambridge, Mass.: Harvard University Press, 2007).

9. Timothy Morton, *The Ecological Thought* (Cambridge, Mass.: Harvard University Press, 2010).

10. Bennett, *Vibrant Matter*; and Hasana Sharp, *Spinoza and the Politics of Renaturalization* (Chicago: Chicago University Press, 2011).

11. For more on this, see Bernard Stiegler, *Technics and Time, 1: The Fault of Epimetheus*, trans. Richard Beardsworth and George Collins (Stanford, Calif.: Stanford University Press, 1998).

12. See Susan Oyama, *The Ontogeny of Information: Developmental Systems and Evolution* (Durham, N.C.: Duke University Press, 2000).

13. Umberto Eco, *A Theory of Semiotics* (Bloomington: Indiana University Press, 1979), 7.

14. Bennett, *Vibrant Matter*, 95–98.

15. Levi R. Bryant, "Wilderness Ontology," in *Preternatural*, ed. Celina Jeffery (Brooklyn: punctum books, 2012).

16. For more on the role that geography plays in the form societies take, see Jared Diamond, *Guns, Germs, and Steel: The Fates of Human Societies* (New York: Norton, 1999); and Fernand Braudel, *Civilization and Capitalism, 14th–18th Century*, vol. 1 of *The Structure of Everyday Life* (Berkeley: University of California Press, 1992).

17. For a thumbnail sketch of what such an analysis would look like in practice and a brief discussion of the ontology presupposed by this chapter, see Levi R. Bryant, "Machine-Oriented Ontology: Towards a Pan-Mechanism," Larval Subjects, http://larvalsubjects.wordpress.com/2012/06/21/machine-oriented-ontology-towards-a-pan-mechanism/.

18. Sharp, *Spinoza and the Politics of Renaturalization*.

19. For an ecological, developmental, nondeterminist, antireductionist account of how biology is imbricated in social formations, see Levi R. Bryant, *The Democracy of Objects* (Ann Arbor, Mich.: Open Humanities Press, 2011), chap. 5; Oyama, *Ontogeny of Information*; and Kim Sterelny, *Thought in a Hostile World: The Evolution of Human Cognition* (Malden, Mass.: Blackwell, 2003).

20. Gilles Deleuze and Claire Parnet, *Dialogues*, trans. Hugh Tomlinson and Barbara Habberjam (New York: Columbia University Press, 1987), 44.

21. Bryant, *Democracy of Objects*, chap. 2.

22. For an account of machinic ontology, see Bryant, "Machine-Oriented Ontology." Here, of course, machines are not to be confused with rigid machines like computers and automobiles. Such machines are only one species of machines.

23. See Jennifer James, "Ecomelancholia: Slavery, War, and Black Ecological Imaginings, in *Environmental Criticism for the Twenty-First Century*, ed. Stephanie LeMenager, Teresa Shewry, and Ken Hiltner (New York, Routledge, 2011), 163–67.

24. See Levi R. Bryant, "Terraism," Larval Subjects, http://larvalsubjects.word press.com/2011/10/04/terraism/.

25. See, for example, Theodor Adorno and Max Horkheimer, *The Dialectic of Enlightenment*, trans. Edmund Jephcott (Stanford, Calif.: Stanford University Press, 2007).

26. See Jared Diamond, *Collapse: How Societies Choose to Fail or Succeed* (New York: Penguin, 2011).

X-Ray

TIMOTHY MORTON

> . . . like God taking a photograph . . .
>
> —*Empire of the Sun*

Going "beyond green" means going beyond nature, which is only an anthropocentric construct, even and especially to the extent that it appears to lie entirely outside the human domain. Nature is the reduction of nonhuman beings to their aesthetic appearance for humans. What is required, contrary to mainstream environmentalism—a term that is curiously close to *sexism* and *racism*—is ecology without nature. What exists according to this view? What exists are strange, uncanny beings, some of whom are alive, some of whom are not, and all of whom are uneasily difficult to specify as living, dead, inorganic, organic, undead. One of those beings is us. We are an entity among the grass, the gravestones, moldering bones, sunlight, and insects.

One way to imagine ecology without nature is to think about how we humans see only a certain bandwidth of light. Ultraviolet and infrared are invisible to us. Perhaps the ultimate example of invisible light would be X-rays, also known as gamma rays. X-rays confuse the commonsense difference between light and matter, since they can directly wound and destroy life, even as they illuminate it, brighter than bright. An X-ray photon is a terrific example of a nonhuman that has agency—it is evidently not alive, yet it is evidently agential.

The Critique of Pure Reason, Immanuel Kant's First Critique, opened an era of philosophy in which two things became apparent. First, there was a gigantic yet inaccessible ocean of mind below the usual, well-worn truths and truisms of traditional metaphysics, which now seemed like islands floating on this giant ocean, rather than solid dry land. By which I simply mean that, for instance, I can measure the width of this page, with various devices. But what, exactly, *is* measurement? What *is* number? What on earth are the conditions of possibility for me to be able to measure anything at all?[1] All of a sudden, there is a strange gap in the real. It is as if within thinking itself, thought glinted through like the flickering light of some deep ocean in a crack in the pavement on some city far inland.

Thus throughout this chapter, when I use the terms *depth* or *deep,* I shall be referring not to some more real material substrate of things but to the radical withdrawal of things, a withdrawal that is a condition of their reality. What I am given, as Kant argues, are phenomena, never things in themselves.

Philosophy has been navigating the ocean of reason ever since, discovering all kinds of strange fish in the region Kant thought was pure space and pure time—the fish of asserting, promising, loving, hating: the *phenomenological* fish discovered by Edmund Husserl, for instance.[2] Below this region where shoals of intentional objects such as desires and wishes sport, is a darker, colder region of *Angst* through which the submarine of Martin Heidegger—perhaps we should say the U-boat—navigates.[3] We are far below the ocean now, far below the "merely" given, the islands of understanding we took to be true propositions, such as "Everything must have a cause." And deeper still, undetected by the Heideggerian U-boat, accessible only by bathysphere and only under great pressure, is a vast coral reef of actually existing beings that this chapter, being an exercise in *object-oriented ontology,* will call *objects,* but we might as well call them *entities* or *things.* These things are not the assumed givens that seemed to populate the Isles of Understanding far above the depths. They are strange, withdrawn beings, forever departing from one another—we are one of them, so they depart from us, too—yet forever sending out signals, like an octopus squirting out ink: signals such as form, color, spatiality, temporality . . . Each entity is its very own Plato's cave, radiating shadows, an isotope that sends out strange waves of itself in every direction. *Ecology* just is the coexistence of these strangers and their strange iridescence.

The moment at which Kant published the First Critique was the moment of *correlationism,* namely, the moment at which philosophy in the West decided that it could not talk directly about things in themselves (the

Kantian *Ding an sich*), only access to things, and human access at that.[4] The ocean was just too deep and too vast. It was the ocean of what Kant calls *a priori synthetic judgment,* the fact that I have intuitions such as time and space, without reference to fingers or clocks. Since then, philosophy, culture, criticism, and science (yes, even science) have been swallowed up in correlationism. Consider quantum theory, whose Standard Model argues that things are real only when they are measured. The measuring device—an apparatus of some kind such as a photographic place—takes the place of the human correlator, but the argument is the same, Protagoras-like one: *man (the measurer) is the measure of all things.* Things are caught in a circle: they are real because they are measured, because measuring measures them. And the humanities thereby ceded a giant area—the area of non-human beings—to science, happy to occupy its ever-shrinking island on the ocean of reason, constantly about to be inundated by the global warming of science and technology, with its ever-encroaching waves of nihilism.

I use the global warming metaphor deliberately, since it is at this very moment, the late eighteenth century, when humans begin to deposit a thin layer of carbon in earth's crust. This carbon layer can now be detected far below in the Arctic ice and in deep lakes. How uncannily ironic, that at the very same time as Western humans are arguing that we have no direct access to the world, we are intervening in it more directly than ever before. I find these two facts to be halves of a torn whole—they seem intuitively to go together. This moment is now called the Anthropocene after Paul Crutzen, who invented the term. The term is ironic in another sense, because this is the moment at which nonhuman beings—including the being we are a part of, the colossal *biosphere*—begin to make decisive contact with humans, from the very depths of the ocean of reason. The very science and technology that allows human history to intervene in geologic time—this should be an intrinsically terrifying thought—also allows us to know entities that many religions, indigenous cultures, and our own intellectual and spiritual ancestors have long known.

Ecological awareness, then, is the ironic, even poetically just, result of the torn whole I mention in the previous paragraph. It is the consequence of nihilistic probing into nonhuman reality (realities), and the simultaneous speak-no-evil gesture of correlationism, which decides humans cannot directly talk about reality.

X-rays mark a second decisive moment in the Anthropocene known as The Great Acceleration. The Great Acceleration began in 1945 when the Trinity, Hiroshima, and Nagasaki bombs (called The Gadget, Little Boy, and Fat Man) deposited a layer of radioactive materials throughout earth's crust. X-rays are part of the electromagnetic spectrum, but humans cannot see them. Indeed, as far as X-rays go, the boot is very much on the other foot. They see you. They see you so intensely that in sufficient quantities they kill you. X-rays (also known as gamma rays) give the lie to the artificial division between *perceiving* and *causing* that has plagued philosophy and ideology since at least the Kantian turn. In an age of ecological awareness, the idea that the perceptual dimension is a neutral field is ended, partly by lethal entities that make up that very dimension itself. The time of nuclear materials and global warming is a time of lethal illumination.

Radiation is a being that is strange enough and vast enough—and at another scale, tiny enough—relative to us humans to shed some light (pun intended) on the coral reef of objects that lies far below the ocean of reason, an ocean that some thought was bottomless or that just led to a void. It is, as Heidegger argued, *underneath* or *within* nihilism itself, below the depths of the ocean, at which what his favorite poet Friedrich Hölderlin called *the saving power* grows, not on the fragile islands of givenness up on the surface.[5] The saving power to which Heidegger is referring is the capacity to push humans out of the modernity that is coterminous with the Anthropocene, into a time of ecological coexistence, that is, a time at which this fact of coexistence becomes woven into human politics, philosophy, and culture. The saving power is the homeopathic quality of reason—it destroys and forces us to know, at one and the same time. The Kantian ocean of reason is both poison and cure, since finally it uncovers beings that are too deep for reason to flood with light. Like characters walking around a Möbius strip, modern humans find themselves in a truly postmodern temporality, that is, the current era in which the thought of extinction and global warming impinges on the smallest conversation at the bus stop, even when it is unspoken.

Within nihilism, because the islands of metaphysical presence on the surface will not last for long: they are riddled with holes and at any moment could sink into the waves. Radiation provides us with an evocative way to think what all beings are—not metaphysically present, that is, not constantly

"there" under the watchful eye of a god or of me, the measurer, not composed of or validated by some more real thing. The deep problem with the
metaphysics of presence is not logocentrism, as Jacques Derrida argued,
Derrida's work being a small region of the larger view of object-oriented
ontology (OOO). The deep problem is that it posits some things as more
real than others and thus involves thinking in beliefs that can never be fully
fleshed out as thoughts. This is the case whether we are talking about fundamental particles (atomism) or rhizomes (fluid atomism) or God as first
cause: some being underlies other beings, making them real.[6]

Consider how this leads to nihilism, in both directions: first, downward.
This page is not really a page, it is a rectangle of paper. This rectangle of
paper is not really a paper rectangle, it is an assemblage of pulped wood
chips. These pulped wood chips are not really pulped wood chips, they are
plant cells. These plant cells are not really plant cells, they are congeries of
organic molecules. These organic molecules are not really organic molecules, but rather assemblages of atoms. They are not really atoms, they are
subatomic particles in a quantum foam. It is not really quantum foam, it is
probability waves in a void. The void becomes more real than all the things
that supposedly emerge out of it. "In the beginning, the world was without
form and void . . ." (Genesis): standard theism is not so different, silencing
the rumbling of the formless nothingness in this biblical sentence, replacing it with the pure void that becomes divided into itself by the Logos.

Now let us try the same thought experiment upward—notice that we
can probably insert various different concepts and terms in the course of
our ascent, according to taste. It is not really a page, it is a cultural construct
called "page" by contemporary human culture. It is not contemporary
human culture, it is a discursive formation. It is not really a discursive formation, it is an assemblage of ideologically interpellated humans. It is not
really an assemblage of ideologically interpellated humans, it is just me,
who validates all the levels below. It is not really me, I am a circulation of
desire. It is not really a circulation of desire, it is a self-positing act. It is not
really a self-positing act, it is the self-reference of the void, the void counting itself as one. We seem to have arrived at the void again, a void that is by
definition more real than all the levels below it.

Humans have been playing this game of upward and downward reduction (*overmining* and *undermining*) since at least the pre-Socratics.[7] The

impingement of strange entities such as global warming and radiation on human history demands that we try to unlearn this habit. These beings confront us with the fact that a being is not simply reducible to smaller, or more fundamental, realities, or to the History or mind that is measuring, seeing, or assessing that being. The ocean of reason sends out gamma rays that irradiate objects, annihilating them into subatomic splatter. Humans have very powerful weapons, both conceptual and technological, and for related reasons. Without sufficient access to the real, philosophy is able to proceed as if the gigantic explosions coming from New Mexico or Nevada are of no consequence. This ironic (painfully ironic) state of affairs was the main subject of Theodor Adorno's critique of totality and totalitarianism, from within a certain Marxism that recognized that the modern subject was equipped with very dangerous weaponry. For the main danger, for Adorno and for any philosophical view that notices how attitudes are not simply an optional extra but built into ideas themselves, is what G. W. F. Hegel describes as *beautiful soul syndrome*.[8]

Beautiful soul syndrome is the quintessentially modern tendency to see reality and myself as fundamentally different, and furthermore to see reality as evil or corrupt: "I'm okay, you're not okay," in the reworked words of the old self-help book. Such an attitude *directly is* the evil that it perceives over yonder, argues Hegel. Evil is the gaze that sees evil as a thing to be eradicated, a pathological symptom to be excised. This is the umbrella subject position of modernity. Whether one is a vegetarian or a fundamentalist, an end-times Christian or simply a flaneur, the world is seen predominantly as a product "over there," suspicious, seductive, slightly or terribly evil. The beautiful soul fails to acknowledge the ugliness that underwrites its seeming beauty. The disavowal of its own "evil," shifting and ambiguous perception, is the cause of what it sees over yonder in the world. We see here a direct example of what quantum theory also tells us, at another level of reality, about "perceiving" or "measuring": that it is a form of causation. It is clear that when a gamma ray is incident on a crystal lattice, it releases electrons from the lattice, *causing* it to burst into light.[9] At a certain level, it becomes evident that to see, to illuminate, is to cause. The beautiful soul is trapped in a correlationist view of reality, which contains two components: (1) (human) subject over here, world over there; and (2) perception severed from causality. One can see the world without having an effect on it.

Yet this very seeing is itself a causal property. If the world is evil, I might as well fly a plane into it or escape from it into the forest, or into heroin, that first very successful product of Bayer. From my opium-like height, I can contemplate the sins of the poor fools who scuttle around on the earth's surface, like larvae.[10] I fail to see how I am still on earth, though perhaps (at least I feel that I am) floating above it at high altitude. I have failed to grasp the truth already thought in Hegel, that ideas come bundled with attitudes, that they code for how one thinks them, and that to do philosophy is thus also to explore attitudes and subjectivities, or in other words to do phenomenology. I am therefore incapable of understanding the essential insight of Husserl, that what I think and how I think it form an inseparable phenomenological whole, like a fish swimming in the ocean of reason that Kant discovered below the islands of prefabricated concepts. For in the immortal words of the great phenomenologist Buckaroo Banzai, "Wherever you go, there you are."

It seems that however many bombs I explode in the desert, I am still observing reality as if through a glass screen. I apply this attitude to the very quantum theory that underwrites my experimentation with gamma rays. My Standard Model says that when a measuring device interacts with a quantum system—say some gamma rays and a crystal lattice—it becomes entangled with it, so that it is not further analyzable. Any statement about the reality of what is happening is impossible. The real thing, whatever it is, disappears beyond the glass screen of my measuring. Really I do not even see the bomb exploding, I see reflections on the glass, traces in the cloud chamber.

Yet something is bugging me. For it seems as if I still exist, and these quantum fluctuations in the void—how do they go about their business if they have no reality? There must be some material support, some anchor for my theory. There must therefore be a subatomic particle that gives mass to the others. I shall call it the Higgs boson. Now give me $100 million and I will find this Higgs boson. I have not found it yet, but if you give me some more time and some more money, I shall increase the teravolts and you will surely see it.

My argument is not predicated on the nonexistence or existence of the Higgs boson, which was in one sense not in question as this chapter was being written. Something like the Higgs has now been discovered. The problem is that the data seem to make the view of quantum theory that the Higgs was supposed to underwrite quite problematic: there may be two Higgs-type particles, many predicted particles that support the model have not appeared, and so on. Or, the particle discovered is valid, but undermines the coherence and "naturalness" of physical laws. These problems aside, what I am observing is that correlationism, like hysteria, needs a physical supplement for its view. The view that measurement is more real that what is measured requires, as its perverse supplement, some physical entity that underscores the system. Correlationism is inherently unstable, tending toward idealism (Hegel, whom on this score I do not follow), or classic materialism, as if Kant had never noticed that threatening crack in the real at the beginning of the Anthropocene. This instability is accompanied by a necessary violence in the experimental and social realm, as correlationism tries to justify the impossible, to square the circle: a violence all the more violent for being seen as "mere" measurement, as "mere" perception, free from the tyranny of the old metaphysical truisms. I hesitate to quote Gandalf, for fear of being dismissed by the lobby whom I am criticizing here, but his words to Saruman do seem rather apposite: "He that breaks a thing to find out what it is has left the path of wisdom."[11] If, to use Heidegger's example, I break a piece of chalk in half to find out what it is, I now have two problems, in the shape of two pieces of chalk.[12] When I split light and discover the X-ray band, I have a big problem. I have discovered how light can be a weapon. (Gandalf is criticizing Saruman's analogy for his change from "Saruman the White" to "Saruman of Many Colours"— "the white light can be broken.")[13]

A more honest approach, which I take to be the OOO approach, and indeed a less violent approach, would be to accept the finitude of the human–world correlate, but not its exceptionalism. In other words, there is, as Kant argues, a crack in the real, but this crack is not unique to humans or to other sentient beings. It is common to relations between cups and saucers, raindrops and windows, bacon and eggs, black holes and Hawking radiation, gamma rays and crystal lattices. Thus OOO preserves a devastating insight of Kant's—that there are realms of thought that transcend reality in a radical way—while refusing to buy into the attitude that construes the human, the living, or even the sentient as a unique or even special force in the universe that must be handled with correlationist kid gloves.

The transcendence Kant discovers between understanding and reason is located, for OOO, on the ontological inside of a thing, any old thing, say a Styrofoam cup. The cup transcends its appearance for me, who is handling it, looking at it, drinking out of it. Yet this transcendence is not in some region beyond time and space, beyond the cup—this transcendence *just is the cup,* its excess over any appearance-for some entity, including itself. This is evidently the case with X-rays, because their minuscule (the most minuscule) wavelength allows for significant Doppler shifting at high velocities. Just as an approaching car seems to scream past in a descending curve of sound, so an approaching gamma ray will be Doppler shifted to a lower-seeming frequency.[14] It is also the case with X-ray emitting particles. Consider the notion of an *isotope,* a type of atom that is similar yet different from its normal self (Greek, *iso,* "equal to"). In beta decay, for instance, X-rays are released precisely because an atom's electronic state has suddenly changed from a charge Z to a charge $Z+1$, since an electron has left the nucleus at close to the speed of light. The atom is now in an excited state and emits energy in the X-ray region. An isotope is inherently unstable, which is what gives radioactive materials their *half-life,* the time during which they radiate the most energy. OOO claims that in a sense radioactive materials embody a property shared by all beings whatsoever: *beings emit isotopes of themselves,* appearances that differ from their essence. This idea is not unlike Lucretius's notion that causality operates because of the way in which atoms emit what he calls *simulacra.*[15]

At this level, the notion "particle" is not to be distinguished from the concept of light as such. Light, that primordial medium of perception, is a kind of particle, a photon. Furthermore, quantum particles are not simply "hard elastic spheres" that bounce off one another like David Hume's billiard balls. Rather, they are better described as wave packets, blobs of wave that might as well be unique particles.[16] Thus when one particle encounters another, there is a *scattering* of energy, since the entire region of what is called *quantum potential* in which the scattering occurs is best thought as acting as a unit, that is, as a whole.[17] At this scale, a particle cannot be located in a precise region of space-time without being "reduced" to measurability by some incident wave: this is the famous Heisenberg uncertainty principle.[18] As absurd as it sounds to our common sense, then, an object at the quantum scale can be ever so slightly displaced from itself.

This effect might not be limited to the quantum scale, as some recent experiments have shown.[19] OOO allows us to predict that the effect is not simply a result of quantum-scale systems (i.e., systems that are close to what is called the *Planck Length*).

Imagine the cup develops Muppet-like powers of self-expression. What it says about itself, as it lies on the psychoanalyst's couch, *is not itself.* There is a gap between a thing and its appearance, a gap that has nothing to do with the supposed scholastic one between a thing and its properties—the gap that Kant himself had eliminated. This is a much more fundamental gap, compared with which all the worry about the matter of the cup versus its form is just banter. On this view, the OOO one, the material causes of the cup (to speak Aristotelian for a moment) are on exactly the same level as its formal causes, its shape, color, and so on. This leads to the insight that *perceiving and causing are one and the same,* which leads us back to our gamma ray, which has a causal effect on things precisely insofar as it measures or "perceives" them.

What we took to be a gigantic ocean of nothingness that was unique to humans as they voyaged through it in the Heideggerian U-boat was actually a fluctuating, myriad emanation of waves of aesthetic causality emanating from the sparkling objects at the very bottom of the ocean, the OOO objects. Recall that a few pages ago it was established that there was no separation between appearance and causality—indeed the agency of X-rays depends on there being no separation. The abyss of reason is in fact an abyss of causality. What I glimpse in my intuition concerning a priori synthetic judgment just is my uniqueness, my unspeakable unicity, which I cannot directly access or speak. Yet I can think it. At first this unicity is thought to be a uniform ocean of existential weirdness, like Emmanuel Levinas's *there is* (the *il y a*), the mere existence of a thing. Yet as I look closer, I find that this vagueness has a specific waveform, even a color and a shape—it oscillates with gravity waves that pull at me. Where are these waves coming from? From objects, which emit space and time themselves, as Albert Einstein predicted. What I took to be the depths of the ocean of reason, the dark uncanny region of *Angst* and the *there is* below the playful Husserlian fish of intentions sporting toward the upper reaches, is in fact something I have been seeing *upside down.* The whole ocean (reason, intention, being-there, space, time) is being *emanated* by the sparkling coral reef of real things that, from modernity's point of view, is absurd or non-existent. Yet the logic of Heidegger's tool analysis convinces me that there must be a coral reef down there, even if his own submarine cannot withstand the pressure required to force thinking down to that level, against the buoyancy of correlationism.

Furthermore, look—*that is me down there,* I am on this coral reef, too. I, a human subject, am part of this coral reef! What I took to be my separate or exceptional self, peering down into the water, was just a refraction that was always already happening at the bottom of the ocean. It is like being a character in the film *Sphere.*[20] A group of scientists discovers an alien entity, a gigantic scintillating sphere, at the very bottom of the ocean. Unwittingly they enter it, and unwittingly everything that happens next is a mind projection, based on their having already entered the sphere. Everything that we are thinking about reason, givenness, existence, being, and time is happening at the bottom of the ocean, and it was only a fiction that we were peering in from the surface. Remember? The surface was never really there: the metaphysical islands were made of shifting sands that the Kantian ocean has overwhelmed.

Let me reiterate the remark I made about *depth* a little earlier. As a metaphor for the withdrawn aspect of a thing, depth does not mean "a substrate that is more real because it is more constantly present." In fact, it means something like the inverse of that. Depth is dark, absent from my (and anything else's) phenomenal space, to the extent that it is real.

This is the long journey of OOO, beneath correlationism, beneath nihilism—beyond, so to speak, the human-correlated electromagnetic bandwidth, into the realm of invisible light. No wonder it is a journey that not many are willing to take, which seems absurd on the face of it. Yet I hope that I have given some reasons why the journey might be taken, and some sense of the validity of such a journey. The culture that discovered how to create gamma rays must somehow get over itself, for the sake of itself and all the other beings that inhabit it, willy-nilly: DNA, snails, aquifers, and bonobos. It cannot bomb itself back to the past, back to a prenuclear age; nor can it bomb itself back to a pre-Kantian age—at least not in both cases without astonishing, unthinkable violence. There is no reverse gear because it is impossible to unthink a thought. Somehow we must convince ourselves that the *journey beneath nihilism* is thinkable, then possible, then necessary. Only then will humans be able to coexist in a nonviolent way with as many (other) beings as possible.

What does this coexistence look like? Philosophically, it means appreciating, even enjoying, the inconsistency of a thing. A thing is fundamentally, irreducibly inconsistent, since a gap is hardwired into the very conditions of possibility of a thing's existence as such. The existence of a thing is the existence of a *rift* between essence and appearance, a rift not locatable in ontically given regions. I can examine the Styrofoam cup for all eternity— it could even examine itself—and its essence would never be grasped, in thought, word, or deed. A thing just is a fresh inconsistency in the world.

To destroy, on these terms, is to *reduce to consistency.* When I take the cup simply as a thing-for-me, I have reduced it to a consistent human use-value (or exchange-value), forgetting or dismissing the photons and mosquitoes that also make use of it. If I really want to analyze it, perhaps I should burn the cup—or fire photons at it. What would happen if I subject the cup to a sufficiently potent gamma ray burst? Just as I reduce the cup to my anthropomorphic needs when I think of it or use it as this Styrofoam-cup-for-me, so the gamma rays reduce the cup to an X-ray-morphic parody of a cup, in all likelihood just a pile of cinders. The X-rays now have a consistent, X-ray-centric picture of the cup. The same happens if you keep on and on taking X-rays of my skeleton. Eventually I die of cancer, but you have some astonishingly accurate photos of my insides for safekeeping.

At the quantum scale, the danger of an X-ray or gamma ray to another entity has to do with its powerful skills of *barrier penetration.* At this scale, "solidity" just means the intensity of the *resistance wells* in an object. The reason that I associate objects with relative degrees of hardness and solidity is due to my galumphing, macro-scale experiences of being unable to put my fingers through a solid oak table, for instance. At the quantum scale, however, waves are encountering other waves. If a wave is powerful enough, it can burst through a resistance well, penetrating the nucleus of an atom and releasing a proton. This means that an incident wave packet is narrow enough to enter a region between the peaks of waves of resistance. The resulting state is *metastable*—many interactions are occurring, but in a reasonably predictable way. This is what it means to be a radioactive nucleus, shedding protons.[21] Protons exit the nucleus because the incident energy resonates with them, much in the same way that a glass shatters when an opera singer resonates with it. Enveloping a thing with something like it, something that resonates with it, is what is called *death*, how a thing ends. It is thus plausible that *death is a kind of beauty*, since for Kant beauty is a perfect resonance (*Stimmung*, attunement) between me and some other being.[22] This gives rise to the possibility that a beautiful-enough sound might have lethal properties, a thought that must send a shudder through any fan of shoegaze or black metal.

Now consider that I am also a metastable being composed of limbs, cells, and protons. Because I cannot be reduced to protons, I am still myself—however, I am now seared with gamma rays at an astonishingly intimate level of my being—the nuclei of my very atoms. When this happens frequently enough, I die of radiation sickness or, more slowly, of cancer. I have achieved stability: I have achieved (beautiful) death.

X-rays and gamma rays can penetrate most materials such as flesh and cotton. A heavy metal smock is thick enough to ward off the X-rays I receive at the dentist, but will I remember to be wearing one when a nuclear bomb explodes in my vicinity? The X-ray reduces me to an assemblage of atoms with weak resistance wells. This will, "If used properly" as David Byrne says of nuclear weapons, result in my death.[23]

This reduction of things to souvenirs for some entity or other exploits the rift between essence and appearance. More precisely, it collapses that rift. We can conclude then that the appearance of anything at all is already a kind of souvenir: when we look at a thing we are looking at the past. The withdrawn essence of a thing is futural, to-come, since we cannot locate it anywhere, even in an ontically given future, that is, a future that is n now-points away from "now" taken to be an atom of time with a specific size and shape. This essence will never arrive, but it is the very existence of the thing—it is like Derrida's *arrivant*, the ultimate guest for whom no hospitality can adequately prepare: a strange stranger.

Appearance is the past, essence is the future. What then of the present? It does not exist! What is called *present* is just a region of the past taken to be more real or more intense than the rest of the past. Gigantic and invisible (to humans) beings such as global warming and radiation, beings that last for eons, force us humans to see this uncanny fact, the fact that we cannot draw a line around beings and call them present in some rigorous way—

that the metaphysics of presence, in other words, depends on a notion of presence and present that is inherently spurious. The half-life of plutonium 239, namely, the time it takes for the plutonium to halve the rate at which it emits alpha, beta, and gamma rays, is 24.1 thousand years. That timescale is roughly comparable with the paintings on the walls of the Chauvet cave, the oldest human art we know of. Ethical and political decisions based on self-interest just fail at these scales. This is even if we widen the notion of self to include not just me and my family, not just me and human society, but all the sponges and lichen and dolphins. That far out into the future, the following will be true:

No one will be meaningfully related to me.
The slightest thing I do now will have a profound effect.

Humans urgently need to develop ethical and political theories not based on self-interest. They need reasons to do this—reasons that must entail ontology, the study of what is. OOO provides some of the best reasons developed thus far.

It works like this. Let us begin with the foremost reason. Since there is no intrinsic, ontological difference between me and a sponge cake, there is no reason to consider my human self as a pampered, privileged being set apart in some first-class cabin of existence while all the nonhumans sweat it out in steerage. Second, since there is no thin, rigid boundary between sentient and nonsentient beings, it is at best fruitless to consider only sentient beings when making ethical and political decisions. Third, since there is also no thin, rigid boundary between life and nonlife, it is equally pointless to act only with reference to life, which is at most a spurious metaphysical fiction. Fourth, given the enormous timescale on which plutonium 239 radiates gamma rays, it is likely that an increasing number of beings will be caught in its causal wake. There is no reason not to consider the widest number of beings possible when we make ethical and political decisions. The only justification for this wide consideration is the fact that we can think these beings. The simple fact that we can think nonhumans immediately proves our responsibility to them—no further reasoning is required, including anything about "the web of life" or "the harmony of existence" and so forth.

From what we know about beings, they exist because they are inherently fragile. "Inherently" means that a thing just falls apart, of its own accord, because it is fundamentally rickety. In an ontically given or metaphysically present world, a thing requires another thing to destroy it. In the OOO world, other things just give them a helping hand over the cliff of their own inherent nothingness. A rift between essence and appearance is an evanescent, metastable thing, because time and space are functions of objects, and not the other way around. Even a black hole, the densest object in the universe, eventually exhausts itself through Hawking radiation. Things are impermanent, not because they exist "in" time, but *because they are things*. When I die, I simply become my appearances—your memory of me, some paper in a wastebasket—and my essence is gone; yet this is also true of wastebaskets and memories. The "death" of a thing is nowhere in ontically given space-time: we see paper, we do not see my death; we see fragments of glass, not the glass that was broken. Reality resembles a gigantic charnel ground in which death is everywhere and nowhere. Ecological awareness means making a home in this uncanny garbage heap of death, ghosts, and zombies. Nonviolence is just allowing as many rifts in being (between essence and appearance) to remain as open as possible. In this sense, biodiversity is just a very small region of a much vaster realm of diversity, a realm that has no center or edge, since there is no "top" or "bottom" object, no fundamental particle, no absolute, no History with a capital /h/.

But why should I care at all? Why not just let the whole thing go to hell? There will be plenty of objects around, no matter whether they are Imperial Stormtroopers or Cylons or comets. This is where the principle of irreduction comes in. In the Steven Spielberg movie of *Empire of the Sun,* the boy Jim remarks that the Hiroshima explosion was "Like God taking a photograph": "I learned a new word today. Atom bomb. It was like a white light in the sky. Like God taking a photograph."[24] The very pinnacle of modernity, encapsulated in Robert Oppenheimer's "I am become death, shatterer of worlds," a line from the Bhagavad Gita that he spoke when the Gadget exploded at Trinity, is the arrival of what Heidegger would have called *the last god*—if Heidegger had been able to include nonhumans in his view.[25] Heidegger simply was unable to ascertain how this last god would manifest in the very core of technological enframing.[26] The poison is indeed the saving power, or not. For it is gigantic nonhuman beings—

radioactive materials, global warming, the very layers in earth's crust that open the Anthropocene—which bring about the end of the world. I am calling these gigantic nonhumans *hyperobjects,* objects massively distributed in time and space relative to humans. Hyperobjects bring about the beginning of history, "the other beginning," as Heidegger puts it, outside the metaphysics of presence that has reduced beings to ontic givenness: the names for this givenness are legion and include *hypokeimenon, energeia, substantia, subjectum, subject, object).*[27]

It is almost there in J. M. W. Turner's paintings of the slave ship and Death riding a pale horse: a light that makes everything transparent, that does not so much illuminate as irradiate. Like God taking a photograph: the nonhuman sees us, in the white light of its fireball, hotter than the sun. *Like* God: this is not an endorsement of a scholastic *causa sui* inhabiting a beyond, but a reminder that we are dealing with a physical entity. Yet this is a *weird* physical entity, with all the fateful force of that term. But to what are we listening when we attune to the hyperobject? Is this uncertainty not precisely *what* we are hearing? Is it not the case that the affect delivered to us in the rain, the weird cyclone, the oil slick, is something uncanny?

Notes

1. Immanuel Kant, *Critique of Pure Reason,* trans. J. M. D. Meiklejohn (London: Henry G. Bohn, 1855), 1–18.

2. Edmund Husserl, *Logical Investigations,* trans. J. N. Findlay, ed. Dermot Moran, 2 vols. (London: Routledge, 2006), 2:95–97, 2:97–100, 2:100–104, 2:109–12.

3. Martin Heidegger, *Being and Time,* trans. Joan Stambaugh (Albany: State University of New York Press, 1996), 131–34, 171–72, and especially section 40 (172–78).

4. Quentin Meillassoux, *After Finitude: An Essay on the Necessity of Contingency,* trans. Ray Brassier (New York: Continuum, 2009), 5.

5. Martin Heidegger, *Contributions to Philosophy (From Enowning),* trans. Parvis Emad and Kenneth Maly (Bloomington: Indiana University Press, 1999), 283–93. See also Joan Stambaugh, *The Finitude of Being* (Albany: State University of New York Press, 1992), 139–44.

6. The rhizome is a Deleuzo-Guatarrian concept: see Gilles Deleuze and Félix Guattari, *A Thousand Plateaus: Capitalism and Schizophrenia,* trans. Brian Massumi (Minneapolis: University of Minnesota Press, 1987), 3–25; Sadie Plant, *Zeroes + Ones* (London: Fourth Estate, 1998).

7. Graham Harman, *The Quadruple Object* (Winchester: Zero Books, 2011), 7–20.

8. Georg Wilhelm Friedrich Hegel, *Hegel's Phenomenology of Spirit,* trans. A. V. Miller (Oxford: Oxford University Press, 1977), 383–409.

9. David Bohm, *Quantum Theory* (New York: Dover, 1989), 522–24, 550–54.

10. I take this phrase from François Laruelle, *Philosophies of Difference: A Critical Introduction to Non-Philosophy,* trans. Rocco Gangle (New York: Continuum, 2010), 179.

11. J. R. R. Tolkien, *The Fellowship of the Ring* (Boston: Houghton Mifflin, 1967), 272.

12. Martin Heidegger, *What Is a Thing?,* trans. W. B. Barton and Vera Deutsch, analysis by Eugene T. Gendlin (Chicago: Henry Regnery, 1967), 19.

13. Tolkien, *Fellowship of the Ring,* 272.

14. Bohm, *Quantum Theory,* 33–37.

15. Lucretius, *On the Nature of Things,* trans. William Ellery Leonard, Internet Classics Archive, http://classics.mit.edu/Carus/nature_things.4.iv.html, 4.26–215.

16. Bohm, *Quantum Theory,* 516–17.

17. Ibid., 529–37.

18. Ibid., 99–115.

19. Aaron D. O'Connell et al., "Quantum Ground State and Single Phonon Control of a Mechanical Ground Resonator," *Nature,* March 17, 2010, 697–703.

20. *Sphere* (dir. Barry Levinson; 1998).

21. Bohm, *Quantum Theory,* 294–95.

22. Immanuel Kant, *Critique of Judgment: Including the First Introduction,* trans. Werner Pluhar (Indianapolis: Hackett, 1987), 43–95.

23. Talking Heads, *Stop Making Sense* (Sire Records, 1984), sleeve note.

24. *Empire of the Sun* (dir. Steven Spielberg; 1987).

25. Heidegger, *Contributions,* 283–93. See also Stambaugh, *Finitude of Being,* 139–44. Robert Oppenheimer's line is from the Bhagavad Gita, trans. Swami Nikhilananda (New York: Ramakrishna-Vivekananda Center, 1944). The term *shatterer* rather than *destroyer* first appeared in "The Eternal Apprentice," *Time,* November 8, 1948, http://www.time.com/time/magazine/article/0,9171,853367-8,00.html.

26. Martin Heidegger, "The Question Concerning Technology," *Basic Writings: From "Being and Time" to "The Task of Thinking,"* ed. David Krell (New York: HarperCollins, 1993), 307–41.

27. Heidegger, *What Is a Thing?,* 35, 105.

After Green Ecologies

Prismatic Visions

SERENELLA IOVINO AND SERPIL OPPERMANN

Take a dog, for example. A black-white-and-brown furry little dog. On a shining blue summer day, you take her to a bright green spot and throw her a brand-new yellow tennis ball to retrieve. Over and over again, she will catch the ball and run back to you, her chestnut-haired and purple-and-orange-dressed interspecies playmate. Kneeling down in the terracotta porch, you will give her a nice brown biscuit as a reward, as bees buzz around the yellow Scotch broom bush, just over there, past that crimson bougainvillea. While you—human, dog, and bees—do these things, light is painting in your eyes a full world of colors and meanings. Physically, the mechanisms at work in this *composition* are the same. But then comes the eye.

When it comes to the eye, differences emerge in the painting. On that same summer morning, the dog will not be running on a playground as green as it appears to you. She will not be seeing so many shades of chestnut in your hair or hers. She will not be catching a fluorescent yellow tennis ball or crunch a really brown little treat. For her, the bougainvillea will look a bit darker than crimson, and there will be no striking contrast between the terracotta porch and the gray concrete buildings in the background. Those bees themselves, they will not be enjoying much of the broom's yellow, but rather a greenish-yellow combination of colors, and maybe some ultraviolet.

It is not easy to talk about colors, for disanthropocentrists. Are there colors in the wild blue yonder—absolute, a-perceived colors? Evidently not. Color, like sound, or taste, or any other sensuous apprehension of reality, is not an "objective" phenomenon—if objective phenomena exist at all. As John Locke would say, these are not "primary" qualities of bodies, such as mass or motion. Like taste, or sound, or smell, color results from the combination of physics and physiology. Therefore, if "grey is the fate of colors at twilight,"[1] color, generally taken, is the fate of light when it meets the eye. It is the fate of physics meeting physiology. It is the way waves of energy get hybridized with hybrid layers of biology, stepping from the unseen to the visible.

This is not a simple process, and it testifies to the way light interacts with other matter, producing new levels of material-energetic arrangement. In the natural world, color emerges from the organic molecules' absorption of certain wavelengths of white light. The atoms of grass, ball, hair, flower, and biscuit absorb photons of visible light depending on the matching energy levels, which include quantized electronic energy. In other words, transitions between electronic states are responsible for the colors of things. All this, however, would not be describable in terms of "color" if an eye were not there to perceive it. As Goethe writes, thinking in a pre-Darwinian time, "The eye may be said to owe its existence to light, . . . colour is a law of nature in relation with the sense of sight."[2] Resulting from the coevolution of organism and light, the eye is a biological prism. Like in all things biological, this interaction is organized differently in all living species. We humans see a spectrum that dogs perceive less vividly, and bees see colors that we humans can only imagine.

Nevertheless, all these colors exist and are real. Different and equal at the same time. Can somebody say that my brown is browner than my dog's? Or that my yellow is more real than the bees' yellow? All these colors are here together at once, reminding us how hybrid and multiple the maps of evolution and perception are. They act, exist, and shape together the physical–physiological patterns of the world.

Ecology, per definition, is thinking the copresence through porous boundaries. We share our *oikos*—our home—with nonhuman beings at macroscopic as well as at molecular levels. In this domestic globe, our relationships to these beings are always "otherworldly conversations," as Donna Haraway puts it, an "inter-subjectivity between radically different kinds of subjects."[3] If this is true, maybe the time has also come to frame these conversations into a more encompassing vision, a vision that recasts in ecological ways the dialectics between unity and plurality: a prismatic vision. *Prismatic Ecology* is a way to think and theorize about this vision. The first step here is to extend ecological discourse beyond the mono-chromatic language of green (which, said incidentally, is imperceptible in the eyes of many humans suffering from Daltonism, or the inability to distinguish red from green). To do so, *Prismatic Ecology* engages a sensuous conversation with the readers, taking them progressively "beyond": beyond standardized discourses about *the* color of ecology and beyond colors themselves, showing how unilateral and incomplete is a world perceived only through human eyes.

The ecologies in this book are therefore postgreen and postcolor, which is another way of saying that the fate of ecology is to multiply, and to become posthuman. But, to become posthuman, the discourse of ecology must try to become human first. *Prismatic Ecology,* in fact, does not aim to neutralize the human eye. Quite the opposite: it wants to enrich the spectrum perceived by the human eye and make us aware of it, in ecological terms. It wants to explore the role colors have in building not only the green rhetorics of ecological discourse but also human imagination about life, places, elements, processes, and changes. The prismatic process of border-crossing produces, in other words, an interesting side effect "for human use": the emergence of the chromatic richness and complexity of ecological imagination. From this point of view, the iridescent concept of prismatic ecologies signifies a planet of colors embedded in heterogeneous naturecultures, from the contaminated whiteness of the Arctic and the caked deserts of Africa to the gloomy synesthetic mélanges of urban land-fills populated by creatures that "can oftentimes be the color of antifreeze."[4] As opposed to the compact plenitude implied by green ecology, prismatic ecologies contain both disruptive and harmonic elements, blurring the boundaries between the sylvan spectra of green exegesis and disclosures of dark ecology. The limits of "green criticism," as Jeffrey Cohen pinpoints, are clear: it "emphasizes balance, the innate, the primal, landscapes with few people, macrosystems, the unrefined. What . . . do we make of the air-plane, graves, gamma rays, bacteria, . . . electronic realms, prehistoric flora lingering as plastic refuse, lost supercontinents, parasites, inorganic com-pounds that act like living creatures, species undergoing sudden change?"[5]

Widening the frame of ecocriticism, prismatic ecologies might therefore exemplify a shift in critical concern to be more inclusive of the harmonics and dissonances of the color spectrum in interpreting the world. This new postgreen vision signals a possible culmination of the traditional ecocriticism's interest in "green" ethics and aesthetics.

In terms of the narrative horizons of this spectrum, the suggestions we get from the ecology of colors are that the green elements that have been read as emanatory of the predominant epistemological trends are now being disrupted, but also enhanced by the new discourse that is premised on being committed to the entire planetary palette. This double move, reminiscent of a postmodern paradox, is more mindful of the complex social, environmental, and cultural dynamics that shape human perception and experience of naturecultures. These experiences constitute the storied matter inhabited by countless biological entities and can be seen in the dynamic and interdepending colorations of the flora and fauna, in the "zones of darkness" of the deep seas (Alaimo), in the auroras' "undulating bands of maroon" just like a "firing sky" (Duckert), in the "blackness of objects" (Bryant), in the "signals of 'blue' sensations, feelings, and climates" (Joy), in the dissolving grays where life and nonlife mesh and hybridize (Cohen), and in many other colors of the planet's electromagnetic spectrum variously articulated by the contributors of this volume.

All the storied expanses in these prismatic visions typically highlight a recent shift in critical concern for the world's material, watery, and airy agencies, best defined as posthumanist liaisons between the human and the nonhuman bodies. Color plays a vital role in navigating space for each organism and enables "a direct material engagement" with the ontology of the world.[6] But, more importantly, color is intellectually and socially significant in cultural poetics, in the production of cultural narratives, social practices, meanings, and regimes of power and knowledge.

Consider, for instance, Mediterranean cultures, whose stories are extensively tinted by Homer's legacy of the "wine-dark sea." In a horizon like this, color plays a central role in co-operative configurations between the species and the environment, and between culture and nature, fashioning literary imaginary and social discourses. Many examples can be quoted in this context. In Turkey, the Greater Flamingo colonies get their delicate rosy pink color from carotenoid pigments in the micro-organisms found in Lake Tuz (Salt Lake), one of the largest hypersaline lakes in the world, sharing the same geological properties as the Great Salt Lake in Utah with its algae and limestone, and red-colored classic units containing gypsum crystal and lignite. Again, other resident animals come to mind: white-fronted goose and lesser kestrel, a small falcon with its brown back and gray head and tails; the endangered caretta caretta sea turtles, with their dark yellow-brown shells; the white-feathered dancing "demoiselle crane" that is a significant sacred symbol in Turkish culture, mythology, and folk songs. The color spectrum of biological entities and ecosystems is inextricably enmeshed with the aesthetic palettes of human environmental imagination.

Interpretations of this colorful narrativity entail a new understanding of natural forms as polychromatic agentic forces. We can instantiate this premise from a typically Turkish phenomenon, when the multicolored tulips fill the streets of Istanbul in the springtime. The legacy of the eighteenth-century Tulip Age of the Ottoman Empire today inextricably connects Turkish cultural imaginary to the flower's conspicuous multicolors. Ottoman seals incorporated the tulip, perhaps on a more subtle level invoking the flower's symbolic potency to Anatolia, the land of tulip blossoms. The pervasive "tulip prose" in Turkish literature is an integral part of this long-lasting material–discursive entanglement of human–nonhuman alliance. The Tulip paradigm in Turkish culture reflects the contours of "storied matter." Novels like Buket Uzuner's *İstanbullu* (2008) play with this vision: "If İstanbul was a flower, it was most certainly a tulip."[7] The novel's central character, İstanbul, speaks as narrative agency manifest in its colors: "Blue as hope, green as poison, rosy as dawn, I am İstanbul; I am in the Judas tree, in acacia, in lavender; I am turquoise! I am the unfathomable; the muse of possibility, vitality, creativity."[8] Blurring the line between human subjects and tulips, Judas flowers, and lavender, and anthropomorphizing the city, the intermingled human and nonhuman stories here can be read as voices coming from the prismatic ecology of the city itself. As such, *İstanbullu* is an excellent example of boundary-crossing between humans and nonhumans, where lines are deliberately questioned, dismantled, and redrawn.

Often, however, the pathways of these interchanges are capricious and unpredictable. Ours is a world that also houses toxins, radiation, pesticides, food preservatives, viruses, migrating bacteria, and many human pollutants exist in the most intimate recesses of the earth. In his introduction to this volume, Cohen refers to this polyphonic array as "restless expanse of multihued contaminations, impurities, hybridity, monstrosity, contagion, interruption, hesitation, enmeshment, refraction, unexpected relations, and wonder." A prismatic vision of defined colors here finds its counterpart in a mélange ecology. Here light is puzzled in front of the density of substances, impenetrable density, the density of compost, of toxic rivulets, of silent radioactive deserts, of body cells transformed by contamination. From this perspective, intrinsic to the life of matter, a chorus of muddy impurities supplements "natural" color, calling forth a sensory attentiveness to these often hazardous nonhuman forces, moving our attention from the many-hued variety of animal and plant species to the uncanny alienness of pollutants and chemicals.

The "coexistence of these strangers and their strange iridescence," as Morton writes in his chapter, signals the inevitable fate of the Anthropocene: ironically, while liberating many people from hardships and needs, technoscientific advancement has created new forms of oppression for human and nonhuman natures. But, as Bruno Latour has noted, "To conceive of humanity and technology as polar opposites is, in effect, to wish away humanity: we are sociotechnical animals."[9] Inseparable from the nonhumans, whether they are bacteria, viruses, or other agencies within the body, the water we drink, the plants we eat, the dogs we play and coevolve with, the human is always already "more" than itself. Like every living thing, the human is essentially co-opted, hybridized, and entangled with alien beings, always in negotiations with other agencies, other bodies, and other natures.

This leads us back to the picture sketched at the beginning: a prismatic ecology as an intermediary for otherworldly conversations, a postgreen, postcolor, posthuman ecology. After revealing the limits of green discourse, the encompassing vision of prismatic ecology shows that a world exists also in the absence of colors, a world after or before, or simply apart from, colors. To envisage this world as a segment of our evolutionary story is easy, if we recall the ironic imagination of postmodern narratives. Italo Calvino, for example, in his fictive cosmology populated by primeval matter, energy fluxes, and weird spatial creatures, represents this world without colors as "a bit monotonous . . . but restful, all the same." In this pre-atmospheric landscape, you "could go for miles and miles at top speed, the way you can move when there isn't any air about, and all [you] could see was gray upon gray."[10]

A pre-/postcolor world is not only a matter of fiction, though. It is here. It is the world of submarine creatures, as Alaimo shows in her chapter; or the confusing agency of X-rays, which erases the difference of light and matter altogether, as Morton demonstrates in his contribution.

As critical eyes, prismatic ecologies explore and define the topographies of the world's hybridizations. These ecologies, to quote Duckert's words on maroon, do not "lift the curtain of relations to decipher a language or catalog its components but to shine on the folds of coexistence, and to find our shared, co-implicated, and more-than-human selves rolling around in ethereal undulations."[11] To see the threads of such coexistence, these "critical eyes" have to elicit the dialectical dance between the elements and the whole, exactly as the prism elicits the color spectrum hybridized in white light. The prism can play with light in the same way evolution plays with life: creating a multiplicity of forms from one apparent singularity. Instead of "e pluribus unum," the motto of this game is "ex uno plura." However, the dynamics of this play are not exactly the same: through evolution, life and matter are differentiated, melted together, and recomposed into new units. Through the prismatic lens, instead, light is diffracted and decomposed. This has a powerful impact on ecocultural theory, especially when a holistic impetus to overthrow human mastery is pushed to the point of denying any value to human-related approaches. As a corrective corollary, prismatic ecologies suggest that we see indeed through our eyes, but that the eyes that see the world are not necessarily only ours. Seeing this, prismatic ecologies can theorize a pluralist vision interpreting the world as the result of endless mediations and combinations.

Colors and forms express the things' interplay with light in relation to the eye. As Goethe says in his *Theory of Colors,* "Colours are acts of light, its active and passive modifications."[12] But light is visible only there, where an eye is, and every eye is a prism. Having eyes, humans are prismatic beings, beings who see—with senses or mind—and beings who theorize: "Every act of seeing leads to consideration, consideration to reflection, reflection to combination, and thus it may be said that in every attentive look on nature we always theorize."[13] By deconstructing conventional cultural discourses and unitary images of "nature," prismatic ecologies theorize the way our human gaze participates in a world of alterity and likeness. In that it is aware about the ex-centricity (i.e., noncentrality) of its position, the (human) eye of prismatic ecologies sees both colors and white light, acknowledging differences and similarities, and producing meaningful forms as compositions of elements that are "formally distinct, but ontologically one."[14]

For this reason, the disanthropocentric and posthumanist mode of prismatic ecologies is not at odds with a renewed and ecological form of humanism, a nonanthropocentric humanism. While refusing the supremacy of the human and assessing difference as evolutionary source of value and creativity, a nonanthropocentric humanism debunks ontological hierarchies and rejects totalizing moral systems. Like an ethical/ontological prism, this vision reveals the landscapes of our partnerships, building new narratives of hybridity, participation, and coevolution.

With the postmodern wit of his philosophical prose, Calvino offers an example of this hybrid and coevolutionary partnership via Mr. Palomar, his ironic alter ego. Mr. Palomar is perfectly aware that the phenomena we experience are completely subordinated to our subjective perception. Lying on a beach, he observes the world around him:

> As the sun sinks toward the sunset, the incandescent-white
> reflection acquires gold and copper tones. . . . His upside-down
> gaze now contemplates the straying clouds and the hills clouded
> with woods. . . . But nothing of what he sees exists in nature: the
> sun does not set, the sea does not have this color, the shapes are
> not those that the light cast on his retina. With unnatural
> movements of his limbs, he is floating among phantoms. . . .
> Does nature not exist?[15]

This question is (tentatively) answered in a chapter titled "The world looks at the world," as Mr. Palomar asks, "How can you look at something and set your own ego aside? Whose eyes are doing the looking? . . . Perhaps the 'I,' the ego, is simply the window through which the world looks at the world. To look at itself the world needs the eye (and the eyeglasses) of Mr. Palomar."[16]

If nature exists, it needs eyes, and "I"'s, and hands, and minds, and eyeglasses, to look at itself. Beyond the color green there is an ecology that hosts zombies, bioluminescence, aurora borealis, and gamma rays. In the disanthropocentric horizon of this ecology, turning our prismatic "eye/I" into a tool of reciprocity is the only way we have to see the world. The world, this alien home, exists here and there; in grains of sand, in wildflowers, in antifreeze-colored dragonflies, in dog biscuits and fluorescent tennis balls, in the color of your skin, Reader; in all the hues of gray, and any other color, in all the manifold forms of life and nonlife that incessantly interact before (and after) our eyes.

Notes

1. Jeffrey J. Cohen, "Grey," this volume.

2. Johann Wolfgang Goethe, *The Theory of Colours,* trans. Charles L. Eastlake (New York: Dover, 2006), xxvi–xxvii.

3. Donna Haraway, "Otherworldly Conversations; Terran Topics; Local Terms," in *The Haraway Reader* (London: Routledge, 2004), 143.

4. Robert Sullivan, *The Meadowlands: Wilderness Adventures on the Edge of New York City* (London: Granta Books, 2006), 18.

5. Jeffrey J. Cohen, "Introduction: Ecology's Rainbow," this volume.

6. Karen Barad, *Meeting the Universe Halfway: Quantum Physics and the Entanglement of Matter and Meaning* (Durham, N.C.: Duke University Press, 2007), 49.

7. Buket Uzuner, *İstanbullu,* trans. Kenneth J. Dakan (Istanbul: Everest, 2008), 377.

8. Ibid., 2.

9. Bruno Latour, *Pandora's Hope: Essays on the Reality of Science Studies* (Cambridge, Mass.: Harvard University Press, 1999), 214.

10. Italo Calvino, *The Complete Cosmicomics,* trans. Martin McLaughlin, Tim Parks, and William Weaver (New York: Penguin Books, 2010), 49.

11. Lowell Duckert, "Maroon," this volume.

12. Goethe, *Theory of Colours,* xvii.

13. Ibid., xxvi–xxvii.

14. Gilles Deleuze, *Expressionism in Philosophy: Spinoza,* trans. Martin Joughin (New York: Zone Books, 1992), 67.

15. Italo Calvino, *Mr. Palomar,* trans. William Weaver (San Diego: Harcourt Brace, 1985), 16.

16. Ibid., 114.

CONTRIBUTORS

STACY ALAIMO is professor of English and distinguished teaching professor at the University of Texas at Arlington. Her publications include *Undomesticated Ground: Recasting Nature as Feminist Space, Material Feminisms* (edited with Susan J. Hekman), and *Bodily Natures: Science, Environment, and the Material Self.* She is working on a book tentatively titled "Sea Creatures and the Limits of Animal Studies: Science, Aesthetics, Ethics."

LEVI R. BRYANT is professor of philosophy at Collin College and a former Lacanian psychoanalyst. He is author of *Difference and Givenness: Deleuze's Transcendental Empiricism and the Ontology of Immanence* and *The Democracy of Objects* and coeditor (with Nick Srnicek and Graham Harman) of *The Speculative Turn: Continental Materialism/Realism.* He has written numerous essays on Gilles Deleuze, Alain Badiou, Jacques Lacan, and Slavoj Žižek and is a leading theorist in the object-oriented ontology movement.

LAWRENCE BUELL recently retired after many years as a professor of English at Harvard University. He is the author of *The Environmental Imagination: Thoreau, Nature Writing, and the Formation of American Culture; Writing for an Endangered World: Literature, Culture, and Environment in the United States and Beyond;* and *The Future of Environmental Criticism: Environmental Crisis and Literary Imagination.*

JEFFREY JEROME COHEN is professor of English and director of the Medieval and Early Modern Studies Institute at George Washington University. His books include *Monster Theory: Reading Culture* (Minnesota,

1996); *Of Giants* (Minnesota, 1999); *Medieval Identity Machines* (Minnesota, 2003); *Hybridity, Identity, and Monstrosity in Medieval Britain;* and *Animal, Vegetable, Mineral: Ethics and Objects.* He is completing *Stories of Stone: An Ecology of the Inhuman* (Minnesota, 2015).

LOWELL DUCKERT is assistant professor of English at West Virginia University. With Jeffrey Jerome Cohen, he is editor of "Ecomaterialism," a special issue of *postmedieval: a journal of medieval cultural studies.* He writes on glaciers, swamps, and rain and is molding a book project on early modern waterscapes and actor network theory.

GRAHAM HARMAN is distinguished university professor at the American University in Cairo. He is the author of *Tool-Being, Guerrilla Metaphysics, Heidegger Explained, Prince of Networks, Towards Speculative Realism, Circus Philosophicus, L'Objet quadruple, Quentin Meillassoux: Philosophy in the Making, The Prince and the Wolf* (with Bruno Latour and Peter Erdélyi), and *Weird Realism: Lovecraft and Philosophy.*

BERND HERZOGENRATH is professor of American literature and culture at Goethe University of Frankfurt/Main, Germany. He is the author of *An American Body|Politic: A Deleuzian Approach* and editor of *The Farthest Place: The Music of John Luther Adams* and *Time and History in Deleuze and Serres.* He is planning a project, *cinapses: thinking|film,* that brings together scholars from film studies, philosophy, and the neurosciences.

SERENELLA IOVINO is professor of comparative literature at the University of Turin (Italy) and research fellow of the Alexander-von-Humboldt Stiftung. She is past president of the European Association for the Study of Literature, Culture, and Environment, and the author of four books and numerous essays on environmental philosophy, landscape ethics, ecofeminism, ecological literary theory, and German classical philosophy. With Serpil Oppermann, she is coeditor of *Material Ecocriticism.*

EILEEN A. JOY is a specialist in Old English literary studies and cultural studies, with interests in poetry and poetics, historiography, ethics, affects, embodiments, queer studies, the politics of friendship, speculative realism, and the posthuman. She has published numerous essays and books and is the lead ingenitor of the BABEL Working Group, coeditor of *postmedieval: a journal of medieval cultural studies,* coeditor of *O-Zone: A Journal of Object-Oriented Studies,* and director of punctum books.

ROBERT MCRUER is professor and chair of English at George Washington University. He is the author of *Crip Theory: Cultural Signs of Queerness and Disability* and *The Queer Renaissance: Contemporary American Literature and the Reinvention of Lesbian and Gay Identities,* and coeditor of *Sex and Disability.*

TOBIAS MENELY is assistant professor of English at Miami University. He is working on a project on the climatological unconscious.

STEVE MENTZ is professor of English at St. John's University in New York City. He is the author of *At the Bottom of Shakespeare's Ocean* and *Romance for Sale in Early Modern England* as well as coeditor of *Rogues and Early Modern English Culture.* He blogs at http://www.stevementz.com.

TIMOTHY MORTON is Rita Shea Guffey Chair of English at Rice University. He is the author of *Hyperobjects: Philosophy and Ecology after the End of the World* (Minnesota, 2013); *Realist Magic: Objects, Ontology, Causality; The Ecological Thought; Ecology without Nature;* and seven other books and eighty essays on philosophy, ecology, literature, food, and music. He blogs regularly at http://www.ecologywithoutnature.blogspot.com.

VIN NARDIZZI is associate professor of English at the University of British Columbia. He is the author of *Wooden Os: Shakespeare's Theatres and England's Trees.* He has edited *Queer Renaissance Historiography: Backward Gaze* (with Stephen Guy-Bray and Will Stockton) and *The Indistinct Human in Renaissance Literature* (with Jean E. Feerick).

SERPIL OPPERMANN is professor of English at Hacettepe University, Ankara. She is coeditor of *The Future of Ecocriticism: New Horizons;* editor of the first collection of ecocritical essays in Turkish, *Ekoeleştiri: Çevre ve Edebiyat;* and coeditor (with Greta Gaard) of *International Perspectives in Feminist Ecocriticism.* With Serenella Iovino she has edited *Material Ecocriticism,* and she is working with Simon C. Estok on a book about new ecocritical pathways in international ecocriticism.

MARGARET RONDA is assistant professor of English at Rutgers University. She is working on a study of poetry and obsolescence in the twentieth century.

WILL STOCKTON is associate professor of English at Clemson University. He is the author of *Playing Dirty: Sexuality and Waste in Early Modern Comedy* (Minnesota, 2011) and coeditor of *Queer Renaissance Historiography: Backward Gaze* and *Sex before Sex: Figuring the Act in Early Modern England* (Minnesota, 2013).

ALLAN STOEKL is professor of French and comparative literature at Penn State University. He has translated a number of works by authors such as Georges Bataille, Maurice Blanchot, and Paul Fournel. He is the author of *Bataille's Peak: Energy, Religion, and Postsustainability* (Minnesota, 2007), which shows an ecological turn.

BEN WOODARD is a PhD candidate at the Theory Centre at the University of Western Ontario. He is the author of *Slime Dynamics* and *On an Ungrounded Earth: Towards a New Geophilosophy.*

JULIAN YATES is associate professor of English and material culture studies at the University of Delaware. His first book, *Error, Misuse, Failure: Object Lessons from the English Renaissance* (Minnesota, 2003), examined the social and textual lives of relics, portrait miniatures, the printed page, and secret hiding places in Renaissance England and was a finalist for the MLA Best First Book Prize. His recent work focuses on questions of ecology, genre, and reading in Renaissance English literature and beyond.

INDEX